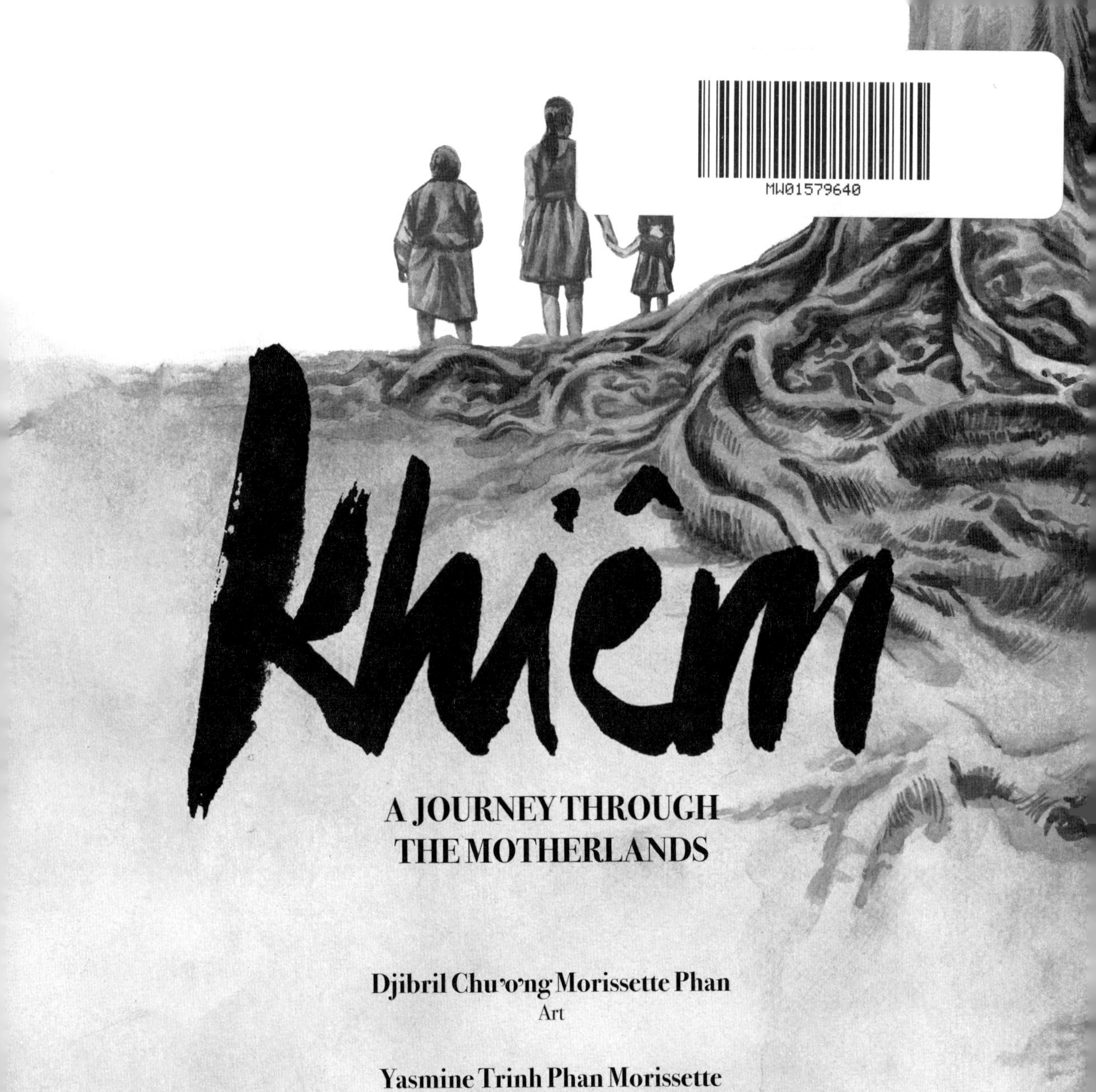

Khiêm

A JOURNEY THROUGH THE MOTHERLANDS

Djibril Chương Morissette Phan
Art

Yasmine Trinh Phan Morissette
Story

Nikki San Pedro
Adaptation

Fabrice Sapolsky
Editor

FAIRSQUARE COMICS

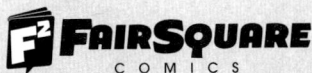

KHIÊM
VOLUME ONE. First Printing.

This title is a publication of FairSquare Comics, LLC.
418 Canal St, New Smyrna Beach, FL, 32168
Copyright © 2024 FairSquare Comics LLC. All Rights Reserved.

Originally published in French under the following title:
KHIÊM, Terres Maternelles by Glénat Québec.
© Copyright © 2020 Les Éditions Glénat Québec, inc.
Published under license.

The story and characters presented in this publication are fictional.
No portion of this book can be reproduced by any means without the
express consent of Éditions Glénat Québec or FairSquare Comics, LLC.

PRINTED IN CANADA

CEO & PUBLISHER | Fabrice Sapolsky
BRAND AMBASSADORS & CO-OWNERS |
Kristal Adams Sapolsky, Ethan Sapolsky

LETTERING & DESIGN | FairSquare Studio
PROOFREADING | Nikki San Pedro
PUBLICITY | Tara Lehmann, taral.lehmann@gmail.com
CONTACT | info@fairsquarecomics.com, +1 (888) 307-0211

COMICS FROM THE REST OF US
WWW.FAIRSQUARECOMICS.COM

INTRODUCTION

This project was born several years ago when our mother translated the life writings of her own mother, whom we never had the chance to meet, into French. We then set out together, my mother, my brother and myself, in search of a narrative framework that could reconstruct our family history. We had to put the events of the past in order to understand how my grandmother's life and mine could be so different.

All our lives, my brother and I had heard of Vietnam as a distant part of ourselves, even though our mother, uncles and aunts in Montreal spared no effort to immerse us in Vietnamese culture. KHIÊM motivated us to cross continents and pick up the pieces of a history too precious to be forgotten. This story took us to Vietnam, then to California, to meet this great family we only knew in writing.

It's a tribute to family, to our resilient mothers, to all those who have experienced uprooting, and to the generations of hybrids that have come from it. In the course of this adventure, I've come to understand the importance of the love that unites a family, and how privileged I am to be part of a clan that protects, uplifts and supports me. I hope this story speaks to those who have to build their camp and form bonds with people who become family in time.

Yasmine Phan Morissette

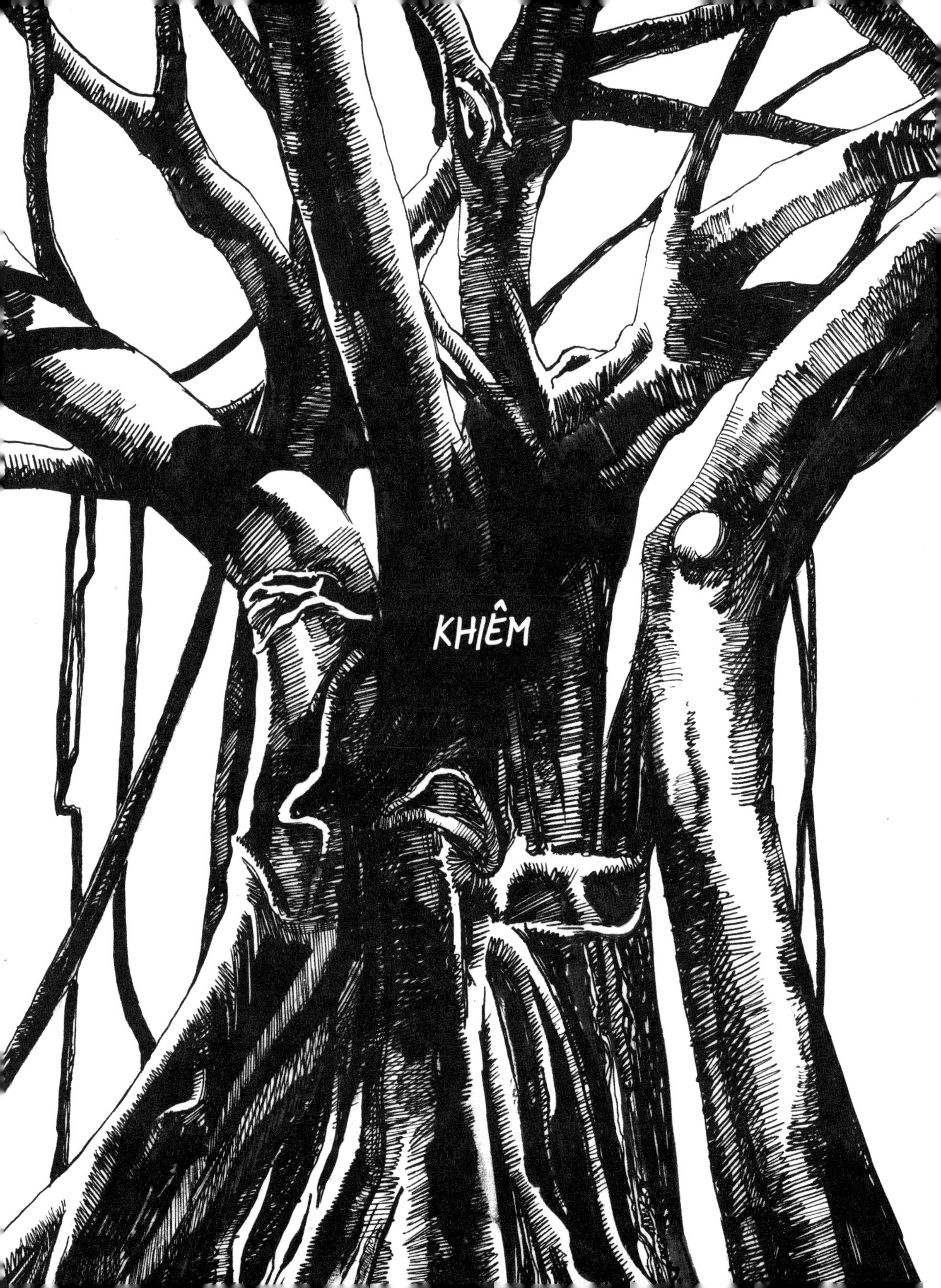
KHIÊM

CHAPTER 1

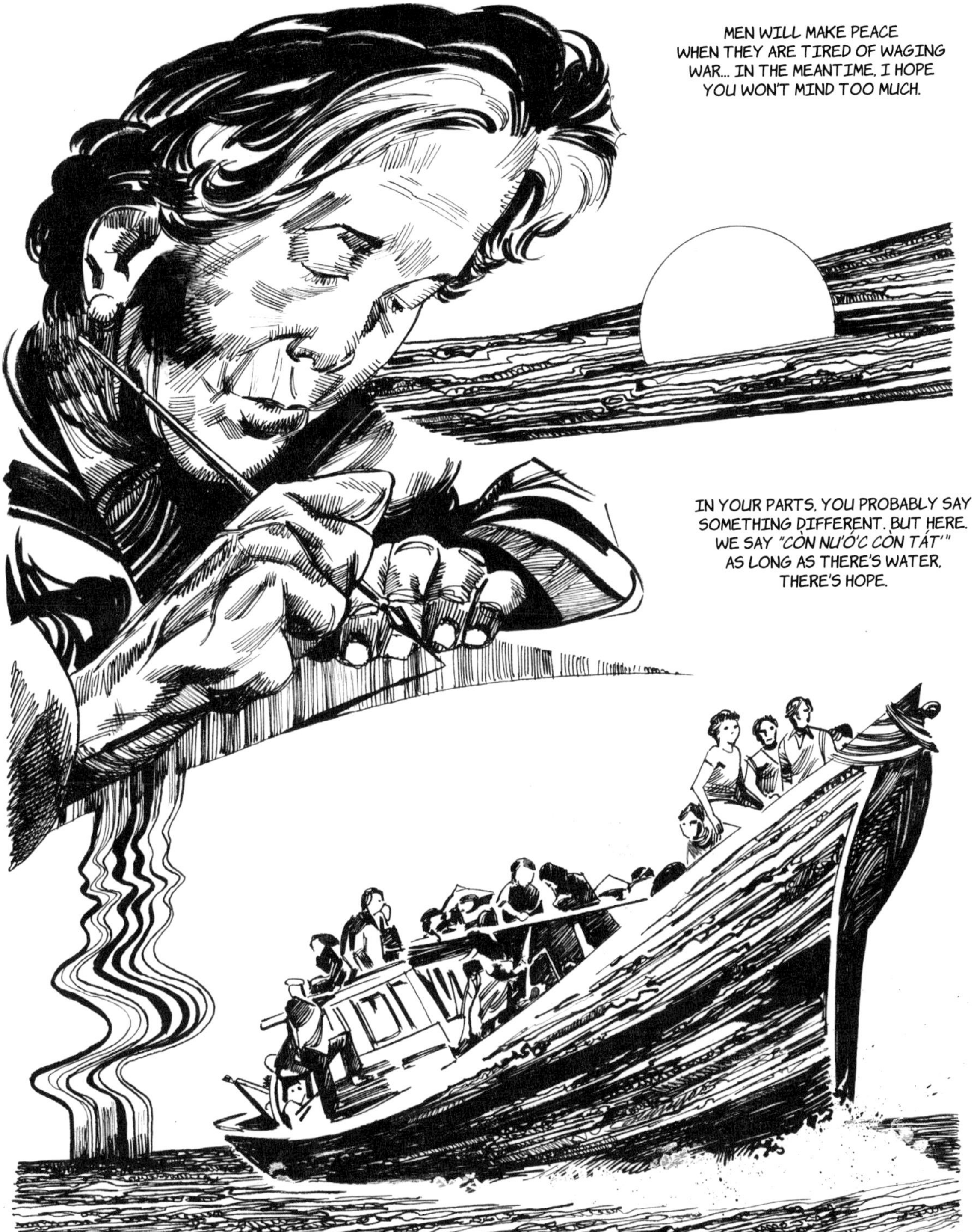
MEN WILL MAKE PEACE WHEN THEY ARE TIRED OF WAGING WAR... IN THE MEANTIME, I HOPE YOU WON'T MIND TOO MUCH.
IN YOUR PARTS, YOU PROBABLY SAY SOMETHING DIFFERENT. BUT HERE, WE SAY "CÒN NƯỚC CÒN TÁT'" AS LONG AS THERE'S WATER, THERE'S HOPE.

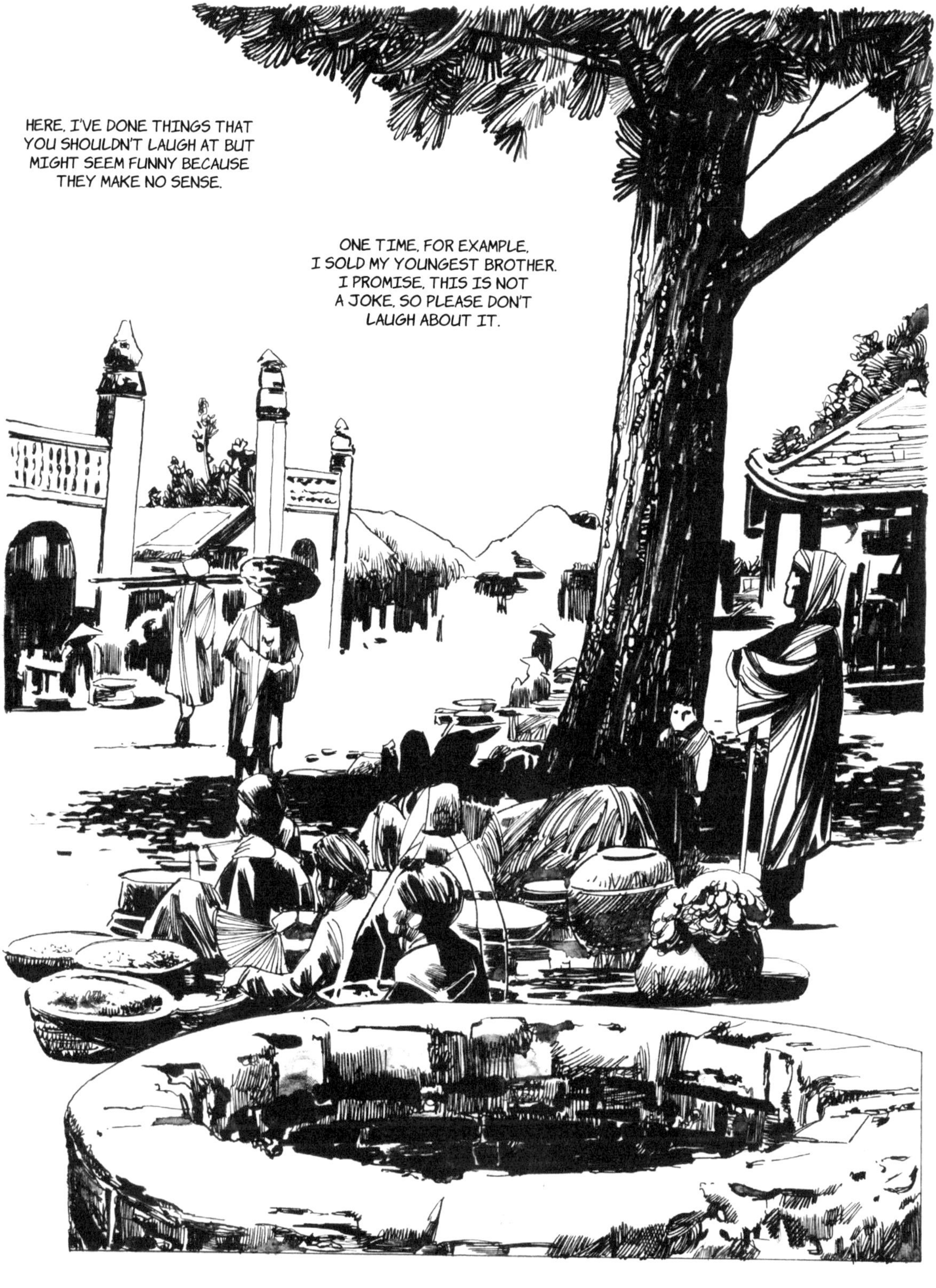
HERE, I'VE DONE THINGS THAT YOU SHOULDN'T LAUGH AT BUT MIGHT SEEM FUNNY BECAUSE THEY MAKE NO SENSE.
ONE TIME, FOR EXAMPLE, I SOLD MY YOUNGEST BROTHER. I PROMISE, THIS IS NOT A JOKE, SO PLEASE DON'T LAUGH ABOUT IT.

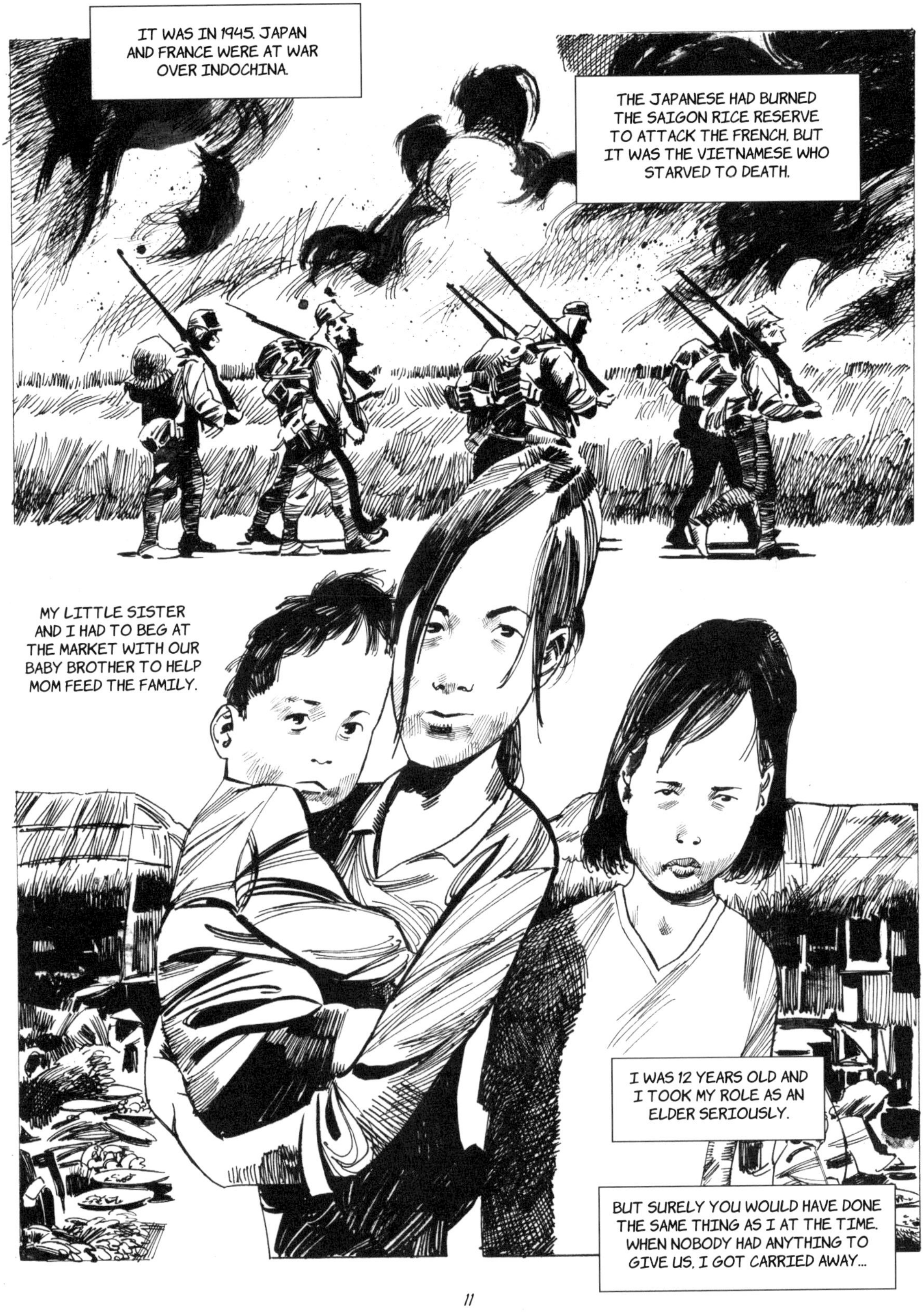
IT WAS IN 1945. JAPAN AND FRANCE WERE AT WAR OVER INDOCHINA.
THE JAPANESE HAD BURNED THE SAIGON RICE RESERVE TO ATTACK THE FRENCH, BUT IT WAS THE VIETNAMESE WHO STARVED TO DEATH.
MY LITTLE SISTER AND I HAD TO BEG AT THE MARKET WITH OUR BABY BROTHER TO HELP MOM FEED THE FAMILY.
I WAS 12 YEARS OLD AND I TOOK MY ROLE AS AN ELDER SERIOUSLY.
BUT SURELY YOU WOULD HAVE DONE THE SAME THING AS I AT THE TIME. WHEN NOBODY HAD ANYTHING TO GIVE US, I GOT CARRIED AWAY...

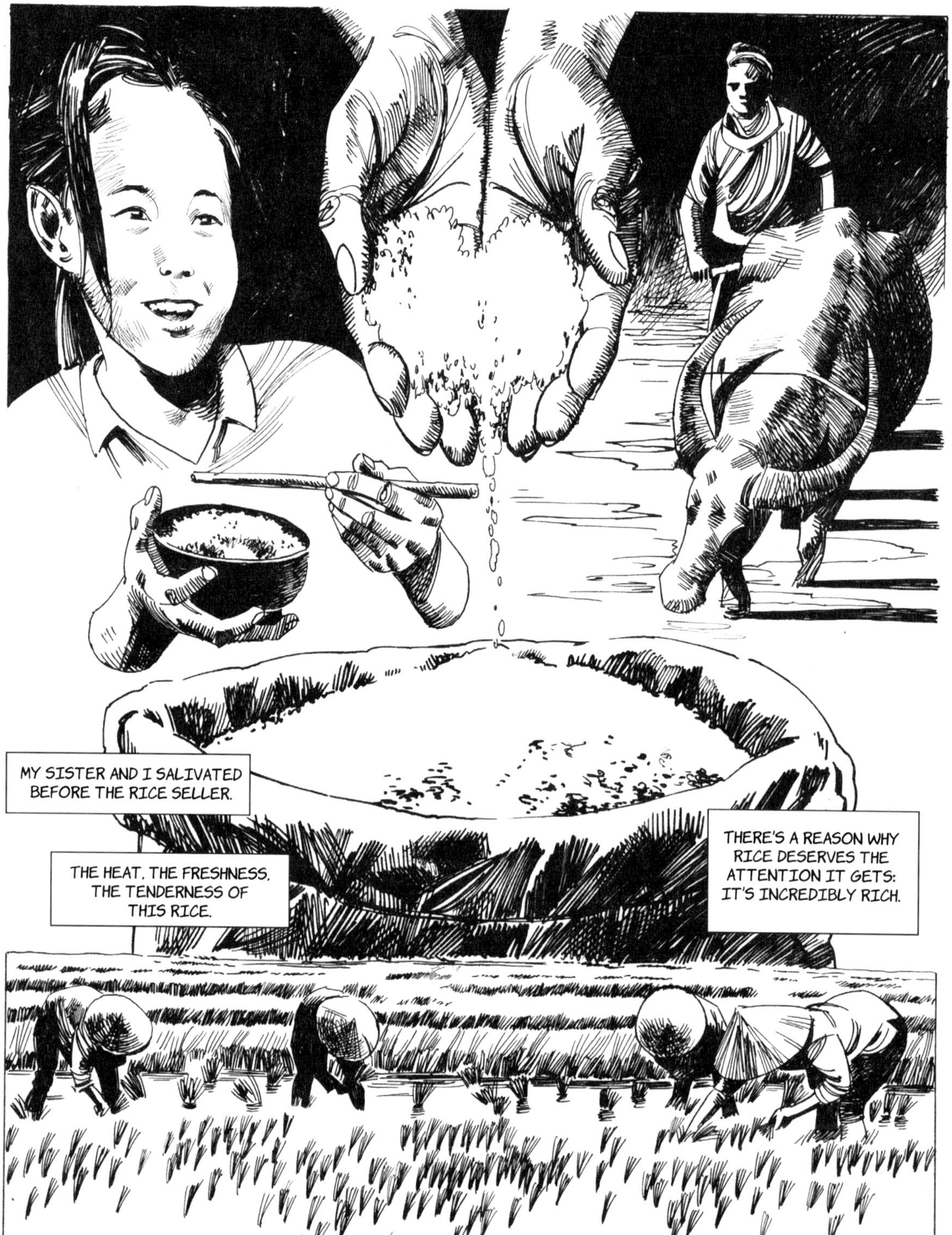
MY SISTER AND I SALIVATED BEFORE THE RICE SELLER.
THE HEAT, THE FRESHNESS, THE TENDERNESS OF THIS RICE.
THERE'S A REASON WHY RICE DESERVES THE ATTENTION IT GETS: IT'S INCREDIBLY RICH.

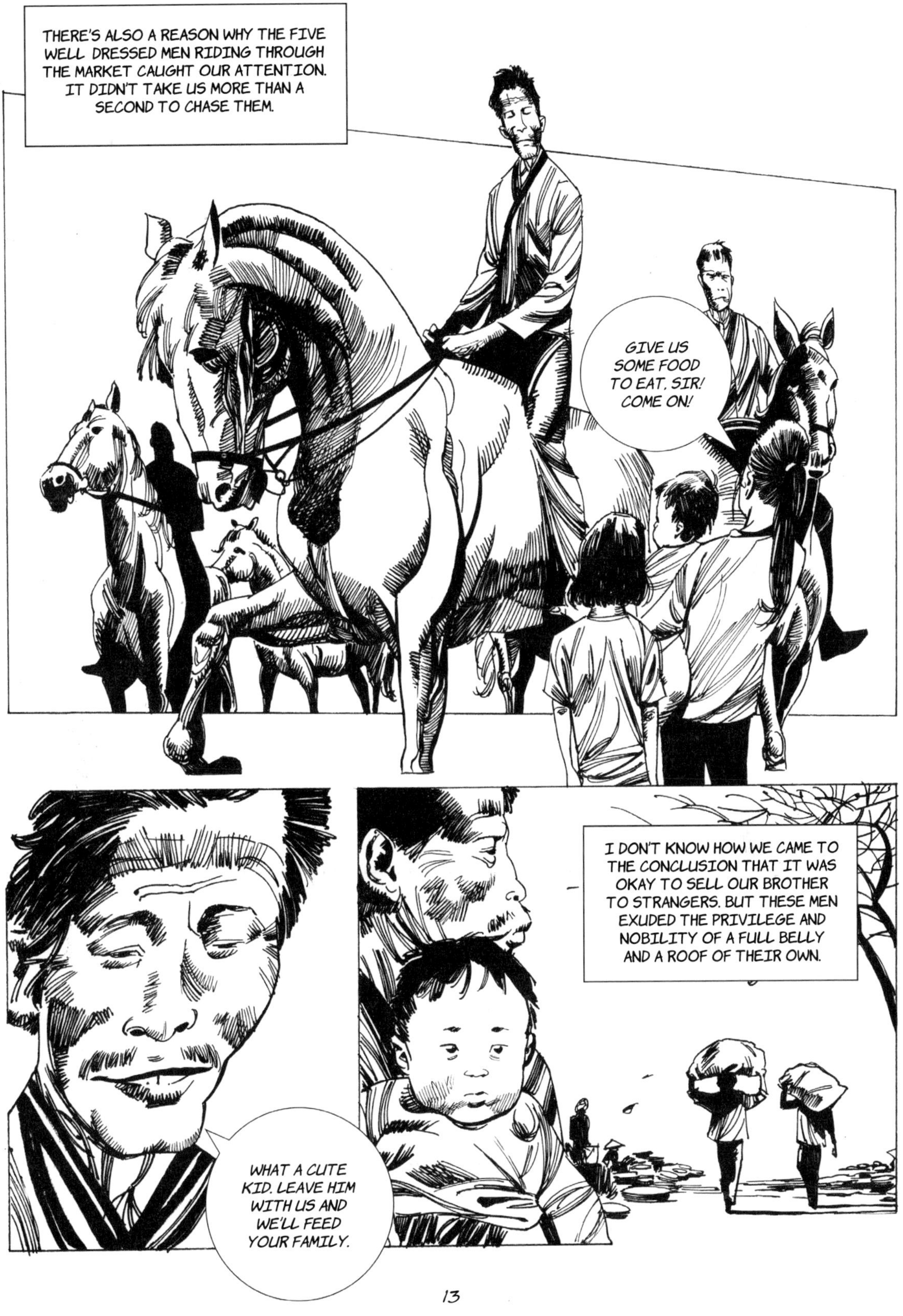
THERE'S ALSO A REASON WHY THE FIVE WELL DRESSED MEN RIDING THROUGH THE MARKET CAUGHT OUR ATTENTION. IT DIDN'T TAKE US MORE THAN A SECOND TO CHASE THEM.
GIVE US SOME FOOD TO EAT, SIR! COME ON!
WHAT A CUTE KID. LEAVE HIM WITH US AND WE'LL FEED YOUR FAMILY.
I DON'T KNOW HOW WE CAME TO THE CONCLUSION THAT IT WAS OKAY TO SELL OUR BROTHER TO STRANGERS. BUT THESE MEN EXUDED THE PRIVILEGE AND NOBILITY OF A FULL BELLY AND A ROOF OF THEIR OWN.

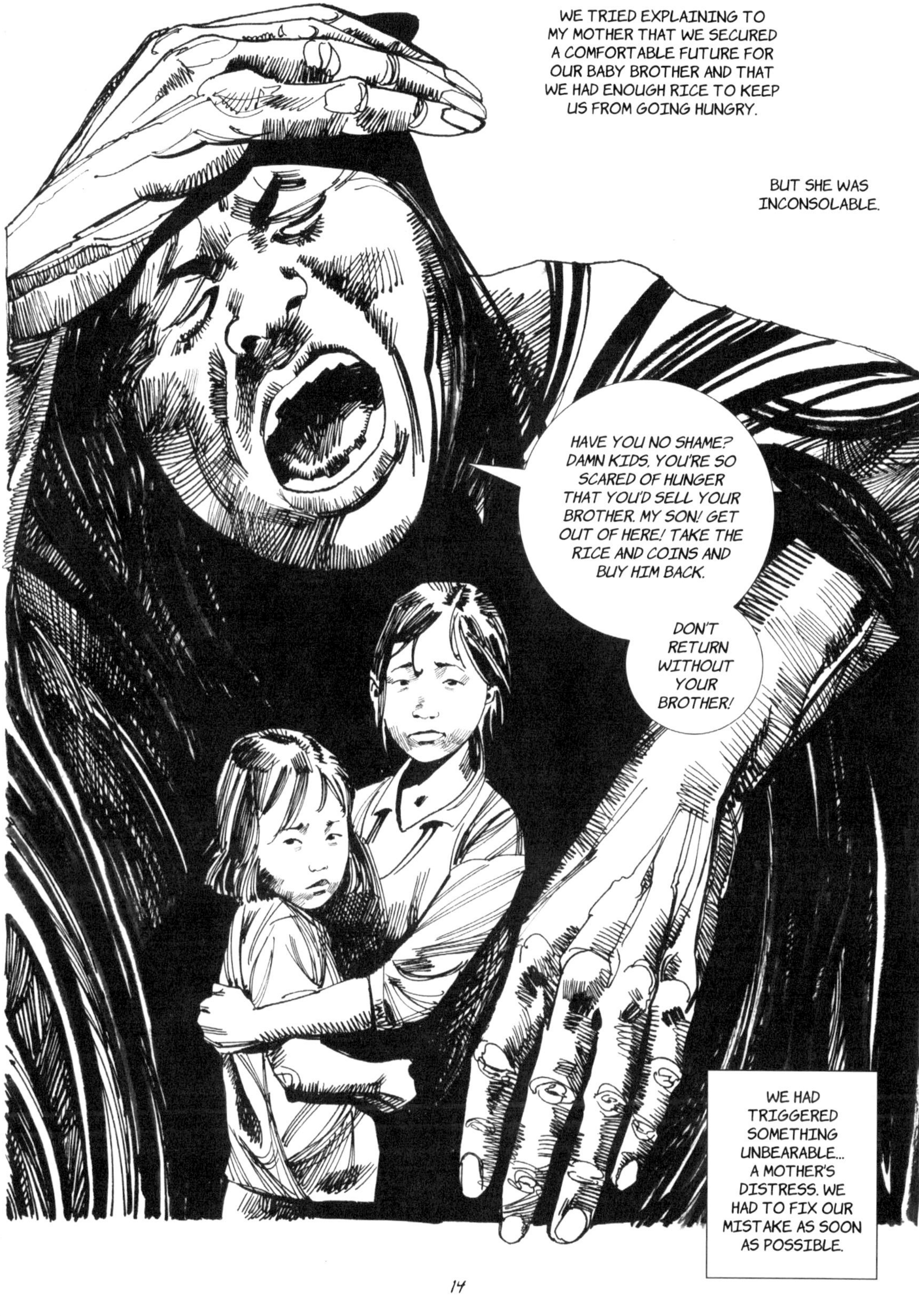
WE TRIED EXPLAINING TO MY MOTHER THAT WE SECURED A COMFORTABLE FUTURE FOR OUR BABY BROTHER AND THAT WE HAD ENOUGH RICE TO KEEP US FROM GOING HUNGRY.
BUT SHE WAS INCONSOLABLE.
HAVE YOU NO SHAME? DAMN KIDS. YOU'RE SO SCARED OF HUNGER THAT YOU'D SELL YOUR BROTHER. MY SON! GET OUT OF HERE! TAKE THE RICE AND COINS AND BUY HIM BACK.
DON'T RETURN WITHOUT YOUR BROTHER!
WE HAD TRIGGERED SOMETHING UNBEARABLE... A MOTHER'S DISTRESS. WE HAD TO FIX OUR MISTAKE AS SOON AS POSSIBLE.

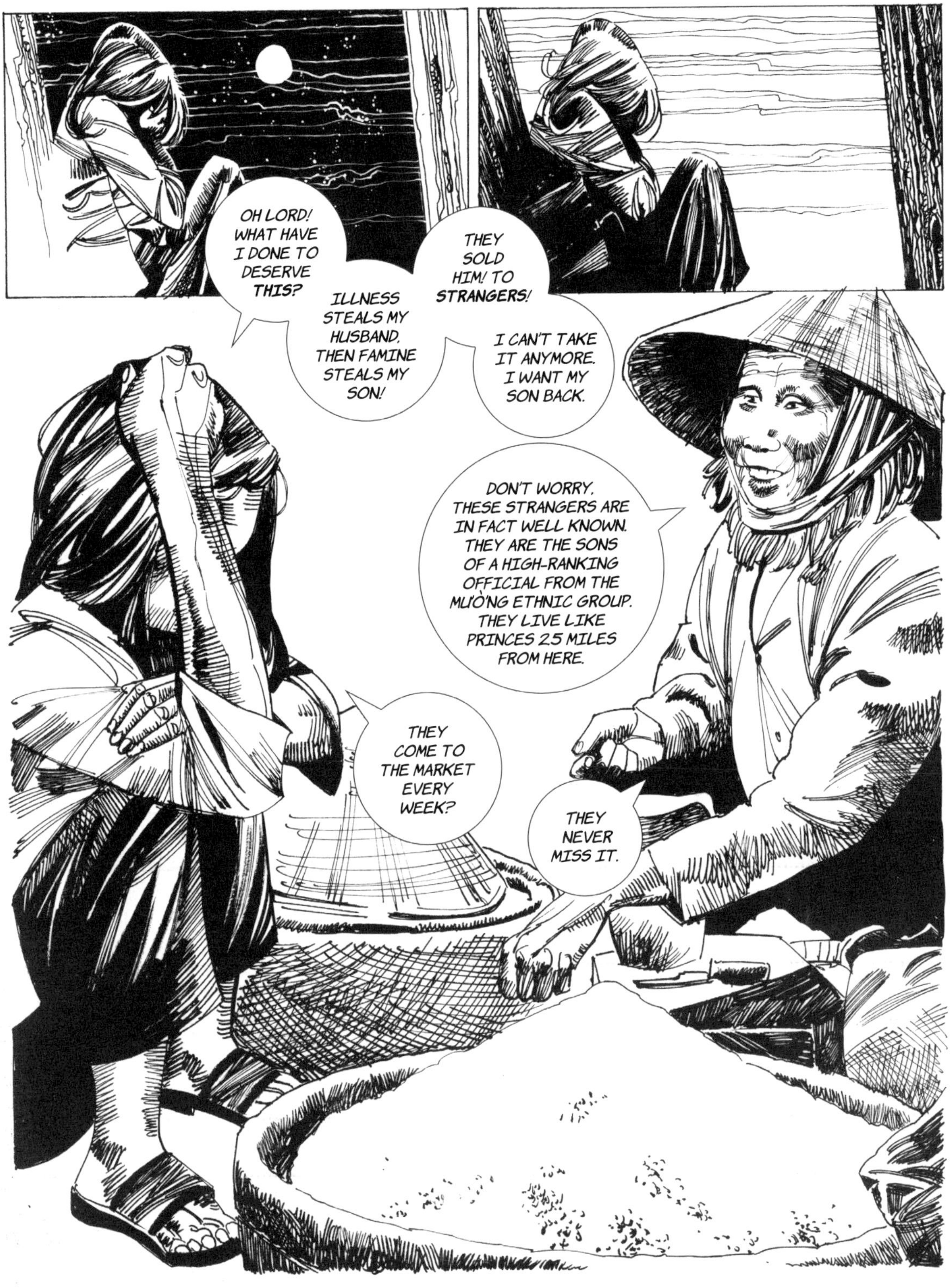
OH LORD! WHAT HAVE I DONE TO DESERVE **THIS?**
THEY SOLD HIM! TO **STRANGERS!**
ILLNESS STEALS MY HUSBAND, THEN FAMINE STEALS MY SON!
I CAN'T TAKE IT ANYMORE. I WANT MY SON BACK.
DON'T WORRY, THESE STRANGERS ARE IN FACT WELL KNOWN. THEY ARE THE SONS OF A HIGH-RANKING OFFICIAL FROM THE MƯỜNG ETHNIC GROUP. THEY LIVE LIKE PRINCES 25 MILES FROM HERE.
THEY COME TO THE MARKET EVERY WEEK?
THEY NEVER MISS IT.

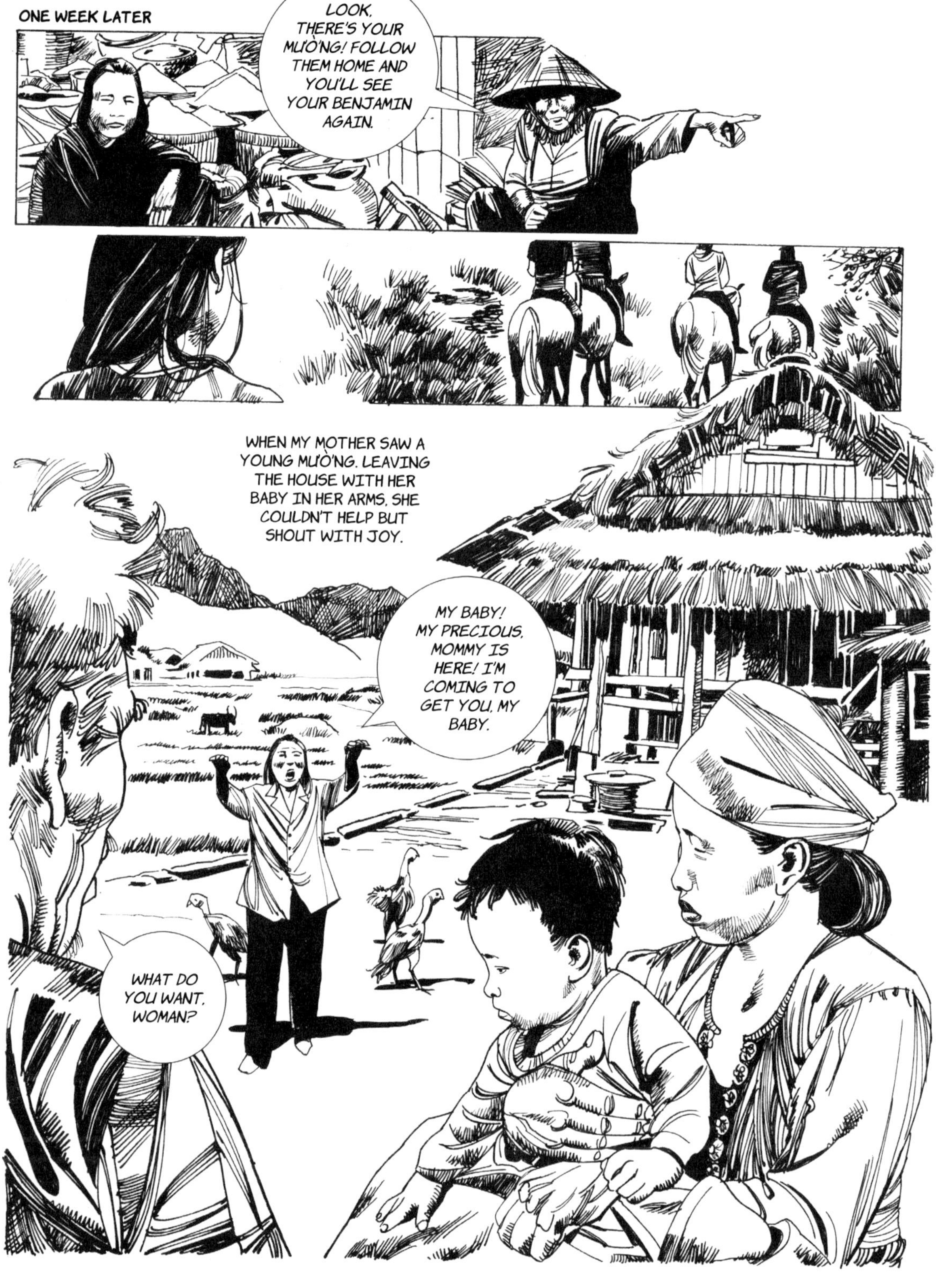
ONE WEEK LATER
LOOK, THERE'S YOUR MƯỜNG! FOLLOW THEM HOME AND YOU'LL SEE YOUR BENJAMIN AGAIN.
WHEN MY MOTHER SAW A YOUNG MƯỜNG, LEAVING THE HOUSE WITH HER BABY IN HER ARMS, SHE COULDN'T HELP BUT SHOUT WITH JOY.
MY BABY! MY PRECIOUS, MOMMY IS HERE! I'M COMING TO GET YOU, MY BABY.
WHAT DO YOU WANT, WOMAN?

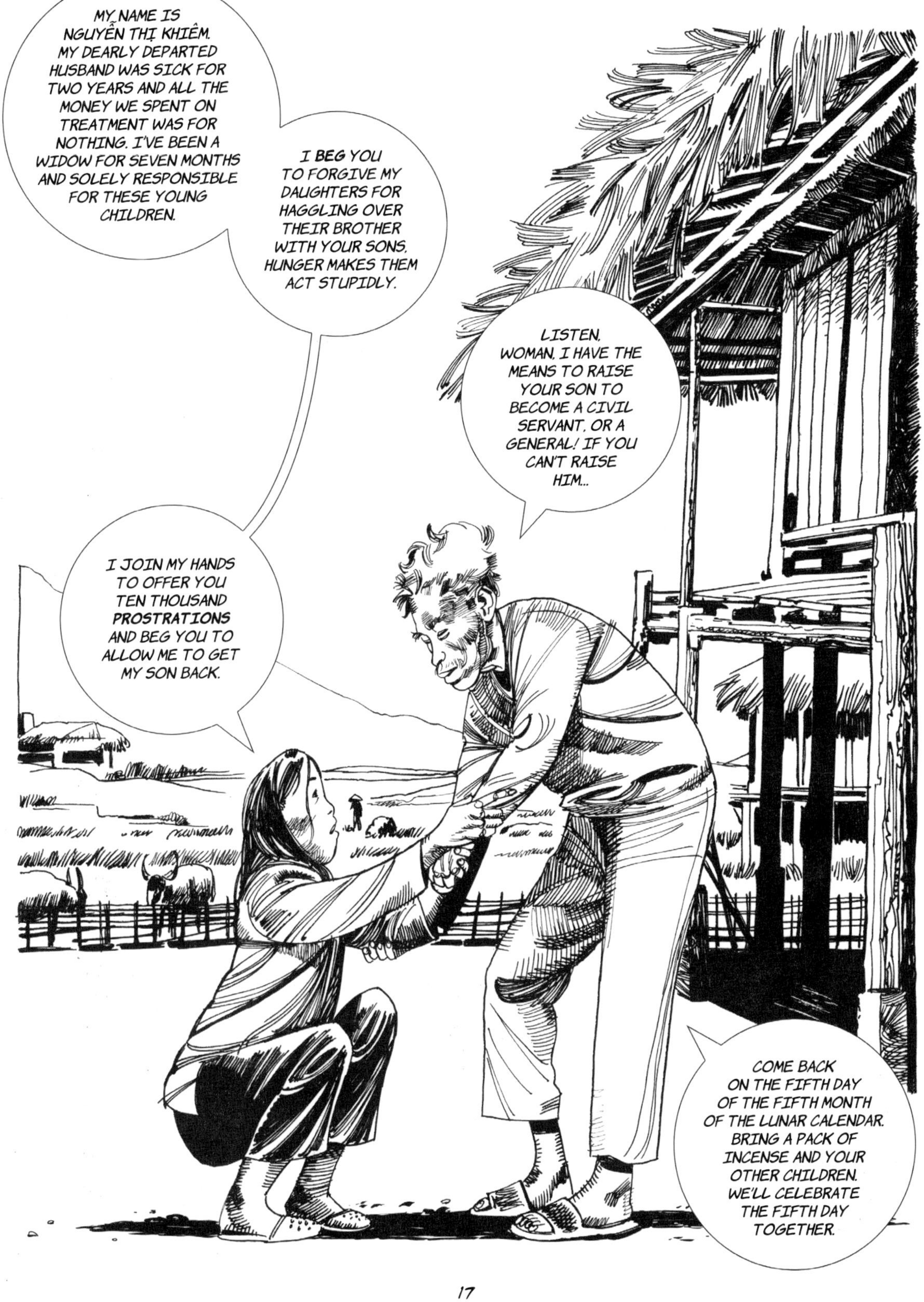
MY NAME IS NGUYỄN THỊ KHIÊM. MY DEARLY DEPARTED HUSBAND WAS SICK FOR TWO YEARS AND ALL THE MONEY WE SPENT ON TREATMENT WAS FOR NOTHING. I'VE BEEN A WIDOW FOR SEVEN MONTHS AND SOLELY RESPONSIBLE FOR THESE YOUNG CHILDREN.
I **BEG** YOU TO FORGIVE MY DAUGHTERS FOR HAGGLING OVER THEIR BROTHER WITH YOUR SONS. HUNGER MAKES THEM ACT STUPIDLY.
I JOIN MY HANDS TO OFFER YOU TEN THOUSAND **PROSTRATIONS** AND BEG YOU TO ALLOW ME TO GET MY SON BACK.
LISTEN, WOMAN, I HAVE THE MEANS TO RAISE YOUR SON TO BECOME A CIVIL SERVANT, OR A GENERAL! IF YOU CAN'T RAISE HIM...
COME BACK ON THE FIFTH DAY OF THE FIFTH MONTH OF THE LUNAR CALENDAR. BRING A PACK OF INCENSE AND YOUR OTHER CHILDREN. WE'LL CELEBRATE THE FIFTH DAY TOGETHER.

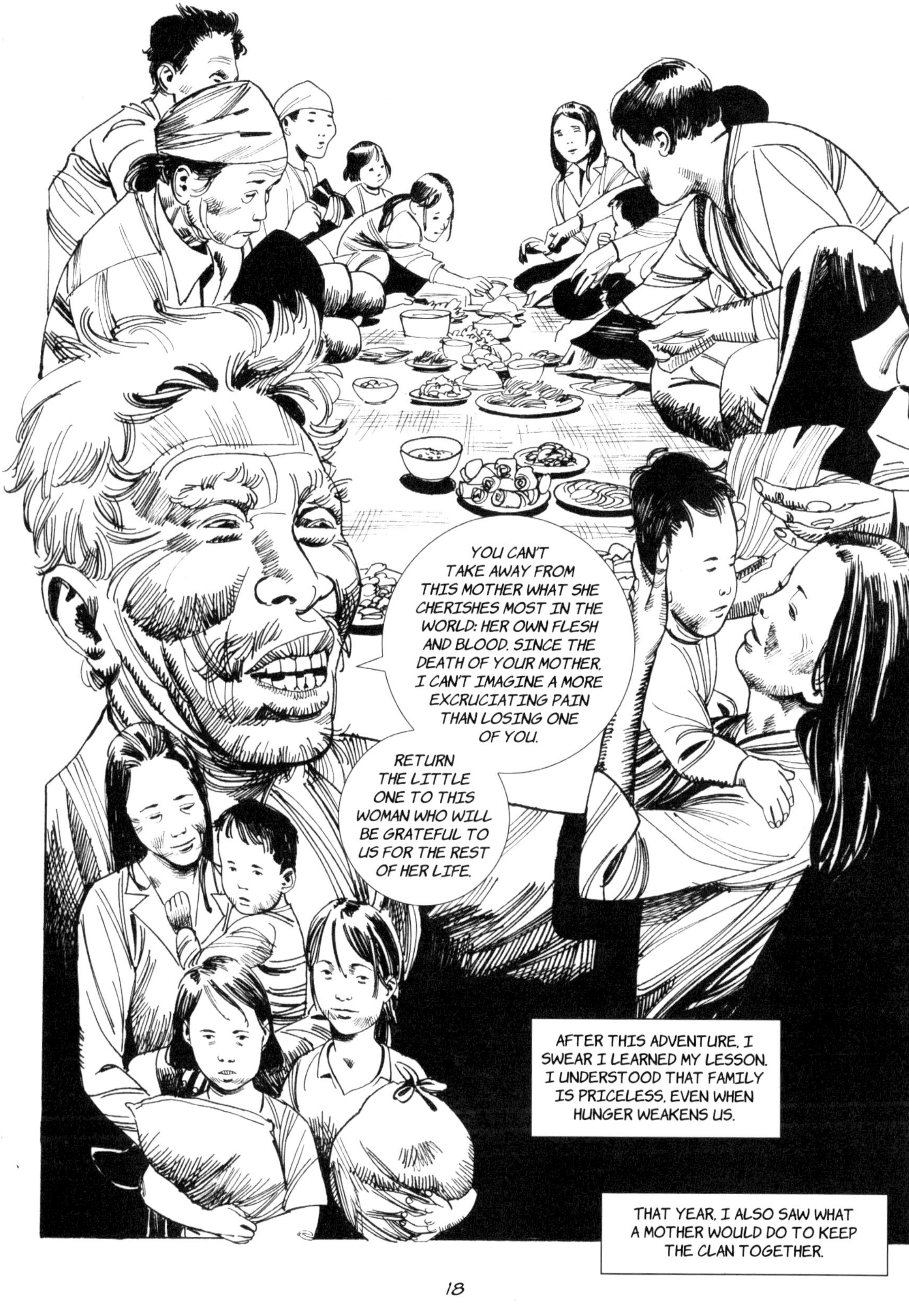
YOU CAN'T TAKE AWAY FROM THIS MOTHER WHAT SHE CHERISHES MOST IN THE WORLD: HER OWN FLESH AND BLOOD. SINCE THE DEATH OF YOUR MOTHER, I CAN'T IMAGINE A MORE EXCRUCIATING PAIN THAN LOSING ONE OF YOU.
RETURN THE LITTLE ONE TO THIS WOMAN WHO WILL BE GRATEFUL TO US FOR THE REST OF HER LIFE.
AFTER THIS ADVENTURE, I SWEAR I LEARNED MY LESSON. I UNDERSTOOD THAT FAMILY IS PRICELESS, EVEN WHEN HUNGER WEAKENS US.
THAT YEAR, I ALSO SAW WHAT A MOTHER WOULD DO TO KEEP THE CLAN TOGETHER.

CHAPTER 2

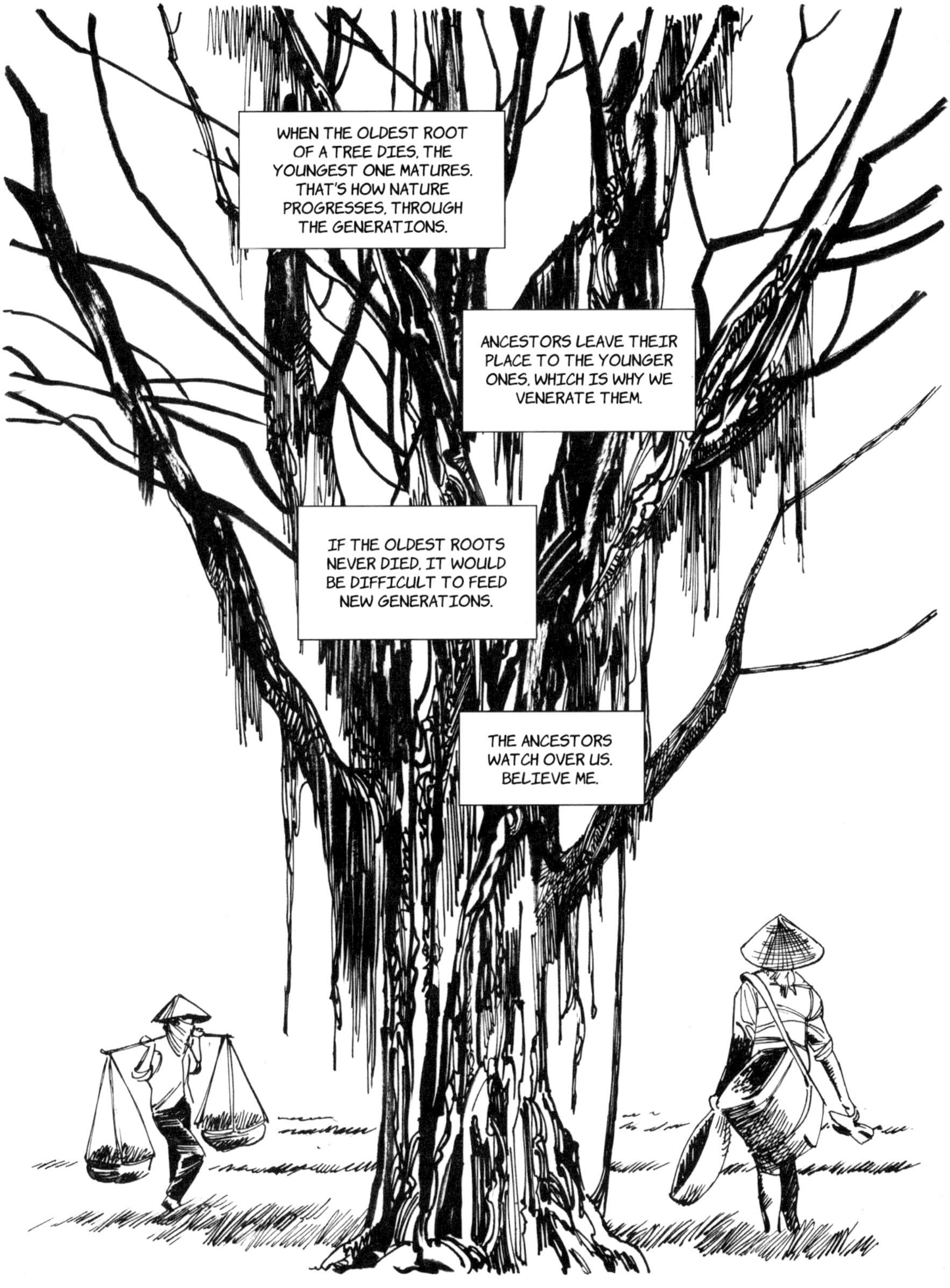
WHEN THE OLDEST ROOT OF A TREE DIES, THE YOUNGEST ONE MATURES. THAT'S HOW NATURE PROGRESSES, THROUGH THE GENERATIONS.
ANCESTORS LEAVE THEIR PLACE TO THE YOUNGER ONES, WHICH IS WHY WE VENERATE THEM.
IF THE OLDEST ROOTS NEVER DIED, IT WOULD BE DIFFICULT TO FEED NEW GENERATIONS.
THE ANCESTORS WATCH OVER US. BELIEVE ME.

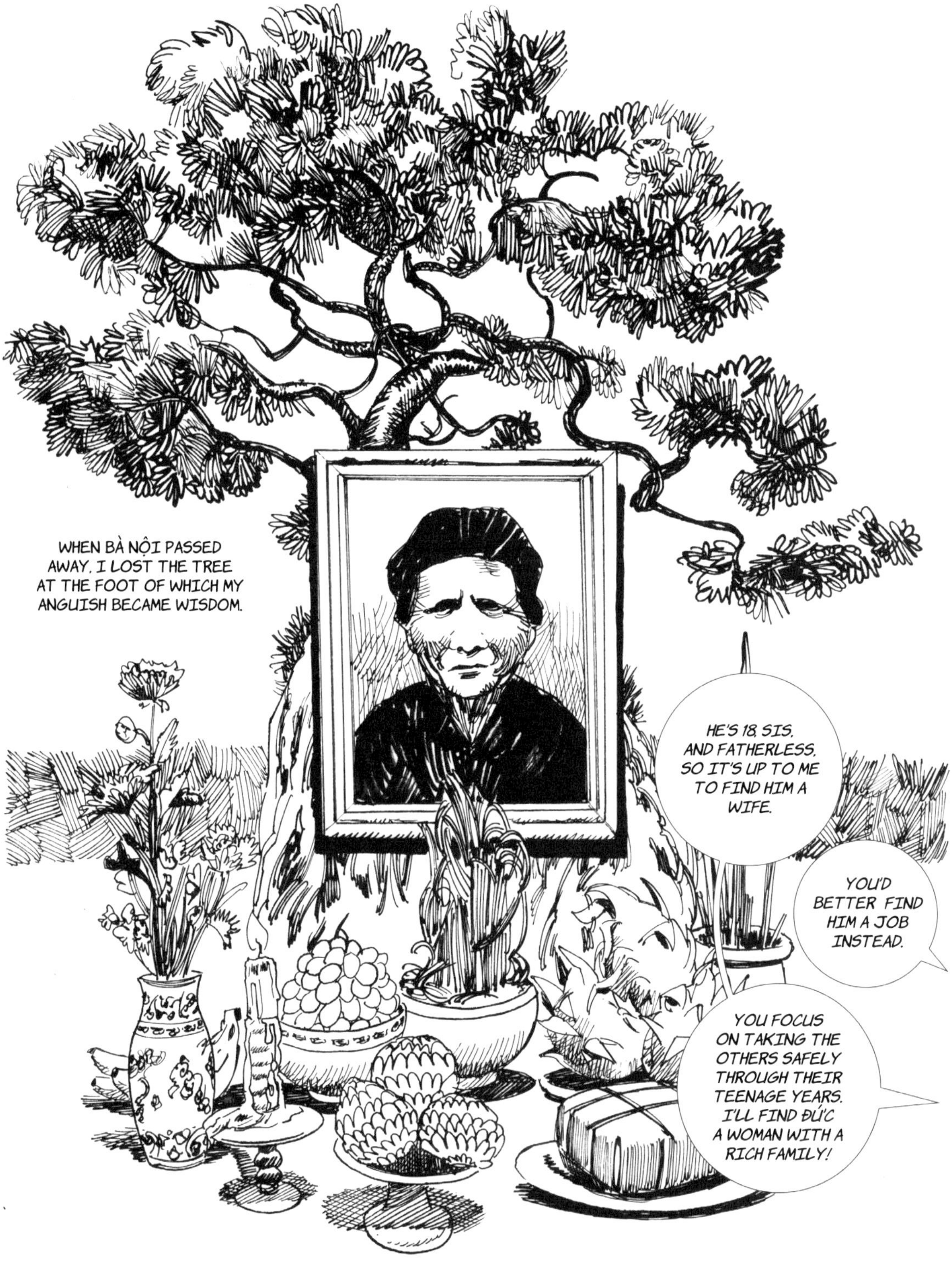
WHEN BÀ NỘI PASSED AWAY, I LOST THE TREE AT THE FOOT OF WHICH MY ANGUISH BECAME WISDOM.
HE'S 18, SIS, AND FATHERLESS, SO IT'S UP TO ME TO FIND HIM A WIFE.
YOU'D BETTER FIND HIM A JOB INSTEAD.
YOU FOCUS ON TAKING THE OTHERS SAFELY THROUGH THEIR TEENAGE YEARS. I'LL FIND ĐỨC A WOMAN WITH A RICH FAMILY!

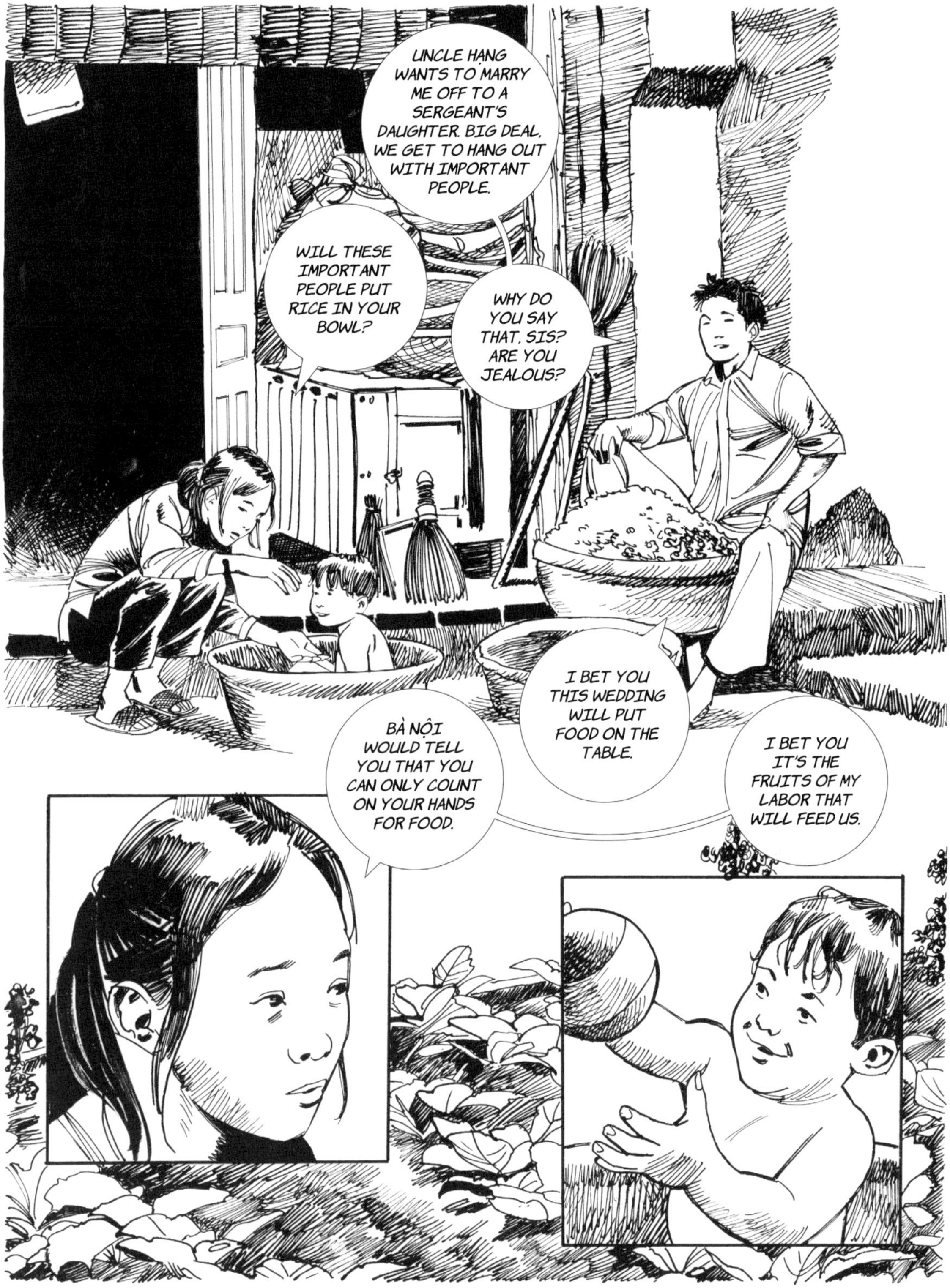
UNCLE HẠNG WANTS TO MARRY ME OFF TO A SERGEANT'S DAUGHTER. BIG DEAL. WE GET TO HANG OUT WITH IMPORTANT PEOPLE.
WILL THESE IMPORTANT PEOPLE PUT RICE IN YOUR BOWL?
WHY DO YOU SAY THAT, SIS? ARE YOU JEALOUS?
I BET YOU THIS WEDDING WILL PUT FOOD ON THE TABLE.
BÀ NỘI WOULD TELL YOU THAT YOU CAN ONLY COUNT ON YOUR HANDS FOR FOOD.
I BET YOU IT'S THE FRUITS OF MY LABOR THAT WILL FEED US.

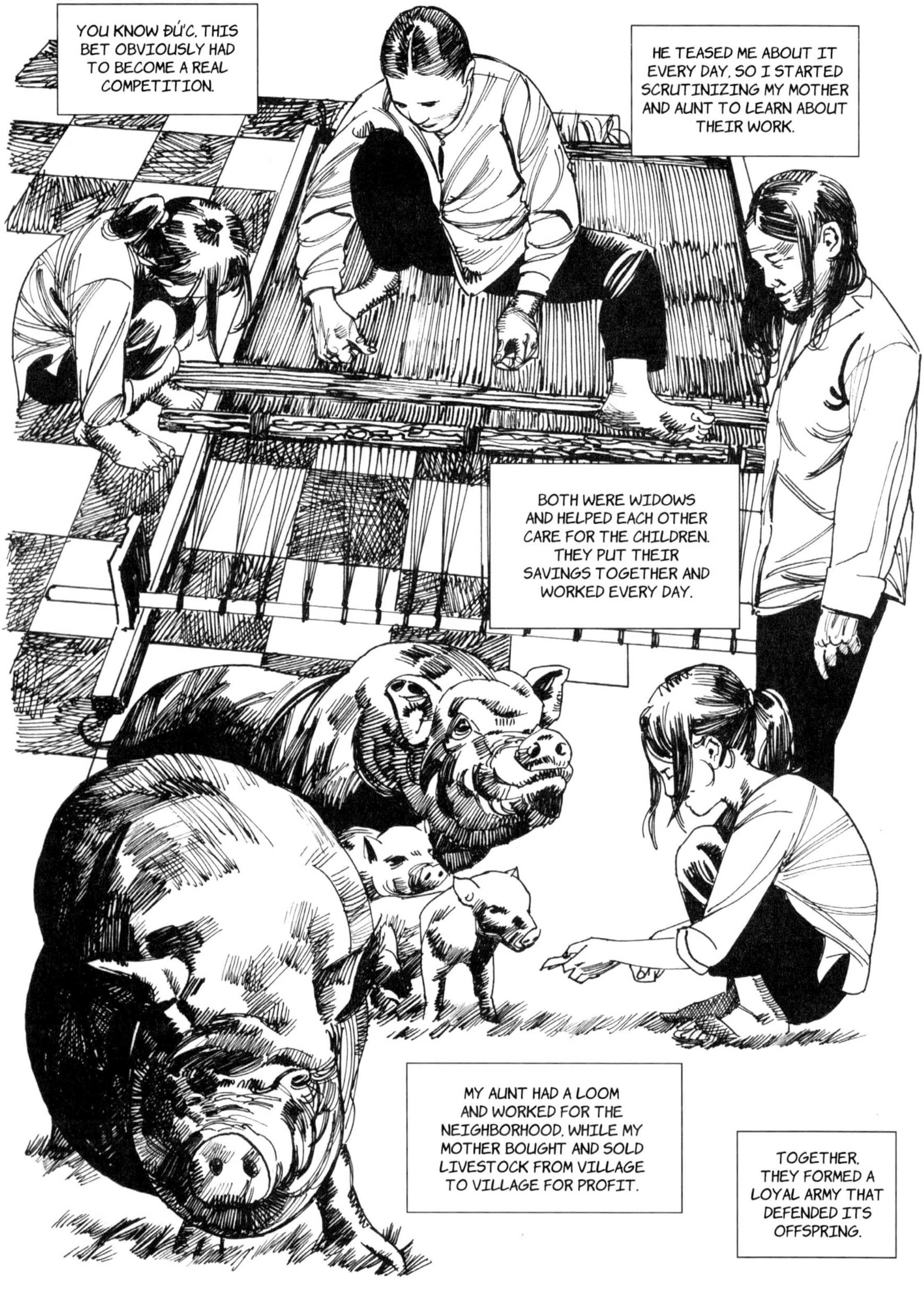
YOU KNOW ĐỨC, THIS BET OBVIOUSLY HAD TO BECOME A REAL COMPETITION.
HE TEASED ME ABOUT IT EVERY DAY, SO I STARTED SCRUTINIZING MY MOTHER AND AUNT TO LEARN ABOUT THEIR WORK.
BOTH WERE WIDOWS AND HELPED EACH OTHER CARE FOR THE CHILDREN. THEY PUT THEIR SAVINGS TOGETHER AND WORKED EVERY DAY.
MY AUNT HAD A LOOM AND WORKED FOR THE NEIGHBORHOOD, WHILE MY MOTHER BOUGHT AND SOLD LIVESTOCK FROM VILLAGE TO VILLAGE FOR PROFIT.
TOGETHER, THEY FORMED A LOYAL ARMY THAT DEFENDED ITS OFFSPRING.

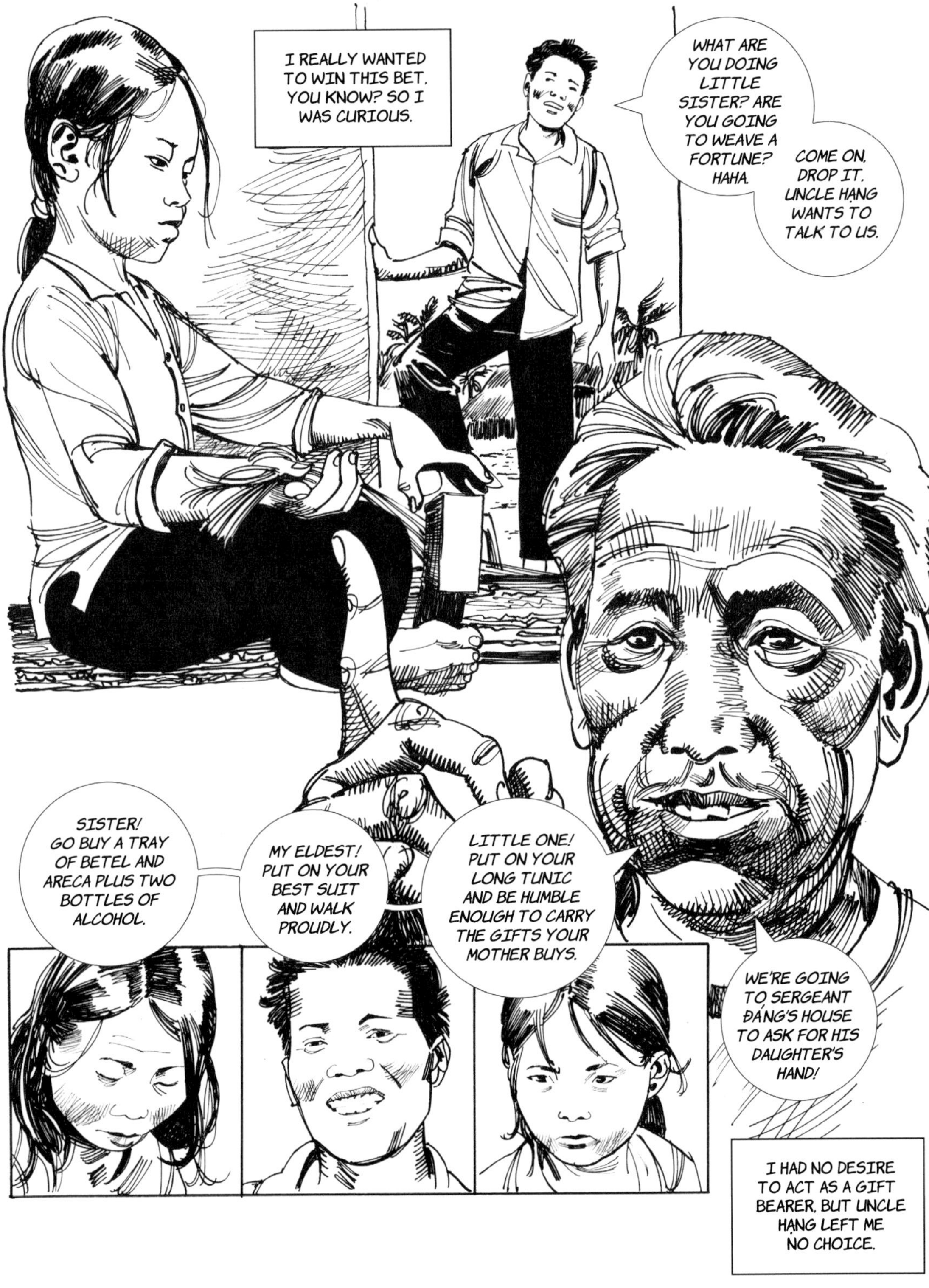
I REALLY WANTED TO WIN THIS BET, YOU KNOW? SO I WAS CURIOUS.
WHAT ARE YOU DOING LITTLE SISTER? ARE YOU GOING TO WEAVE A FORTUNE? HAHA.
COME ON, DROP IT, UNCLE HẠNG WANTS TO TALK TO US.
SISTER! GO BUY A TRAY OF BETEL AND ARECA PLUS TWO BOTTLES OF ALCOHOL.
MY ELDEST! PUT ON YOUR BEST SUIT AND WALK PROUDLY.
LITTLE ONE! PUT ON YOUR LONG TUNIC AND BE HUMBLE ENOUGH TO CARRY THE GIFTS YOUR MOTHER BUYS.
WE'RE GOING TO SERGEANT ĐÁNG'S HOUSE TO ASK FOR HIS DAUGHTER'S HAND!
I HAD NO DESIRE TO ACT AS A GIFT BEARER, BUT UNCLE HẠNG LEFT ME NO CHOICE.

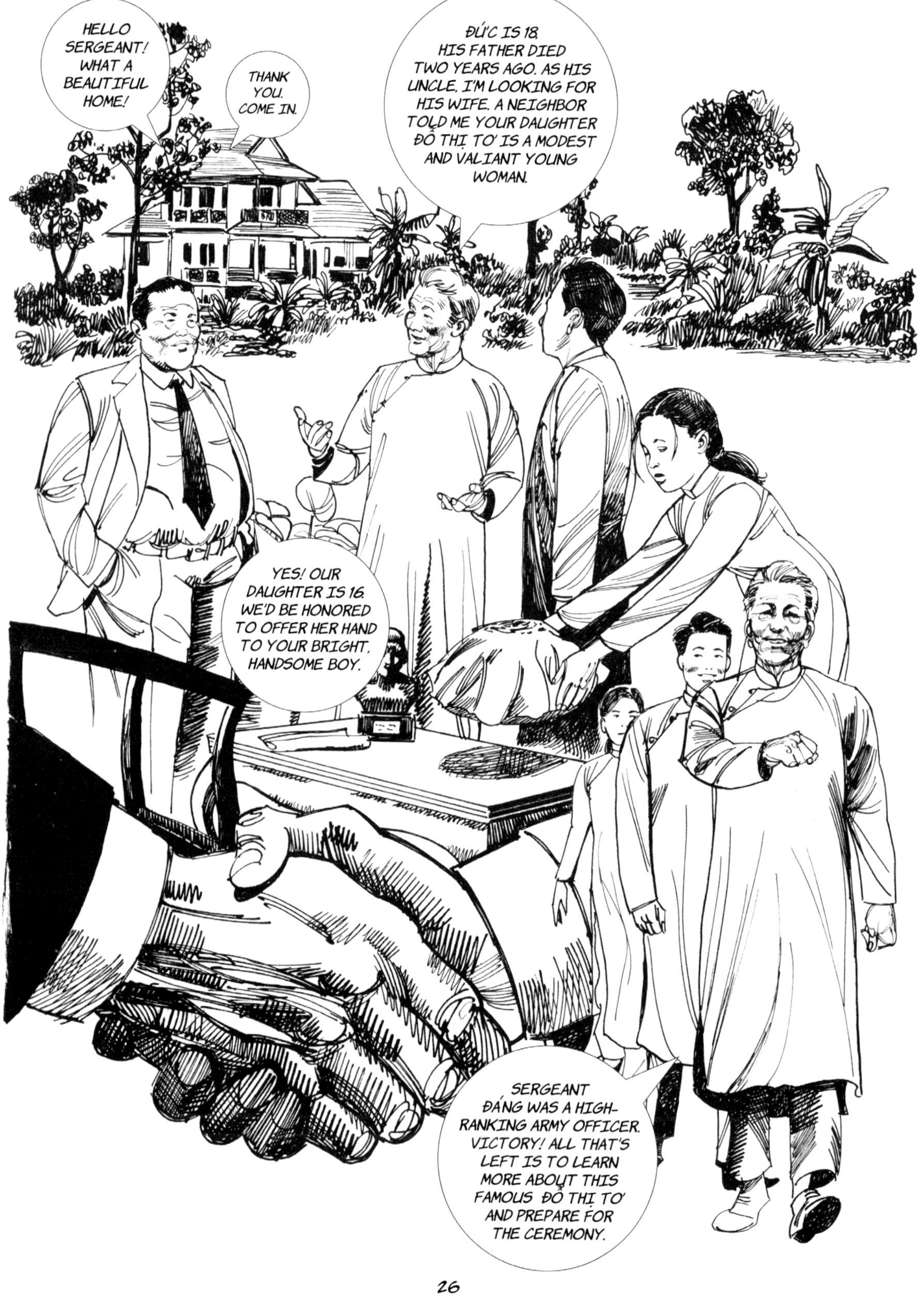
HELLO SERGEANT! WHAT A BEAUTIFUL HOME!
THANK YOU. COME IN.
ĐỨC IS 18. HIS FATHER DIED TWO YEARS AGO. AS HIS UNCLE, I'M LOOKING FOR HIS WIFE. A NEIGHBOR TOLD ME YOUR DAUGHTER ĐỖ THỊ TƠ IS A MODEST AND VALIANT YOUNG WOMAN.
YES! OUR DAUGHTER IS 16. WE'D BE HONORED TO OFFER HER HAND TO YOUR BRIGHT, HANDSOME BOY.
SERGEANT ĐẶNG WAS A HIGH-RANKING ARMY OFFICER. VICTORY! ALL THAT'S LEFT IS TO LEARN MORE ABOUT THIS FAMOUS ĐỖ THỊ TƠ AND PREPARE FOR THE CEREMONY.

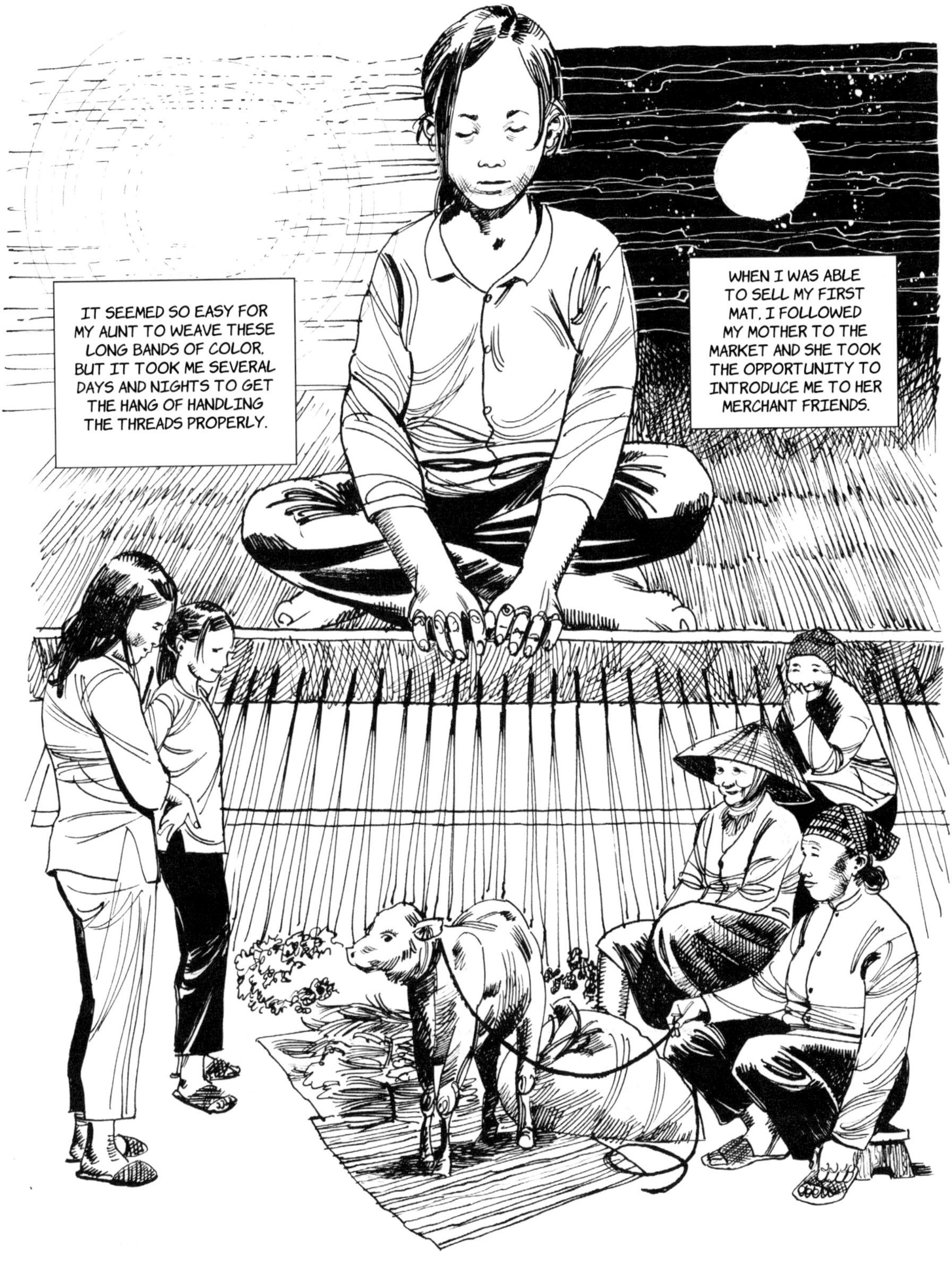
IT SEEMED SO EASY FOR MY AUNT TO WEAVE THESE LONG BANDS OF COLOR, BUT IT TOOK ME SEVERAL DAYS AND NIGHTS TO GET THE HANG OF HANDLING THE THREADS PROPERLY.
WHEN I WAS ABLE TO SELL MY FIRST MAT, I FOLLOWED MY MOTHER TO THE MARKET AND SHE TOOK THE OPPORTUNITY TO INTRODUCE ME TO HER MERCHANT FRIENDS.

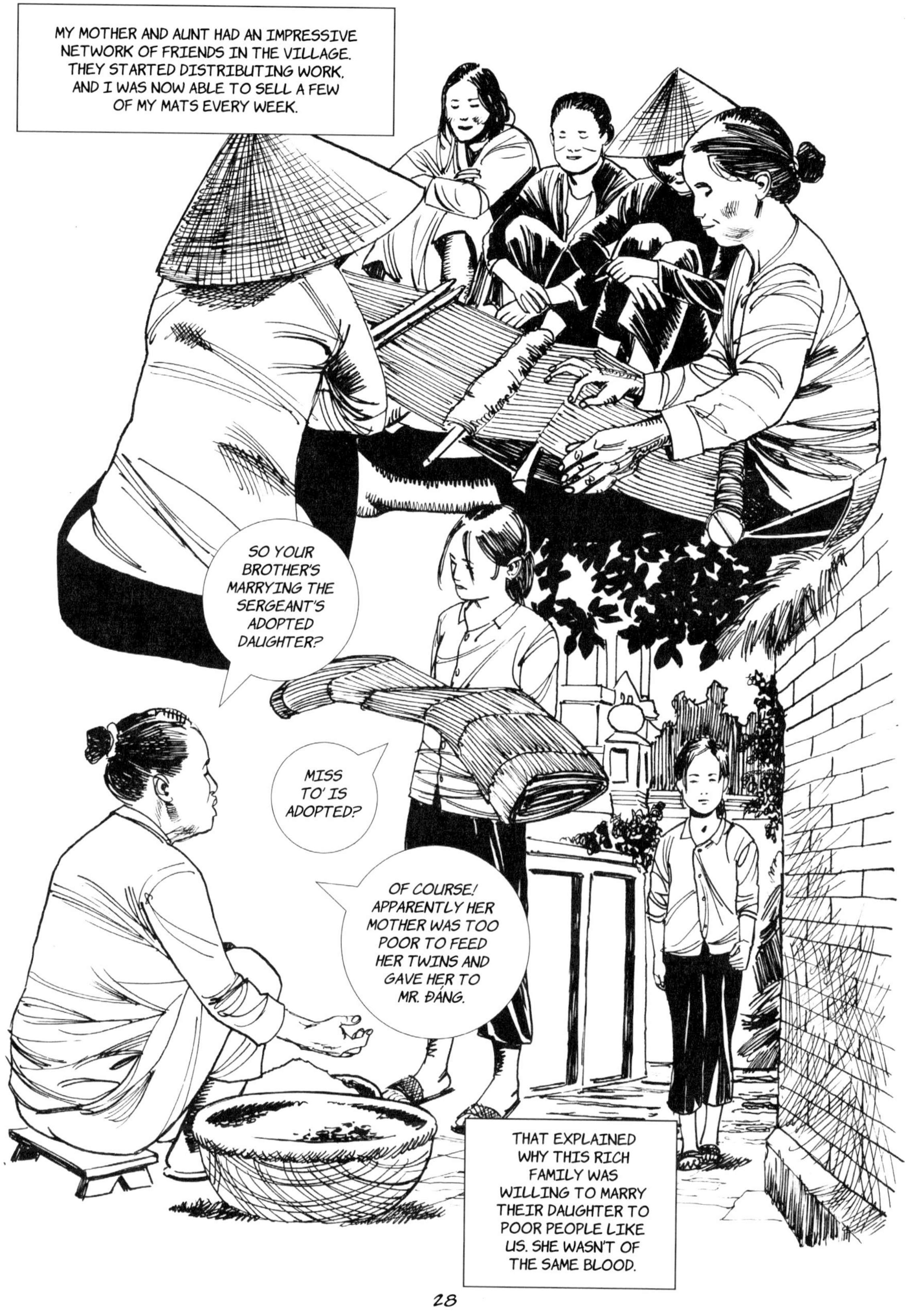
MY MOTHER AND AUNT HAD AN IMPRESSIVE NETWORK OF FRIENDS IN THE VILLAGE. THEY STARTED DISTRIBUTING WORK, AND I WAS NOW ABLE TO SELL A FEW OF MY MATS EVERY WEEK.
SO YOUR BROTHER'S MARRYING THE SERGEANT'S ADOPTED DAUGHTER?
MISS TO' IS ADOPTED?
OF COURSE! APPARENTLY HER MOTHER WAS TOO POOR TO FEED HER TWINS AND GAVE HER TO MR. ĐÁNG.
THAT EXPLAINED WHY THIS RICH FAMILY WAS WILLING TO MARRY THEIR DAUGHTER TO POOR PEOPLE LIKE US. SHE WASN'T OF THE SAME BLOOD.

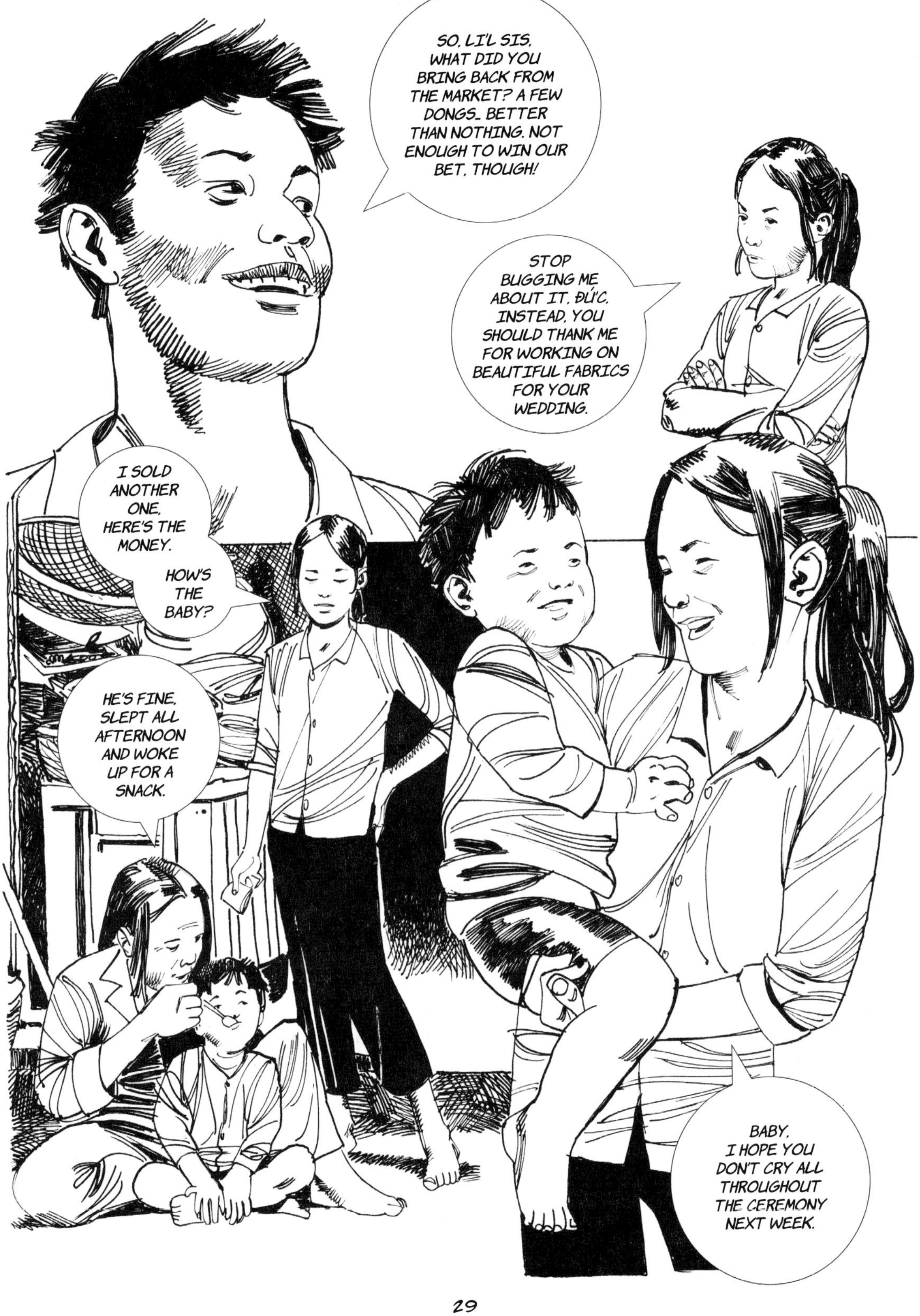
SO, LI'L SIS, WHAT DID YOU BRING BACK FROM THE MARKET? A FEW DONGS... BETTER THAN NOTHING. NOT ENOUGH TO WIN OUR BET, THOUGH!
STOP BUGGING ME ABOUT IT, ĐỨC. INSTEAD, YOU SHOULD THANK ME FOR WORKING ON BEAUTIFUL FABRICS FOR YOUR WEDDING.
I SOLD ANOTHER ONE, HERE'S THE MONEY.
HOW'S THE BABY?
HE'S FINE, SLEPT ALL AFTERNOON AND WOKE UP FOR A SNACK.
BABY, I HOPE YOU DON'T CRY ALL THROUGHOUT THE CEREMONY NEXT WEEK.

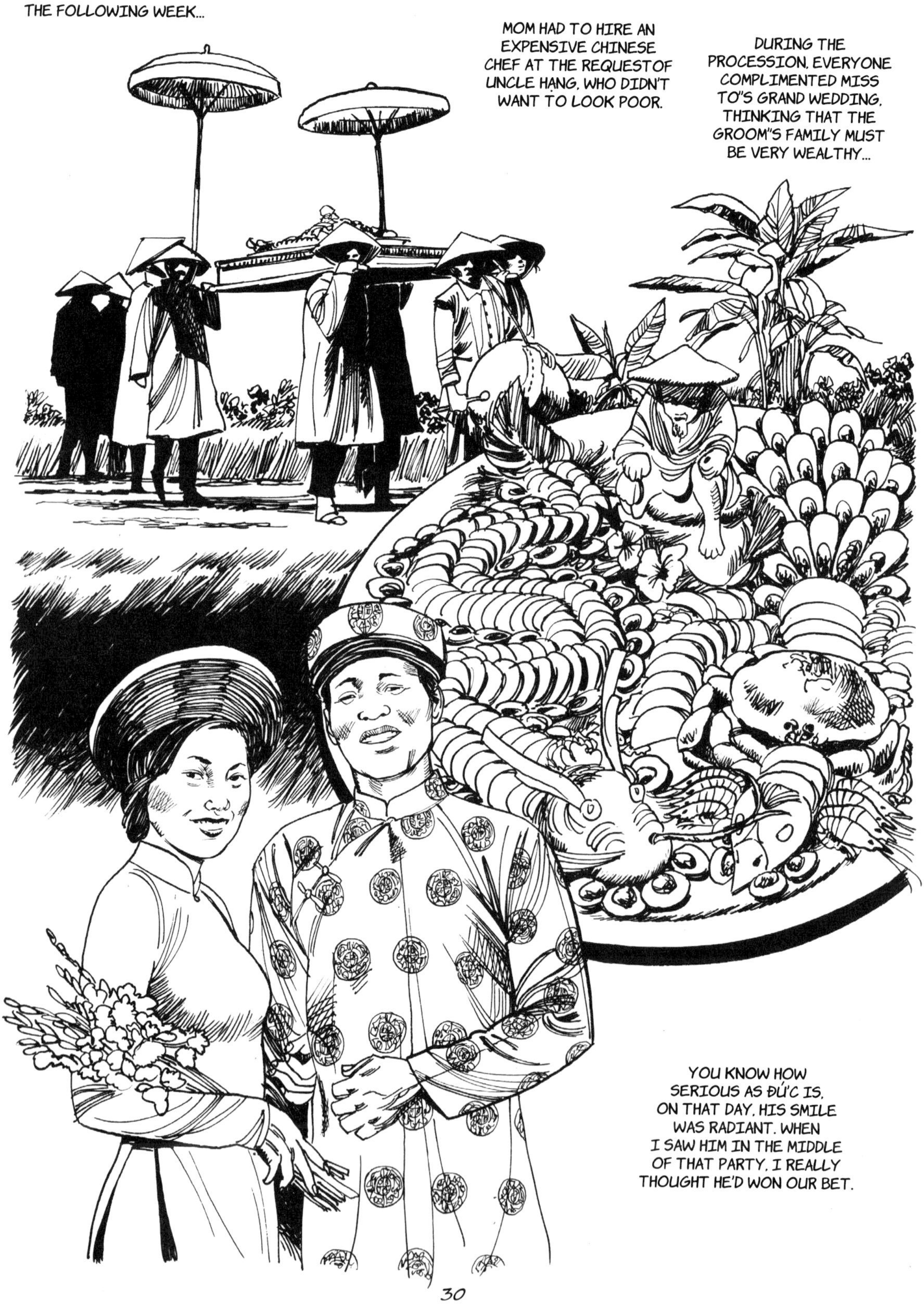
THE FOLLOWING WEEK...
MOM HAD TO HIRE AN EXPENSIVE CHINESE CHEF AT THE REQUESTOF UNCLE HẠNG, WHO DIDN'T WANT TO LOOK POOR.
DURING THE PROCESSION, EVERYONE COMPLIMENTED MISS TO"S GRAND WEDDING, THINKING THAT THE GROOM"S FAMILY MUST BE VERY WEALTHY...
YOU KNOW HOW SERIOUS AS ĐỨC IS. ON THAT DAY, HIS SMILE WAS RADIANT. WHEN I SAW HIM IN THE MIDDLE OF THAT PARTY, I REALLY THOUGHT HE'D WON OUR BET.

CHAPTER 3

THE FEELING OF BEING RICH AND IMPORTANT FADED QUICKLY AFTER THE WEDDING.

THE CEREMONY HAD COST US A LOT OF MONEY, AND IT WAS OUR MAT MONEY THAT FINANCED IT.

NOBODY HAD WON THE BET.

DESPITE ALL THESE ALLIANCES AND ALL MY MOTHER'S EFFORTS TO KEEP THE FAMILY TOGETHER, SHE COULDN'T PROTECT ME FROM THE LONELINESS THAT AWAITED ME.

IT WAS AT 15 THAT I FOUND MYSELF ALONE... ARE YOU BEGINNING TO UNDERSTAND WHY I'M WRITING YOU THESE LETTERS?

A FEW MONTHS LATER...

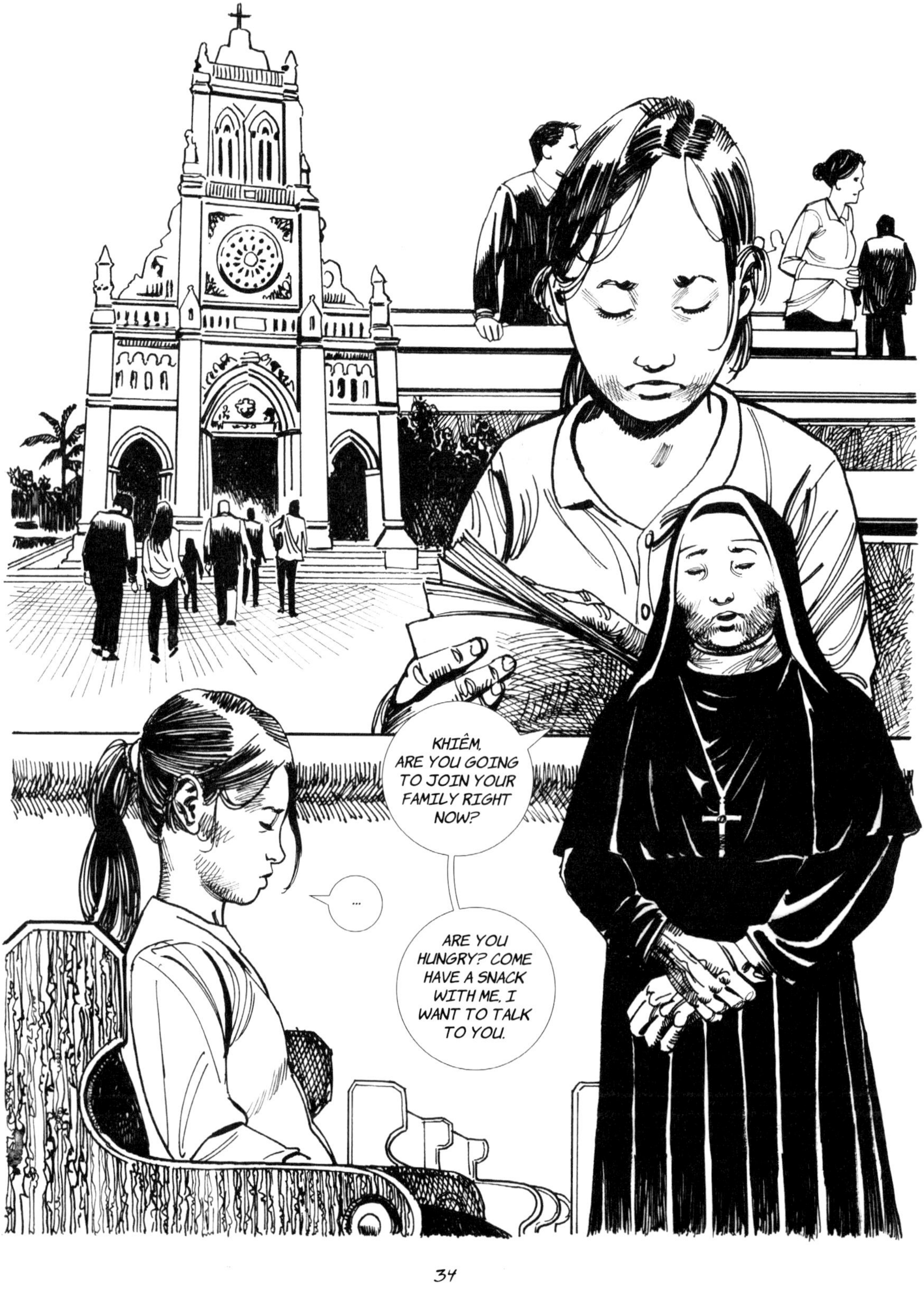
KHIÊM, ARE YOU GOING TO JOIN YOUR FAMILY RIGHT NOW?
...
ARE YOU HUNGRY? COME HAVE A SNACK WITH ME. I WANT TO TALK TO YOU.

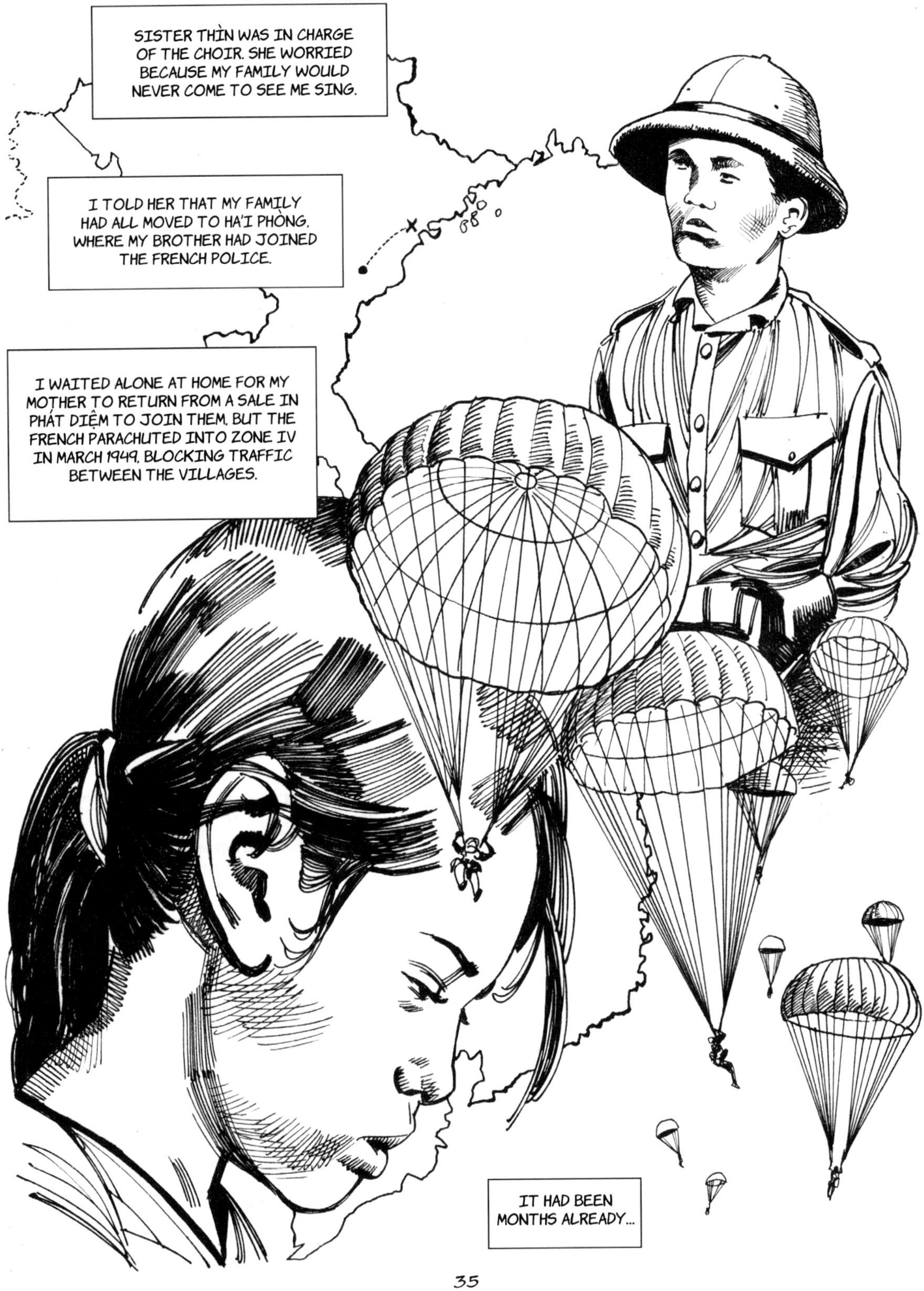
SISTER THÌN WAS IN CHARGE OF THE CHOIR. SHE WORRIED BECAUSE MY FAMILY WOULD NEVER COME TO SEE ME SING.
I TOLD HER THAT MY FAMILY HAD ALL MOVED TO HẢI PHÒNG, WHERE MY BROTHER HAD JOINED THE FRENCH POLICE.
I WAITED ALONE AT HOME FOR MY MOTHER TO RETURN FROM A SALE IN PHÁT DIỆM TO JOIN THEM, BUT THE FRENCH PARACHUTED INTO ZONE IV IN MARCH 1949, BLOCKING TRAFFIC BETWEEN THE VILLAGES.
IT HAD BEEN MONTHS ALREADY...

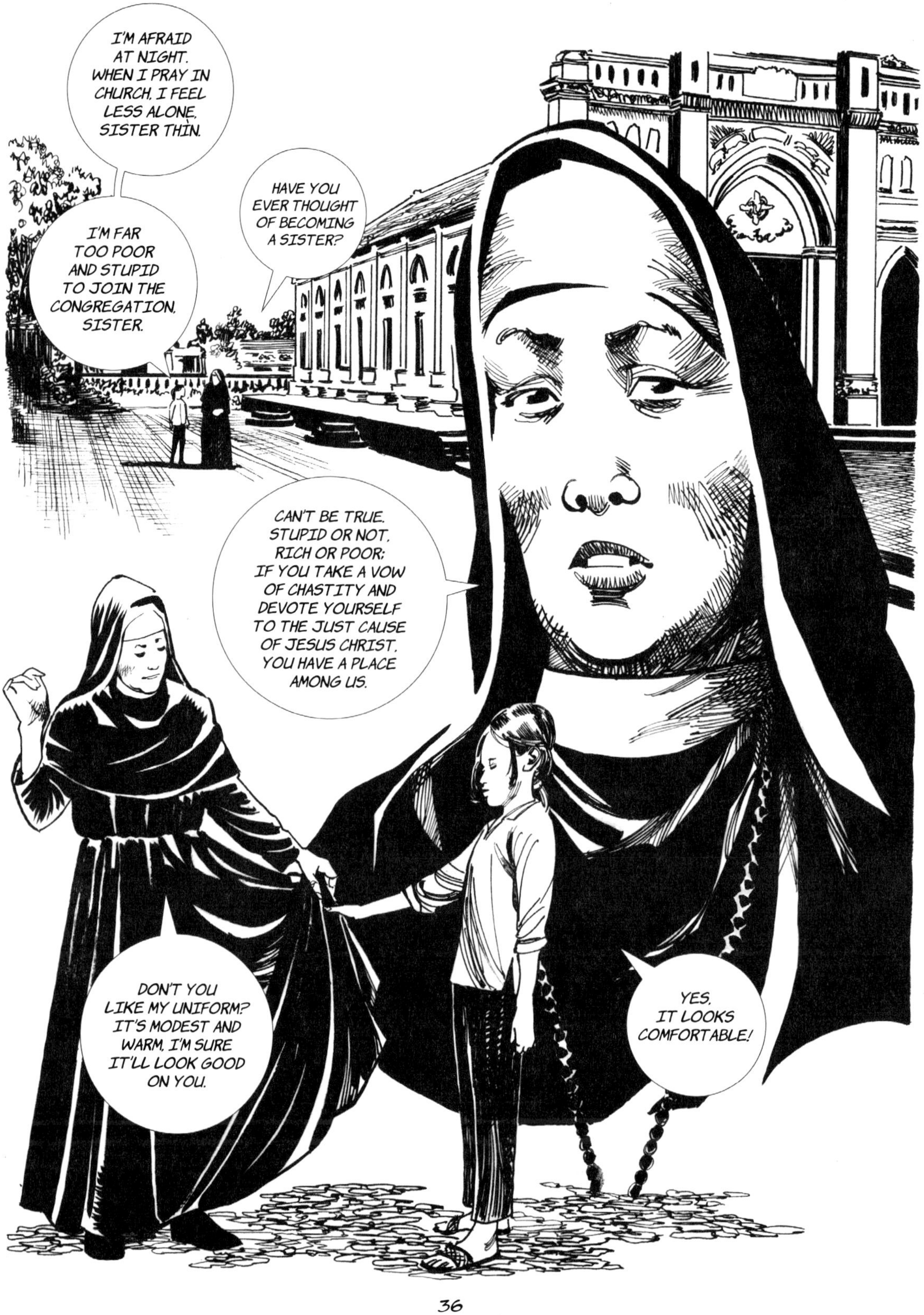
I'M AFRAID AT NIGHT. WHEN I PRAY IN CHURCH, I FEEL LESS ALONE, SISTER THÌN.
HAVE YOU EVER THOUGHT OF BECOMING A SISTER?
I'M FAR TOO POOR AND STUPID TO JOIN THE CONGREGATION, SISTER.
CAN'T BE TRUE. STUPID OR NOT, RICH OR POOR; IF YOU TAKE A VOW OF CHASTITY AND DEVOTE YOURSELF TO THE JUST CAUSE OF JESUS CHRIST, YOU HAVE A PLACE AMONG US.
DON'T YOU LIKE MY UNIFORM? IT'S MODEST AND WARM. I'M SURE IT'LL LOOK GOOD ON YOU.
YES, IT LOOKS COMFORTABLE!

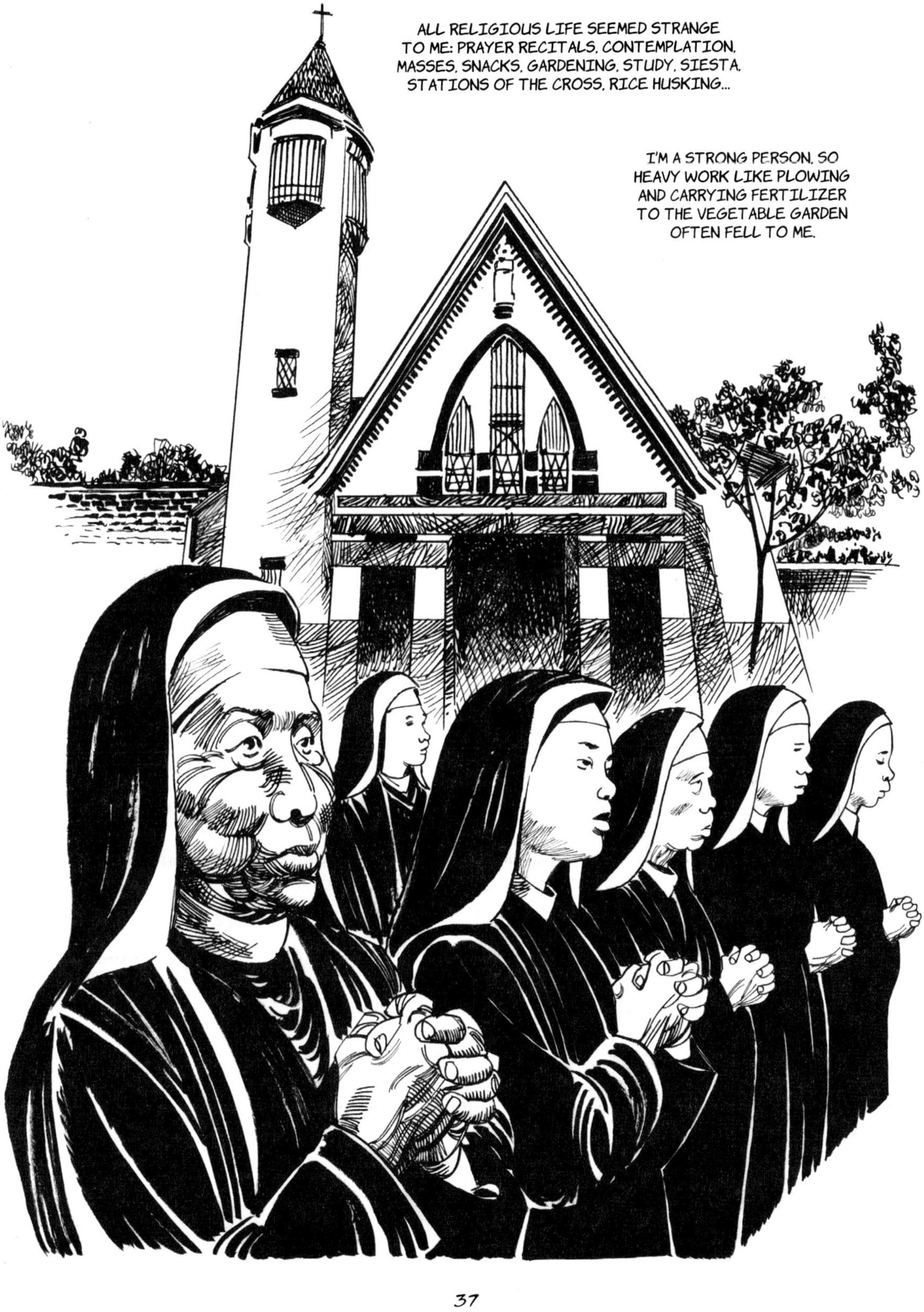
ALL RELIGIOUS LIFE SEEMED STRANGE TO ME: PRAYER RECITALS, CONTEMPLATION, MASSES, SNACKS, GARDENING, STUDY, SIESTA, STATIONS OF THE CROSS, RICE HUSKING...
I'M A STRONG PERSON, SO HEAVY WORK LIKE PLOWING AND CARRYING FERTILIZER TO THE VEGETABLE GARDEN OFTEN FELL TO ME.

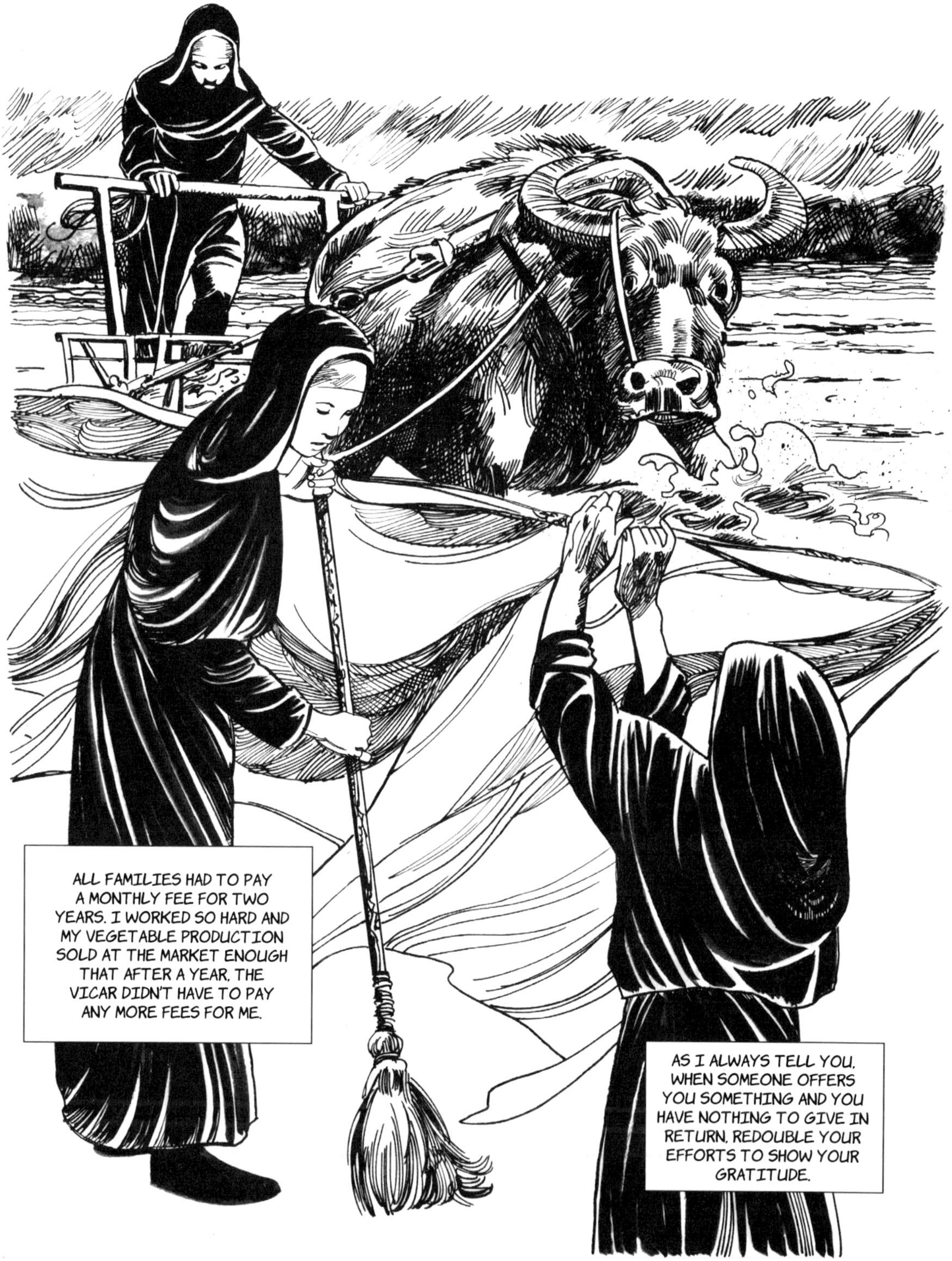
ALL FAMILIES HAD TO PAY A MONTHLY FEE FOR TWO YEARS. I WORKED SO HARD AND MY VEGETABLE PRODUCTION SOLD AT THE MARKET ENOUGH THAT AFTER A YEAR, THE VICAR DIDN'T HAVE TO PAY ANY MORE FEES FOR ME.
AS I ALWAYS TELL YOU, WHEN SOMEONE OFFERS YOU SOMETHING AND YOU HAVE NOTHING TO GIVE IN RETURN, REDOUBLE YOUR EFFORTS TO SHOW YOUR GRATITUDE.

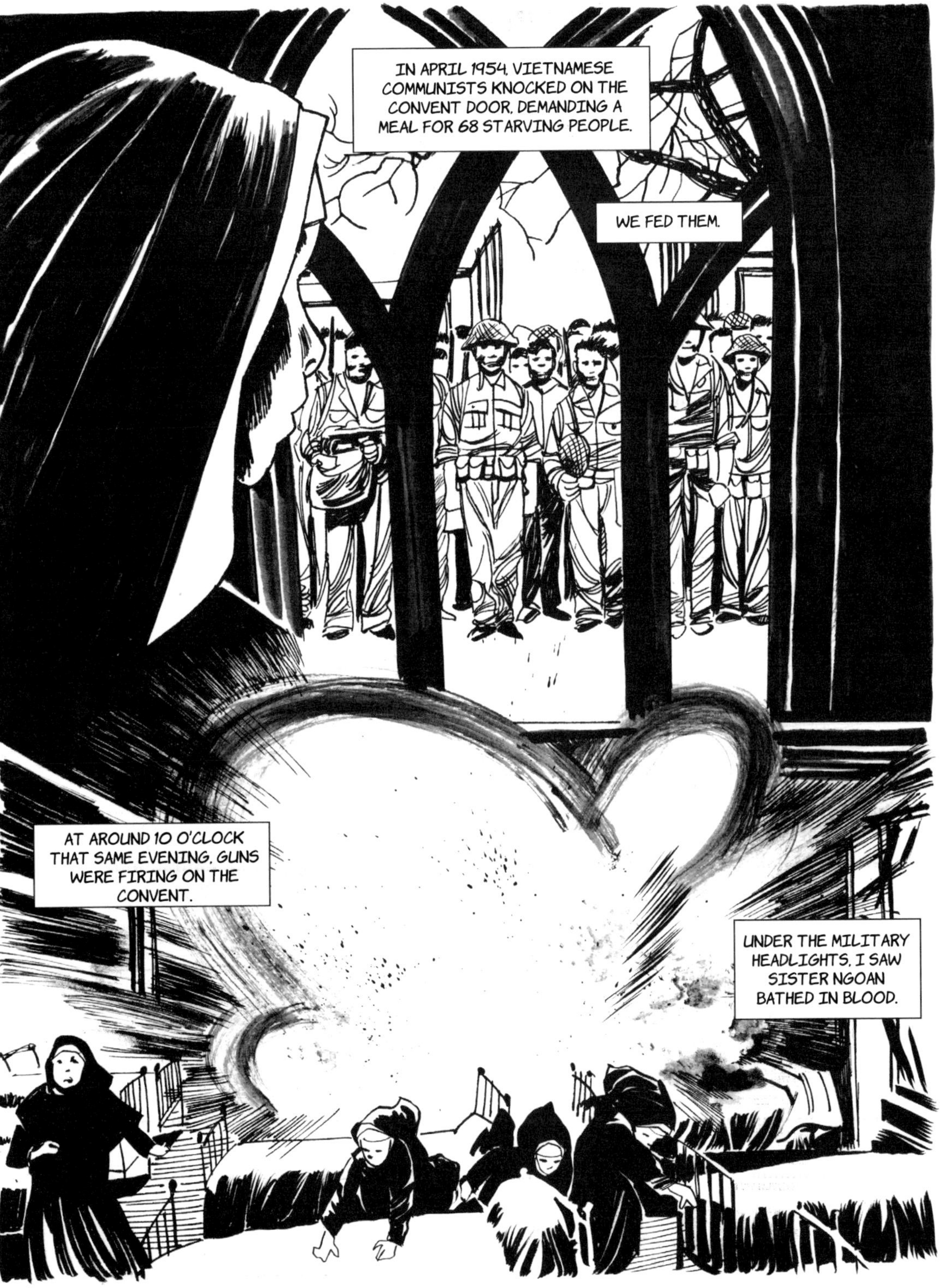
IN APRIL 1954, VIETNAMESE COMMUNISTS KNOCKED ON THE CONVENT DOOR, DEMANDING A MEAL FOR 68 STARVING PEOPLE.
WE FED THEM.
AT AROUND 10 O'CLOCK THAT SAME EVENING, GUNS WERE FIRING ON THE CONVENT.
UNDER THE MILITARY HEADLIGHTS, I SAW SISTER NGOAN BATHED IN BLOOD.

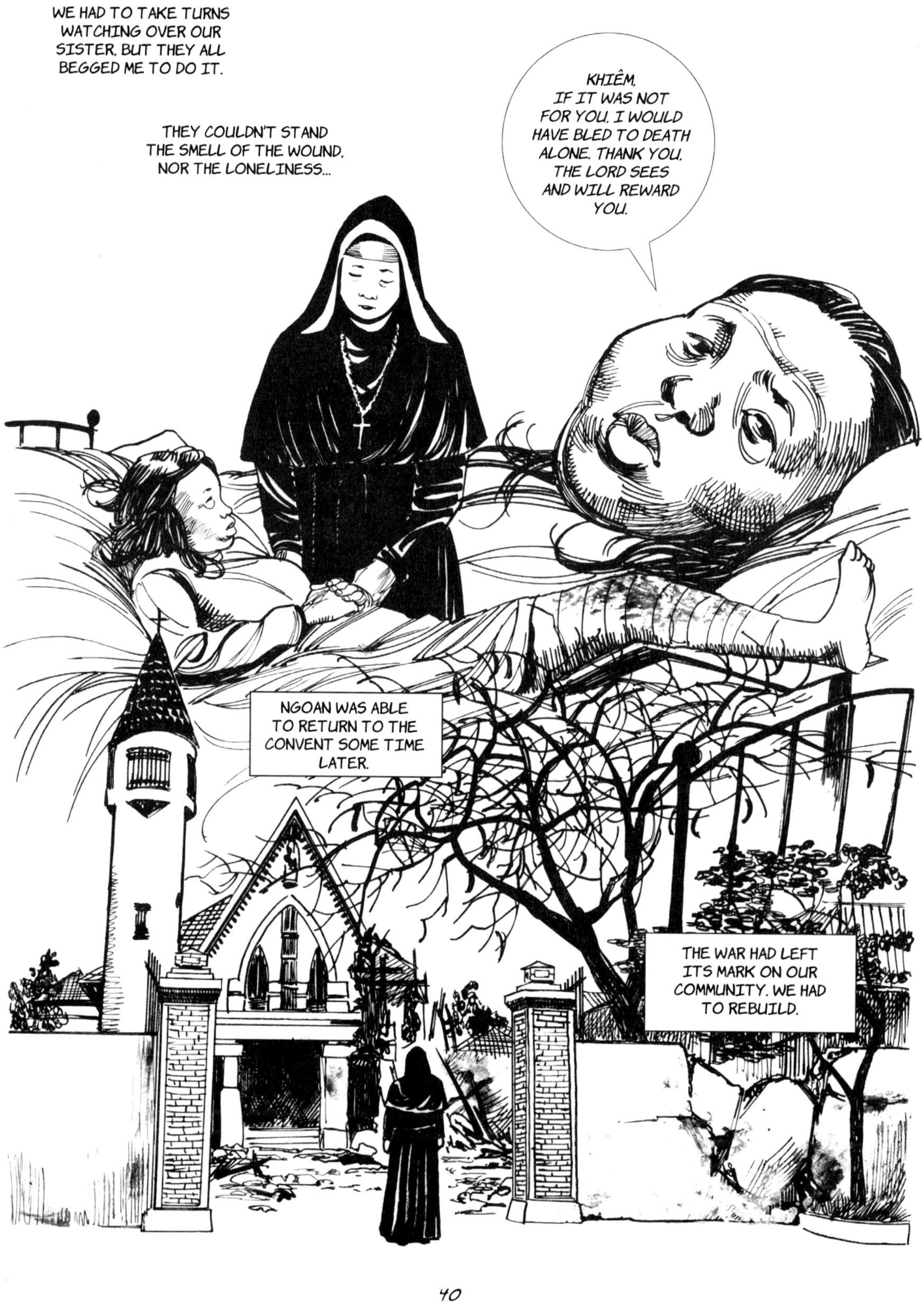
WE HAD TO TAKE TURNS WATCHING OVER OUR SISTER, BUT THEY ALL BEGGED ME TO DO IT.
THEY COULDN'T STAND THE SMELL OF THE WOUND, NOR THE LONELINESS...
KHIÊM, IF IT WAS NOT FOR YOU, I WOULD HAVE BLED TO DEATH ALONE. THANK YOU. THE LORD SEES AND WILL REWARD YOU.
NGOAN WAS ABLE TO RETURN TO THE CONVENT SOME TIME LATER.
THE WAR HAD LEFT ITS MARK ON OUR COMMUNITY. WE HAD TO REBUILD.

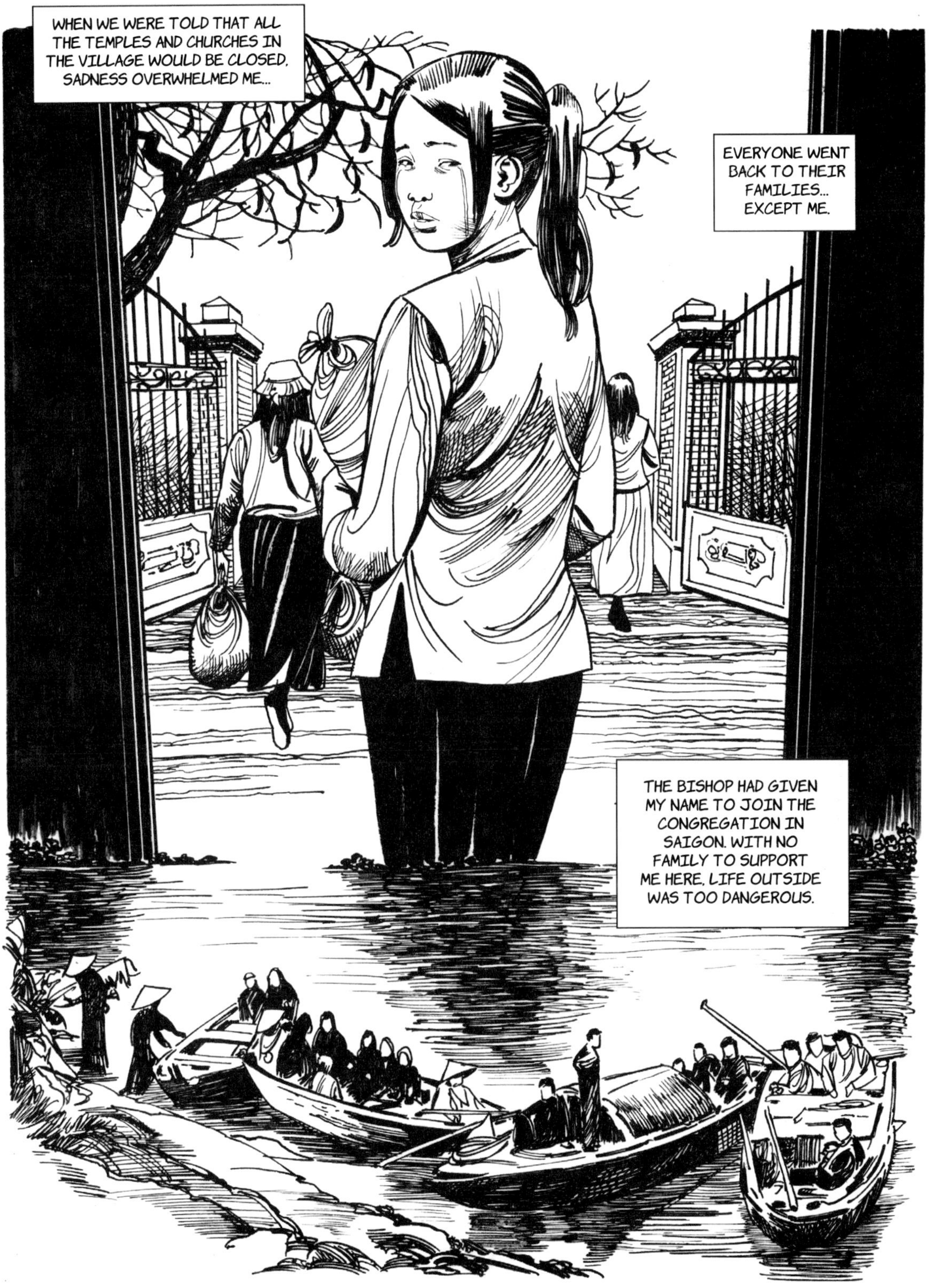
WHEN WE WERE TOLD THAT ALL THE TEMPLES AND CHURCHES IN THE VILLAGE WOULD BE CLOSED, SADNESS OVERWHELMED ME...
EVERYONE WENT BACK TO THEIR FAMILIES... EXCEPT ME.
THE BISHOP HAD GIVEN MY NAME TO JOIN THE CONGREGATION IN SAIGON. WITH NO FAMILY TO SUPPORT ME HERE, LIFE OUTSIDE WAS TOO DANGEROUS.

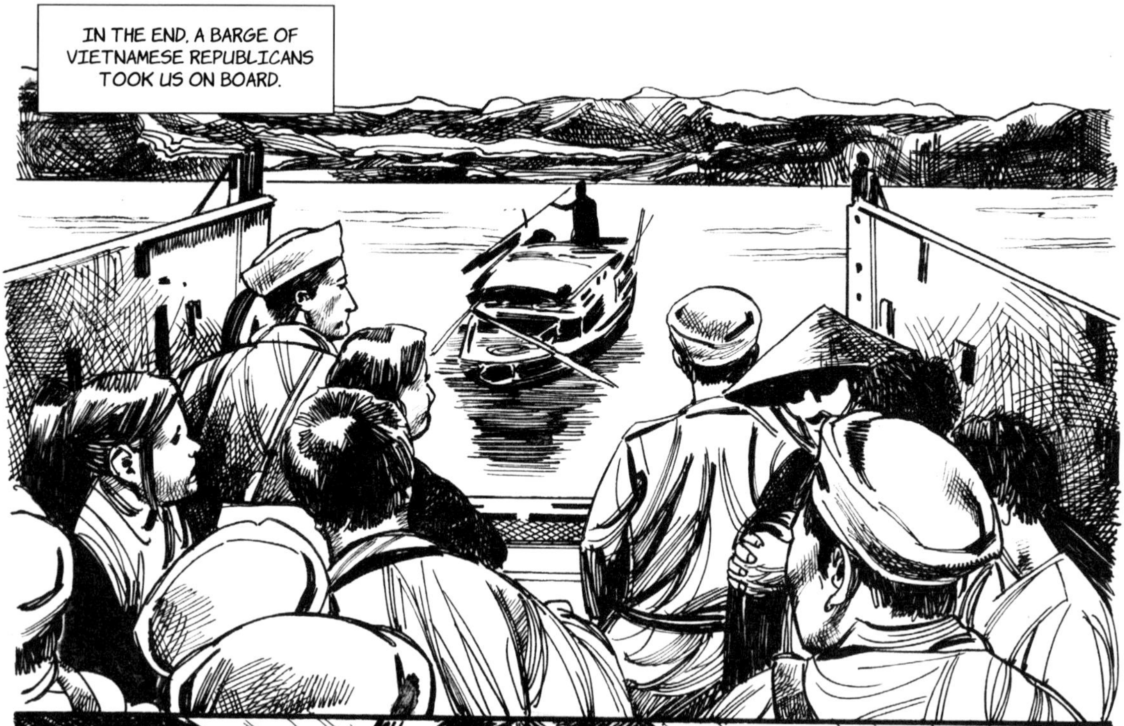
IN THE END, A BARGE OF VIETNAMESE REPUBLICANS TOOK US ON BOARD.

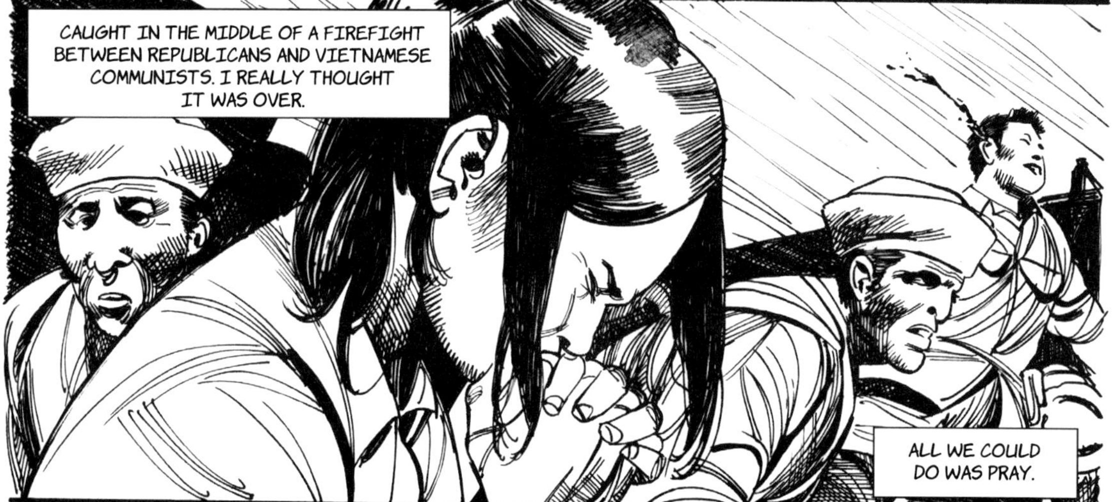
CAUGHT IN THE MIDDLE OF A FIREFIGHT BETWEEN REPUBLICANS AND VIETNAMESE COMMUNISTS. I REALLY THOUGHT IT WAS OVER.
ALL WE COULD DO WAS PRAY.

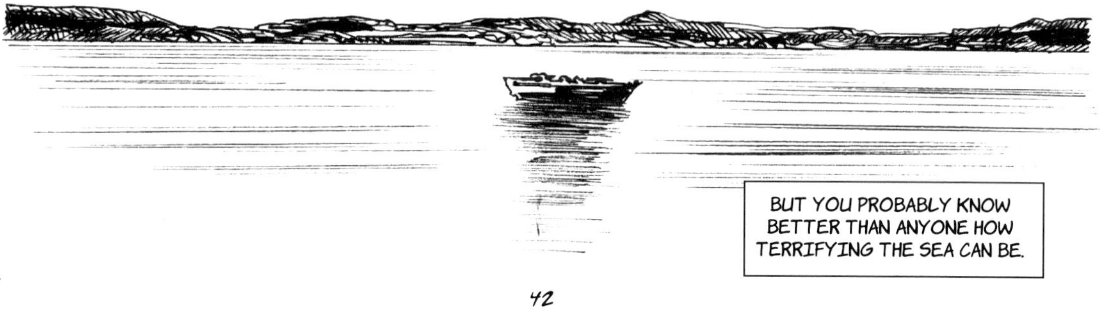
BUT YOU PROBABLY KNOW BETTER THAN ANYONE HOW TERRIFYING THE SEA CAN BE.

CHAPTER 4

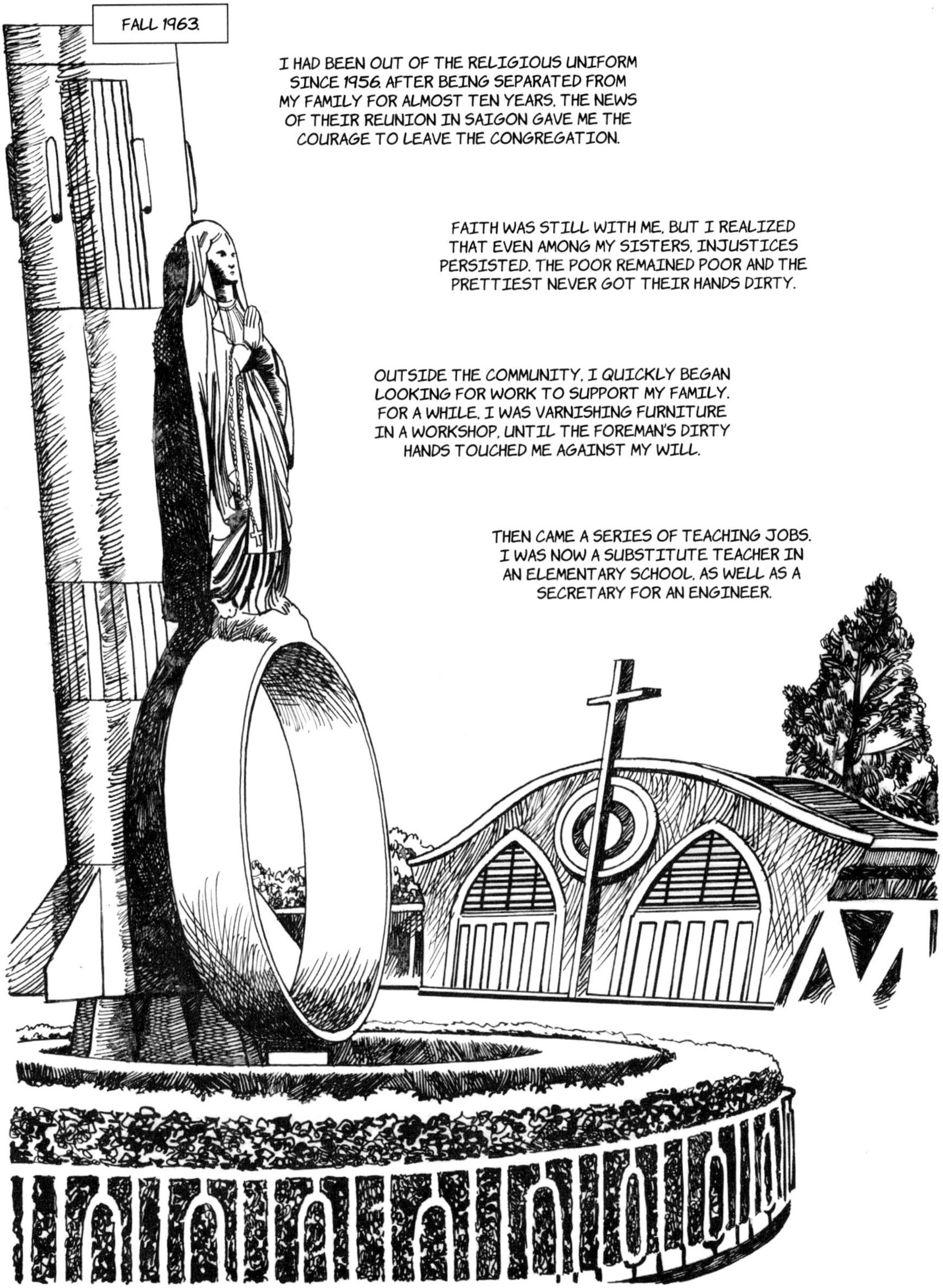
FALL 1963.
I HAD BEEN OUT OF THE RELIGIOUS UNIFORM SINCE 1956. AFTER BEING SEPARATED FROM MY FAMILY FOR ALMOST TEN YEARS, THE NEWS OF THEIR REUNION IN SAIGON GAVE ME THE COURAGE TO LEAVE THE CONGREGATION.
FAITH WAS STILL WITH ME, BUT I REALIZED THAT EVEN AMONG MY SISTERS, INJUSTICES PERSISTED. THE POOR REMAINED POOR AND THE PRETTIEST NEVER GOT THEIR HANDS DIRTY.
OUTSIDE THE COMMUNITY, I QUICKLY BEGAN LOOKING FOR WORK TO SUPPORT MY FAMILY. FOR A WHILE, I WAS VARNISHING FURNITURE IN A WORKSHOP, UNTIL THE FOREMAN'S DIRTY HANDS TOUCHED ME AGAINST MY WILL.
THEN CAME A SERIES OF TEACHING JOBS. I WAS NOW A SUBSTITUTE TEACHER IN AN ELEMENTARY SCHOOL, AS WELL AS A SECRETARY FOR AN ENGINEER.

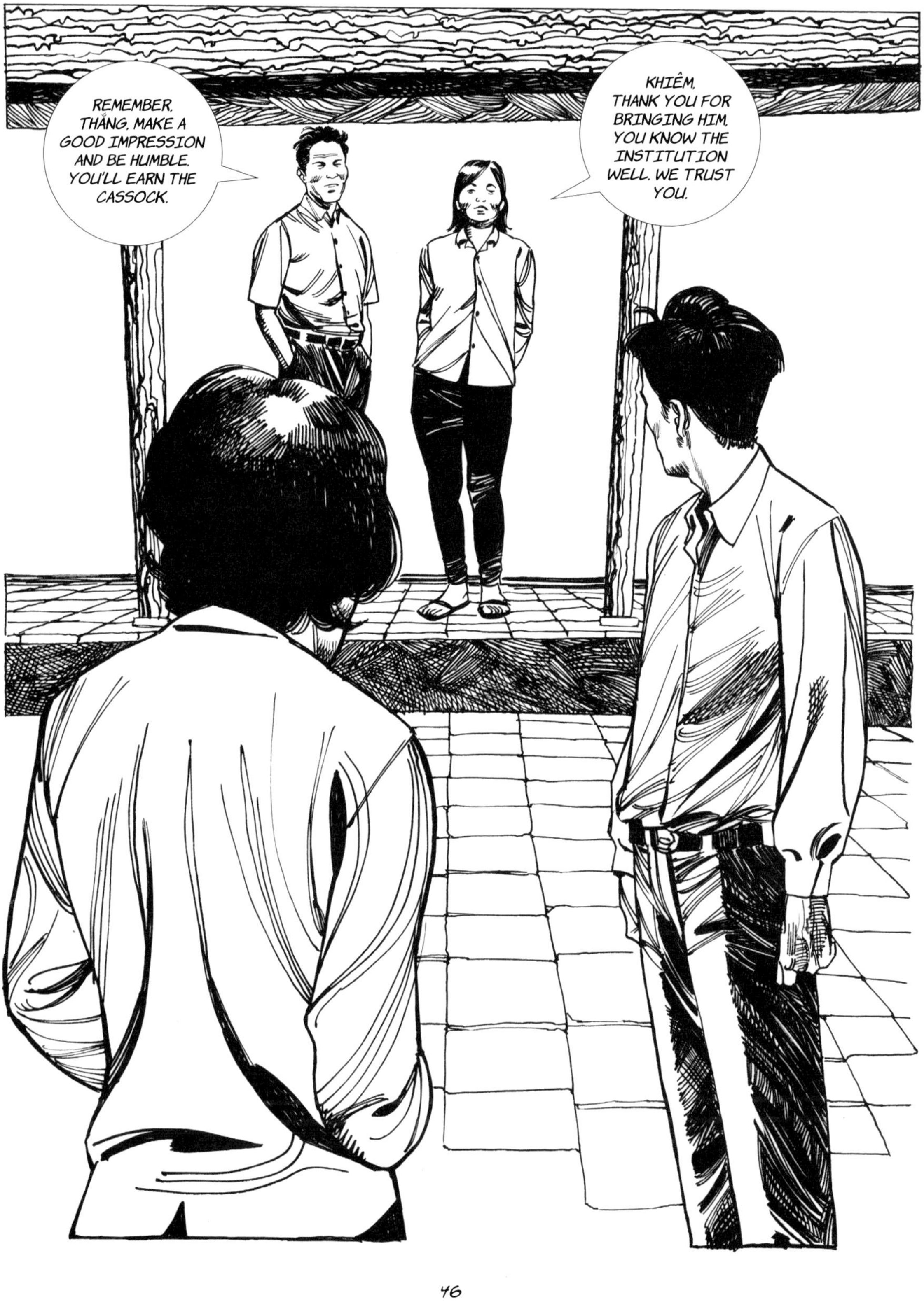
REMEMBER, THẮNG, MAKE A GOOD IMPRESSION AND BE HUMBLE. YOU'LL EARN THE CASSOCK.
KHIÊM, THANK YOU FOR BRINGING HIM, YOU KNOW THE INSTITUTION WELL. WE TRUST YOU.

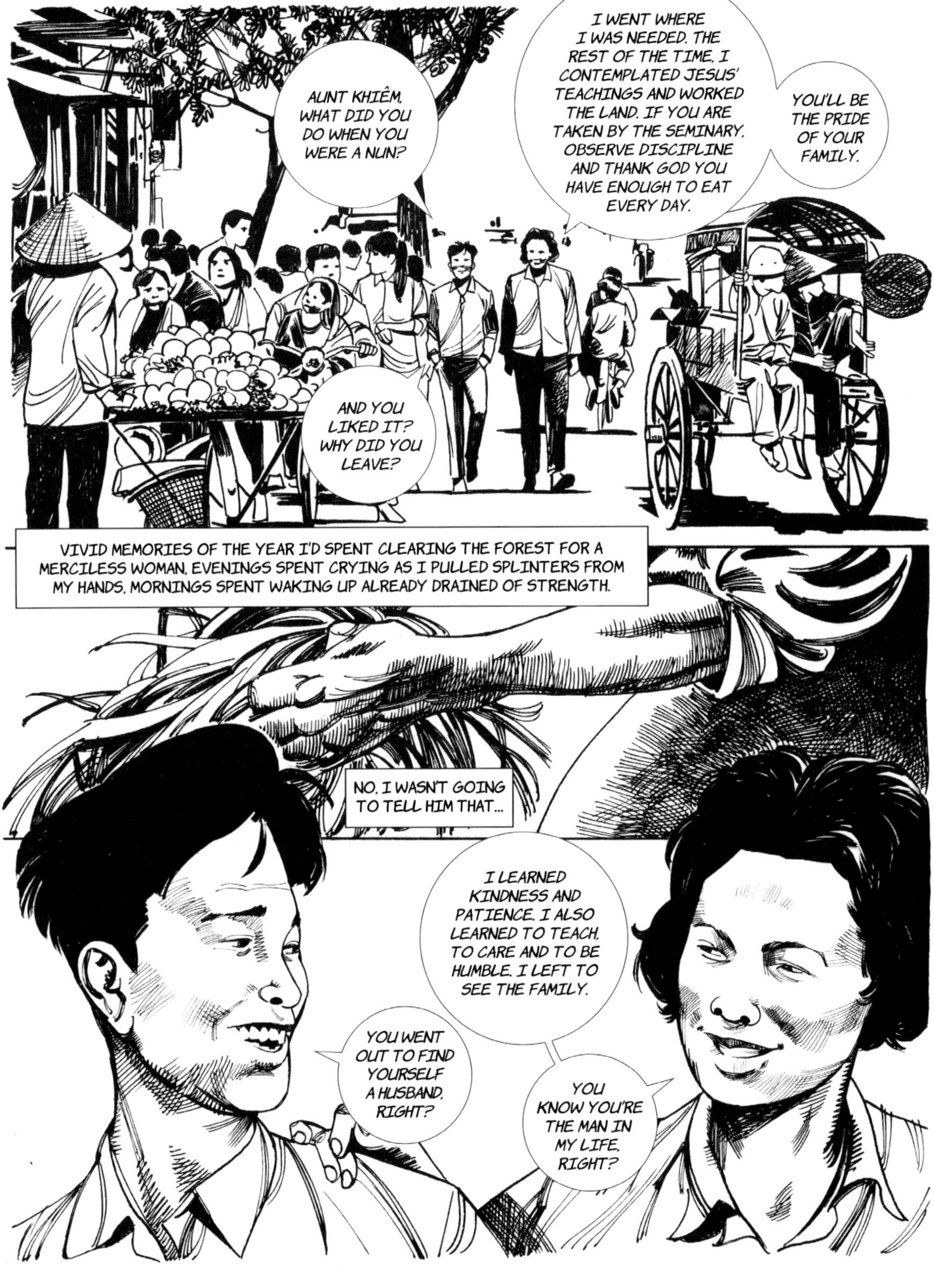
AUNT KHIÊM, WHAT DID YOU DO WHEN YOU WERE A NUN?
I WENT WHERE I WAS NEEDED. THE REST OF THE TIME, I CONTEMPLATED JESUS' TEACHINGS AND WORKED THE LAND. IF YOU ARE TAKEN BY THE SEMINARY, OBSERVE DISCIPLINE AND THANK GOD YOU HAVE ENOUGH TO EAT EVERY DAY.
YOU'LL BE THE PRIDE OF YOUR FAMILY.
AND YOU LIKED IT? WHY DID YOU LEAVE?
VIVID MEMORIES OF THE YEAR I'D SPENT CLEARING THE FOREST FOR A MERCILESS WOMAN, EVENINGS SPENT CRYING AS I PULLED SPLINTERS FROM MY HANDS, MORNINGS SPENT WAKING UP ALREADY DRAINED OF STRENGTH.
NO, I WASN'T GOING TO TELL HIM THAT...
I LEARNED KINDNESS AND PATIENCE. I ALSO LEARNED TO TEACH, TO CARE AND TO BE HUMBLE. I LEFT TO SEE THE FAMILY.
YOU WENT OUT TO FIND YOURSELF A HUSBAND, RIGHT?
YOU KNOW YOU'RE THE MAN IN MY LIFE, RIGHT?

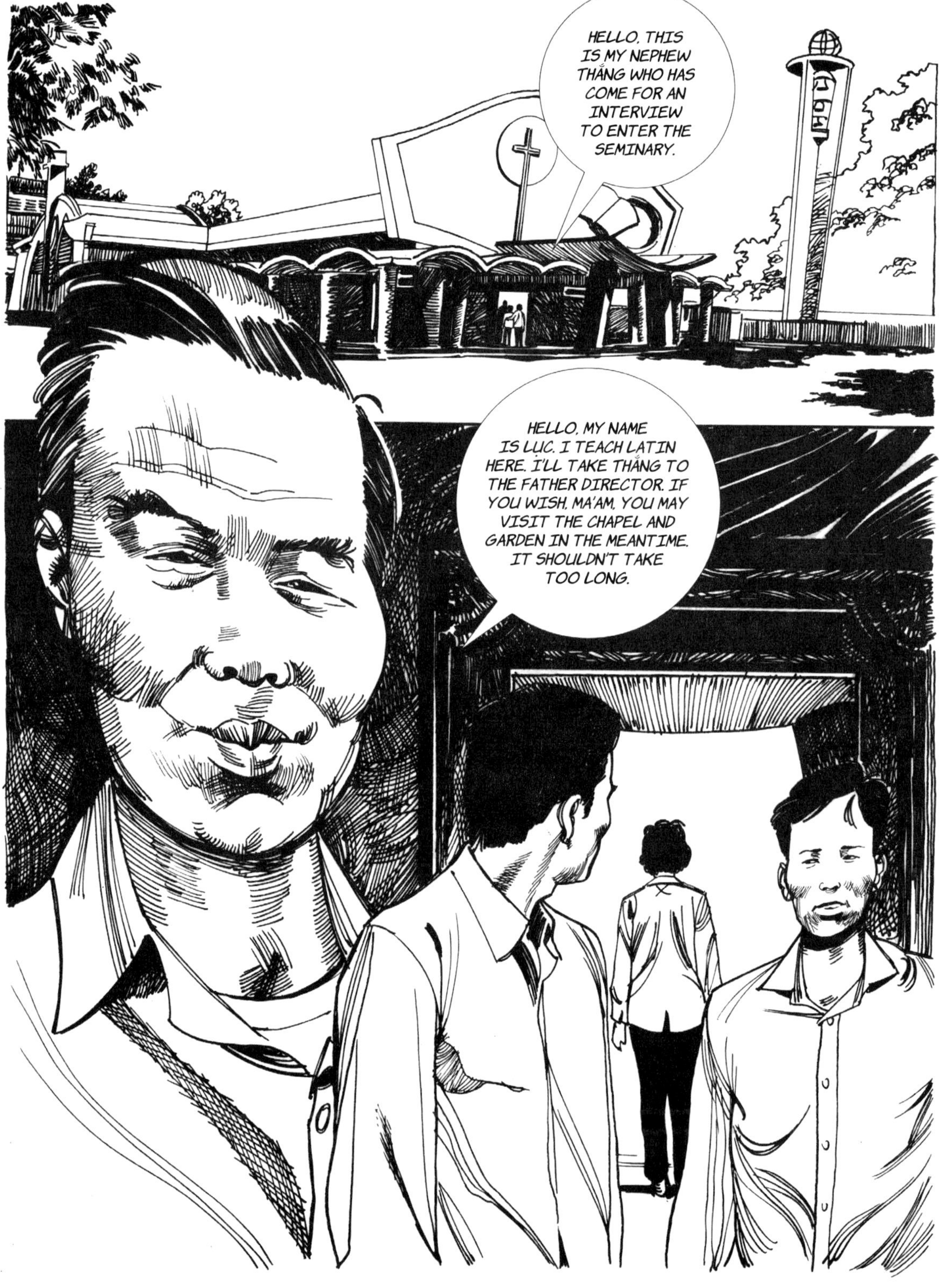
HELLO, THIS IS MY NEPHEW THẮNG WHO HAS COME FOR AN INTERVIEW TO ENTER THE SEMINARY.
HELLO, MY NAME IS LỤC. I TEACH LATIN HERE. I'LL TAKE THẮNG TO THE FATHER DIRECTOR. IF YOU WISH, MA'AM, YOU MAY VISIT THE CHAPEL AND GARDEN IN THE MEANTIME. IT SHOULDN'T TAKE TOO LONG.

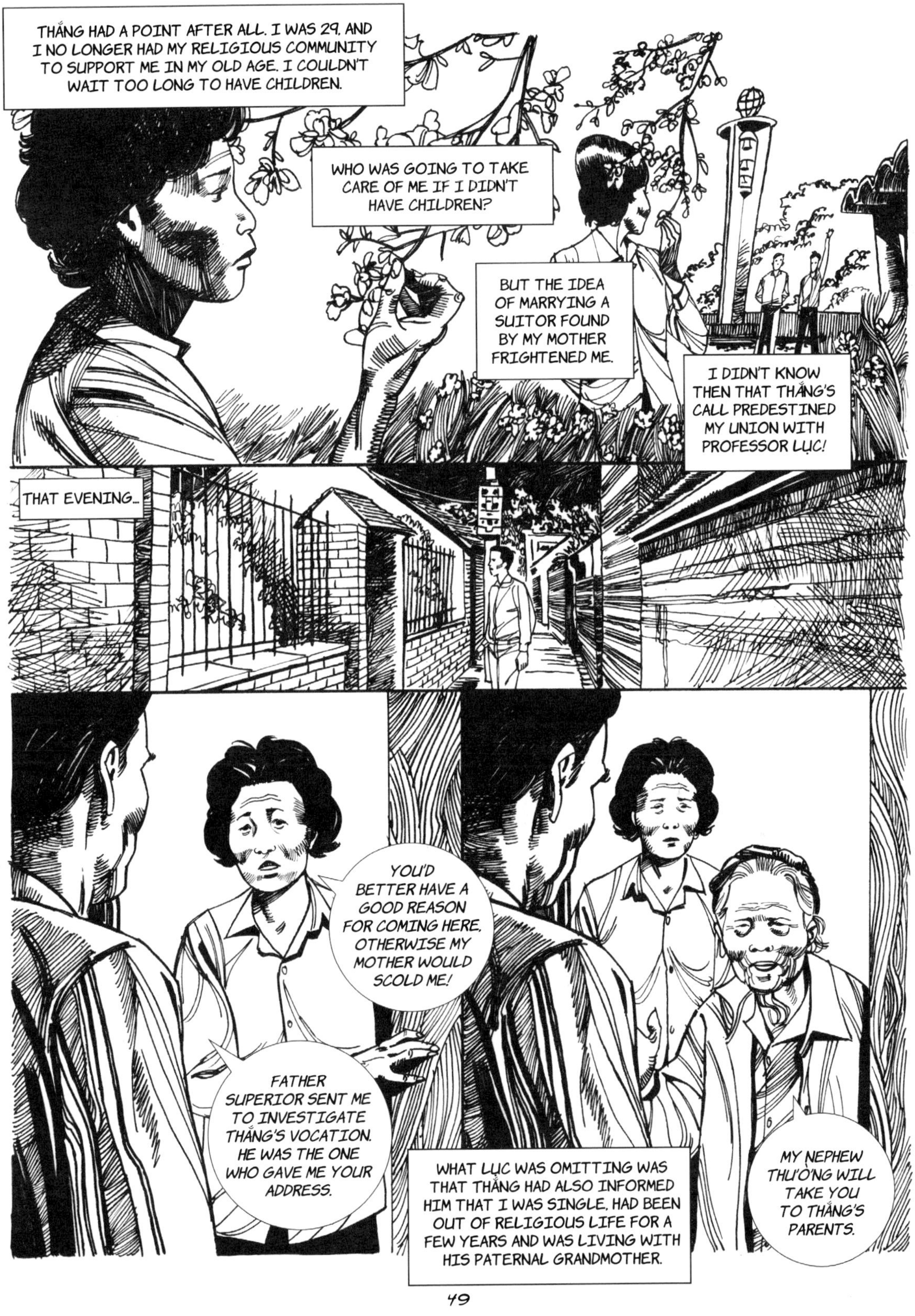
THẮNG HAD A POINT AFTER ALL. I WAS 29, AND I NO LONGER HAD MY RELIGIOUS COMMUNITY TO SUPPORT ME IN MY OLD AGE. I COULDN'T WAIT TOO LONG TO HAVE CHILDREN.
WHO WAS GOING TO TAKE CARE OF ME IF I DIDN'T HAVE CHILDREN?
BUT THE IDEA OF MARRYING A SUITOR FOUND BY MY MOTHER FRIGHTENED ME.
I DIDN'T KNOW THEN THAT THẮNG'S CALL PREDESTINED MY UNION WITH PROFESSOR LỤC!
THAT EVENING...
YOU'D BETTER HAVE A GOOD REASON FOR COMING HERE, OTHERWISE MY MOTHER WOULD SCOLD ME!
FATHER SUPERIOR SENT ME TO INVESTIGATE THẮNG'S VOCATION. HE WAS THE ONE WHO GAVE ME YOUR ADDRESS.
WHAT LỤC WAS OMITTING WAS THAT THẮNG HAD ALSO INFORMED HIM THAT I WAS SINGLE, HAD BEEN OUT OF RELIGIOUS LIFE FOR A FEW YEARS AND WAS LIVING WITH HIS PATERNAL GRANDMOTHER.
MY NEPHEW THƯỜNG WILL TAKE YOU TO THẮNG'S PARENTS.

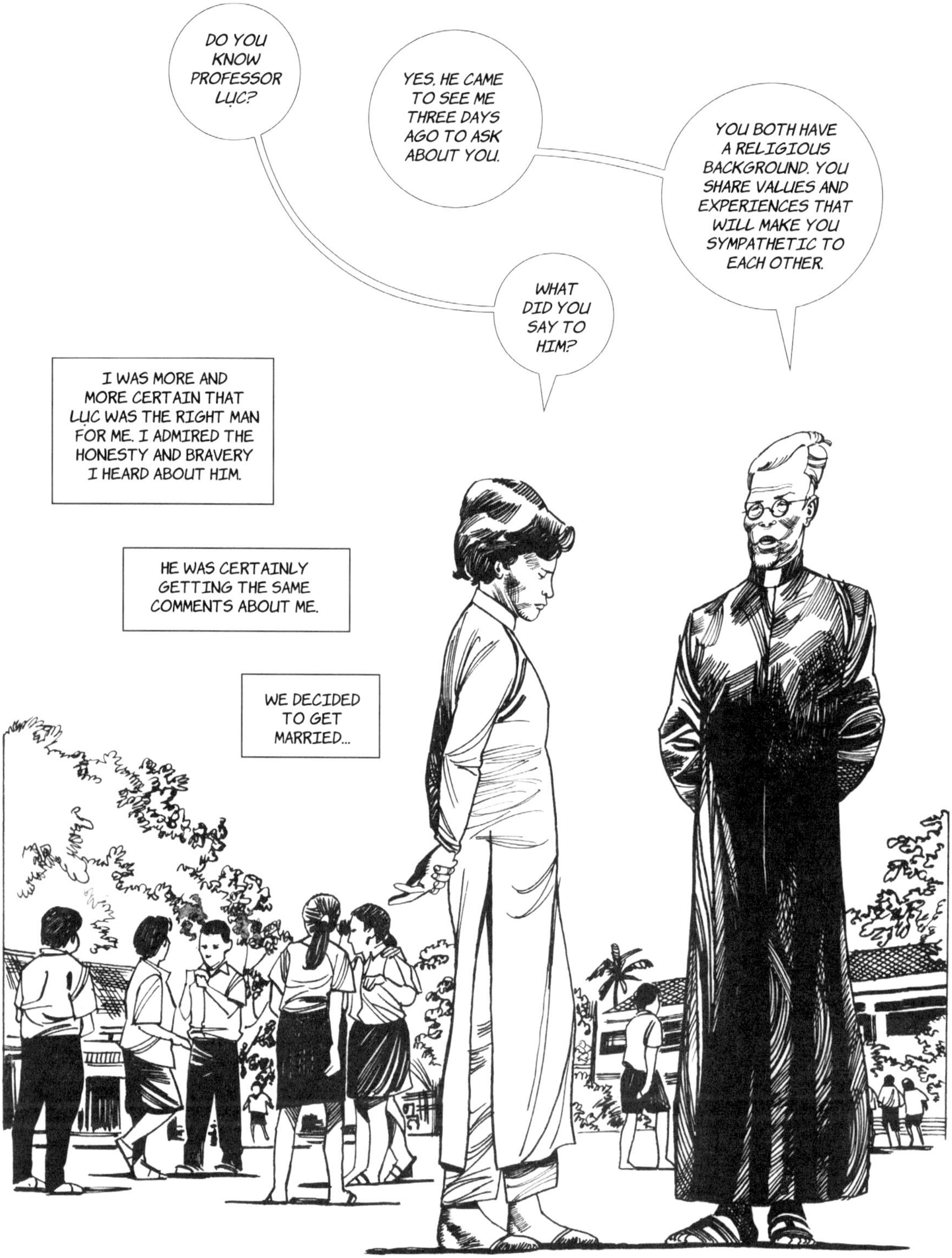
DO YOU KNOW PROFESSOR LỤC?
YES, HE CAME TO SEE ME THREE DAYS AGO TO ASK ABOUT YOU.
WHAT DID YOU SAY TO HIM?
YOU BOTH HAVE A RELIGIOUS BACKGROUND. YOU SHARE VALUES AND EXPERIENCES THAT WILL MAKE YOU SYMPATHETIC TO EACH OTHER.
I WAS MORE AND MORE CERTAIN THAT LỤC WAS THE RIGHT MAN FOR ME. I ADMIRED THE HONESTY AND BRAVERY I HEARD ABOUT HIM.
HE WAS CERTAINLY GETTING THE SAME COMMENTS ABOUT ME.
WE DECIDED TO GET MARRIED...

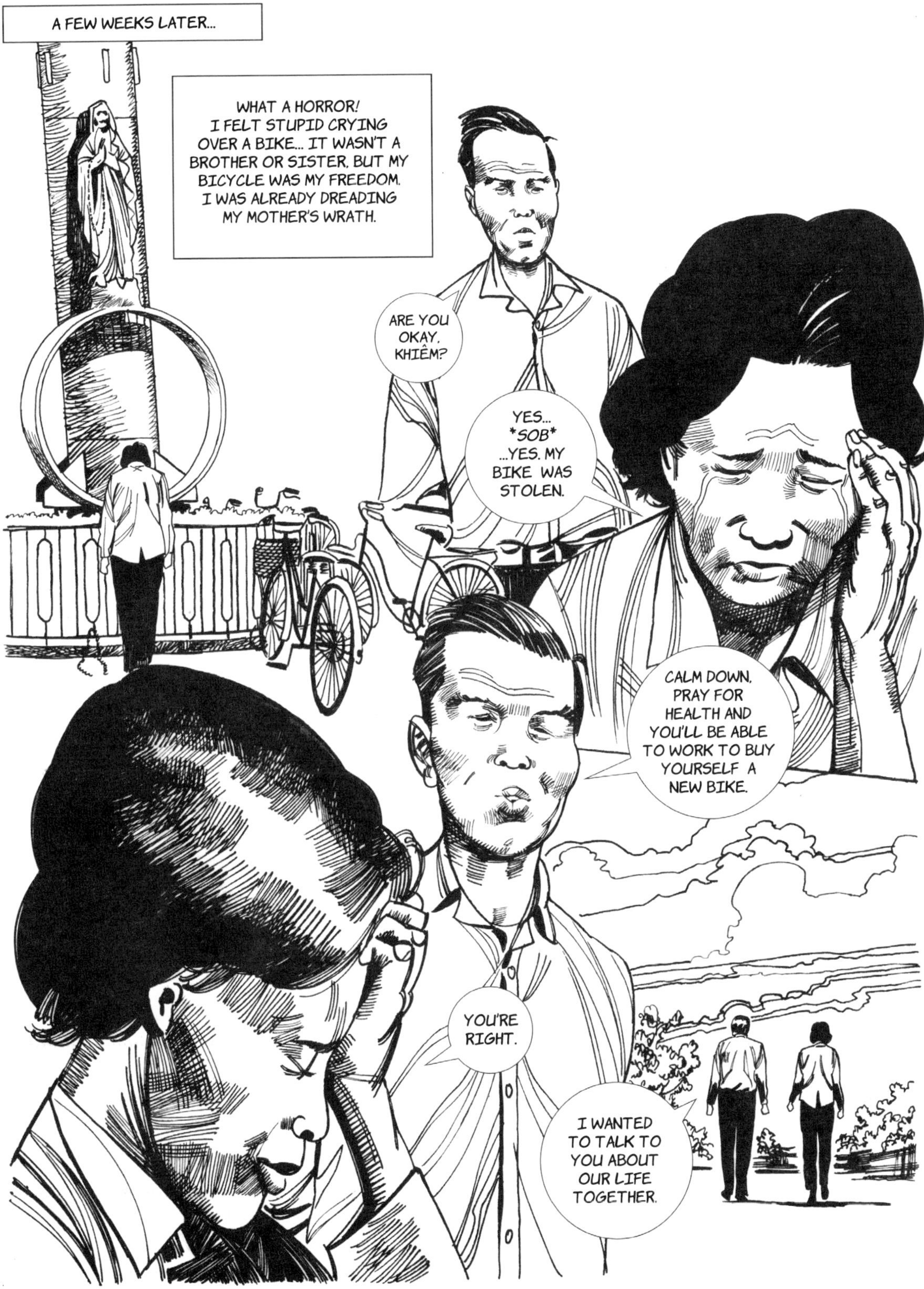
A FEW WEEKS LATER...
WHAT A HORROR! I FELT STUPID CRYING OVER A BIKE... IT WASN'T A BROTHER OR SISTER, BUT MY BICYCLE WAS MY FREEDOM. I WAS ALREADY DREADING MY MOTHER'S WRATH.
ARE YOU OKAY, KHIÊM?
YES... *SOB* ...YES. MY BIKE WAS STOLEN.
CALM DOWN, PRAY FOR HEALTH AND YOU'LL BE ABLE TO WORK TO BUY YOURSELF A NEW BIKE.
YOU'RE RIGHT.
I WANTED TO TALK TO YOU ABOUT OUR LIFE TOGETHER.

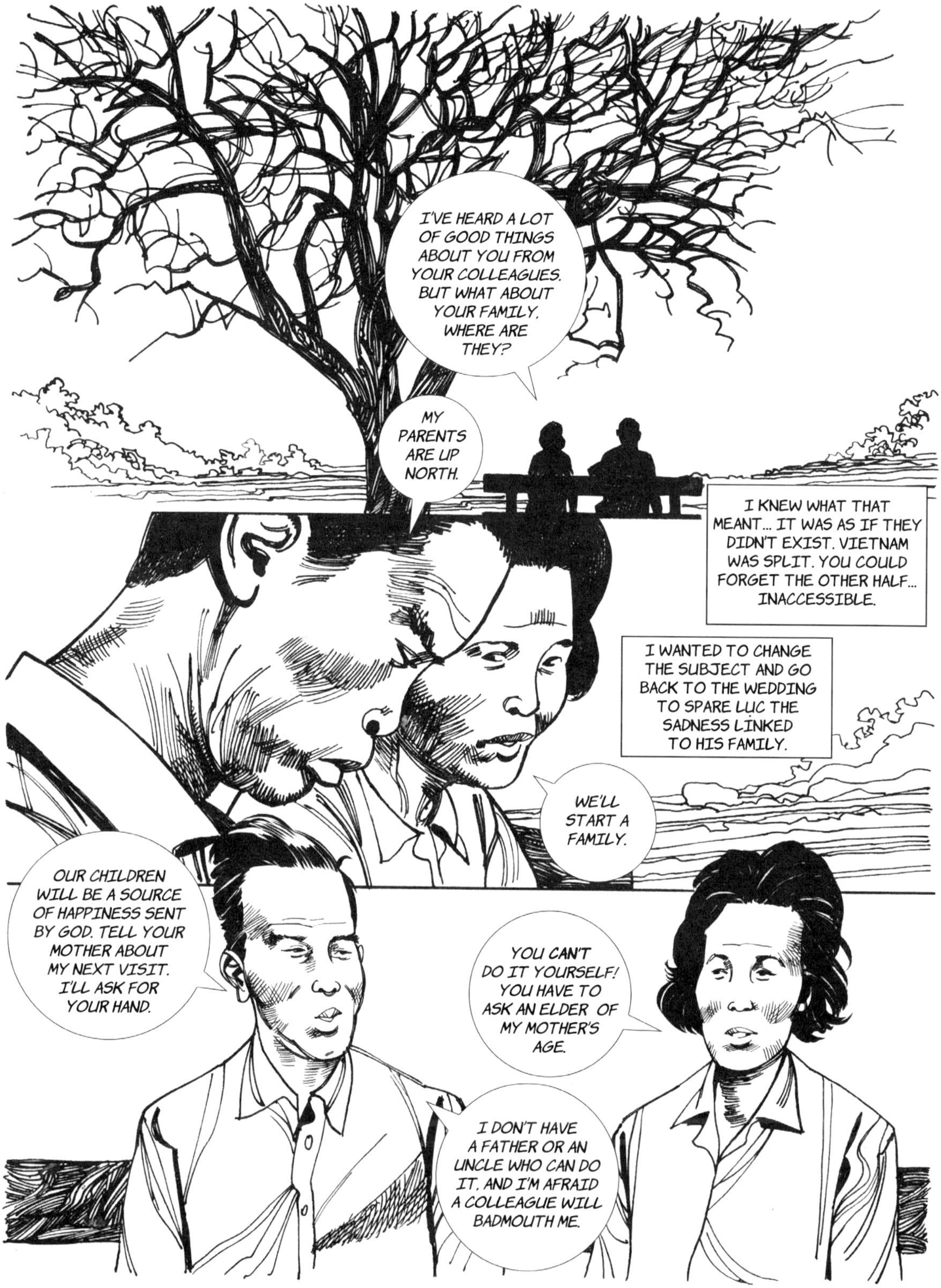
I'VE HEARD A LOT OF GOOD THINGS ABOUT YOU FROM YOUR COLLEAGUES. BUT WHAT ABOUT YOUR FAMILY. WHERE ARE THEY?
MY PARENTS ARE UP NORTH.
I KNEW WHAT THAT MEANT... IT WAS AS IF THEY DIDN'T EXIST. VIETNAM WAS SPLIT. YOU COULD FORGET THE OTHER HALF... INACCESSIBLE.
I WANTED TO CHANGE THE SUBJECT AND GO BACK TO THE WEDDING TO SPARE LUC THE SADNESS LINKED TO HIS FAMILY.
WE'LL START A FAMILY.
OUR CHILDREN WILL BE A SOURCE OF HAPPINESS SENT BY GOD. TELL YOUR MOTHER ABOUT MY NEXT VISIT. I'LL ASK FOR YOUR HAND.
YOU CAN'T DO IT YOURSELF! YOU HAVE TO ASK AN ELDER OF MY MOTHER'S AGE.
I DON'T HAVE A FATHER OR AN UNCLE WHO CAN DO IT. AND I'M AFRAID A COLLEAGUE WILL BADMOUTH ME.

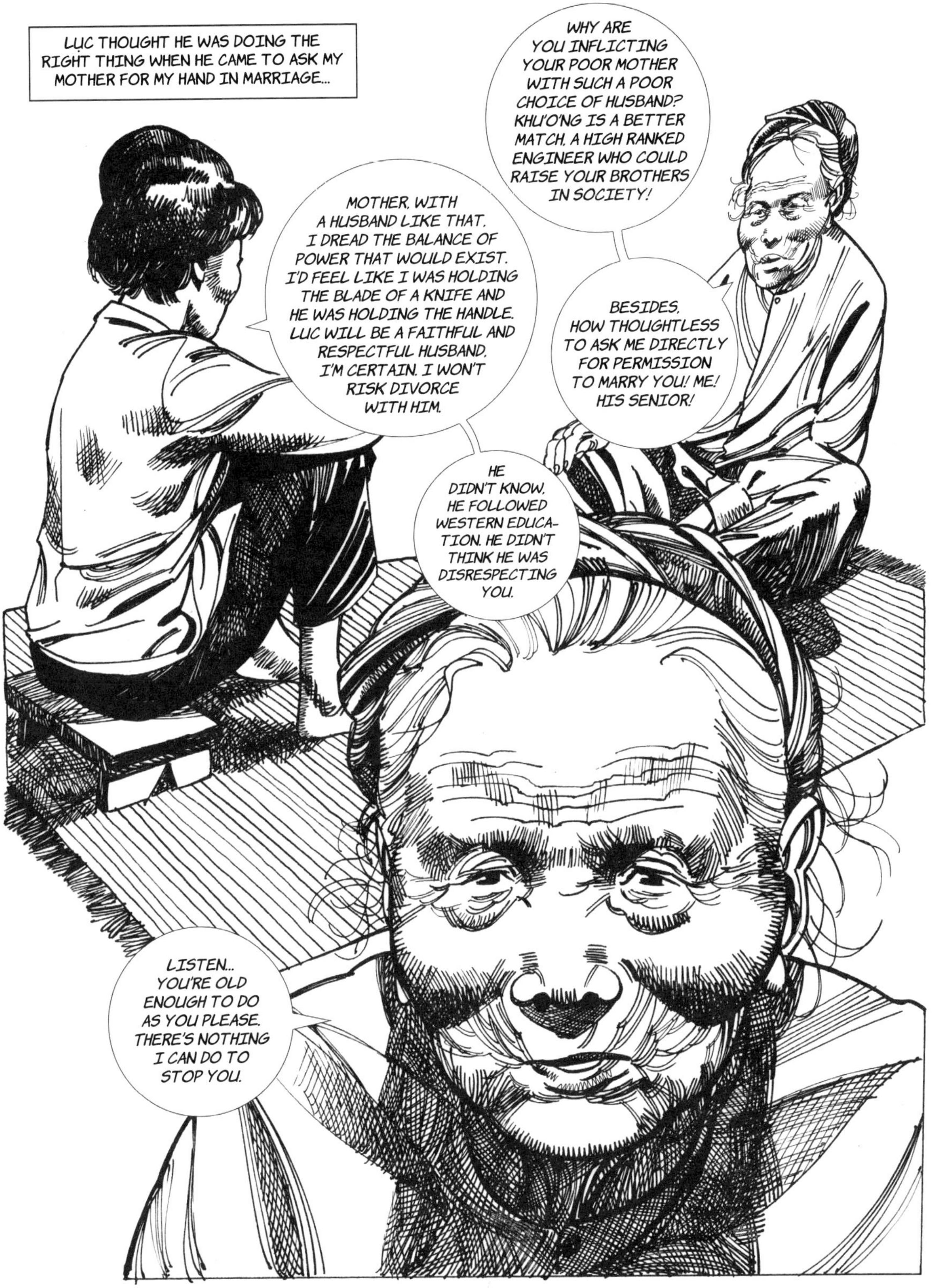
LUC THOUGHT HE WAS DOING THE RIGHT THING WHEN HE CAME TO ASK MY MOTHER FOR MY HAND IN MARRIAGE...
WHY ARE YOU INFLICTING YOUR POOR MOTHER WITH SUCH A POOR CHOICE OF HUSBAND? KHU'O'NG IS A BETTER MATCH, A HIGH RANKED ENGINEER WHO COULD RAISE YOUR BROTHERS IN SOCIETY!
MOTHER, WITH A HUSBAND LIKE THAT, I DREAD THE BALANCE OF POWER THAT WOULD EXIST. I'D FEEL LIKE I WAS HOLDING THE BLADE OF A KNIFE AND HE WAS HOLDING THE HANDLE. LUC WILL BE A FAITHFUL AND RESPECTFUL HUSBAND, I'M CERTAIN. I WON'T RISK DIVORCE WITH HIM.
BESIDES, HOW THOUGHTLESS TO ASK ME DIRECTLY FOR PERMISSION TO MARRY YOU! ME! HIS SENIOR!
HE DIDN'T KNOW, HE FOLLOWED WESTERN EDUCA-TION. HE DIDN'T THINK HE WAS DISRESPECTING YOU.
LISTEN... YOU'RE OLD ENOUGH TO DO AS YOU PLEASE. THERE'S NOTHING I CAN DO TO STOP YOU.

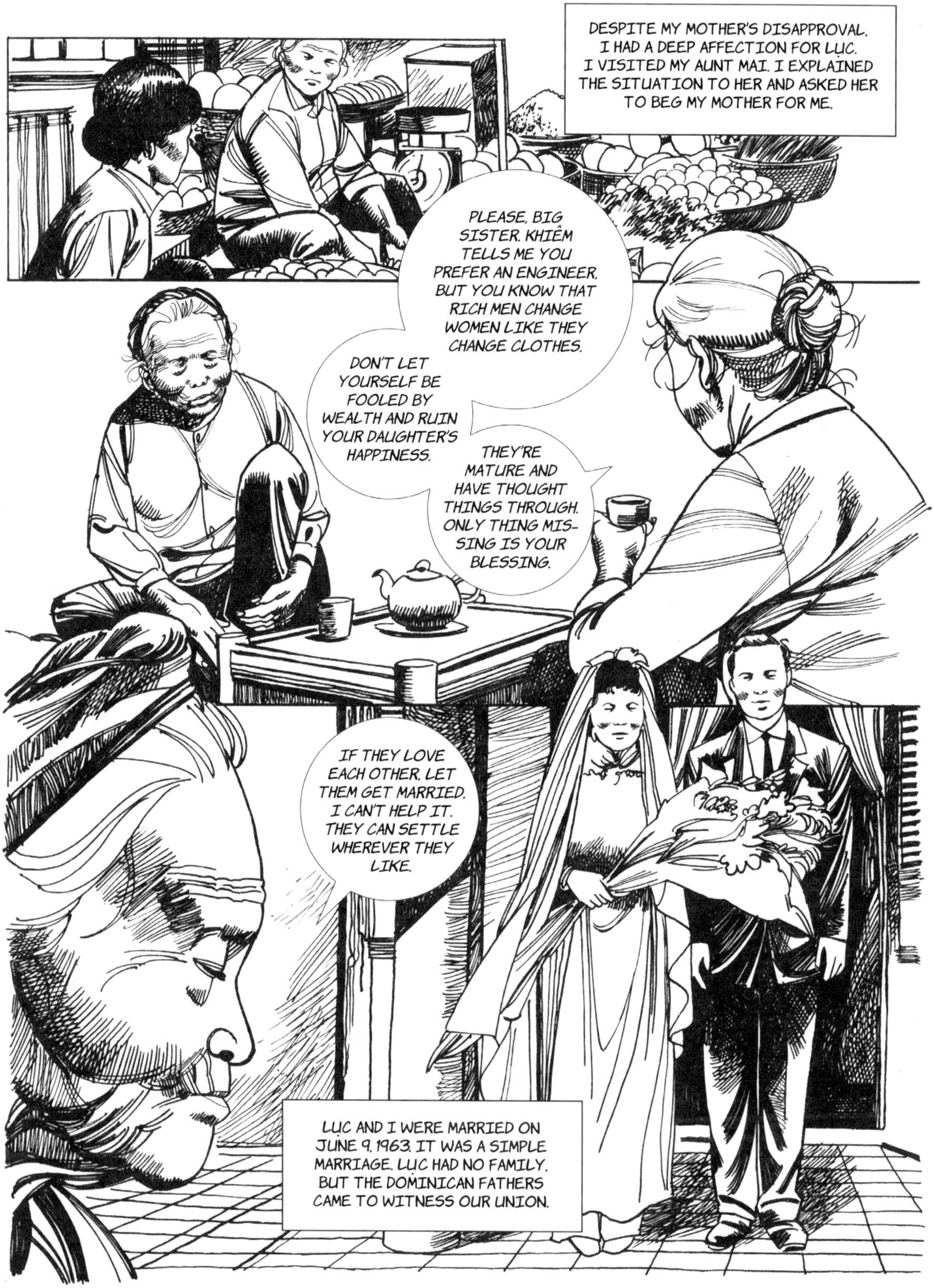
DESPITE MY MOTHER'S DISAPPROVAL, I HAD A DEEP AFFECTION FOR LUC. I VISITED MY AUNT MAI. I EXPLAINED THE SITUATION TO HER AND ASKED HER TO BEG MY MOTHER FOR ME.
PLEASE, BIG SISTER. KHIÊM TELLS ME YOU PREFER AN ENGINEER, BUT YOU KNOW THAT RICH MEN CHANGE WOMEN LIKE THEY CHANGE CLOTHES.
DON'T LET YOURSELF BE FOOLED BY WEALTH AND RUIN YOUR DAUGHTER'S HAPPINESS.
THEY'RE MATURE AND HAVE THOUGHT THINGS THROUGH. ONLY THING MISSING IS YOUR BLESSING.
IF THEY LOVE EACH OTHER, LET THEM GET MARRIED. I CAN'T HELP IT. THEY CAN SETTLE WHEREVER THEY LIKE.
LUC AND I WERE MARRIED ON JUNE 9, 1963. IT WAS A SIMPLE MARRIAGE. LUC HAD NO FAMILY, BUT THE DOMINICAN FATHERS CAME TO WITNESS OUR UNION.

CHAPTER 5

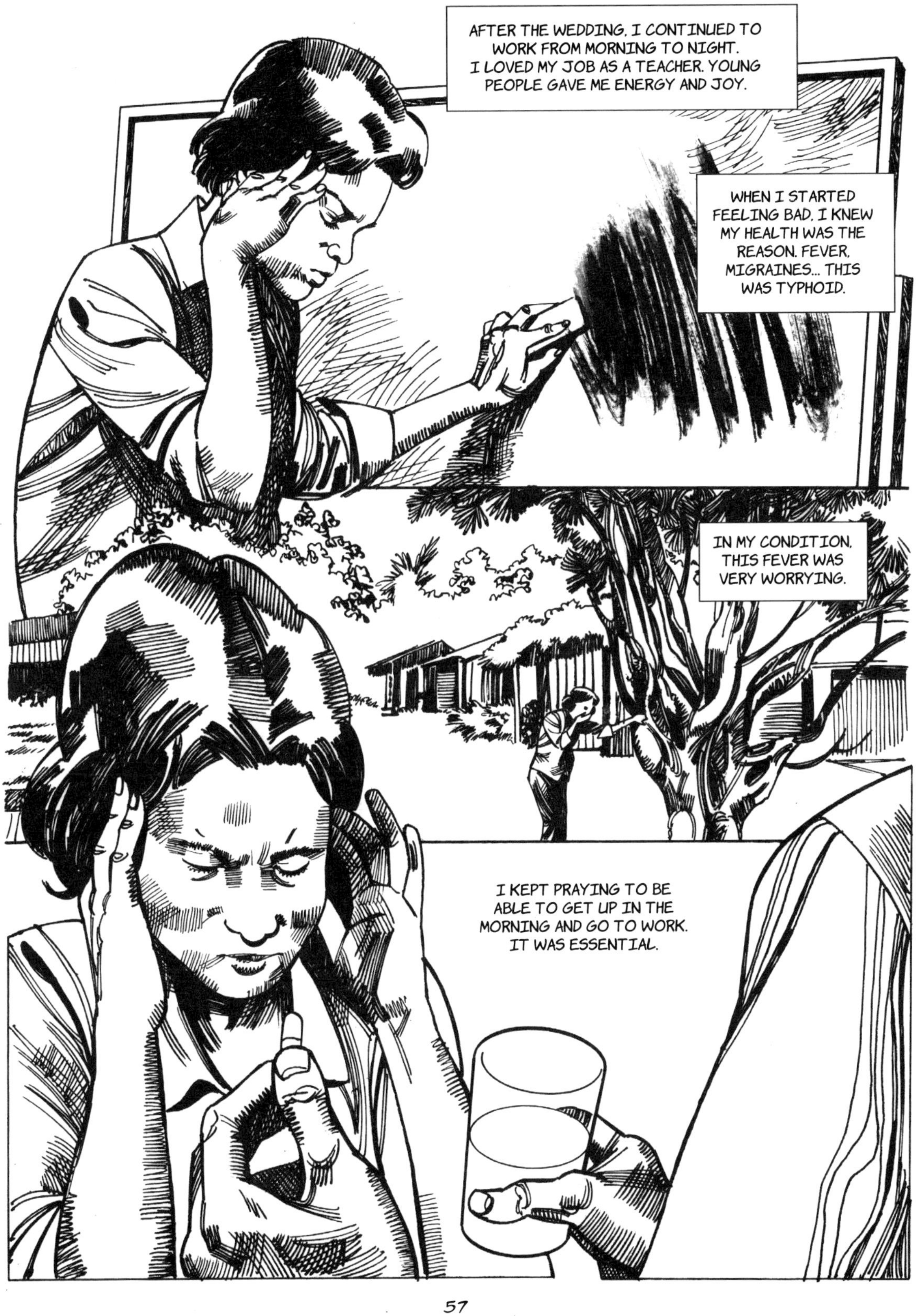
AFTER THE WEDDING, I CONTINUED TO WORK FROM MORNING TO NIGHT. I LOVED MY JOB AS A TEACHER. YOUNG PEOPLE GAVE ME ENERGY AND JOY.
WHEN I STARTED FEELING BAD, I KNEW MY HEALTH WAS THE REASON. FEVER, MIGRAINES... THIS WAS TYPHOID.
IN MY CONDITION, THIS FEVER WAS VERY WORRYING.
I KEPT PRAYING TO BE ABLE TO GET UP IN THE MORNING AND GO TO WORK. IT WAS ESSENTIAL.

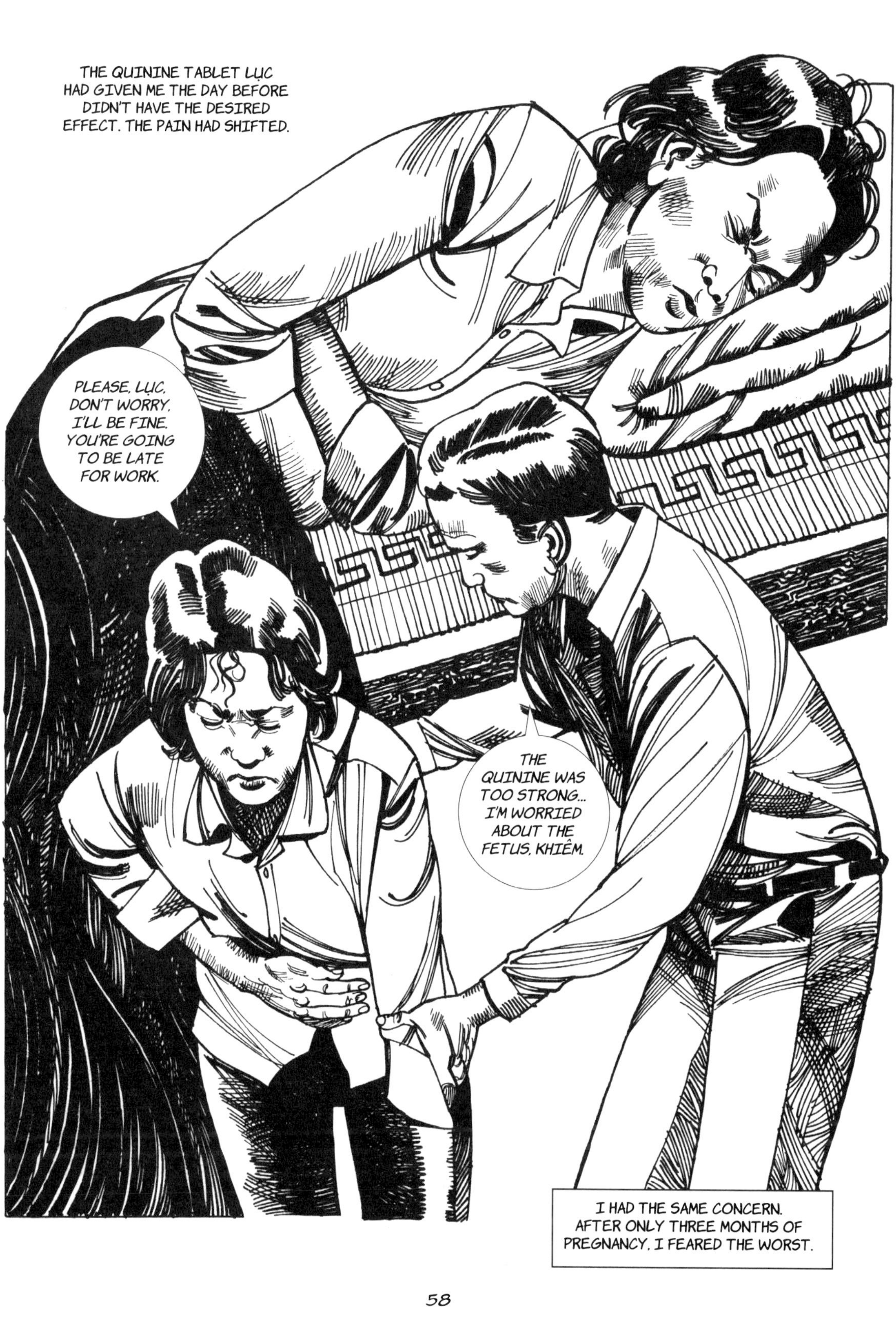
THE QUININE TABLET LỤC HAD GIVEN ME THE DAY BEFORE DIDN'T HAVE THE DESIRED EFFECT. THE PAIN HAD SHIFTED.
PLEASE, LỤC, DON'T WORRY. I'LL BE FINE. YOU'RE GOING TO BE LATE FOR WORK.
THE QUININE WAS TOO STRONG... I'M WORRIED ABOUT THE FETUS, KHIÊM.
I HAD THE SAME CONCERN. AFTER ONLY THREE MONTHS OF PREGNANCY, I FEARED THE WORST.

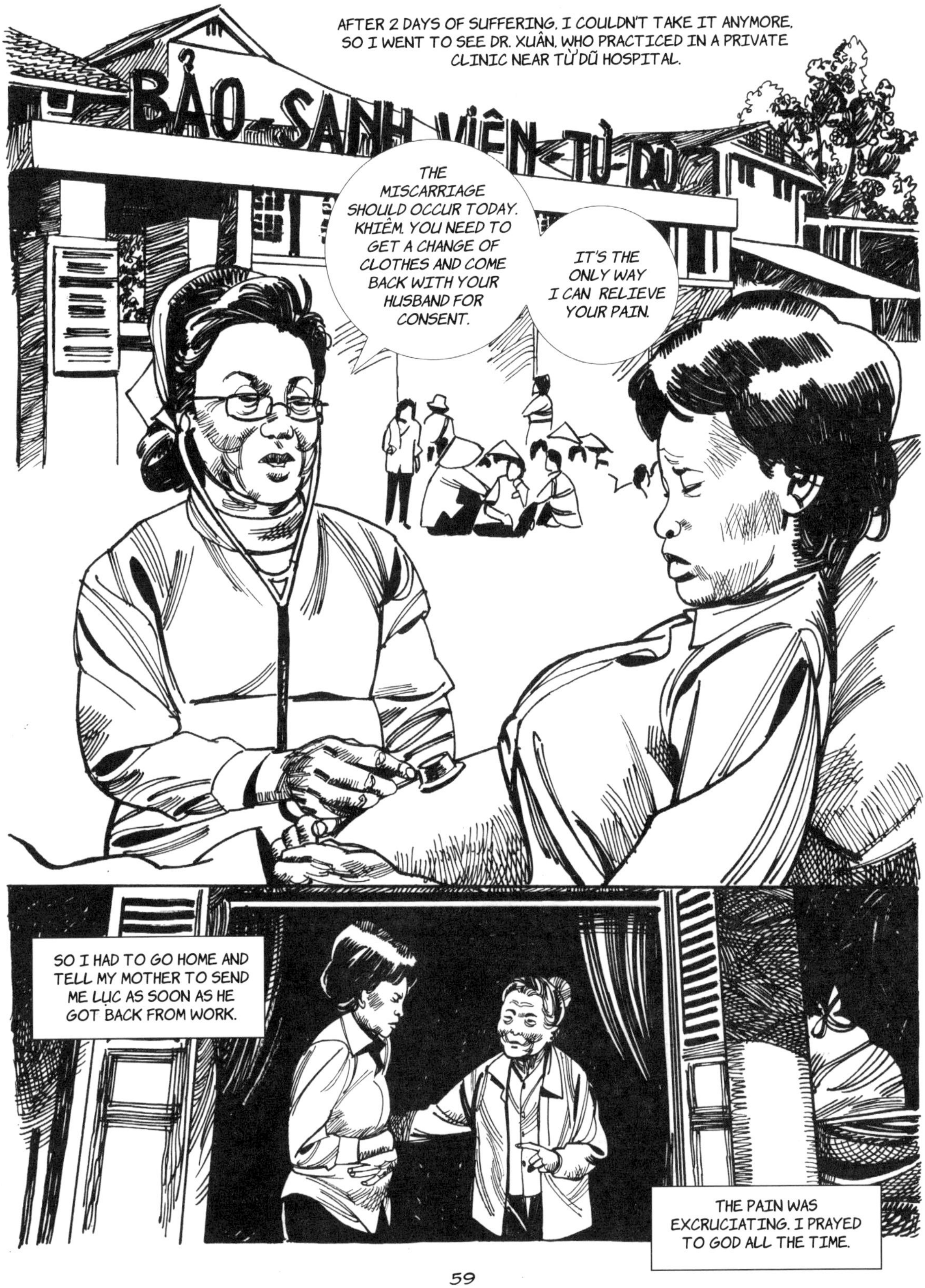
AFTER 2 DAYS OF SUFFERING, I COULDN'T TAKE IT ANYMORE, SO I WENT TO SEE DR. XUÂN, WHO PRACTICED IN A PRIVATE CLINIC NEAR TỪ DŨ HOSPITAL.
BẢO-SANH VIỆN TỪ-DŨ
THE MISCARRIAGE SHOULD OCCUR TODAY. KHIÊM, YOU NEED TO GET A CHANGE OF CLOTHES AND COME BACK WITH YOUR HUSBAND FOR CONSENT.
IT'S THE ONLY WAY I CAN RELIEVE YOUR PAIN.
SO I HAD TO GO HOME AND TELL MY MOTHER TO SEND ME LỤC AS SOON AS HE GOT BACK FROM WORK.
THE PAIN WAS EXCRUCIATING. I PRAYED TO GOD ALL THE TIME.

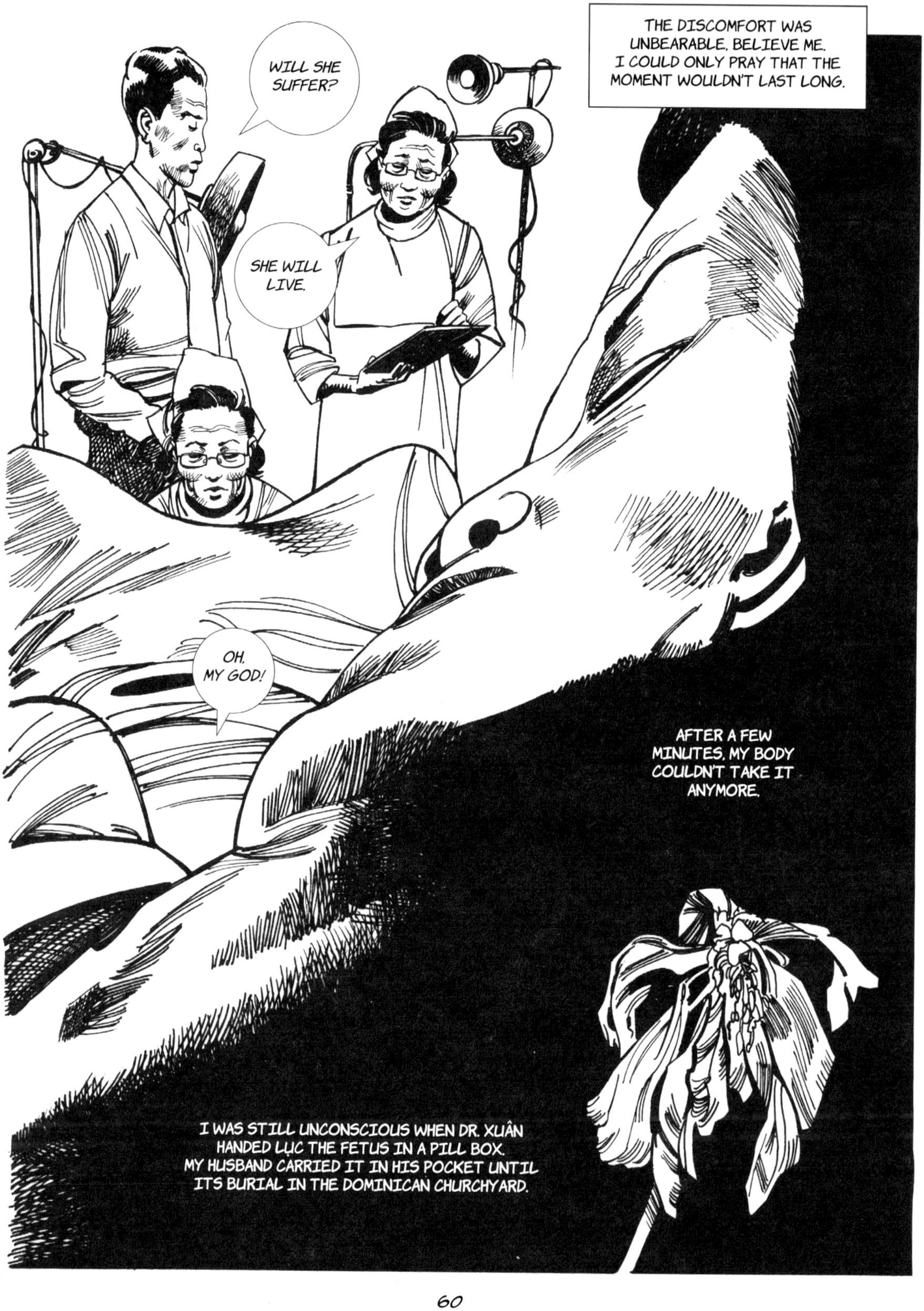
THE DISCOMFORT WAS UNBEARABLE, BELIEVE ME. I COULD ONLY PRAY THAT THE MOMENT WOULDN'T LAST LONG.
WILL SHE SUFFER?
SHE WILL LIVE.
OH, MY GOD!
AFTER A FEW MINUTES, MY BODY COULDN'T TAKE IT ANYMORE.
I WAS STILL UNCONSCIOUS WHEN DR. XUÂN HANDED LỤC THE FETUS IN A PILL BOX. MY HUSBAND CARRIED IT IN HIS POCKET UNTIL ITS BURIAL IN THE DOMINICAN CHURCHYARD.

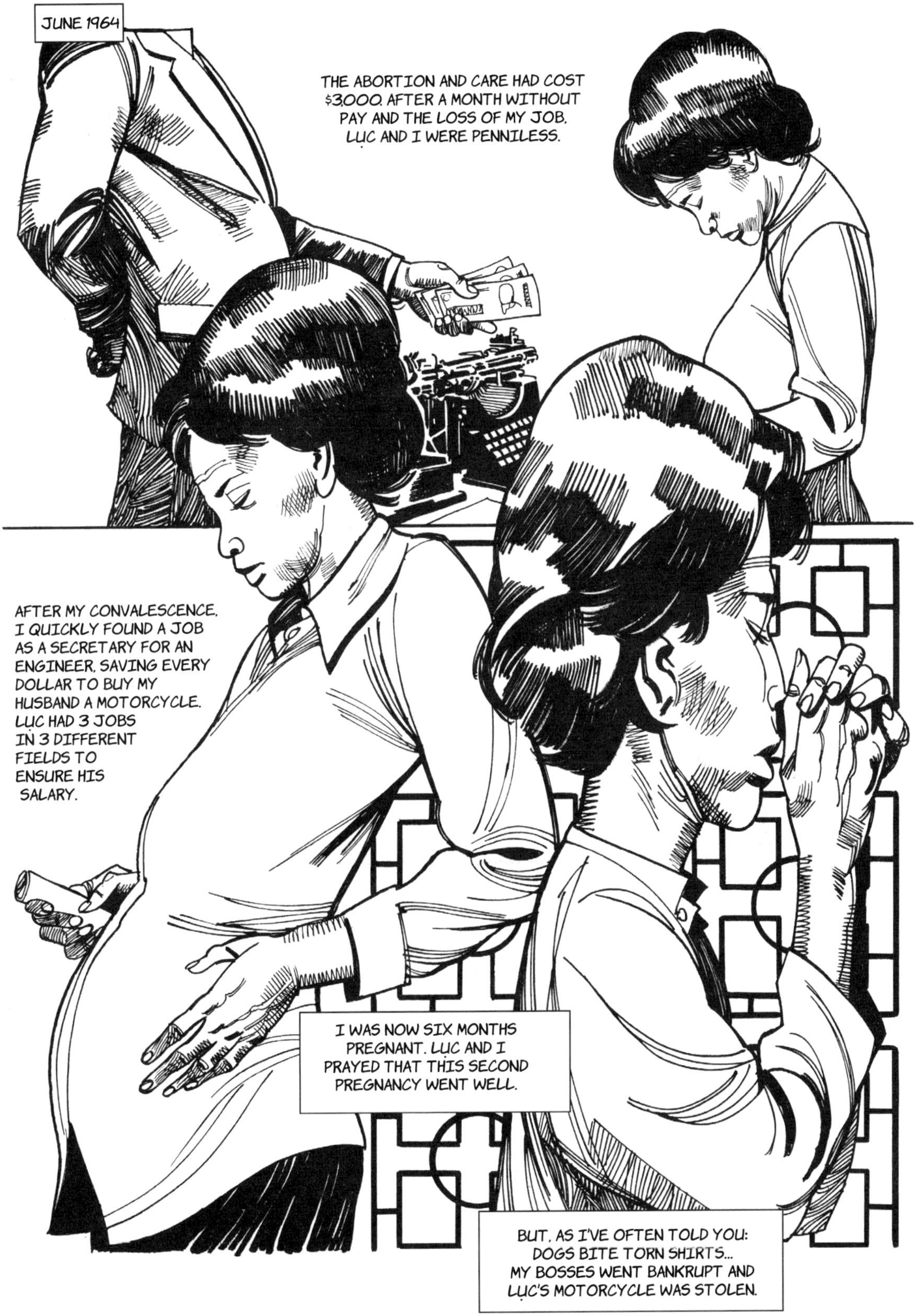
JUNE 1964
THE ABORTION AND CARE HAD COST $3,000. AFTER A MONTH WITHOUT PAY AND THE LOSS OF MY JOB, LUC AND I WERE PENNILESS.
AFTER MY CONVALESCENCE, I QUICKLY FOUND A JOB AS A SECRETARY FOR AN ENGINEER, SAVING EVERY DOLLAR TO BUY MY HUSBAND A MOTORCYCLE. LUC HAD 3 JOBS IN 3 DIFFERENT FIELDS TO ENSURE HIS SALARY.
I WAS NOW SIX MONTHS PREGNANT. LUC AND I PRAYED THAT THIS SECOND PREGNANCY WENT WELL.
BUT, AS I'VE OFTEN TOLD YOU: DOGS BITE TORN SHIRTS... MY BOSSES WENT BANKRUPT AND LUC'S MOTORCYCLE WAS STOLEN.

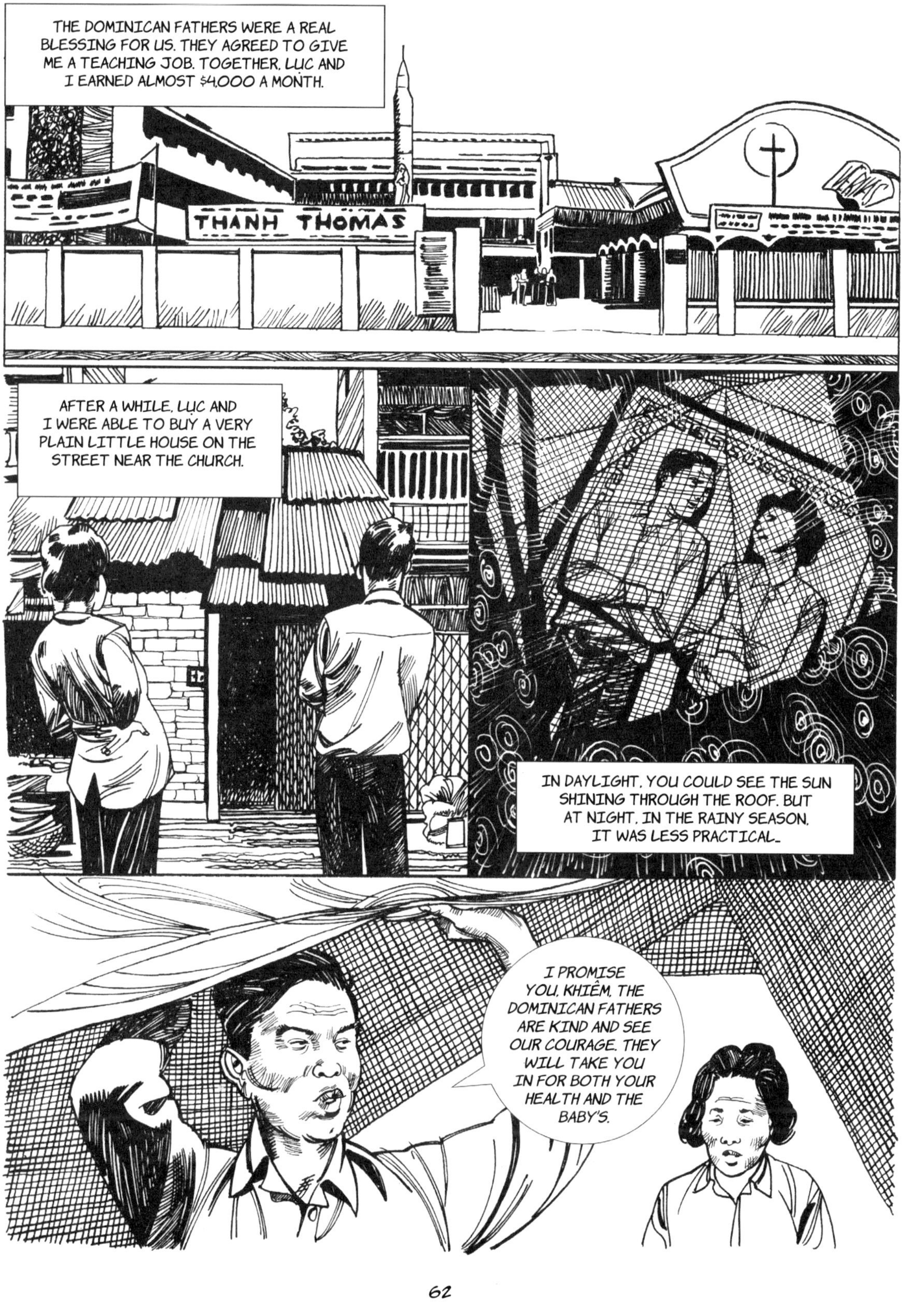
THE DOMINICAN FATHERS WERE A REAL BLESSING FOR US. THEY AGREED TO GIVE ME A TEACHING JOB. TOGETHER, LUC AND I EARNED ALMOST $4,000 A MONTH.
THANH THOMAS
AFTER A WHILE, LUC AND I WERE ABLE TO BUY A VERY PLAIN LITTLE HOUSE ON THE STREET NEAR THE CHURCH.
IN DAYLIGHT, YOU COULD SEE THE SUN SHINING THROUGH THE ROOF. BUT AT NIGHT, IN THE RAINY SEASON, IT WAS LESS PRACTICAL...
I PROMISE YOU, KHIÊM, THE DOMINICAN FATHERS ARE KIND AND SEE OUR COURAGE. THEY WILL TAKE YOU IN FOR BOTH YOUR HEALTH AND THE BABY'S.

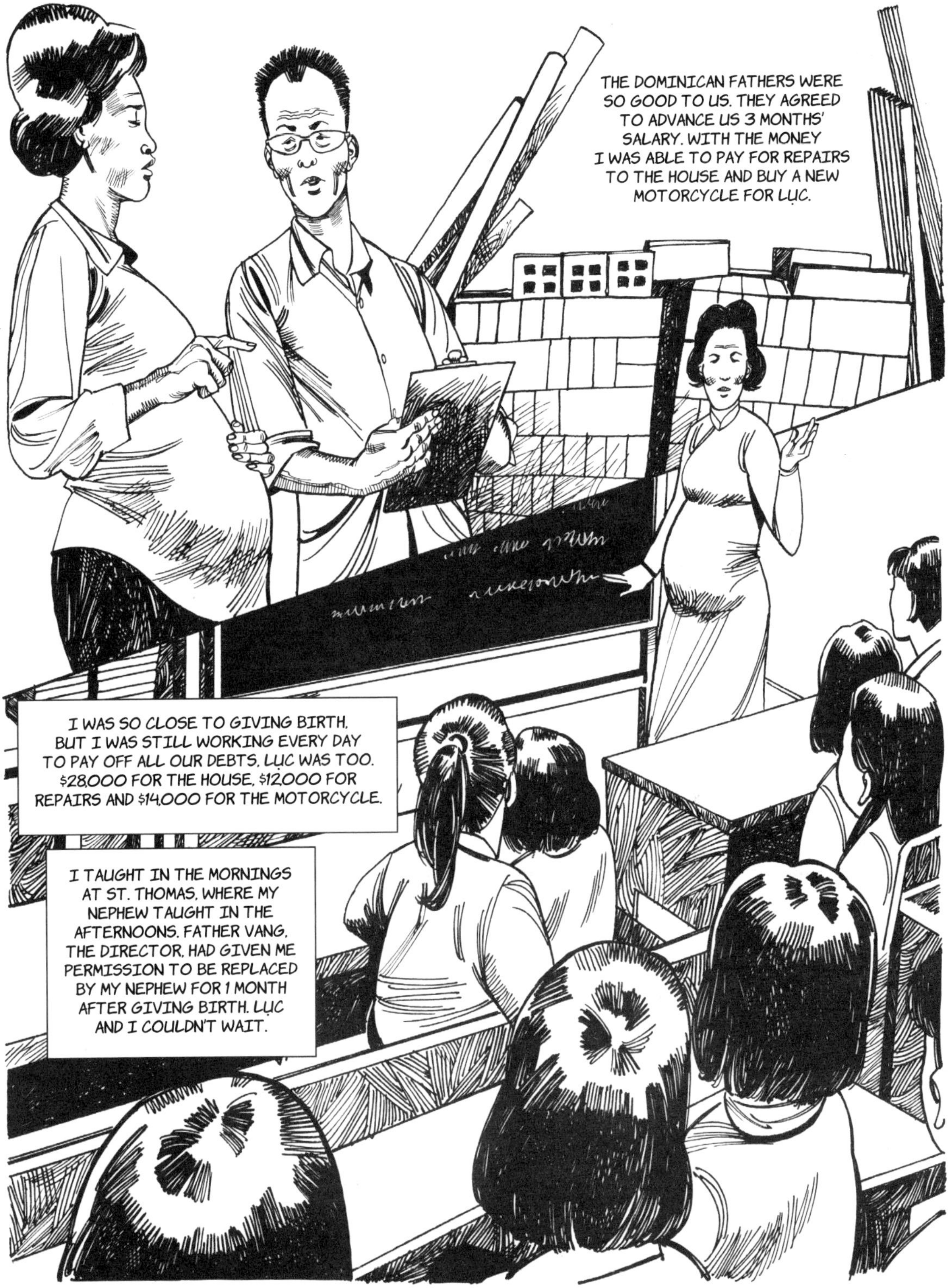
THE DOMINICAN FATHERS WERE SO GOOD TO US. THEY AGREED TO ADVANCE US 3 MONTHS' SALARY. WITH THE MONEY I WAS ABLE TO PAY FOR REPAIRS TO THE HOUSE AND BUY A NEW MOTORCYCLE FOR LỤC.
I WAS SO CLOSE TO GIVING BIRTH, BUT I WAS STILL WORKING EVERY DAY TO PAY OFF ALL OUR DEBTS. LỤC WAS TOO. $28,000 FOR THE HOUSE, $12,000 FOR REPAIRS AND $14,000 FOR THE MOTORCYCLE.
I TAUGHT IN THE MORNINGS AT ST. THOMAS, WHERE MY NEPHEW TAUGHT IN THE AFTERNOONS. FATHER VANG, THE DIRECTOR, HAD GIVEN ME PERMISSION TO BE REPLACED BY MY NEPHEW FOR 1 MONTH AFTER GIVING BIRTH. LỤC AND I COULDN'T WAIT.

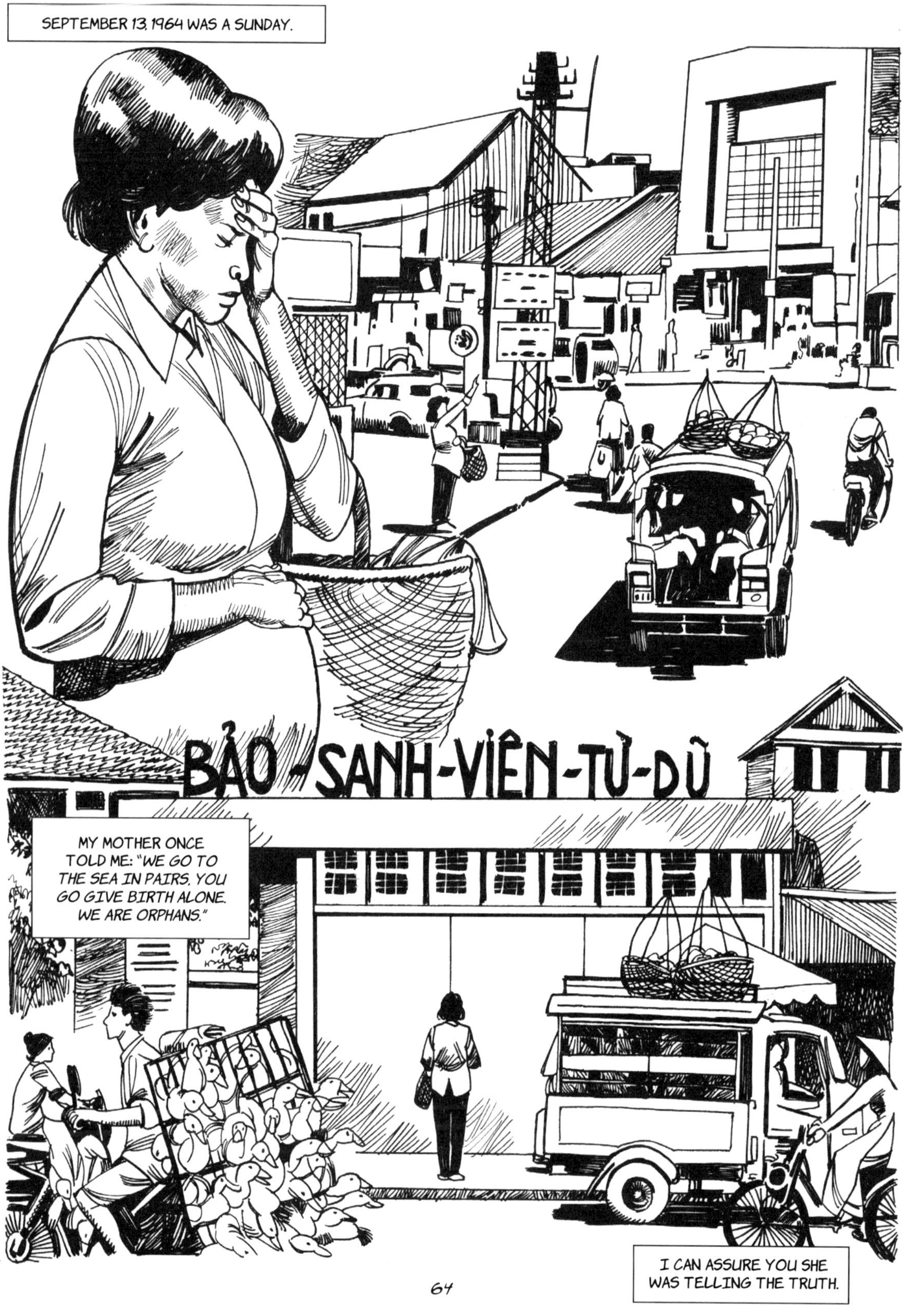
SEPTEMBER 13, 1964 WAS A SUNDAY.
BẢO-SANH-VIÊN-TỪ-DŨ
MY MOTHER ONCE TOLD ME: "WE GO TO THE SEA IN PAIRS, YOU GO GIVE BIRTH ALONE. WE ARE ORPHANS."
I CAN ASSURE YOU SHE WAS TELLING THE TRUTH.

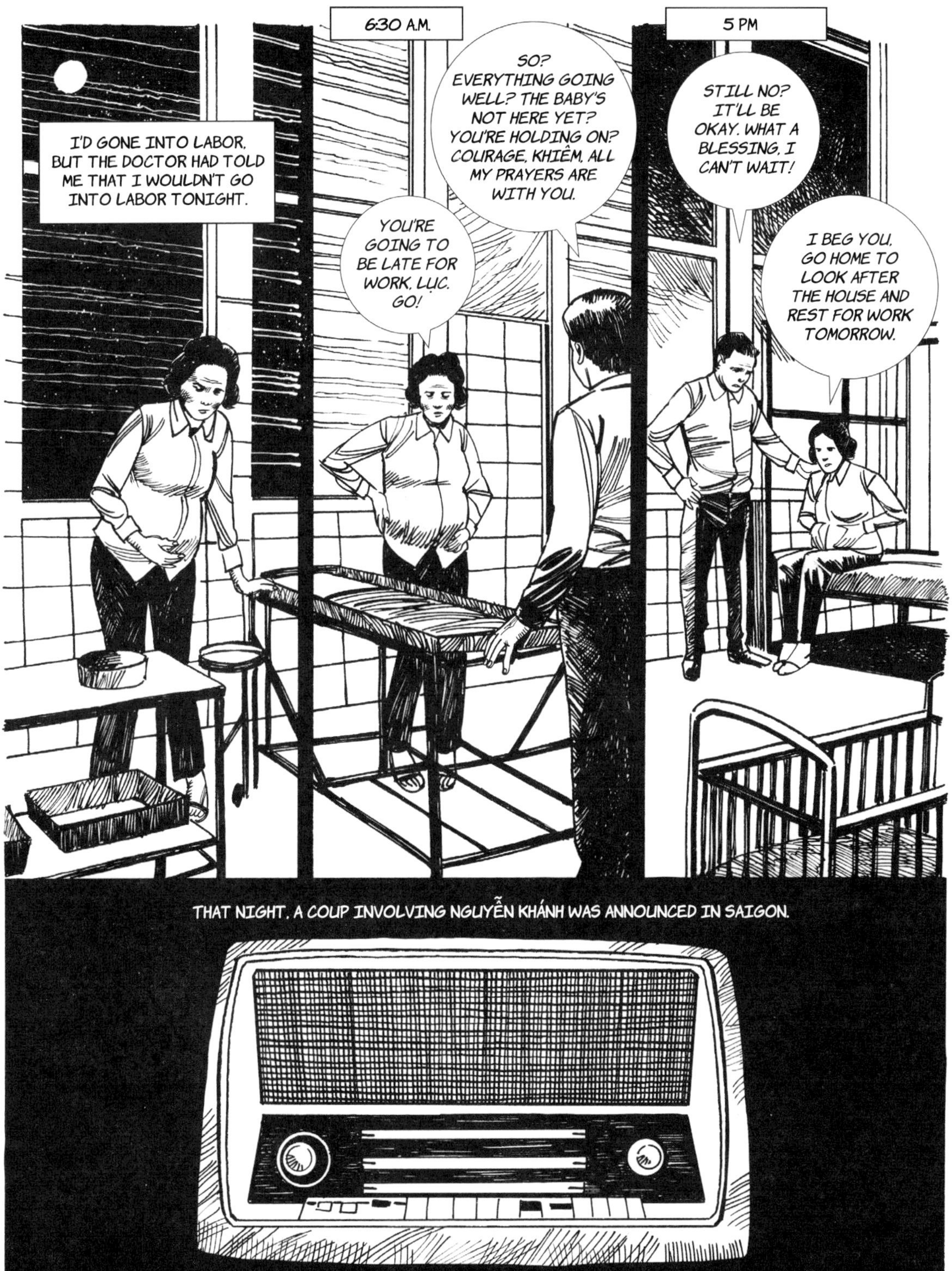
I'D GONE INTO LABOR, BUT THE DOCTOR HAD TOLD ME THAT I WOULDN'T GO INTO LABOR TONIGHT.
6:30 A.M.
YOU'RE GOING TO BE LATE FOR WORK, LỤC. GO!
SO? EVERYTHING GOING WELL? THE BABY'S NOT HERE YET? YOU'RE HOLDING ON? COURAGE, KHIÊM, ALL MY PRAYERS ARE WITH YOU.
5 PM
STILL NO? IT'LL BE OKAY. WHAT A BLESSING, I CAN'T WAIT!
I BEG YOU, GO HOME TO LOOK AFTER THE HOUSE AND REST FOR WORK TOMORROW.
THAT NIGHT, A COUP INVOLVING NGUYỄN KHÁNH WAS ANNOUNCED IN SAIGON.

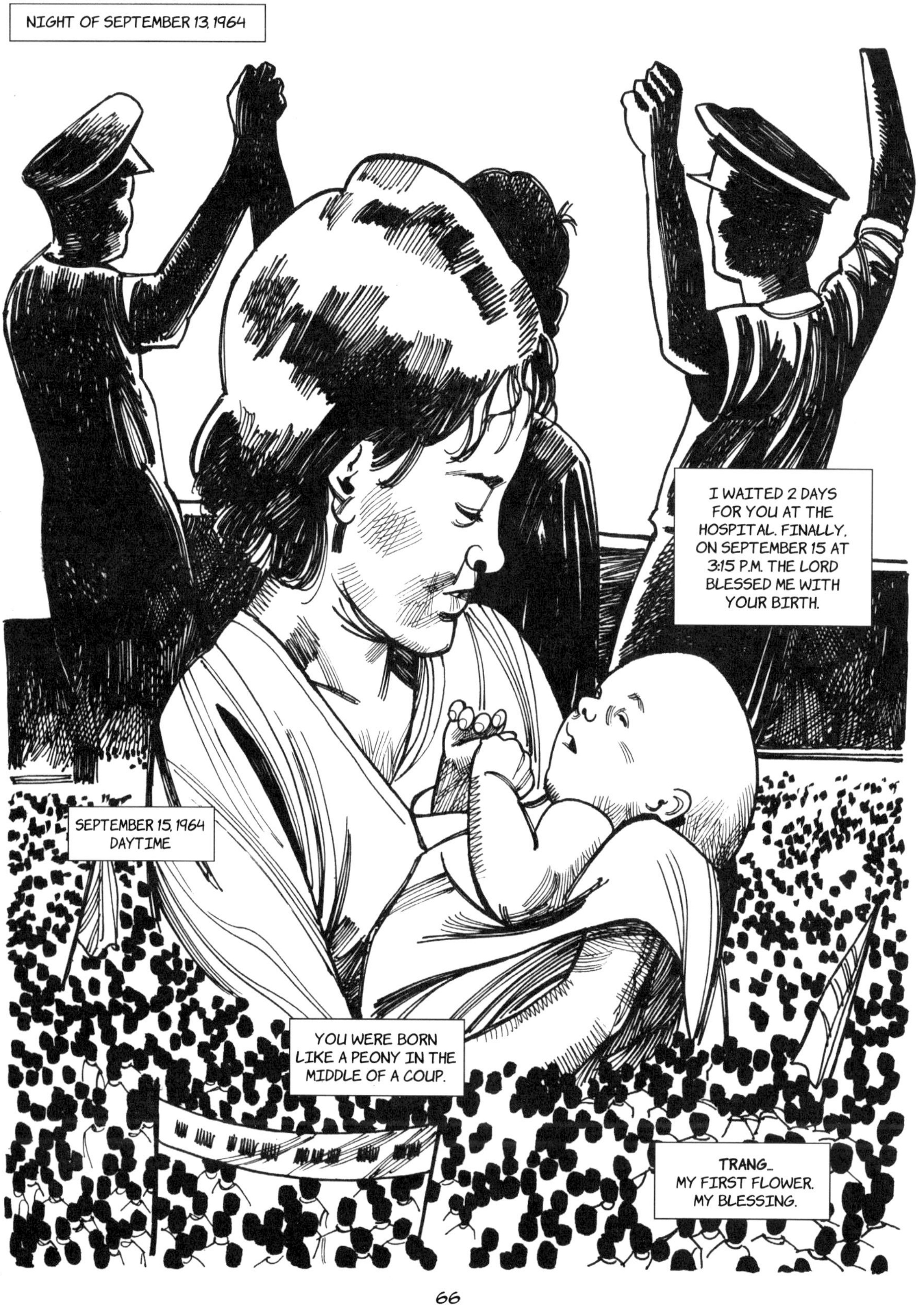
NIGHT OF SEPTEMBER 13, 1964
I WAITED 2 DAYS FOR YOU AT THE HOSPITAL. FINALLY, ON SEPTEMBER 15 AT 3:15 P.M. THE LORD BLESSED ME WITH YOUR BIRTH.
SEPTEMBER 15, 1964 DAYTIME
YOU WERE BORN LIKE A PEONY IN THE MIDDLE OF A COUP.
TRANG... MY FIRST FLOWER. MY BLESSING.

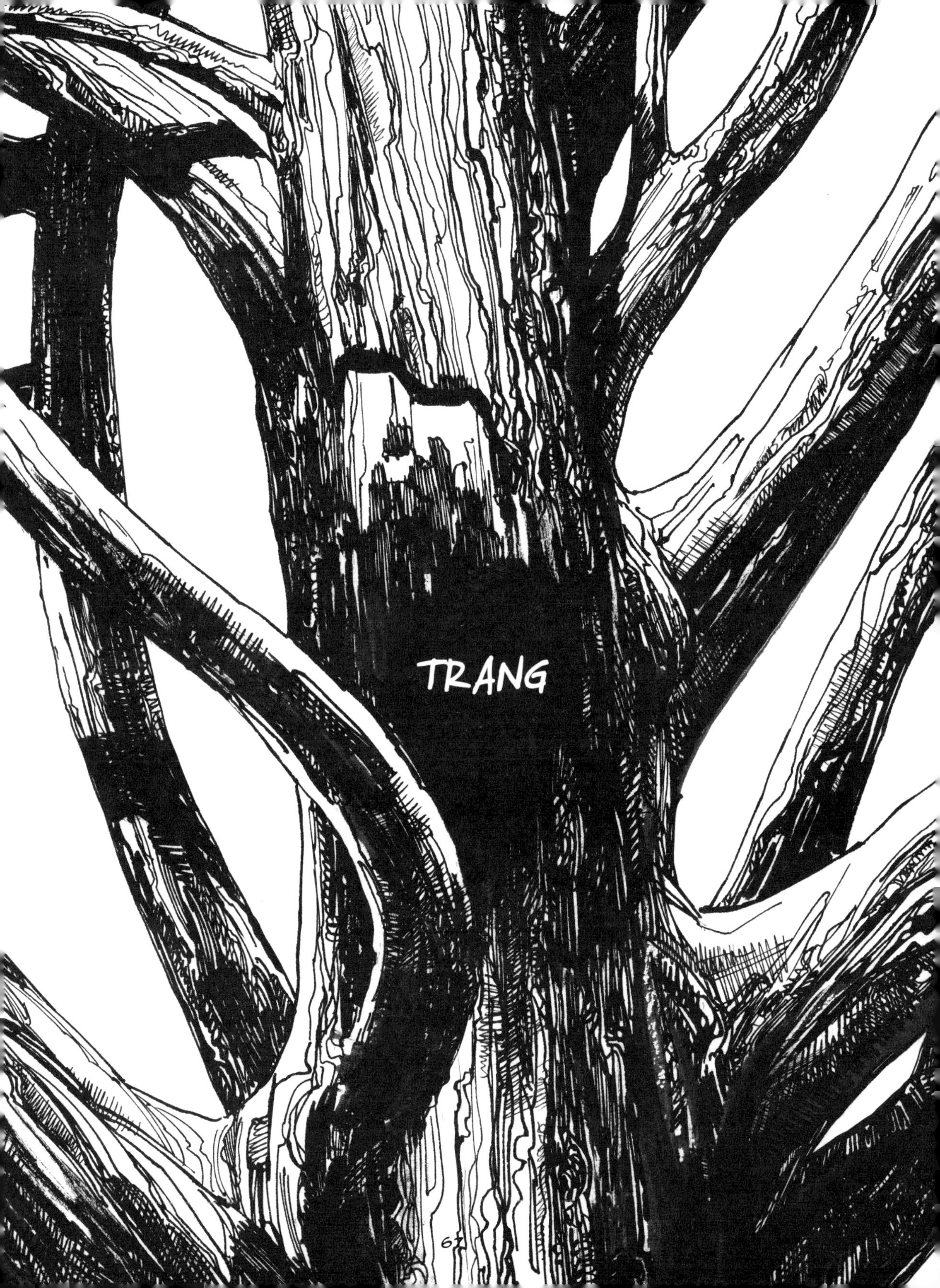
TRANG

CHAPTER 1

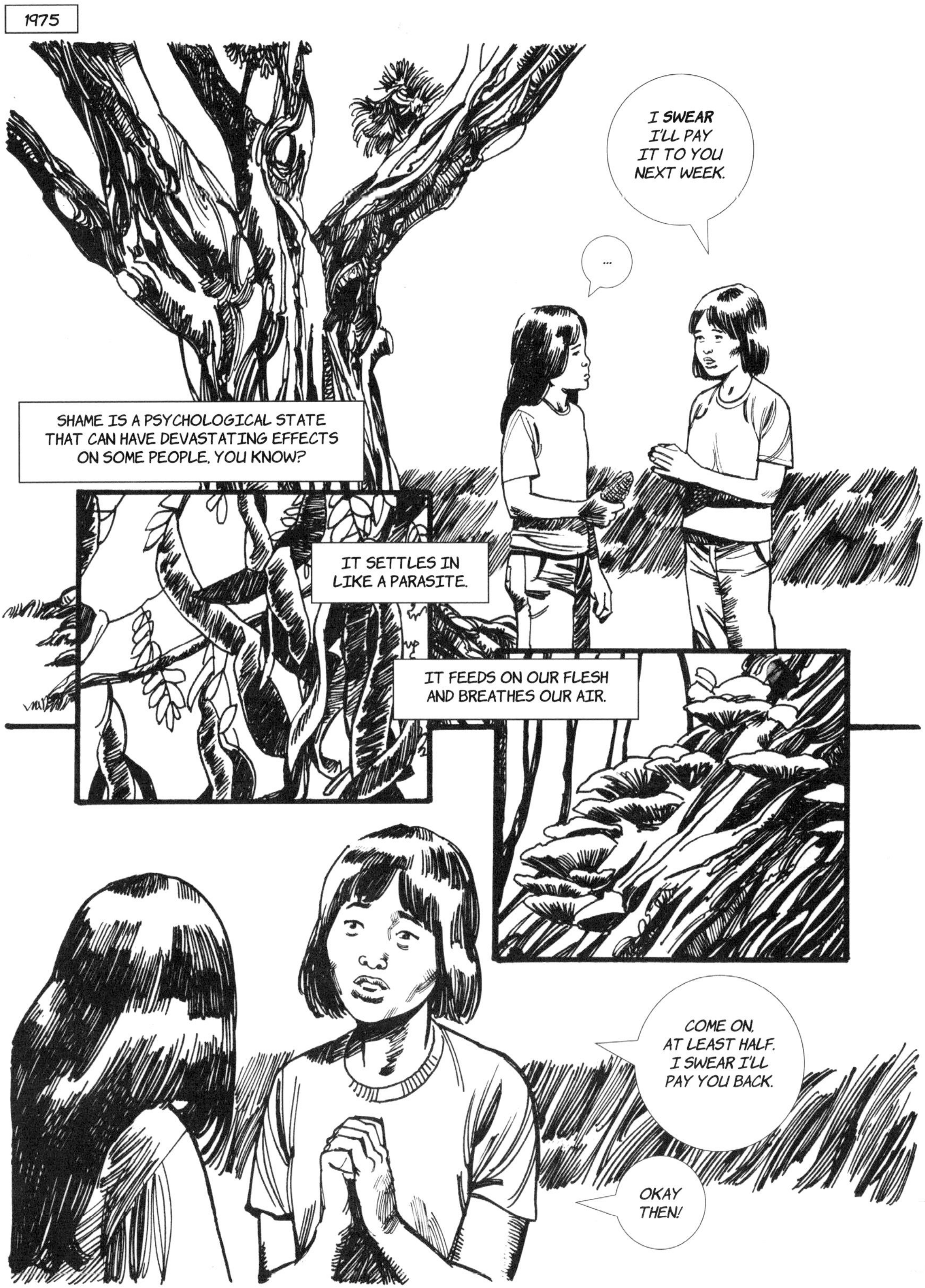

1975
I SWEAR I'LL PAY IT TO YOU NEXT WEEK.
...
SHAME IS A PSYCHOLOGICAL STATE THAT CAN HAVE DEVASTATING EFFECTS ON SOME PEOPLE, YOU KNOW?
IT SETTLES IN LIKE A PARASITE.
IT FEEDS ON OUR FLESH AND BREATHES OUR AIR.
COME ON, AT LEAST HALF. I SWEAR I'LL PAY YOU BACK.
OKAY THEN!

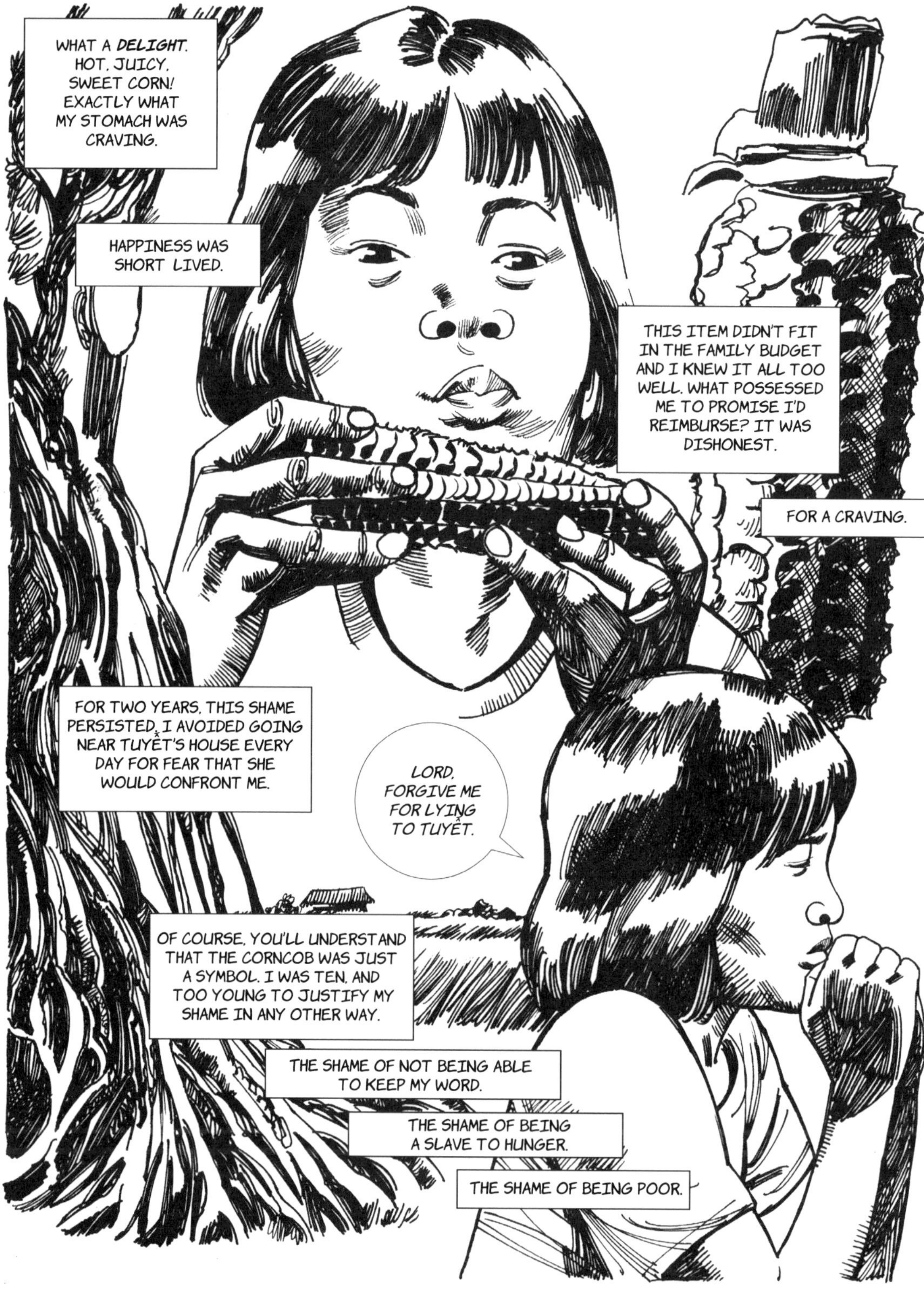
WHAT A DELIGHT. HOT, JUICY, SWEET CORN! EXACTLY WHAT MY STOMACH WAS CRAVING.
HAPPINESS WAS SHORT LIVED.
THIS ITEM DIDN'T FIT IN THE FAMILY BUDGET AND I KNEW IT ALL TOO WELL. WHAT POSSESSED ME TO PROMISE I'D REIMBURSE? IT WAS DISHONEST.
FOR A CRAVING.
FOR TWO YEARS, THIS SHAME PERSISTED. I AVOIDED GOING NEAR TUYẾT'S HOUSE EVERY DAY FOR FEAR THAT SHE WOULD CONFRONT ME.
LORD, FORGIVE ME FOR LYING TO TUYẾT.
OF COURSE, YOU'LL UNDERSTAND THAT THE CORNCOB WAS JUST A SYMBOL. I WAS TEN, AND TOO YOUNG TO JUSTIFY MY SHAME IN ANY OTHER WAY.
THE SHAME OF NOT BEING ABLE TO KEEP MY WORD.
THE SHAME OF BEING A SLAVE TO HUNGER.
THE SHAME OF BEING POOR.

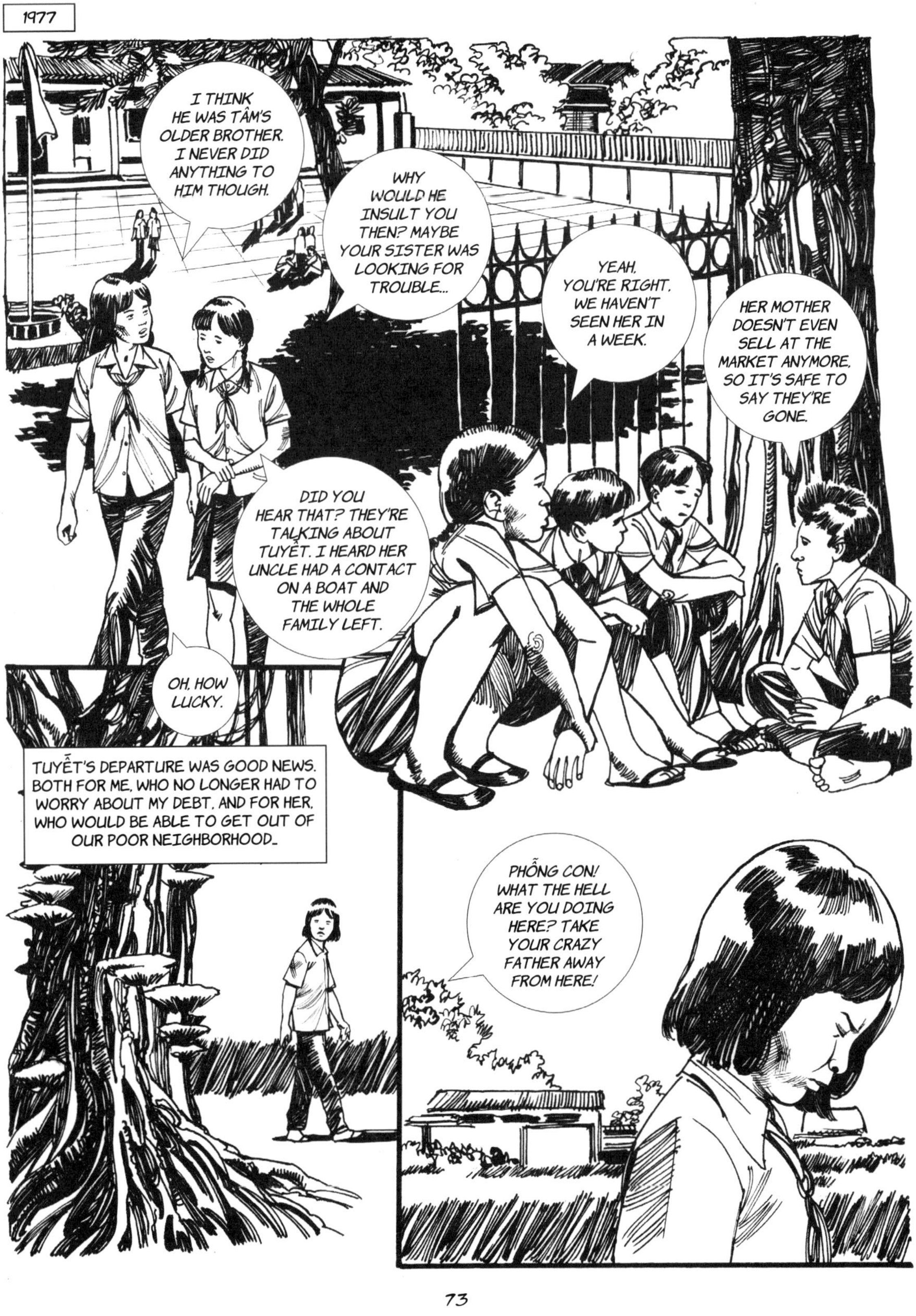
1977
I THINK HE WAS TÂM'S OLDER BROTHER. I NEVER DID ANYTHING TO HIM THOUGH.
WHY WOULD HE INSULT YOU THEN? MAYBE YOUR SISTER WAS LOOKING FOR TROUBLE...
YEAH, YOU'RE RIGHT, WE HAVEN'T SEEN HER IN A WEEK.
HER MOTHER DOESN'T EVEN SELL AT THE MARKET ANYMORE, SO IT'S SAFE TO SAY THEY'RE GONE.
DID YOU HEAR THAT? THEY'RE TALKING ABOUT TUYẾT. I HEARD HER UNCLE HAD A CONTACT ON A BOAT AND THE WHOLE FAMILY LEFT.
OH, HOW LUCKY.
TUYẾT'S DEPARTURE WAS GOOD NEWS. BOTH FOR ME, WHO NO LONGER HAD TO WORRY ABOUT MY DEBT, AND FOR HER, WHO WOULD BE ABLE TO GET OUT OF OUR POOR NEIGHBORHOOD...
PHỖNG CON! WHAT THE HELL ARE YOU DOING HERE? TAKE YOUR CRAZY FATHER AWAY FROM HERE!

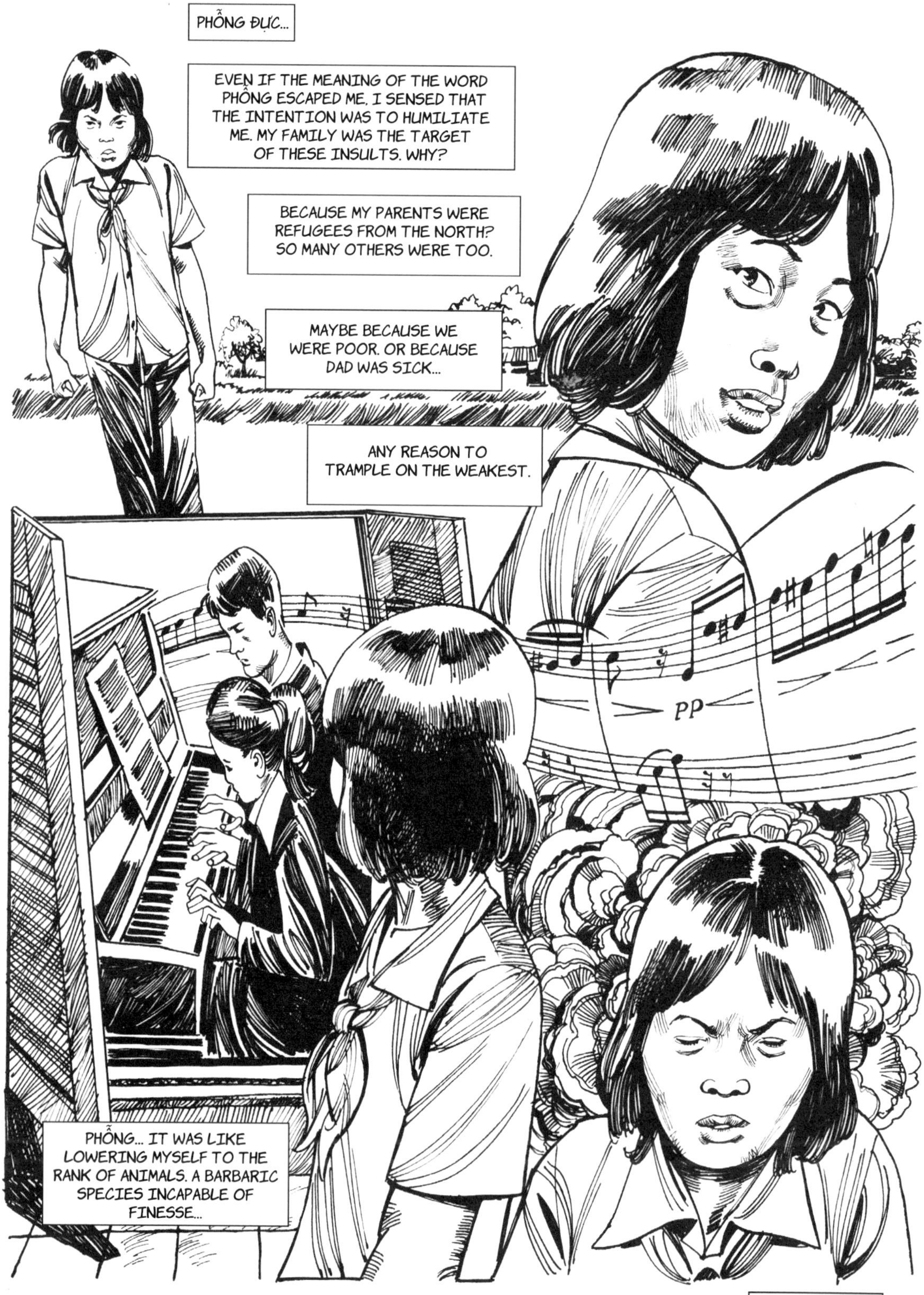
PHỖNG ĐỤC...
EVEN IF THE MEANING OF THE WORD PHỖNG ESCAPED ME, I SENSED THAT THE INTENTION WAS TO HUMILIATE ME. MY FAMILY WAS THE TARGET OF THESE INSULTS. WHY?
BECAUSE MY PARENTS WERE REFUGEES FROM THE NORTH? SO MANY OTHERS WERE TOO.
MAYBE BECAUSE WE WERE POOR. OR BECAUSE DAD WAS SICK...
ANY REASON TO TRAMPLE ON THE WEAKEST.
PP
PHỖNG... IT WAS LIKE LOWERING MYSELF TO THE RANK OF ANIMALS. A BARBARIC SPECIES INCAPABLE OF FINESSE...

...OF MUSIC.

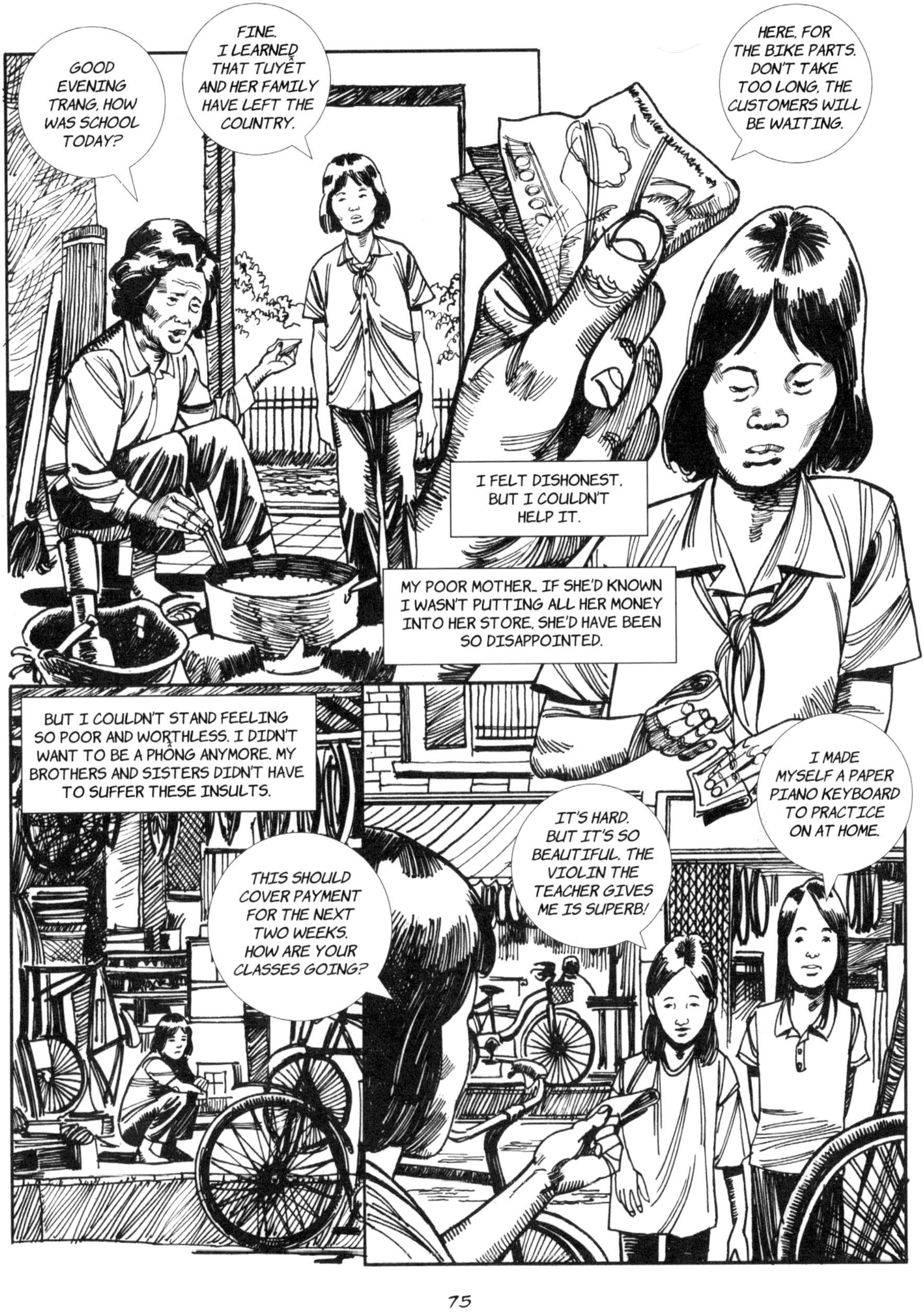
GOOD EVENING TRANG. HOW WAS SCHOOL TODAY?
FINE. I LEARNED THAT TUYẾT AND HER FAMILY HAVE LEFT THE COUNTRY.
HERE, FOR THE BIKE PARTS. DON'T TAKE TOO LONG, THE CUSTOMERS WILL BE WAITING.
I FELT DISHONEST, BUT I COULDN'T HELP IT.
MY POOR MOTHER... IF SHE'D KNOWN I WASN'T PUTTING ALL HER MONEY INTO HER STORE, SHE'D HAVE BEEN SO DISAPPOINTED.
BUT I COULDN'T STAND FEELING SO POOR AND WORTHLESS. I DIDN'T WANT TO BE A PHỒNG ANYMORE. MY BROTHERS AND SISTERS DIDN'T HAVE TO SUFFER THESE INSULTS.
THIS SHOULD COVER PAYMENT FOR THE NEXT TWO WEEKS. HOW ARE YOUR CLASSES GOING?
IT'S HARD. BUT IT'S SO BEAUTIFUL. THE VIOLIN THE TEACHER GIVES ME IS SUPERB!
I MADE MYSELF A PAPER PIANO KEYBOARD TO PRACTICE ON AT HOME.

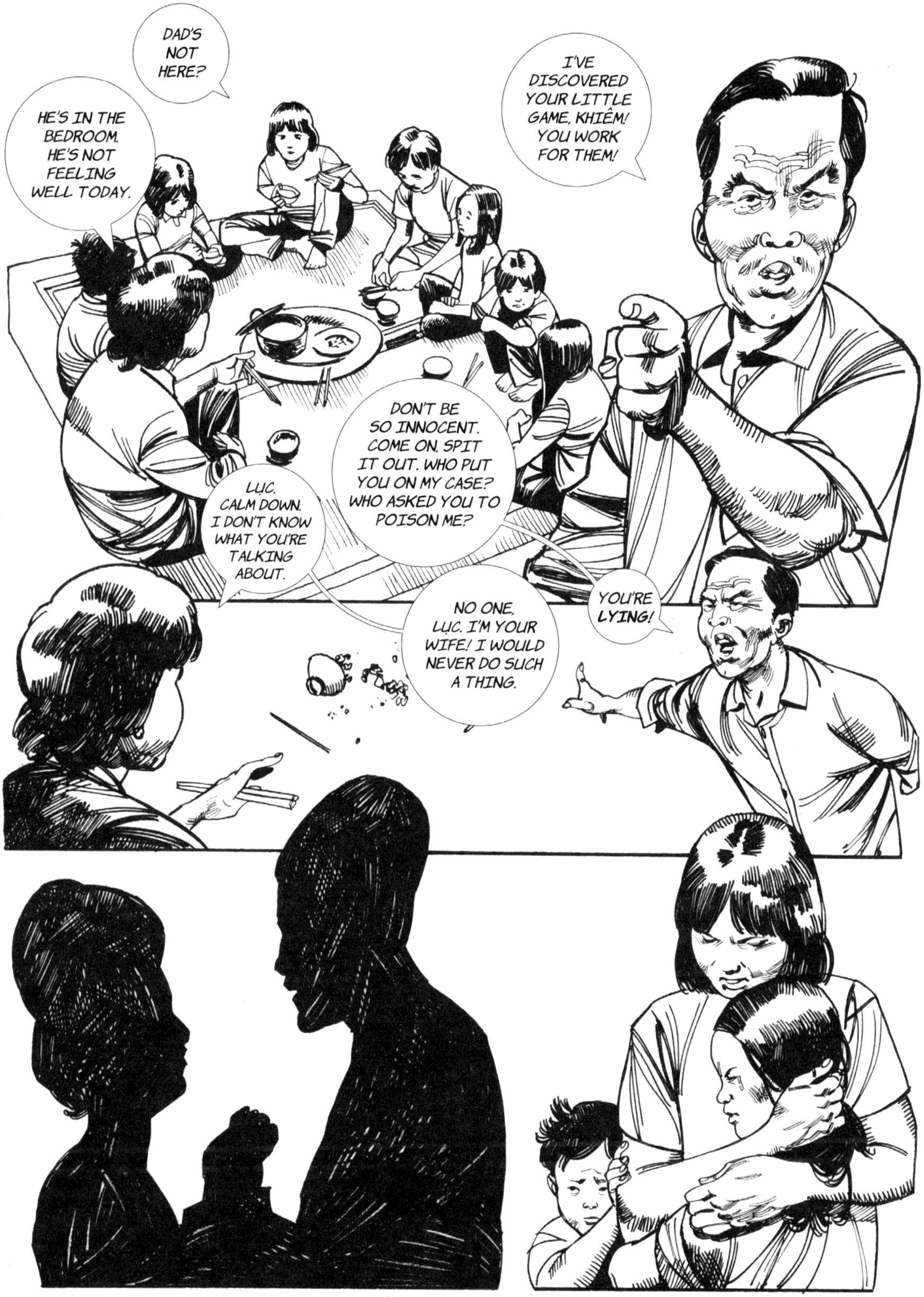
DAD'S NOT HERE?
HE'S IN THE BEDROOM. HE'S NOT FEELING WELL TODAY.
I'VE DISCOVERED YOUR LITTLE GAME, KHIÊM! YOU WORK FOR THEM!
LỤC, CALM DOWN. I DON'T KNOW WHAT YOU'RE TALKING ABOUT.
DON'T BE SO INNOCENT. COME ON, SPIT IT OUT. WHO PUT YOU ON MY CASE? WHO ASKED YOU TO POISON ME?
NO ONE, LỤC. I'M YOUR WIFE! I WOULD NEVER DO SUCH A THING.
YOU'RE **LYING!**

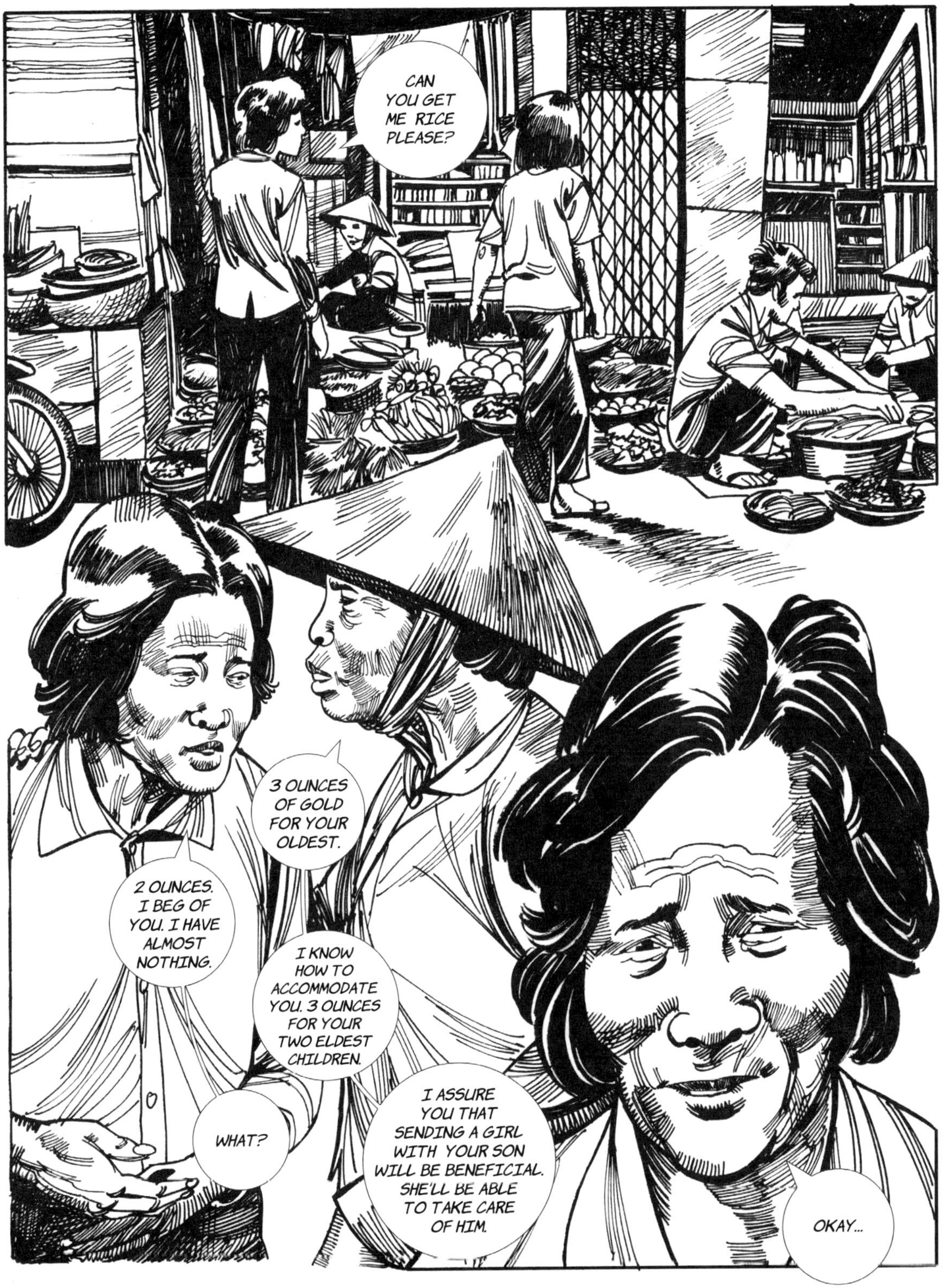
CAN YOU GET ME RICE PLEASE?
3 OUNCES OF GOLD FOR YOUR OLDEST.
2 OUNCES. I BEG OF YOU. I HAVE ALMOST NOTHING.
I KNOW HOW TO ACCOMMODATE YOU. 3 OUNCES FOR YOUR TWO ELDEST CHILDREN.
WHAT?
I ASSURE YOU THAT SENDING A GIRL WITH YOUR SON WILL BE BENEFICIAL. SHE'LL BE ABLE TO TAKE CARE OF HIM.
OKAY...

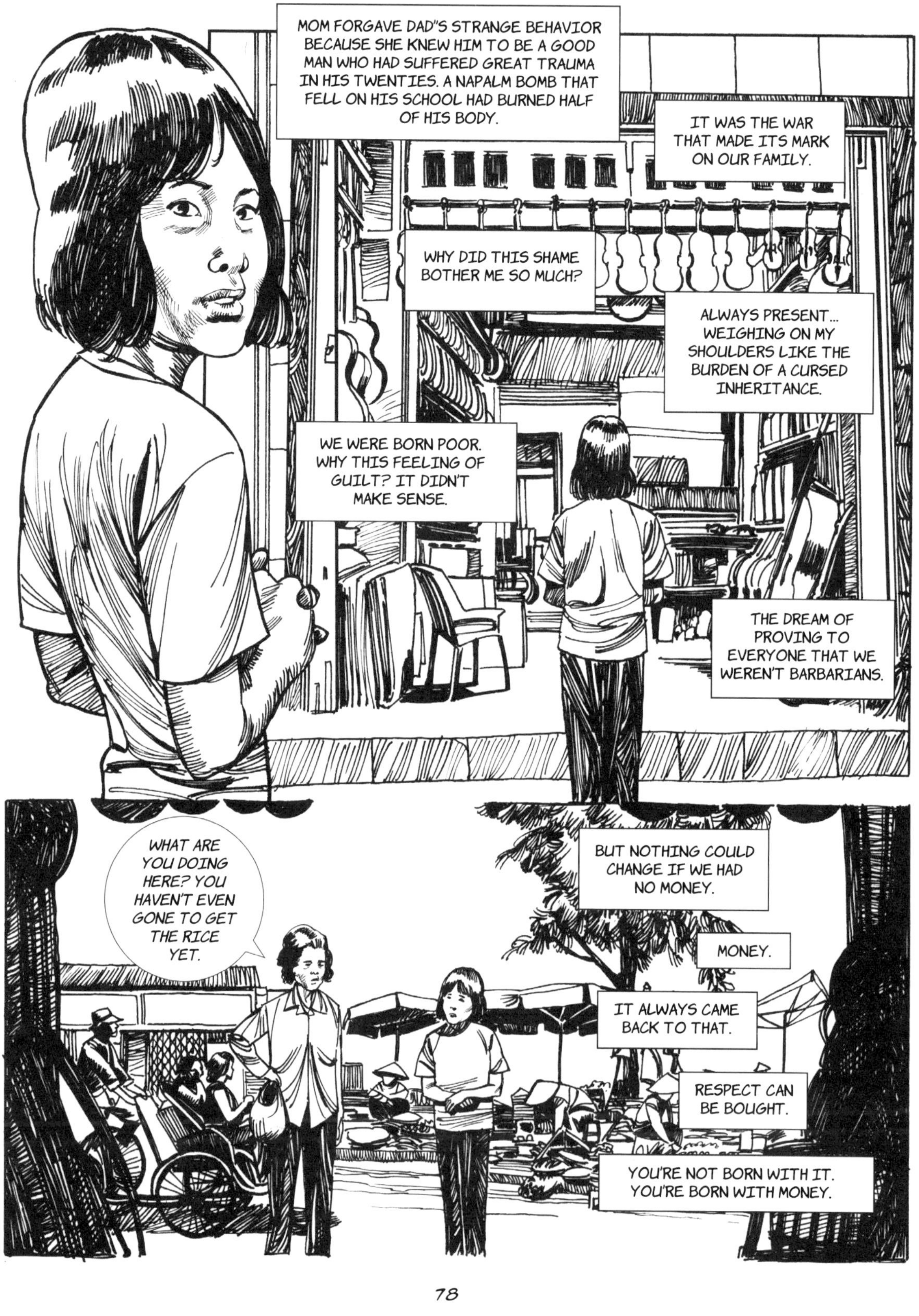
MOM FORGAVE DAD"S STRANGE BEHAVIOR BECAUSE SHE KNEW HIM TO BE A GOOD MAN WHO HAD SUFFERED GREAT TRAUMA IN HIS TWENTIES. A NAPALM BOMB THAT FELL ON HIS SCHOOL HAD BURNED HALF OF HIS BODY.
IT WAS THE WAR THAT MADE ITS MARK ON OUR FAMILY.
WHY DID THIS SHAME BOTHER ME SO MUCH?
ALWAYS PRESENT... WEIGHING ON MY SHOULDERS LIKE THE BURDEN OF A CURSED INHERITANCE.
WE WERE BORN POOR. WHY THIS FEELING OF GUILT? IT DIDN'T MAKE SENSE.
THE DREAM OF PROVING TO EVERYONE THAT WE WEREN'T BARBARIANS.
WHAT ARE YOU DOING HERE? YOU HAVEN'T EVEN GONE TO GET THE RICE YET.
BUT NOTHING COULD CHANGE IF WE HAD NO MONEY.
MONEY.
IT ALWAYS CAME BACK TO THAT.
RESPECT CAN BE BOUGHT.
YOU'RE NOT BORN WITH IT. YOU'RE BORN WITH MONEY.

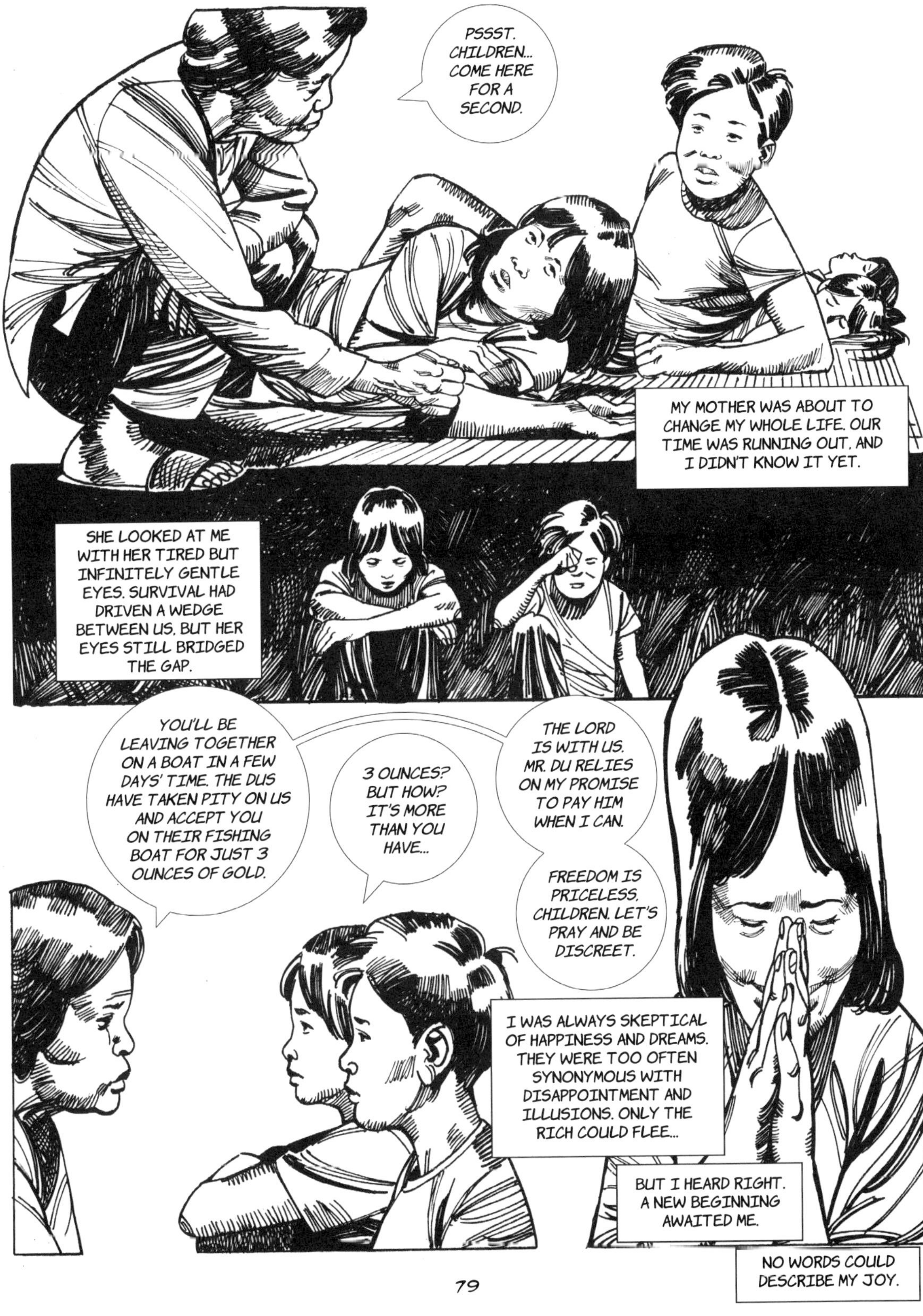
PSSST. CHILDREN... COME HERE FOR A SECOND.
MY MOTHER WAS ABOUT TO CHANGE MY WHOLE LIFE. OUR TIME WAS RUNNING OUT, AND I DIDN'T KNOW IT YET.
SHE LOOKED AT ME WITH HER TIRED BUT INFINITELY GENTLE EYES. SURVIVAL HAD DRIVEN A WEDGE BETWEEN US, BUT HER EYES STILL BRIDGED THE GAP.
YOU'LL BE LEAVING TOGETHER ON A BOAT IN A FEW DAYS' TIME. THE DUS HAVE TAKEN PITY ON US AND ACCEPT YOU ON THEIR FISHING BOAT FOR JUST 3 OUNCES OF GOLD.
3 OUNCES? BUT HOW? IT'S MORE THAN YOU HAVE...
THE LORD IS WITH US. MR. DU RELIES ON MY PROMISE TO PAY HIM WHEN I CAN.
FREEDOM IS PRICELESS, CHILDREN. LET'S PRAY AND BE DISCREET.
I WAS ALWAYS SKEPTICAL OF HAPPINESS AND DREAMS. THEY WERE TOO OFTEN SYNONYMOUS WITH DISAPPOINTMENT AND ILLUSIONS. ONLY THE RICH COULD FLEE...
BUT I HEARD RIGHT. A NEW BEGINNING AWAITED ME.
NO WORDS COULD DESCRIBE MY JOY.

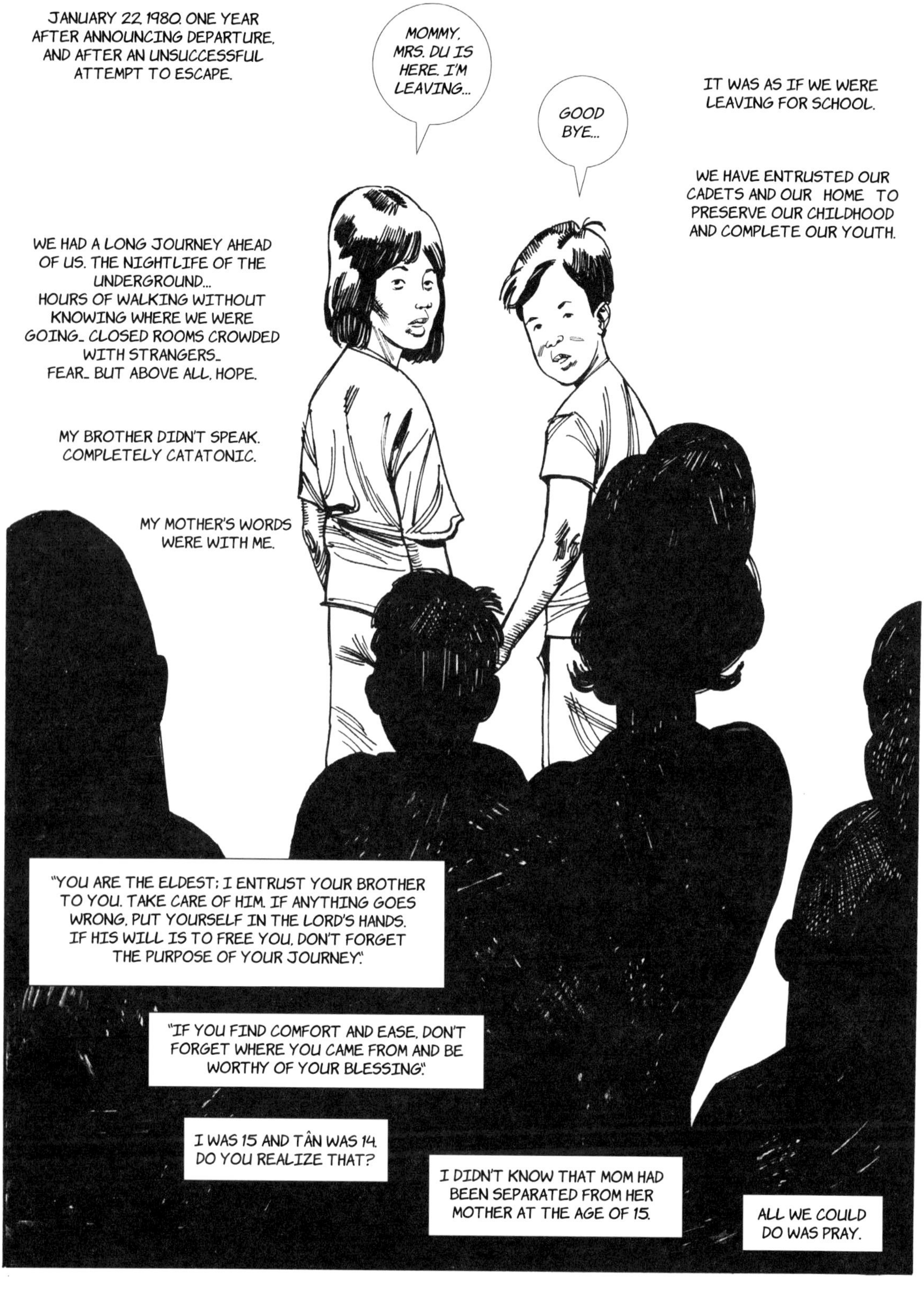

JANUARY 22, 1980. ONE YEAR AFTER ANNOUNCING DEPARTURE, AND AFTER AN UNSUCCESSFUL ATTEMPT TO ESCAPE.
MOMMY, MRS. DU IS HERE. I'M LEAVING...
GOOD BYE...
IT WAS AS IF WE WERE LEAVING FOR SCHOOL.
WE HAVE ENTRUSTED OUR CADETS AND OUR HOME TO PRESERVE OUR CHILDHOOD AND COMPLETE OUR YOUTH.
WE HAD A LONG JOURNEY AHEAD OF US. THE NIGHTLIFE OF THE UNDERGROUND... HOURS OF WALKING WITHOUT KNOWING WHERE WE WERE GOING... CLOSED ROOMS CROWDED WITH STRANGERS... FEAR... BUT ABOVE ALL, HOPE.
MY BROTHER DIDN'T SPEAK. COMPLETELY CATATONIC.
MY MOTHER'S WORDS WERE WITH ME.
"YOU ARE THE ELDEST; I ENTRUST YOUR BROTHER TO YOU. TAKE CARE OF HIM. IF ANYTHING GOES WRONG, PUT YOURSELF IN THE LORD'S HANDS. IF HIS WILL IS TO FREE YOU, DON'T FORGET THE PURPOSE OF YOUR JOURNEY".
"IF YOU FIND COMFORT AND EASE, DON'T FORGET WHERE YOU CAME FROM AND BE WORTHY OF YOUR BLESSING".
I WAS 15 AND TÂN WAS 14. DO YOU REALIZE THAT?
I DIDN'T KNOW THAT MOM HAD BEEN SEPARATED FROM HER MOTHER AT THE AGE OF 15.
ALL WE COULD DO WAS PRAY.

CHAPTER 2

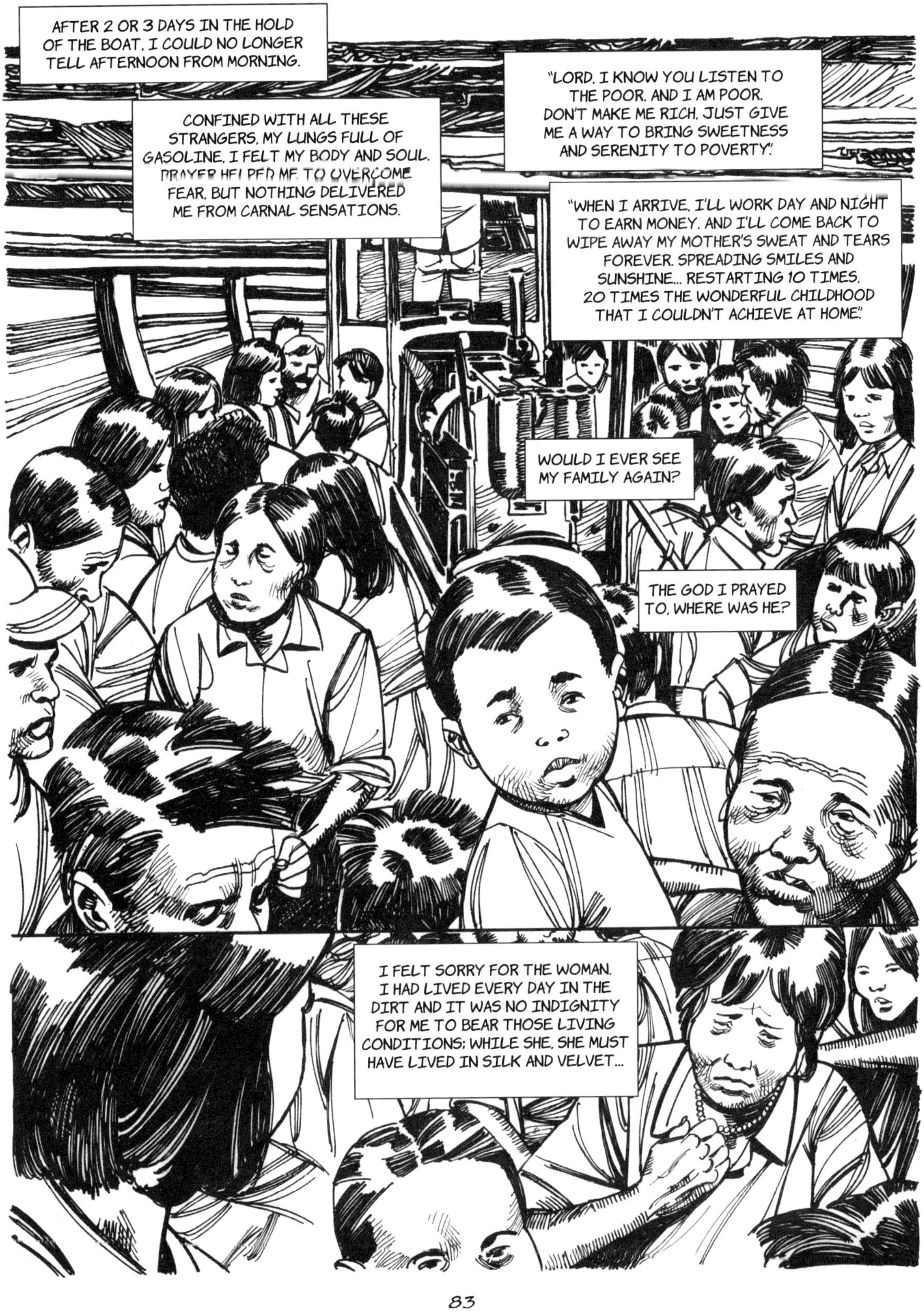
AFTER 2 OR 3 DAYS IN THE HOLD OF THE BOAT, I COULD NO LONGER TELL AFTERNOON FROM MORNING.
CONFINED WITH ALL THESE STRANGERS, MY LUNGS FULL OF GASOLINE, I FELT MY BODY AND SOUL. PRAYER HELPED ME TO OVERCOME FEAR, BUT NOTHING DELIVERED ME FROM CARNAL SENSATIONS.
"LORD, I KNOW YOU LISTEN TO THE POOR. AND I AM POOR. DON'T MAKE ME RICH, JUST GIVE ME A WAY TO BRING SWEETNESS AND SERENITY TO POVERTY."
"WHEN I ARRIVE, I'LL WORK DAY AND NIGHT TO EARN MONEY. AND I'LL COME BACK TO WIPE AWAY MY MOTHER'S SWEAT AND TEARS FOREVER. SPREADING SMILES AND SUNSHINE... RESTARTING 10 TIMES, 20 TIMES THE WONDERFUL CHILDHOOD THAT I COULDN'T ACHIEVE AT HOME."
WOULD I EVER SEE MY FAMILY AGAIN?
THE GOD I PRAYED TO, WHERE WAS HE?
I FELT SORRY FOR THE WOMAN. I HAD LIVED EVERY DAY IN THE DIRT AND IT WAS NO INDIGNITY FOR ME TO BEAR THOSE LIVING CONDITIONS; WHILE SHE, SHE MUST HAVE LIVED IN SILK AND VELVET...

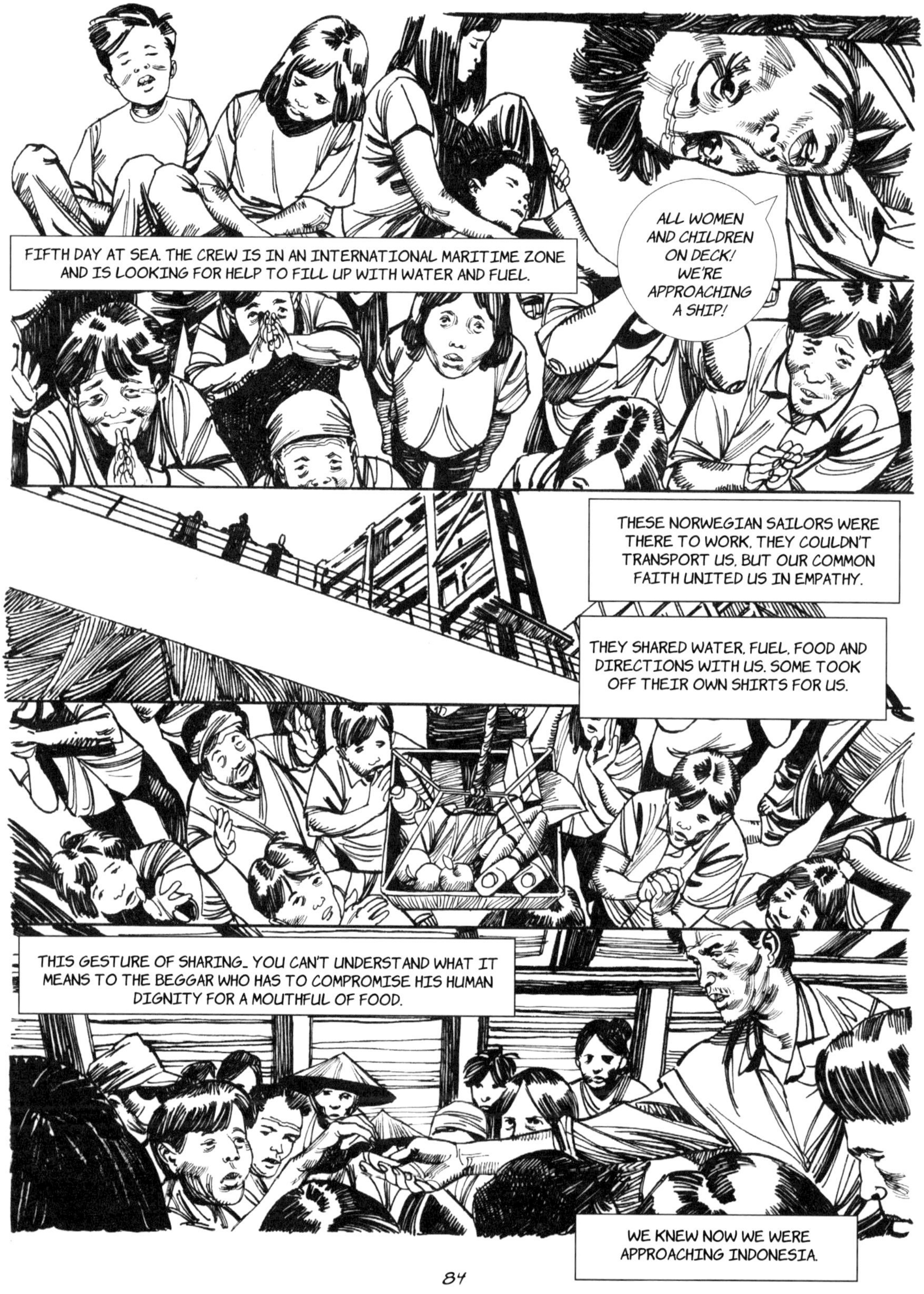
FIFTH DAY AT SEA. THE CREW IS IN AN INTERNATIONAL MARITIME ZONE AND IS LOOKING FOR HELP TO FILL UP WITH WATER AND FUEL.
ALL WOMEN AND CHILDREN ON DECK! WE'RE APPROACHING A SHIP!
THESE NORWEGIAN SAILORS WERE THERE TO WORK. THEY COULDN'T TRANSPORT US, BUT OUR COMMON FAITH UNITED US IN EMPATHY.
THEY SHARED WATER, FUEL, FOOD AND DIRECTIONS WITH US. SOME TOOK OFF THEIR OWN SHIRTS FOR US.
THIS GESTURE OF SHARING... YOU CAN'T UNDERSTAND WHAT IT MEANS TO THE BEGGAR WHO HAS TO COMPROMISE HIS HUMAN DIGNITY FOR A MOUTHFUL OF FOOD.
WE KNEW NOW WE WERE APPROACHING INDONESIA.

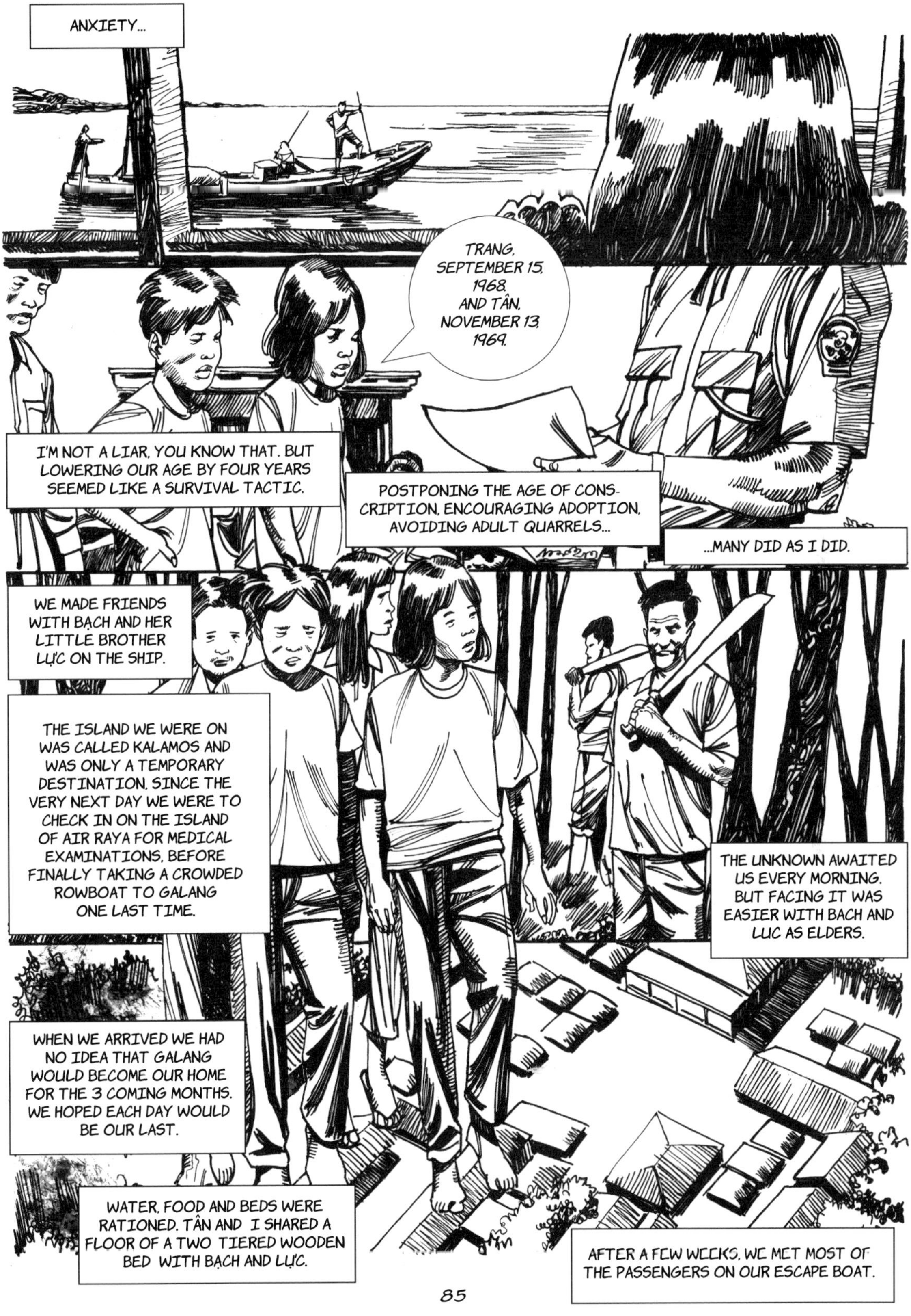
ANXIETY...
TRANG, SEPTEMBER 15, 1968. AND TÂN, NOVEMBER 13, 1969.
I'M NOT A LIAR, YOU KNOW THAT. BUT LOWERING OUR AGE BY FOUR YEARS SEEMED LIKE A SURVIVAL TACTIC.
POSTPONING THE AGE OF CONS-CRIPTION, ENCOURAGING ADOPTION, AVOIDING ADULT QUARRELS...
...MANY DID AS I DID.
WE MADE FRIENDS WITH BẠCH AND HER LITTLE BROTHER LỰC ON THE SHIP.
THE ISLAND WE WERE ON WAS CALLED KALAMOS AND WAS ONLY A TEMPORARY DESTINATION, SINCE THE VERY NEXT DAY WE WERE TO CHECK IN ON THE ISLAND OF AIR RAYA FOR MEDICAL EXAMINATIONS, BEFORE FINALLY TAKING A CROWDED ROWBOAT TO GALANG ONE LAST TIME.
THE UNKNOWN AWAITED US EVERY MORNING. BUT FACING IT WAS EASIER WITH BACH AND LUC AS ELDERS.
WHEN WE ARRIVED WE HAD NO IDEA THAT GALANG WOULD BECOME OUR HOME FOR THE 3 COMING MONTHS. WE HOPED EACH DAY WOULD BE OUR LAST.
WATER, FOOD AND BEDS WERE RATIONED. TÂN AND I SHARED A FLOOR OF A TWO TIERED WOODEN BED WITH BẠCH AND LỰC.
AFTER A FEW WEEKS, WE MET MOST OF THE PASSENGERS ON OUR ESCAPE BOAT.

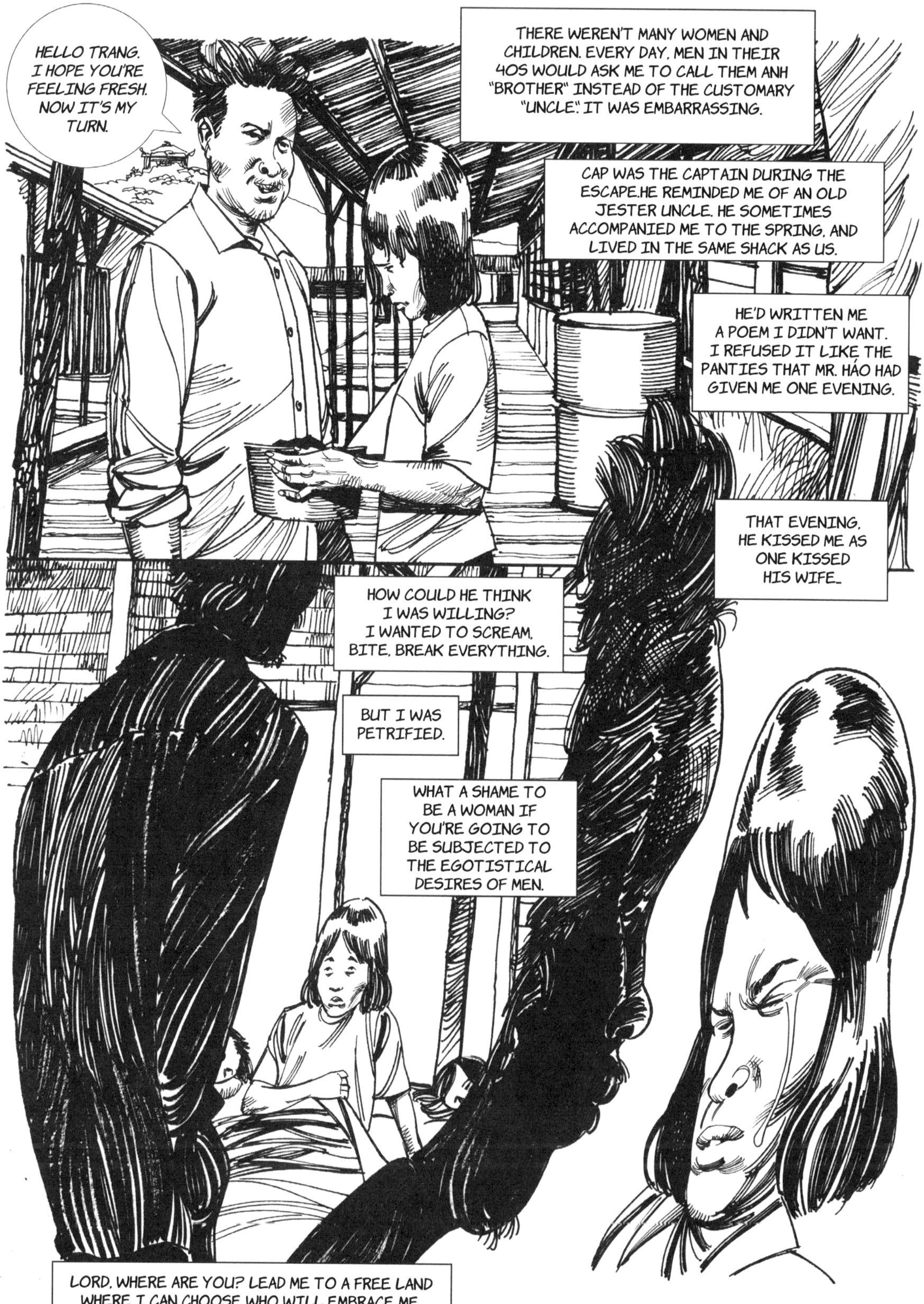
HELLO TRANG. I HOPE YOU'RE FEELING FRESH. NOW IT'S MY TURN.
THERE WEREN'T MANY WOMEN AND CHILDREN. EVERY DAY, MEN IN THEIR 40S WOULD ASK ME TO CALL THEM ANH "BROTHER" INSTEAD OF THE CUSTOMARY "UNCLE." IT WAS EMBARRASSING.
CAP WAS THE CAPTAIN DURING THE ESCAPE.HE REMINDED ME OF AN OLD JESTER UNCLE. HE SOMETIMES ACCOMPANIED ME TO THE SPRING, AND LIVED IN THE SAME SHACK AS US.
HE'D WRITTEN ME A POEM I DIDN'T WANT. I REFUSED IT LIKE THE PANTIES THAT MR. HÁO HAD GIVEN ME ONE EVENING.
THAT EVENING, HE KISSED ME AS ONE KISSED HIS WIFE...
HOW COULD HE THINK I WAS WILLING? I WANTED TO SCREAM, BITE, BREAK EVERYTHING.
BUT I WAS PETRIFIED.
WHAT A SHAME TO BE A WOMAN IF YOU'RE GOING TO BE SUBJECTED TO THE EGOTISTICAL DESIRES OF MEN.
LORD, WHERE ARE YOU? LEAD ME TO A FREE LAND WHERE I CAN CHOOSE WHO WILL EMBRACE ME.

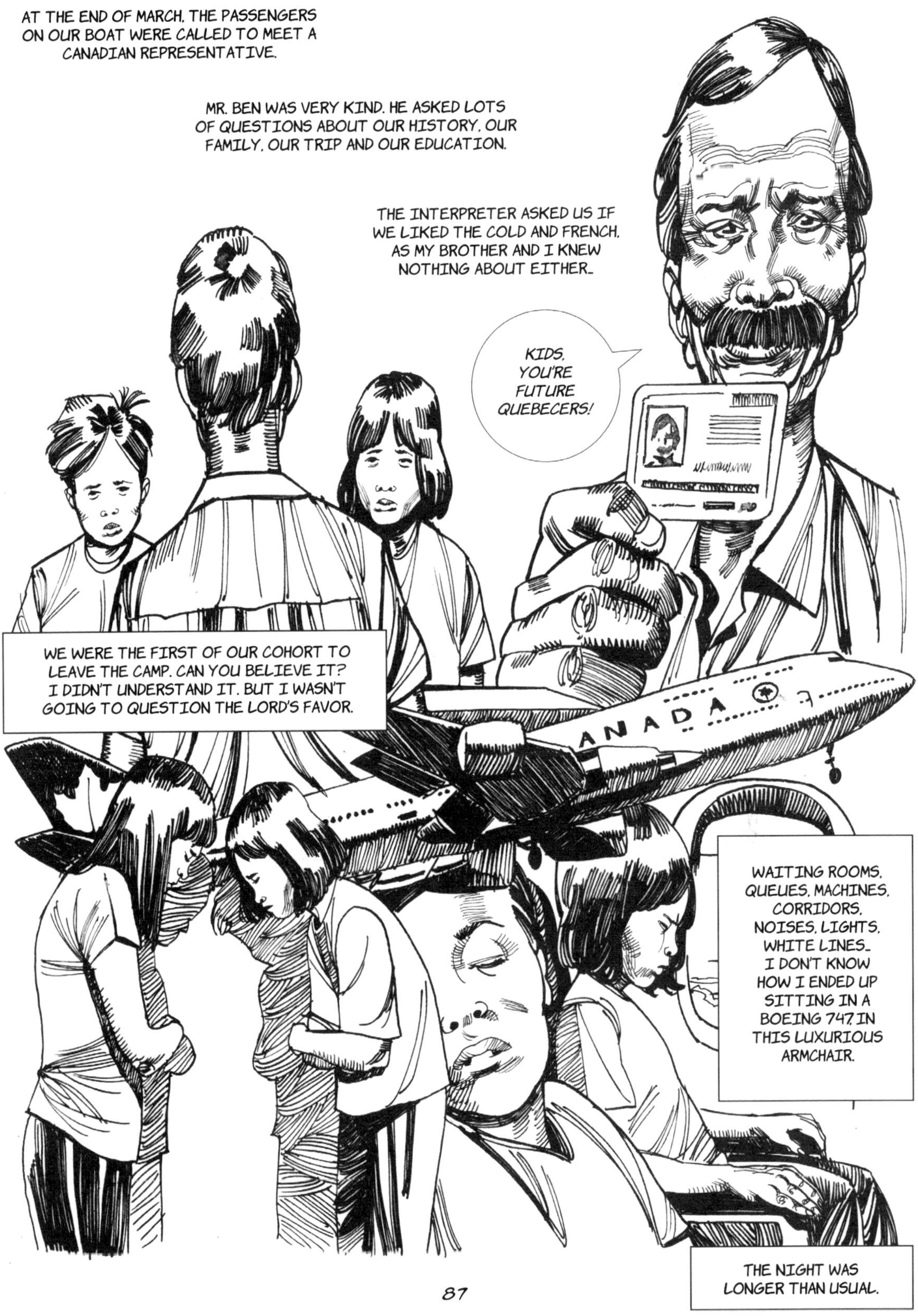
AT THE END OF MARCH, THE PASSENGERS ON OUR BOAT WERE CALLED TO MEET A CANADIAN REPRESENTATIVE.
MR. BEN WAS VERY KIND. HE ASKED LOTS OF QUESTIONS ABOUT OUR HISTORY, OUR FAMILY, OUR TRIP AND OUR EDUCATION.
THE INTERPRETER ASKED US IF WE LIKED THE COLD AND FRENCH, AS MY BROTHER AND I KNEW NOTHING ABOUT EITHER…
KIDS, YOU'RE FUTURE QUEBECERS!
WE WERE THE FIRST OF OUR COHORT TO LEAVE THE CAMP. CAN YOU BELIEVE IT? I DIDN'T UNDERSTAND IT. BUT I WASN'T GOING TO QUESTION THE LORD'S FAVOR.
ANADA
WAITING ROOMS, QUEUES, MACHINES, CORRIDORS, NOISES, LIGHTS, WHITE LINES… I DON'T KNOW HOW I ENDED UP SITTING IN A BOEING 747, IN THIS LUXURIOUS ARMCHAIR.
THE NIGHT WAS LONGER THAN USUAL.

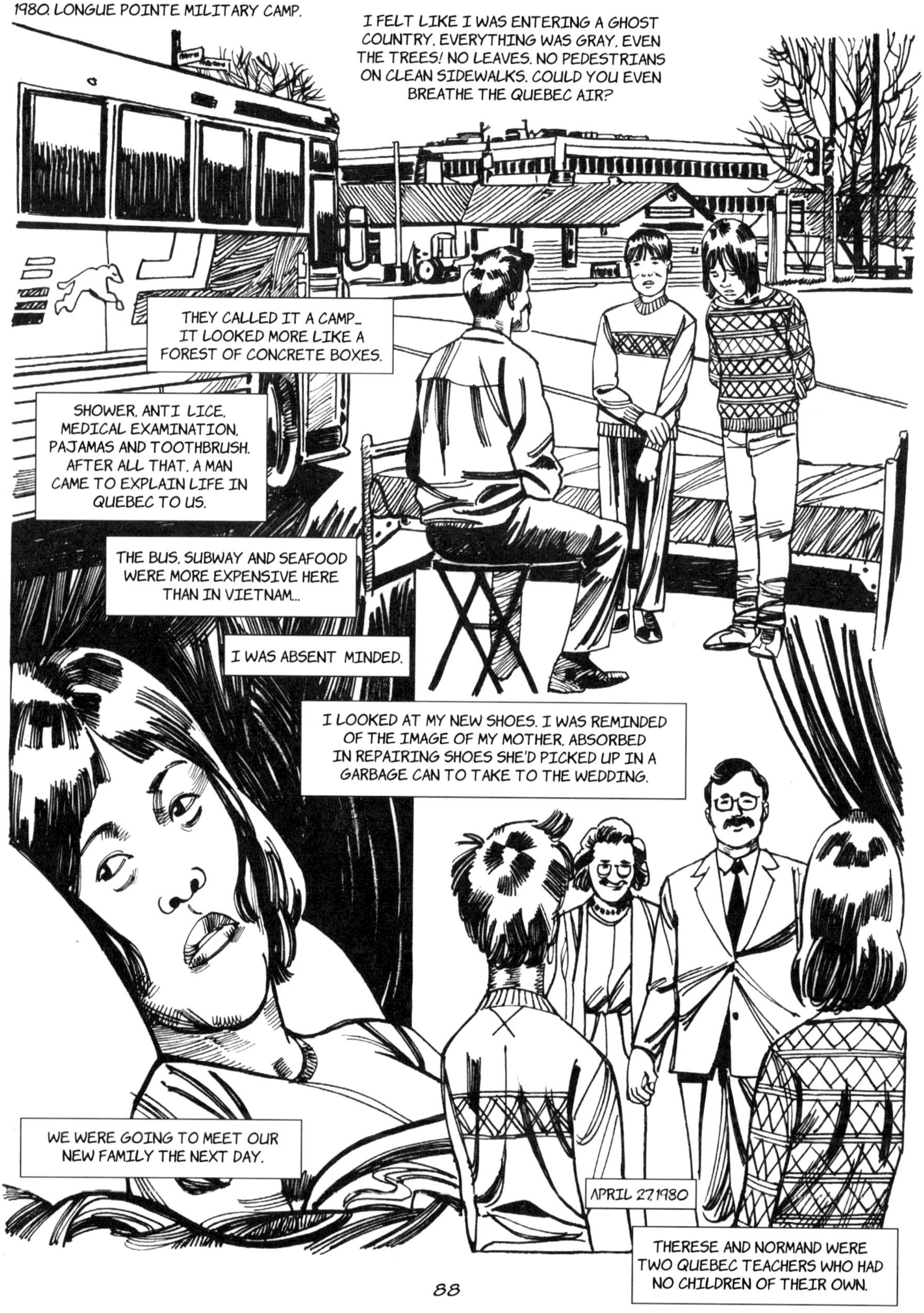
1980. LONGUE POINTE MILITARY CAMP.
I FELT LIKE I WAS ENTERING A GHOST COUNTRY. EVERYTHING WAS GRAY. EVEN THE TREES! NO LEAVES. NO PEDESTRIANS ON CLEAN SIDEWALKS. COULD YOU EVEN BREATHE THE QUEBEC AIR?
THEY CALLED IT A CAMP… IT LOOKED MORE LIKE A FOREST OF CONCRETE BOXES.
SHOWER. ANTI LICE. MEDICAL EXAMINATION. PAJAMAS AND TOOTHBRUSH. AFTER ALL THAT, A MAN CAME TO EXPLAIN LIFE IN QUEBEC TO US.
THE BUS, SUBWAY AND SEAFOOD WERE MORE EXPENSIVE HERE THAN IN VIETNAM…
I WAS ABSENT MINDED.
I LOOKED AT MY NEW SHOES. I WAS REMINDED OF THE IMAGE OF MY MOTHER, ABSORBED IN REPAIRING SHOES SHE'D PICKED UP IN A GARBAGE CAN TO TAKE TO THE WEDDING.
WE WERE GOING TO MEET OUR NEW FAMILY THE NEXT DAY.
APRIL 27, 1980
THERESE AND NORMAND WERE TWO QUEBEC TEACHERS WHO HAD NO CHILDREN OF THEIR OWN.

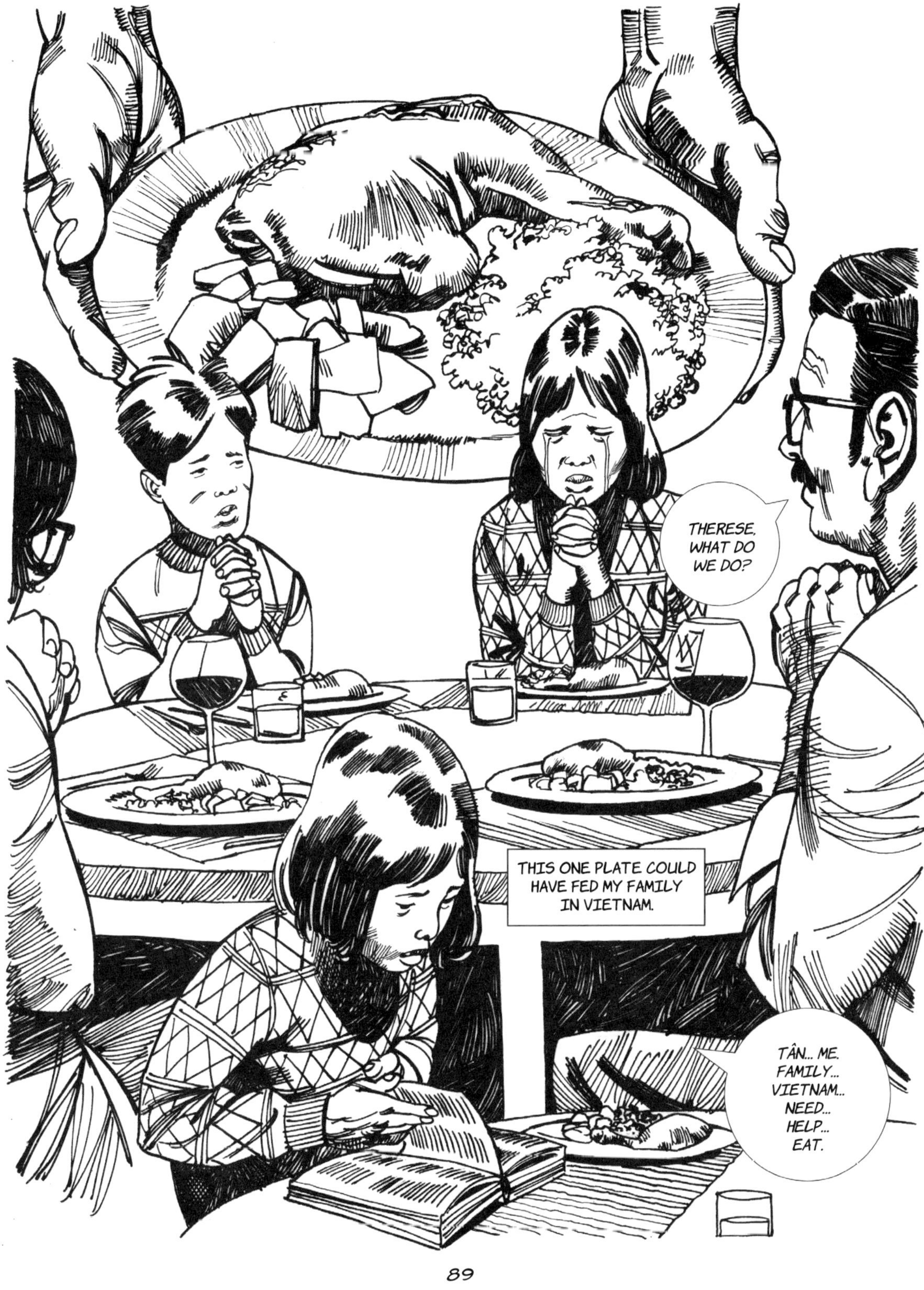
THERESE, WHAT DO WE DO?
THIS ONE PLATE COULD HAVE FED MY FAMILY IN VIETNAM.
TÂN... ME. FAMILY... VIETNAM... NEED... HELP... EAT.

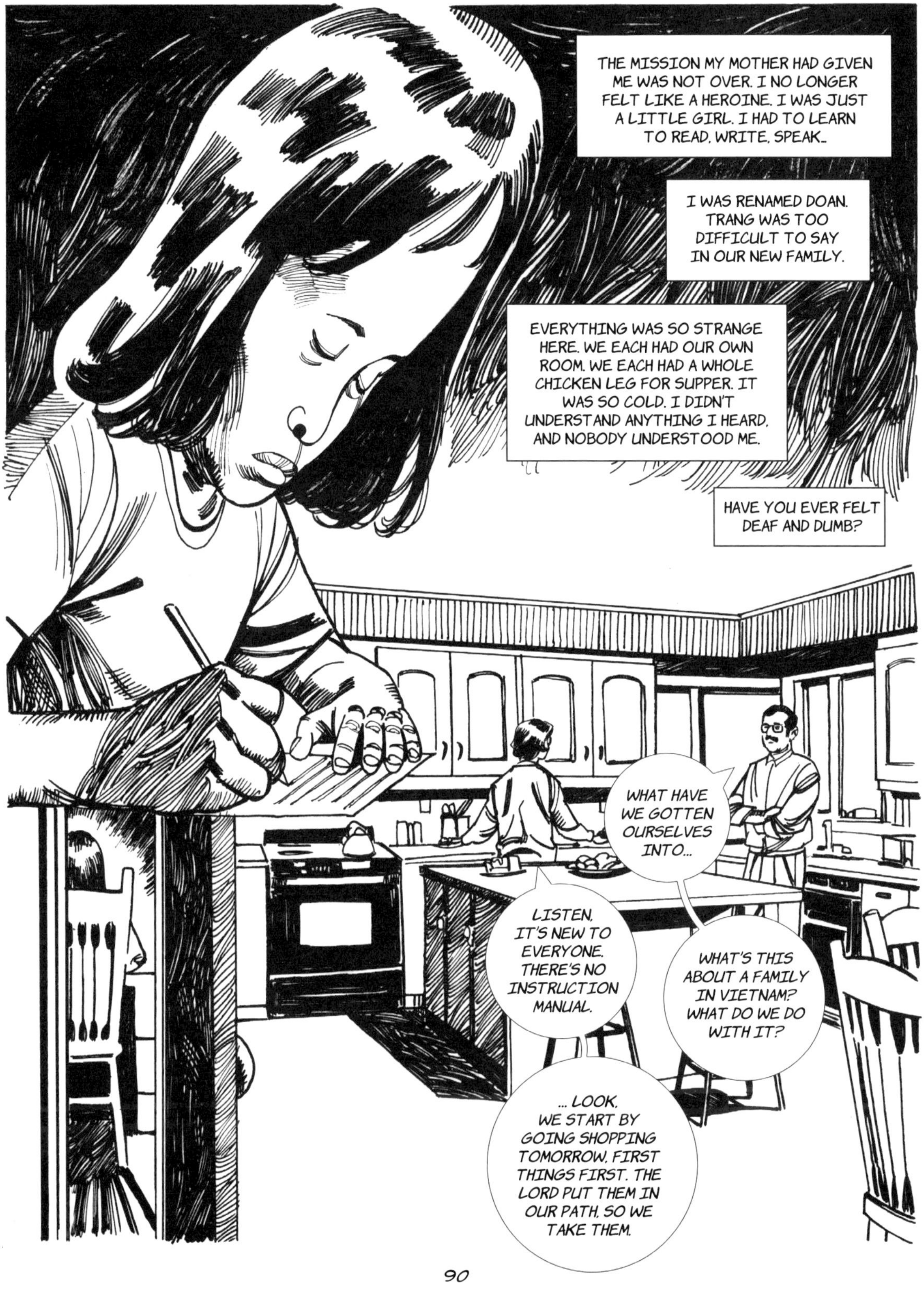

THE MISSION MY MOTHER HAD GIVEN ME WAS NOT OVER. I NO LONGER FELT LIKE A HEROINE. I WAS JUST A LITTLE GIRL. I HAD TO LEARN TO READ, WRITE, SPEAK...
I WAS RENAMED DOAN. TRANG WAS TOO DIFFICULT TO SAY IN OUR NEW FAMILY.
EVERYTHING WAS SO STRANGE HERE. WE EACH HAD OUR OWN ROOM. WE EACH HAD A WHOLE CHICKEN LEG FOR SUPPER. IT WAS SO COLD. I DIDN'T UNDERSTAND ANYTHING I HEARD, AND NOBODY UNDERSTOOD ME.
HAVE YOU EVER FELT DEAF AND DUMB?
WHAT HAVE WE GOTTEN OURSELVES INTO...
LISTEN, IT'S NEW TO EVERYONE. THERE'S NO INSTRUCTION MANUAL.
WHAT'S THIS ABOUT A FAMILY IN VIETNAM? WHAT DO WE DO WITH IT?
... LOOK, WE START BY GOING SHOPPING TOMORROW, FIRST THINGS FIRST. THE LORD PUT THEM IN OUR PATH, SO WE TAKE THEM.

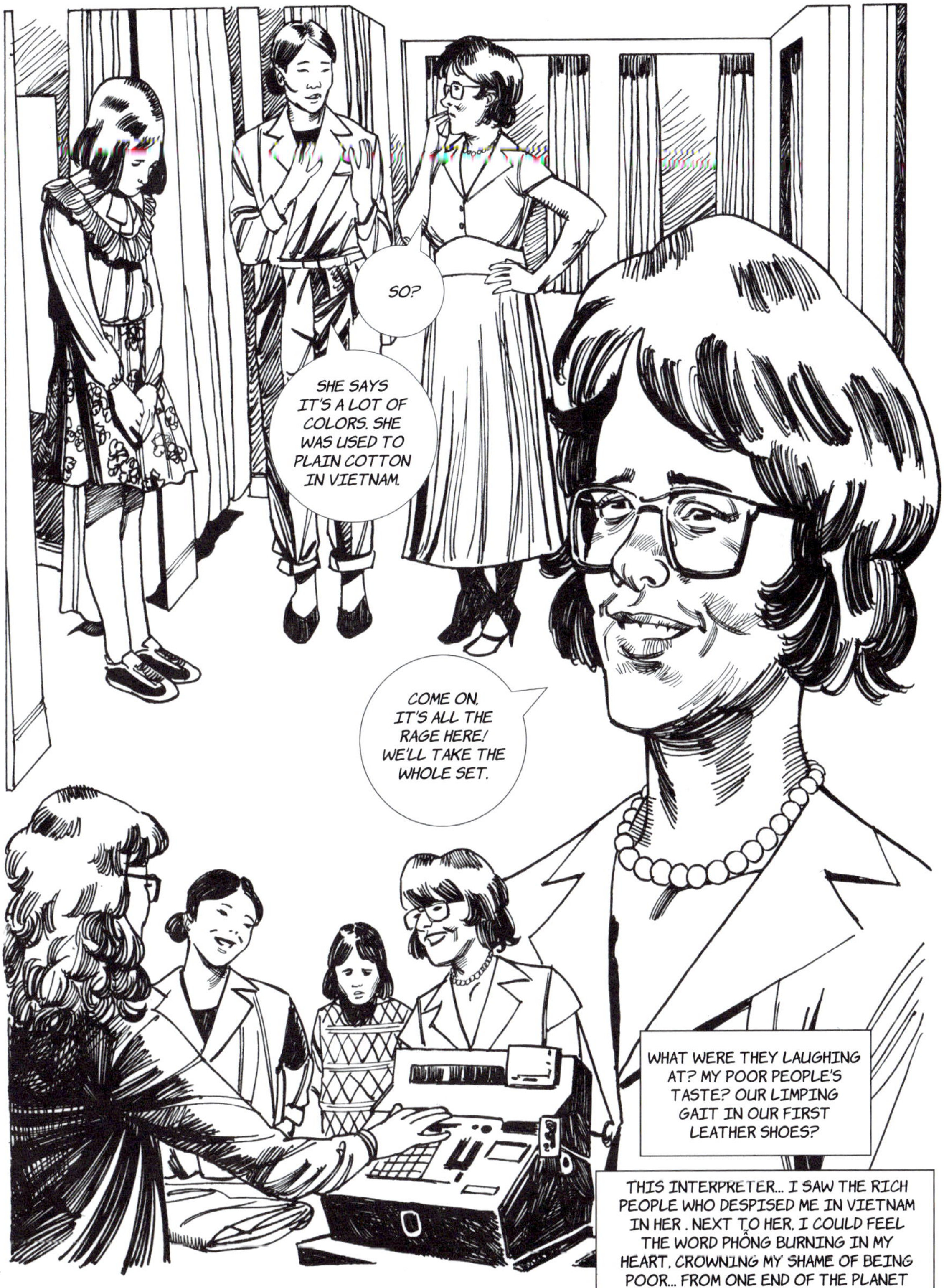
SO?
SHE SAYS IT'S A LOT OF COLORS. SHE WAS USED TO PLAIN COTTON IN VIETNAM.
COME ON, IT'S ALL THE RAGE HERE! WE'LL TAKE THE WHOLE SET.
WHAT WERE THEY LAUGHING AT? MY POOR PEOPLE'S TASTE? OUR LIMPING GAIT IN OUR FIRST LEATHER SHOES?
THIS INTERPRETER... I SAW THE RICH PEOPLE WHO DESPISED ME IN VIETNAM IN HER . NEXT TO HER, I COULD FEEL THE WORD PHỖNG BURNING IN MY HEART, CROWNING MY SHAME OF BEING POOR... FROM ONE END OF THE PLANET TO THE OTHER.

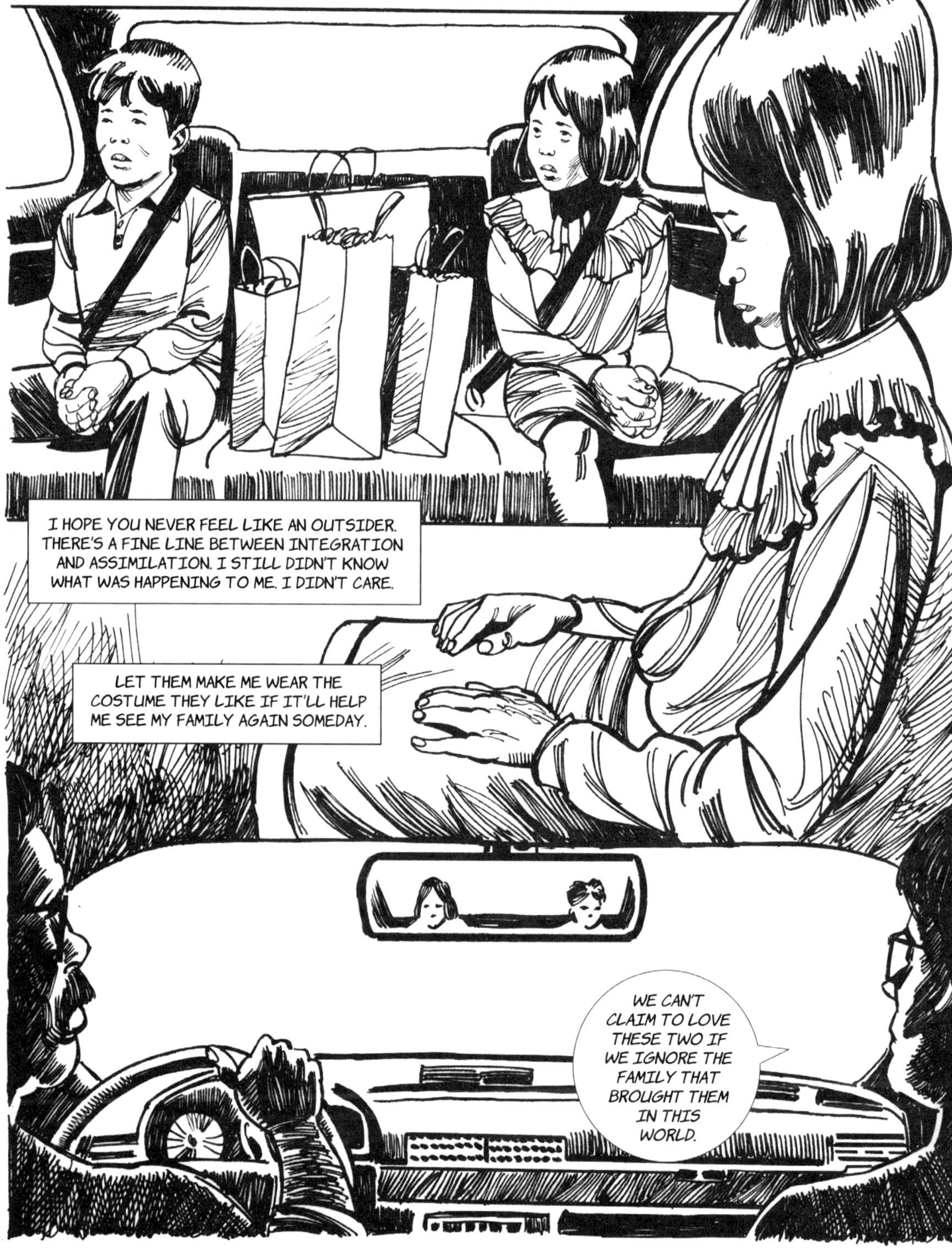
I HOPE YOU NEVER FEEL LIKE AN OUTSIDER. THERE'S A FINE LINE BETWEEN INTEGRATION AND ASSIMILATION. I STILL DIDN'T KNOW WHAT WAS HAPPENING TO ME. I DIDN'T CARE.
LET THEM MAKE ME WEAR THE COSTUME THEY LIKE IF IT'LL HELP ME SEE MY FAMILY AGAIN SOMEDAY.
WE CAN'T CLAIM TO LOVE THESE TWO IF WE IGNORE THE FAMILY THAT BROUGHT THEM IN THIS WORLD.

CHAPTER 3

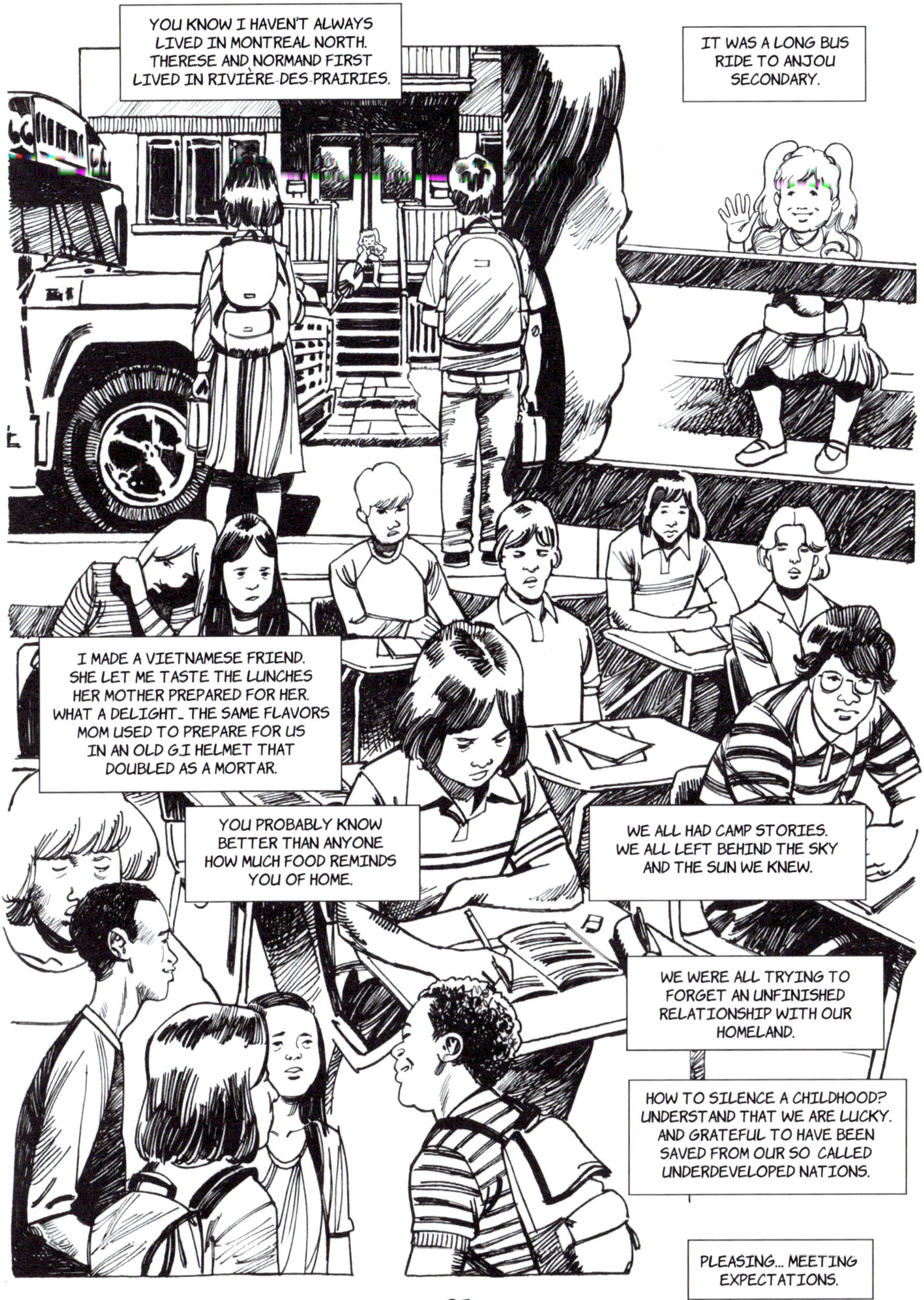
YOU KNOW I HAVEN'T ALWAYS LIVED IN MONTREAL NORTH. THERESE AND NORMAND FIRST LIVED IN RIVIÈRE-DES-PRAIRIES.
IT WAS A LONG BUS RIDE TO ANJOU SECONDARY.
I MADE A VIETNAMESE FRIEND. SHE LET ME TASTE THE LUNCHES HER MOTHER PREPARED FOR HER. WHAT A DELIGHT... THE SAME FLAVORS MOM USED TO PREPARE FOR US IN AN OLD G.I HELMET THAT DOUBLED AS A MORTAR.
YOU PROBABLY KNOW BETTER THAN ANYONE HOW MUCH FOOD REMINDS YOU OF HOME.
WE ALL HAD CAMP STORIES. WE ALL LEFT BEHIND THE SKY AND THE SUN WE KNEW.
WE WERE ALL TRYING TO FORGET AN UNFINISHED RELATIONSHIP WITH OUR HOMELAND.
HOW TO SILENCE A CHILDHOOD? UNDERSTAND THAT WE ARE LUCKY. AND GRATEFUL TO HAVE BEEN SAVED FROM OUR SO CALLED UNDERDEVELOPED NATIONS.
PLEASING... MEETING EXPECTATIONS.

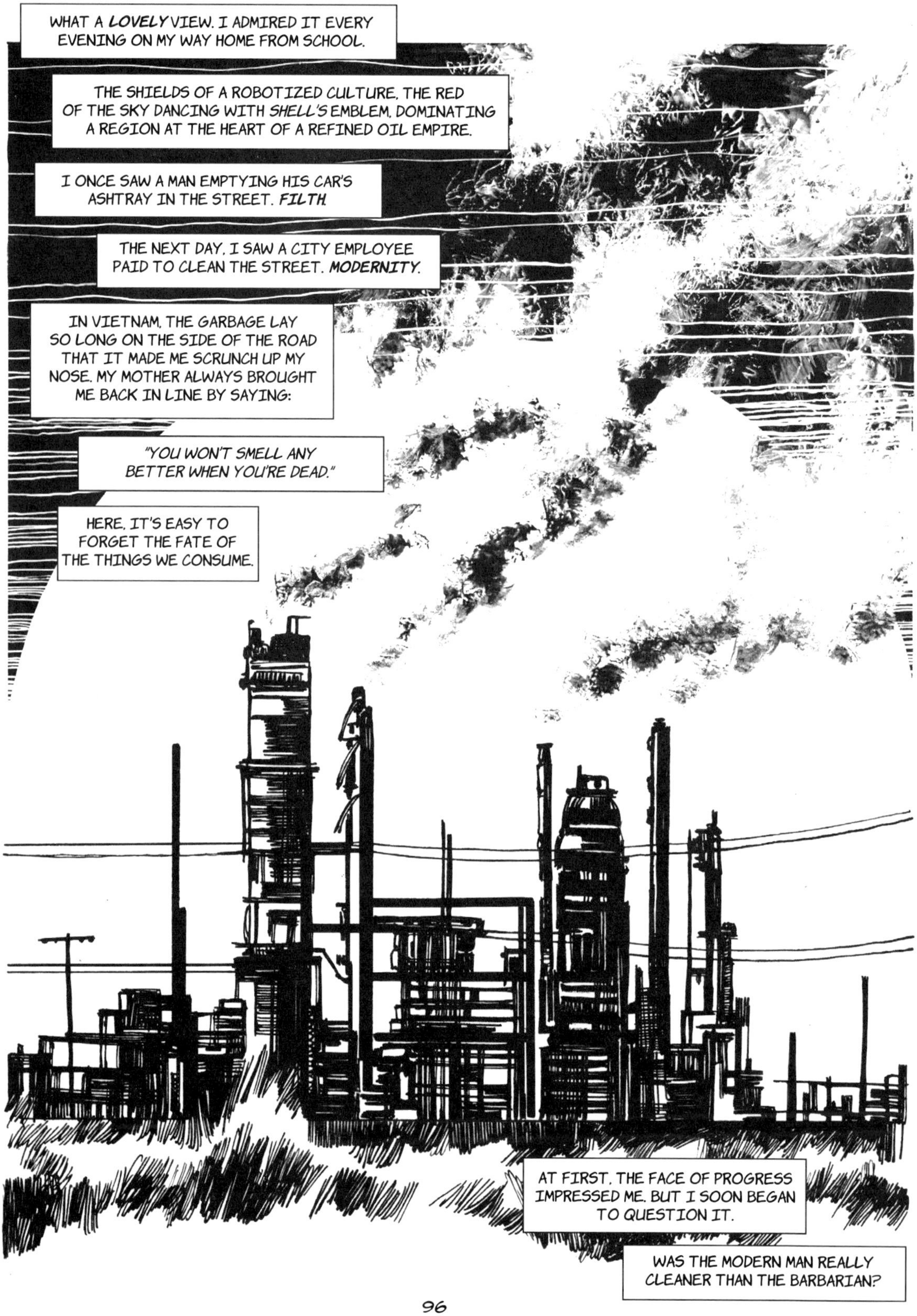
WHAT A **LOVELY** VIEW. I ADMIRED IT EVERY EVENING ON MY WAY HOME FROM SCHOOL.
THE SHIELDS OF A ROBOTIZED CULTURE, THE RED OF THE SKY DANCING WITH *SHELL'S* EMBLEM, DOMINATING A REGION AT THE HEART OF A REFINED OIL EMPIRE.
I ONCE SAW A MAN EMPTYING HIS CAR'S ASHTRAY IN THE STREET. *FILTH.*
THE NEXT DAY, I SAW A CITY EMPLOYEE PAID TO CLEAN THE STREET. ***MODERNITY.***
IN VIETNAM, THE GARBAGE LAY SO LONG ON THE SIDE OF THE ROAD THAT IT MADE ME SCRUNCH UP MY NOSE. MY MOTHER ALWAYS BROUGHT ME BACK IN LINE BY SAYING:
"YOU WON'T SMELL ANY BETTER WHEN YOU'RE DEAD."
HERE, IT'S EASY TO FORGET THE FATE OF THE THINGS WE CONSUME.
AT FIRST, THE FACE OF PROGRESS IMPRESSED ME. BUT I SOON BEGAN TO QUESTION IT.
WAS THE MODERN MAN REALLY CLEANER THAN THE BARBARIAN?

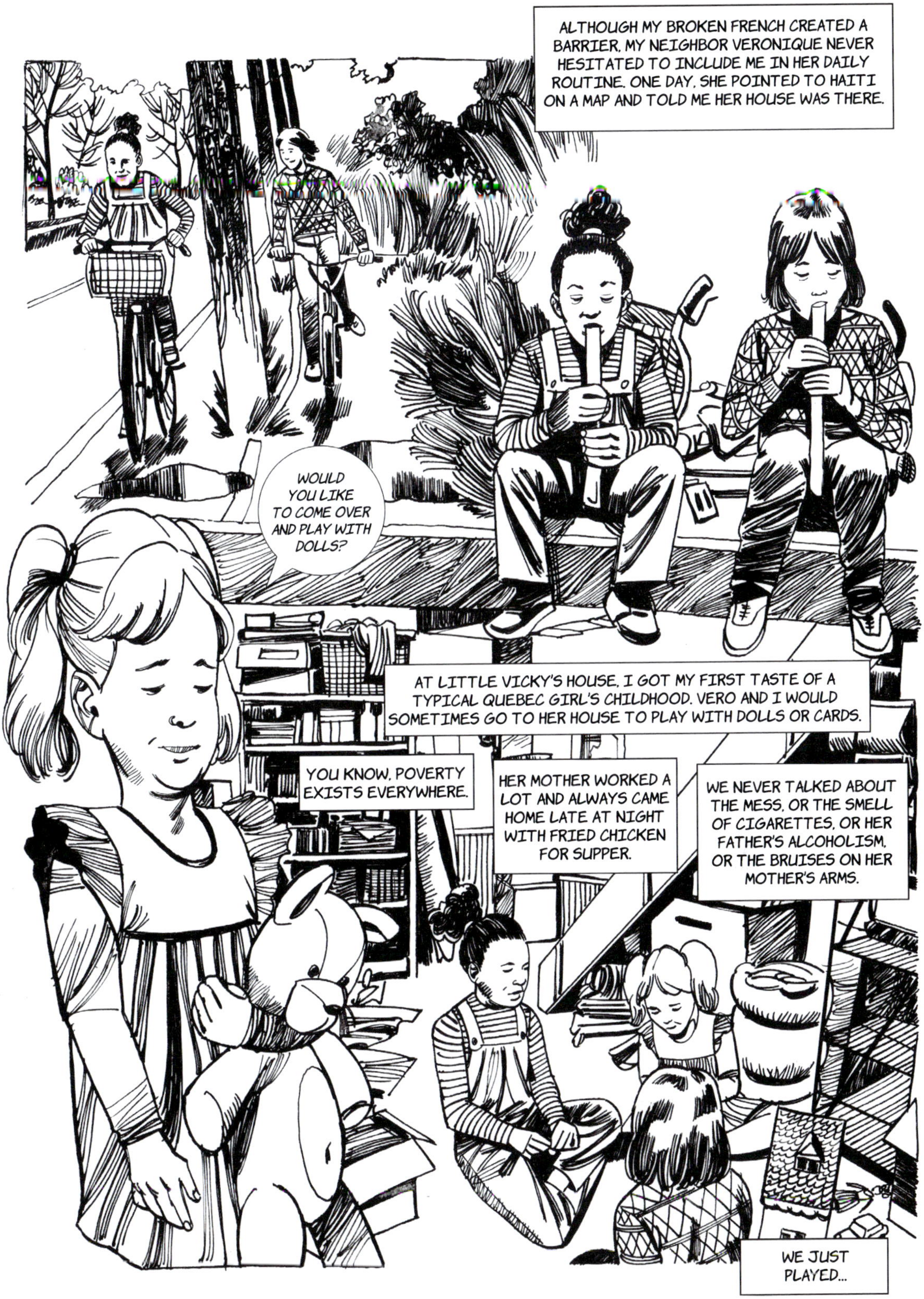
ALTHOUGH MY BROKEN FRENCH CREATED A BARRIER, MY NEIGHBOR VERONIQUE NEVER HESITATED TO INCLUDE ME IN HER DAILY ROUTINE. ONE DAY, SHE POINTED TO HAITI ON A MAP AND TOLD ME HER HOUSE WAS THERE.
WOULD YOU LIKE TO COME OVER AND PLAY WITH DOLLS?
AT LITTLE VICKY'S HOUSE, I GOT MY FIRST TASTE OF A TYPICAL QUEBEC GIRL'S CHILDHOOD. VERO AND I WOULD SOMETIMES GO TO HER HOUSE TO PLAY WITH DOLLS OR CARDS.
YOU KNOW, POVERTY EXISTS EVERYWHERE.
HER MOTHER WORKED A LOT AND ALWAYS CAME HOME LATE AT NIGHT WITH FRIED CHICKEN FOR SUPPER.
WE NEVER TALKED ABOUT THE MESS, OR THE SMELL OF CIGARETTES, OR HER FATHER'S ALCOHOLISM, OR THE BRUISES ON HER MOTHER'S ARMS.
WE JUST PLAYED...

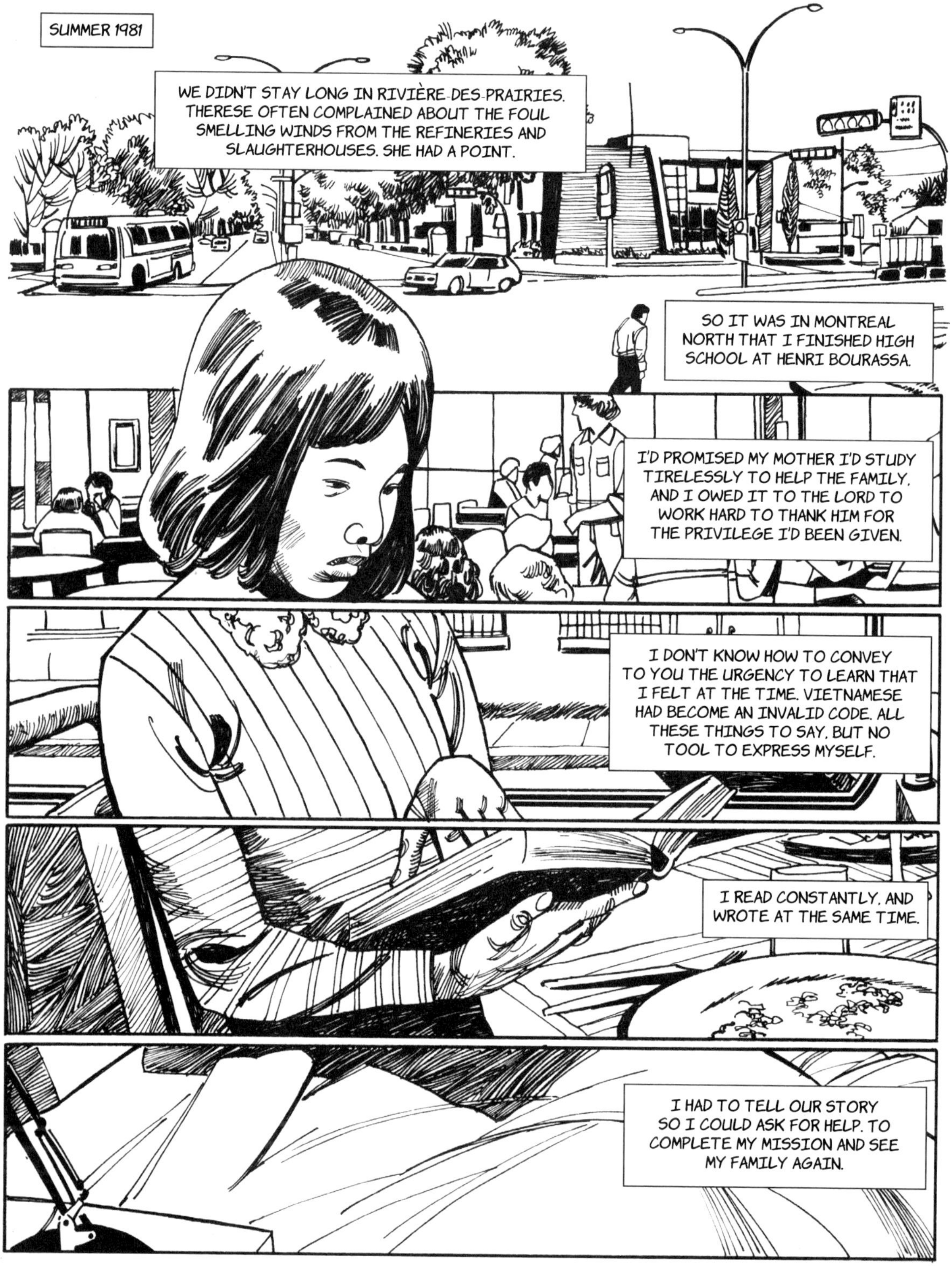
SUMMER 1981
WE DIDN'T STAY LONG IN RIVIÈRE-DES-PRAIRIES. THERESE OFTEN COMPLAINED ABOUT THE FOUL SMELLING WINDS FROM THE REFINERIES AND SLAUGHTERHOUSES. SHE HAD A POINT.
SO IT WAS IN MONTREAL NORTH THAT I FINISHED HIGH SCHOOL AT HENRI BOURASSA.
I'D PROMISED MY MOTHER I'D STUDY TIRELESSLY TO HELP THE FAMILY, AND I OWED IT TO THE LORD TO WORK HARD TO THANK HIM FOR THE PRIVILEGE I'D BEEN GIVEN.
I DON'T KNOW HOW TO CONVEY TO YOU THE URGENCY TO LEARN THAT I FELT AT THE TIME. VIETNAMESE HAD BECOME AN INVALID CODE. ALL THESE THINGS TO SAY, BUT NO TOOL TO EXPRESS MYSELF.
I READ CONSTANTLY, AND WROTE AT THE SAME TIME.
I HAD TO TELL OUR STORY SO I COULD ASK FOR HELP. TO COMPLETE MY MISSION AND SEE MY FAMILY AGAIN.

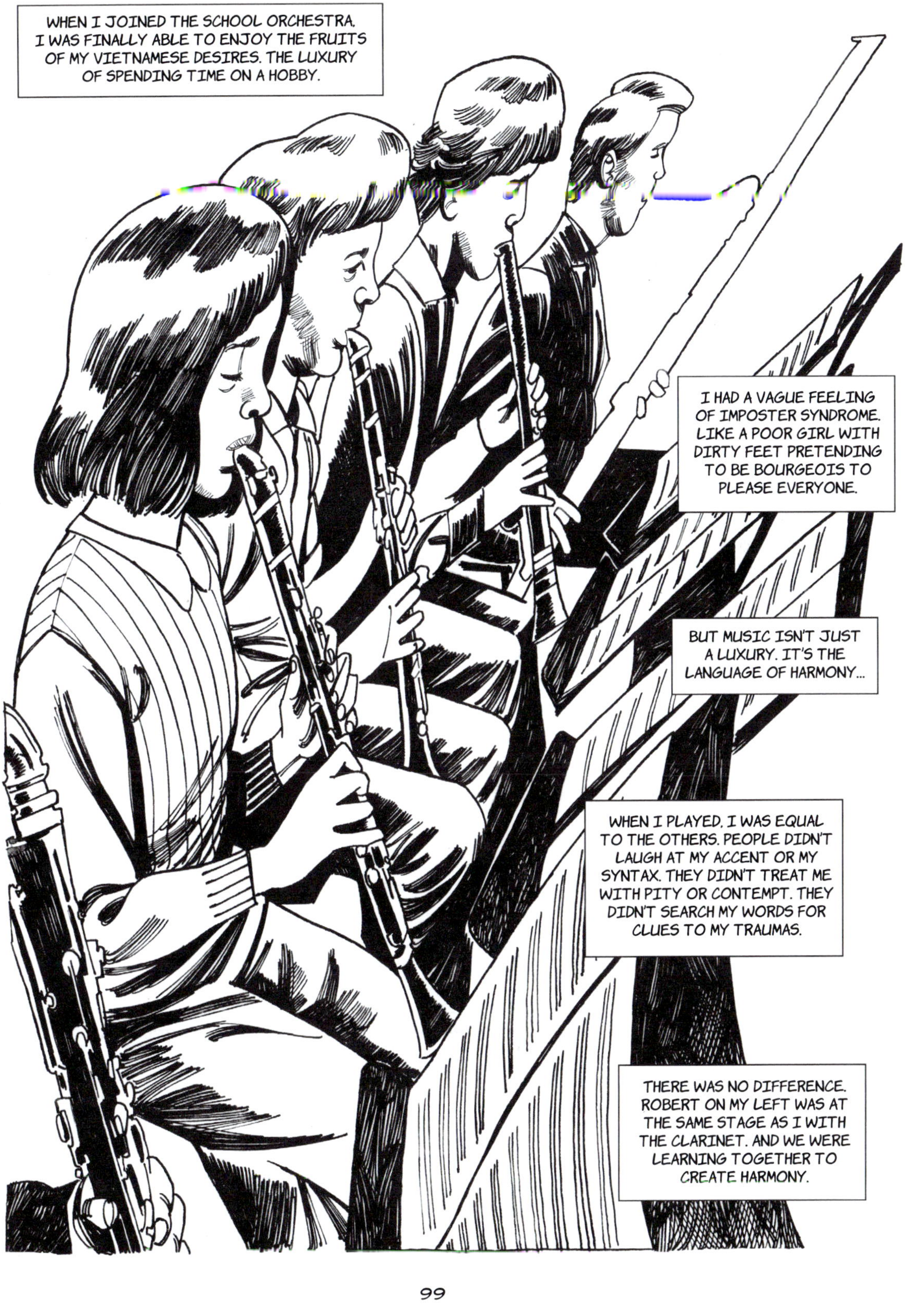
WHEN I JOINED THE SCHOOL ORCHESTRA, I WAS FINALLY ABLE TO ENJOY THE FRUITS OF MY VIETNAMESE DESIRES. THE LUXURY OF SPENDING TIME ON A HOBBY.
I HAD A VAGUE FEELING OF IMPOSTER SYNDROME. LIKE A POOR GIRL WITH DIRTY FEET PRETENDING TO BE BOURGEOIS TO PLEASE EVERYONE.
BUT MUSIC ISN'T JUST A LUXURY. IT'S THE LANGUAGE OF HARMONY...
WHEN I PLAYED, I WAS EQUAL TO THE OTHERS. PEOPLE DIDN'T LAUGH AT MY ACCENT OR MY SYNTAX. THEY DIDN'T TREAT ME WITH PITY OR CONTEMPT. THEY DIDN'T SEARCH MY WORDS FOR CLUES TO MY TRAUMAS.
THERE WAS NO DIFFERENCE. ROBERT ON MY LEFT WAS AT THE SAME STAGE AS I WITH THE CLARINET. AND WE WERE LEARNING TOGETHER TO CREATE HARMONY.

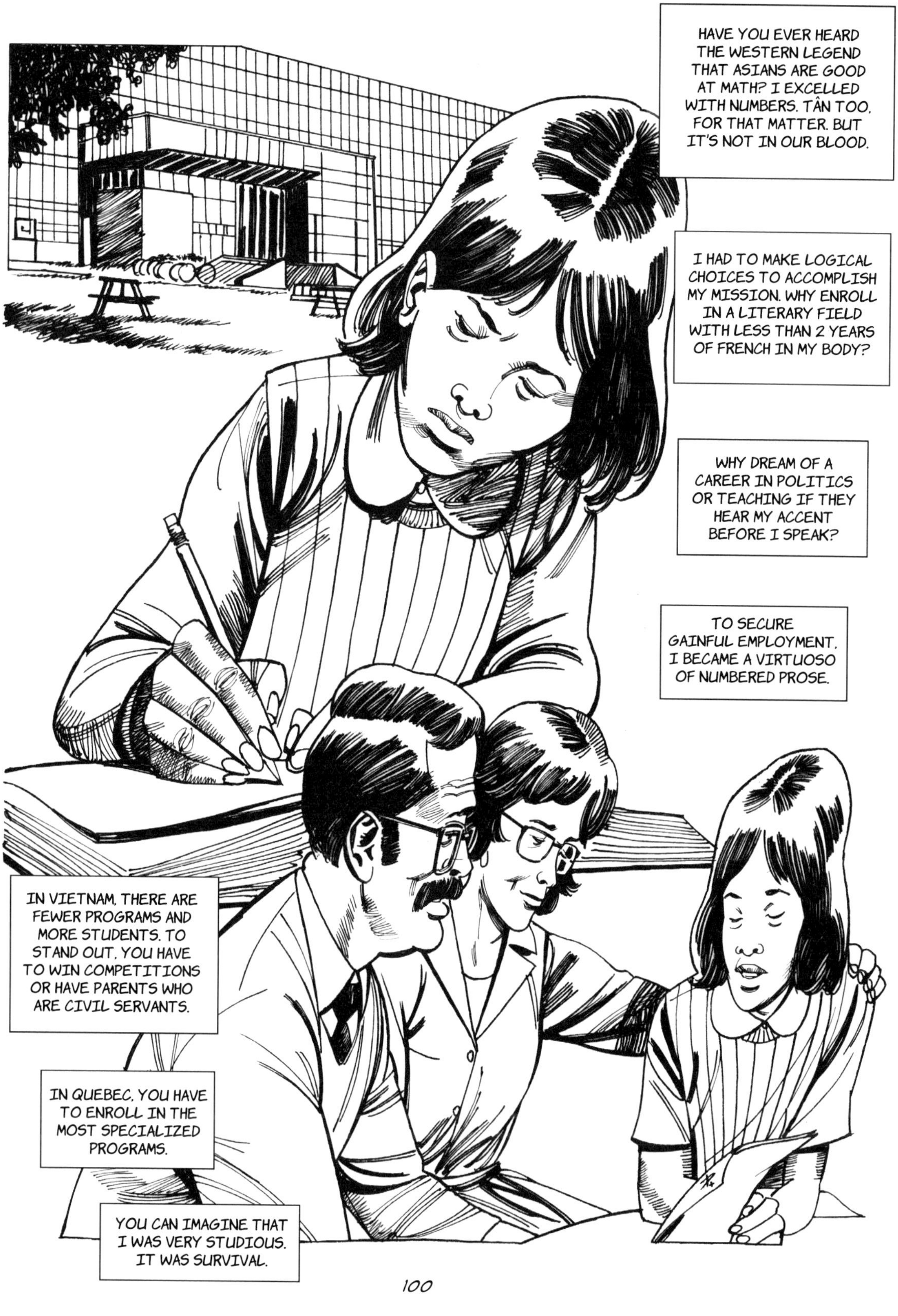
HAVE YOU EVER HEARD THE WESTERN LEGEND THAT ASIANS ARE GOOD AT MATH? I EXCELLED WITH NUMBERS. TÂN TOO, FOR THAT MATTER. BUT IT'S NOT IN OUR BLOOD.
I HAD TO MAKE LOGICAL CHOICES TO ACCOMPLISH MY MISSION. WHY ENROLL IN A LITERARY FIELD WITH LESS THAN 2 YEARS OF FRENCH IN MY BODY?
WHY DREAM OF A CAREER IN POLITICS OR TEACHING IF THEY HEAR MY ACCENT BEFORE I SPEAK?
TO SECURE GAINFUL EMPLOYMENT, I BECAME A VIRTUOSO OF NUMBERED PROSE.
IN VIETNAM, THERE ARE FEWER PROGRAMS AND MORE STUDENTS. TO STAND OUT, YOU HAVE TO WIN COMPETITIONS OR HAVE PARENTS WHO ARE CIVIL SERVANTS.
IN QUEBEC, YOU HAVE TO ENROLL IN THE MOST SPECIALIZED PROGRAMS.
YOU CAN IMAGINE THAT I WAS VERY STUDIOUS. IT WAS SURVIVAL.

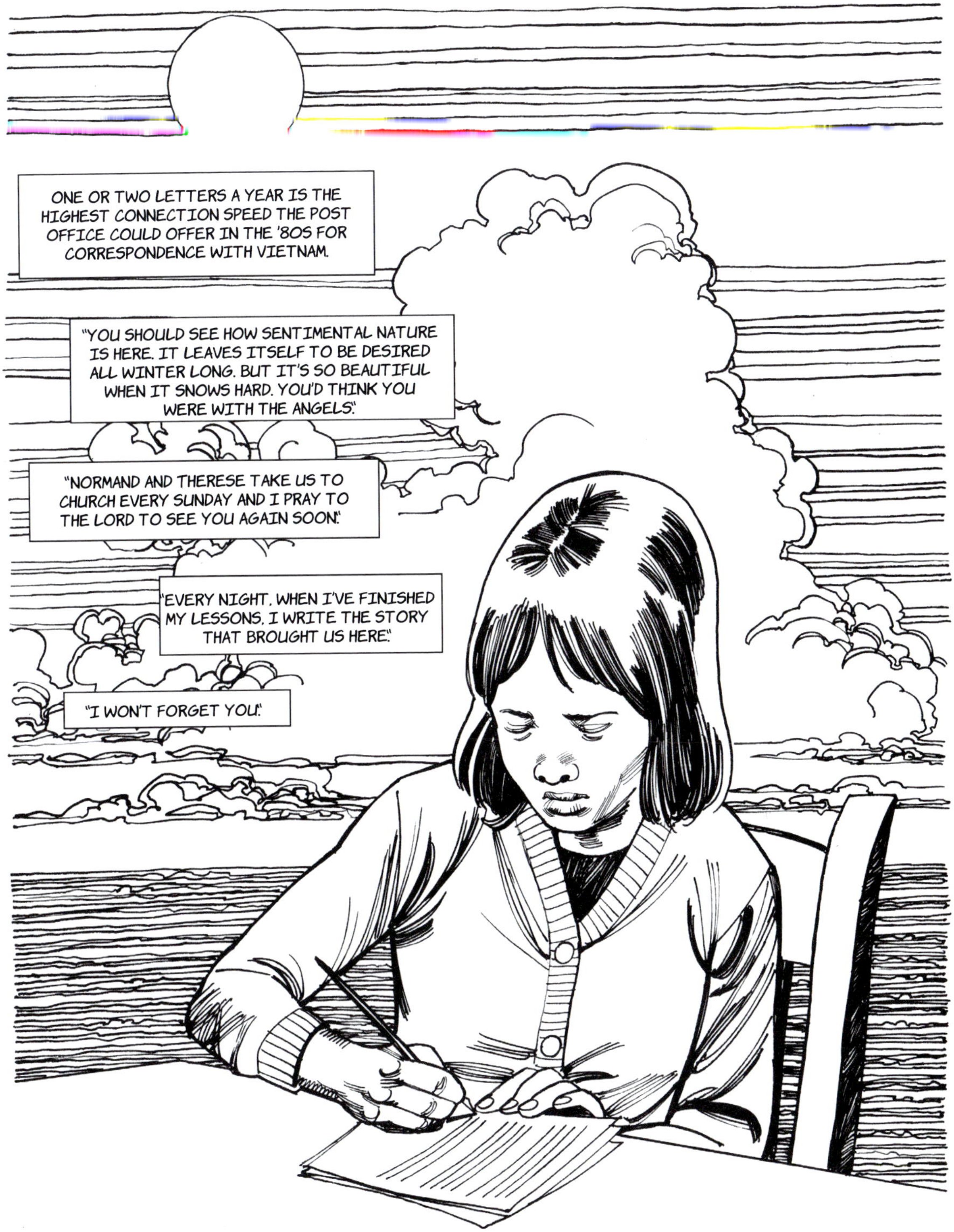
ONE OR TWO LETTERS A YEAR IS THE HIGHEST CONNECTION SPEED THE POST OFFICE COULD OFFER IN THE '80S FOR CORRESPONDENCE WITH VIETNAM.
"YOU SHOULD SEE HOW SENTIMENTAL NATURE IS HERE. IT LEAVES ITSELF TO BE DESIRED ALL WINTER LONG. BUT IT'S SO BEAUTIFUL WHEN IT SNOWS HARD. YOU'D THINK YOU WERE WITH THE ANGELS."
"NORMAND AND THERESE TAKE US TO CHURCH EVERY SUNDAY AND I PRAY TO THE LORD TO SEE YOU AGAIN SOON."
"EVERY NIGHT, WHEN I'VE FINISHED MY LESSONS, I WRITE THE STORY THAT BROUGHT US HERE."
"I WON'T FORGET YOU."

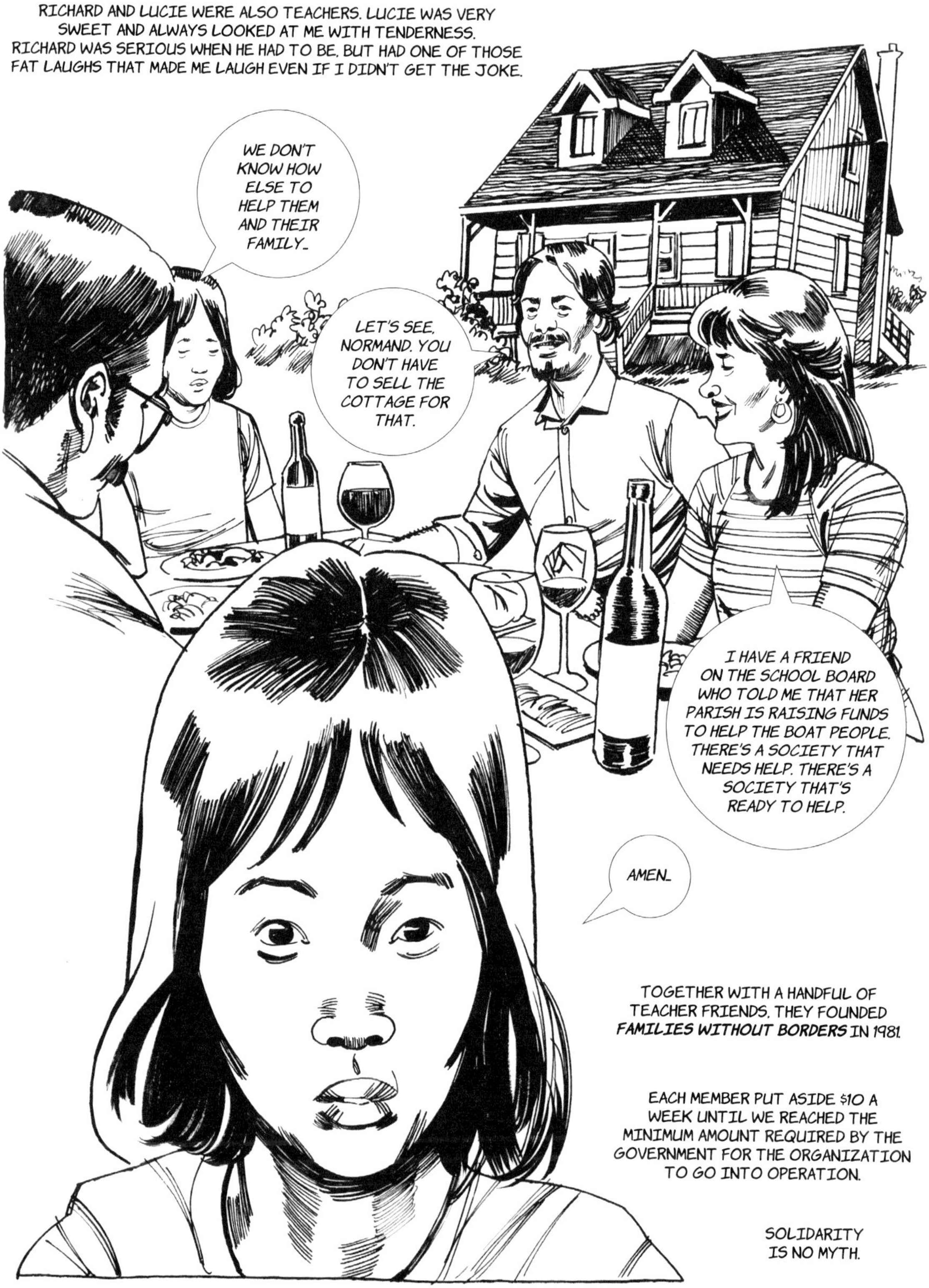
RICHARD AND LUCIE WERE ALSO TEACHERS. LUCIE WAS VERY SWEET AND ALWAYS LOOKED AT ME WITH TENDERNESS. RICHARD WAS SERIOUS WHEN HE HAD TO BE, BUT HAD ONE OF THOSE FAT LAUGHS THAT MADE ME LAUGH EVEN IF I DIDN'T GET THE JOKE.
WE DON'T KNOW HOW ELSE TO HELP THEM AND THEIR FAMILY...
LET'S SEE, NORMAND. YOU DON'T HAVE TO SELL THE COTTAGE FOR THAT.
I HAVE A FRIEND ON THE SCHOOL BOARD WHO TOLD ME THAT HER PARISH IS RAISING FUNDS TO HELP THE BOAT PEOPLE. THERE'S A SOCIETY THAT NEEDS HELP. THERE'S A SOCIETY THAT'S READY TO HELP.
AMEN...
TOGETHER WITH A HANDFUL OF TEACHER FRIENDS, THEY FOUNDED **FAMILIES WITHOUT BORDERS** IN 1981.
EACH MEMBER PUT ASIDE $10 A WEEK UNTIL WE REACHED THE MINIMUM AMOUNT REQUIRED BY THE GOVERNMENT FOR THE ORGANIZATION TO GO INTO OPERATION.
SOLIDARITY IS NO MYTH.

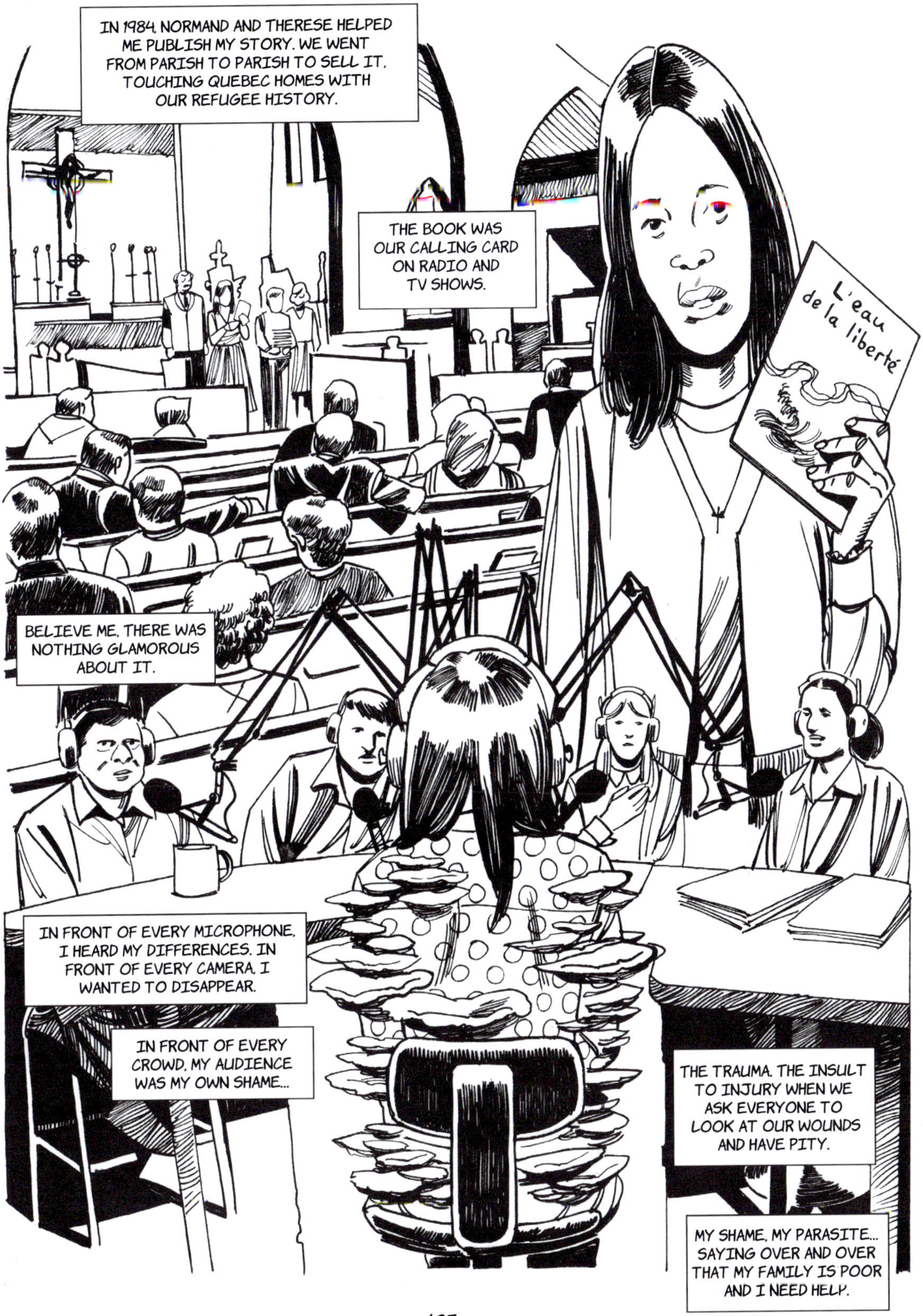
IN 1984, NORMAND AND THERESE HELPED ME PUBLISH MY STORY. WE WENT FROM PARISH TO PARISH TO SELL IT, TOUCHING QUEBEC HOMES WITH OUR REFUGEE HISTORY.
THE BOOK WAS OUR CALLING CARD ON RADIO AND TV SHOWS.
L'eau de la liberté
BELIEVE ME, THERE WAS NOTHING GLAMOROUS ABOUT IT.
IN FRONT OF EVERY MICROPHONE, I HEARD MY DIFFERENCES. IN FRONT OF EVERY CAMERA, I WANTED TO DISAPPEAR.
IN FRONT OF EVERY CROWD, MY AUDIENCE WAS MY OWN SHAME...
THE TRAUMA. THE INSULT TO INJURY WHEN WE ASK EVERYONE TO LOOK AT OUR WOUNDS AND HAVE PITY.
MY SHAME, MY PARASITE... SAYING OVER AND OVER THAT MY FAMILY IS POOR AND I NEED HELP.

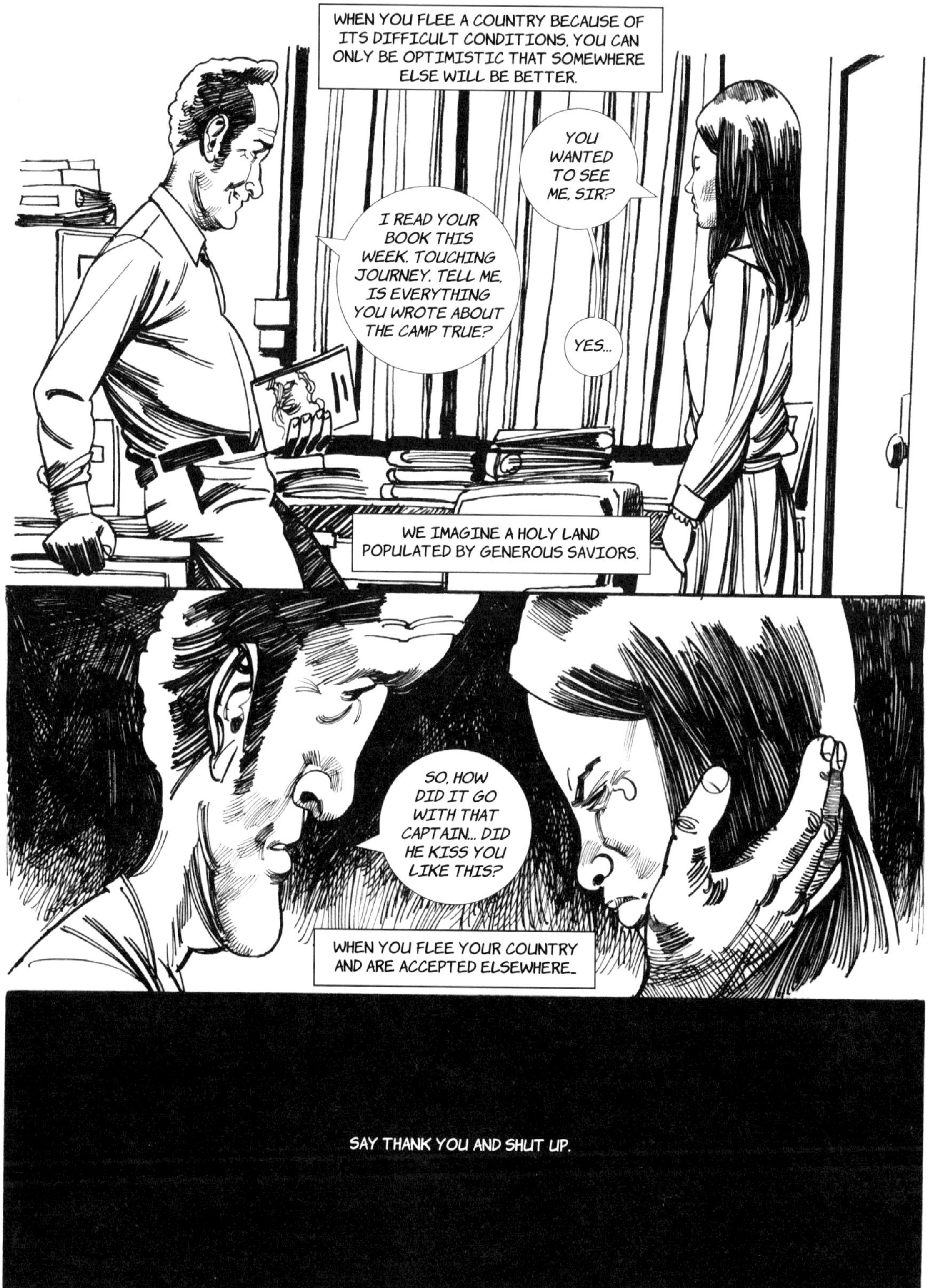
WHEN YOU FLEE A COUNTRY BECAUSE OF ITS DIFFICULT CONDITIONS, YOU CAN ONLY BE OPTIMISTIC THAT SOMEWHERE ELSE WILL BE BETTER.
YOU WANTED TO SEE ME, SIR?
I READ YOUR BOOK THIS WEEK. TOUCHING JOURNEY. TELL ME, IS EVERYTHING YOU WROTE ABOUT THE CAMP TRUE?
YES...
WE IMAGINE A HOLY LAND POPULATED BY GENEROUS SAVIORS.
SO, HOW DID IT GO WITH THAT CAPTAIN... DID HE KISS YOU LIKE THIS?
WHEN YOU FLEE YOUR COUNTRY AND ARE ACCEPTED ELSEWHERE...
SAY THANK YOU AND SHUT UP.

CHAPTER 4

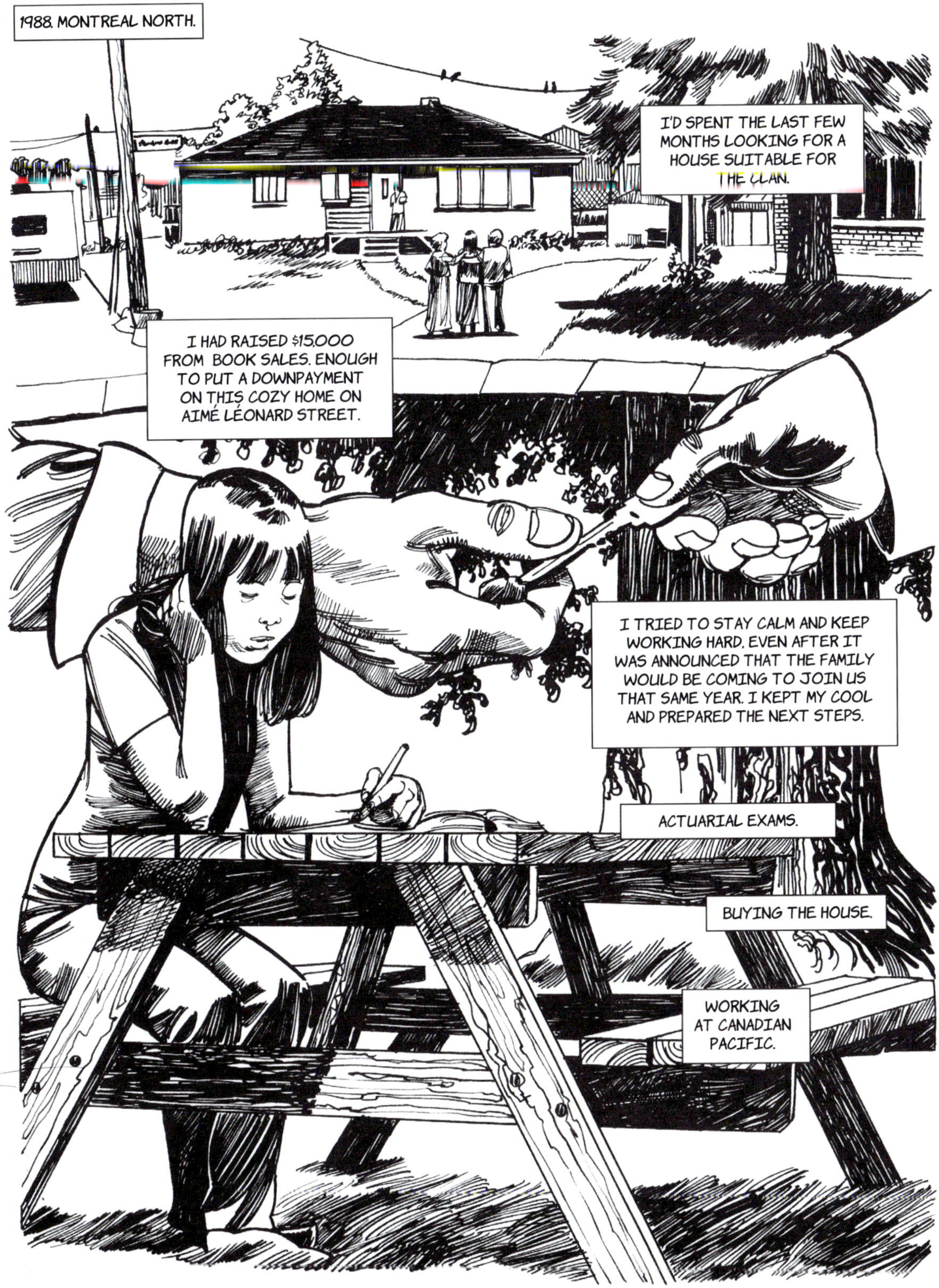
1988. MONTREAL NORTH.
I'D SPENT THE LAST FEW MONTHS LOOKING FOR A HOUSE SUITABLE FOR THE CLAN.
I HAD RAISED $15,000 FROM BOOK SALES. ENOUGH TO PUT A DOWNPAYMENT ON THIS COZY HOME ON AIMÉ LÉONARD STREET.
I TRIED TO STAY CALM AND KEEP WORKING HARD, EVEN AFTER IT WAS ANNOUNCED THAT THE FAMILY WOULD BE COMING TO JOIN US THAT SAME YEAR. I KEPT MY COOL AND PREPARED THE NEXT STEPS.
ACTUARIAL EXAMS.
BUYING THE HOUSE.
WORKING AT CANADIAN PACIFIC.

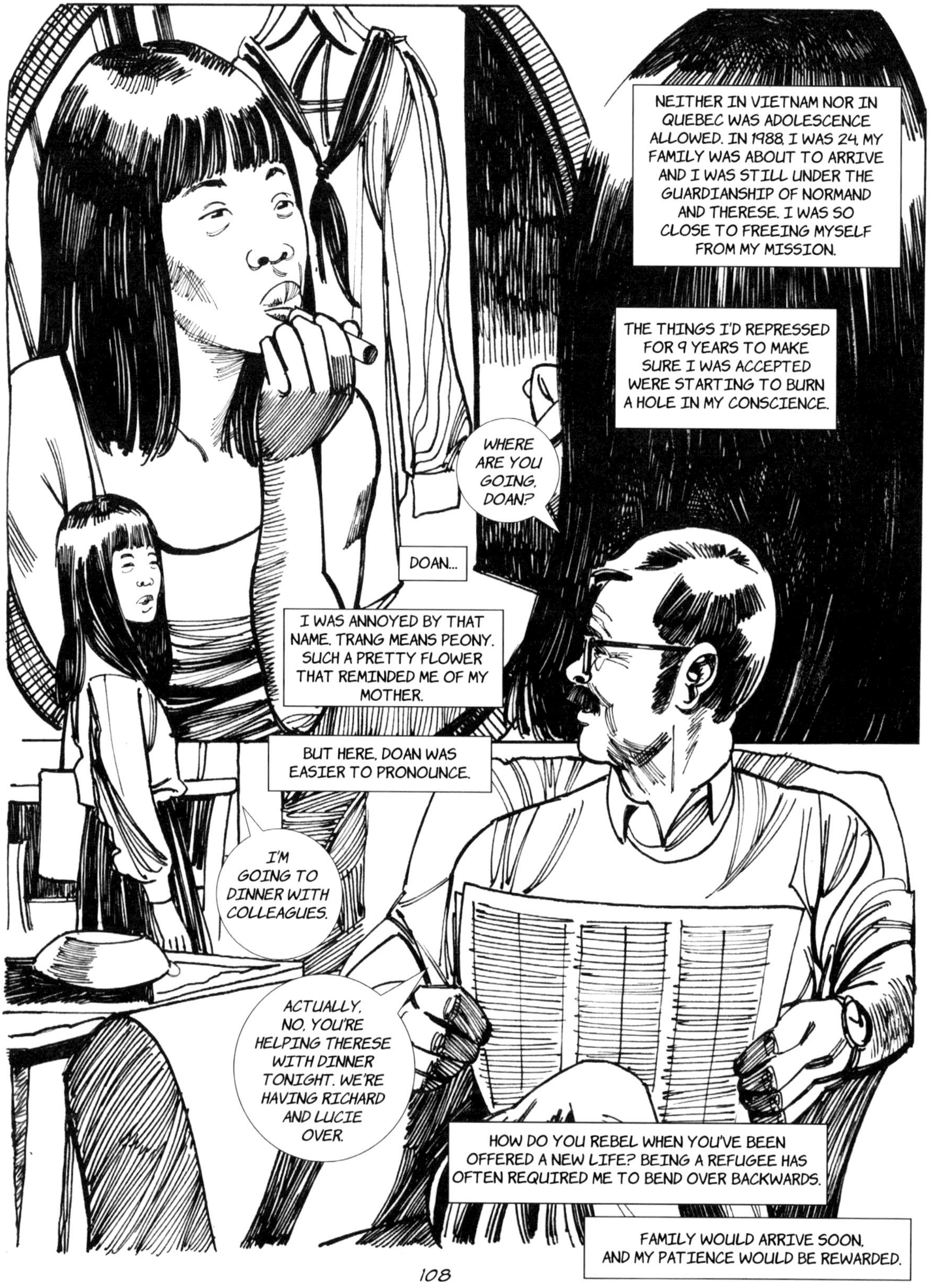
NEITHER IN VIETNAM NOR IN QUEBEC WAS ADOLESCENCE ALLOWED. IN 1988, I WAS 24. MY FAMILY WAS ABOUT TO ARRIVE AND I WAS STILL UNDER THE GUARDIANSHIP OF NORMAND AND THERESE. I WAS SO CLOSE TO FREEING MYSELF FROM MY MISSION.
THE THINGS I'D REPRESSED FOR 9 YEARS TO MAKE SURE I WAS ACCEPTED WERE STARTING TO BURN A HOLE IN MY CONSCIENCE.
WHERE ARE YOU GOING, DOAN?
DOAN...
I WAS ANNOYED BY THAT NAME. TRANG MEANS PEONY. SUCH A PRETTY FLOWER THAT REMINDED ME OF MY MOTHER.
BUT HERE, DOAN WAS EASIER TO PRONOUNCE.
I'M GOING TO DINNER WITH COLLEAGUES.
ACTUALLY, NO, YOU'RE HELPING THERESE WITH DINNER TONIGHT. WE'RE HAVING RICHARD AND LUCIE OVER.
HOW DO YOU REBEL WHEN YOU'VE BEEN OFFERED A NEW LIFE? BEING A REFUGEE HAS OFTEN REQUIRED ME TO BEND OVER BACKWARDS.
FAMILY WOULD ARRIVE SOON, AND MY PATIENCE WOULD BE REWARDED.

DECEMBER 14, 1988

IF THESE WOMEN COULD SPEAK...

MOVED BY THE SUFFERING OF YOUNG MOTHERS WHO GAVE UP THEIR BABIES FOR ADOPTION AT THE ORPHANAGE WHERE SHE WORKED, THERESE HAD ALSO TAKEN THE RELIGIOUS PATH.

SHE EVENTUALLY LEFT THE HABIT AND BECAME A TEACHER. TO GET AWAY FROM THE HIERARCHY, GET CLOSER TO CHILDREN. MY TWO MOTHERS HAD A LOT IN COMMON.

LOVE AND HOPE HAD DRIVEN ONE OF THEM TO SEPARATE FROM HER DAUGHTER AND SON.

LOVE AND HOPE HAD DRIVEN THE OTHER TO WELCOME THEM.

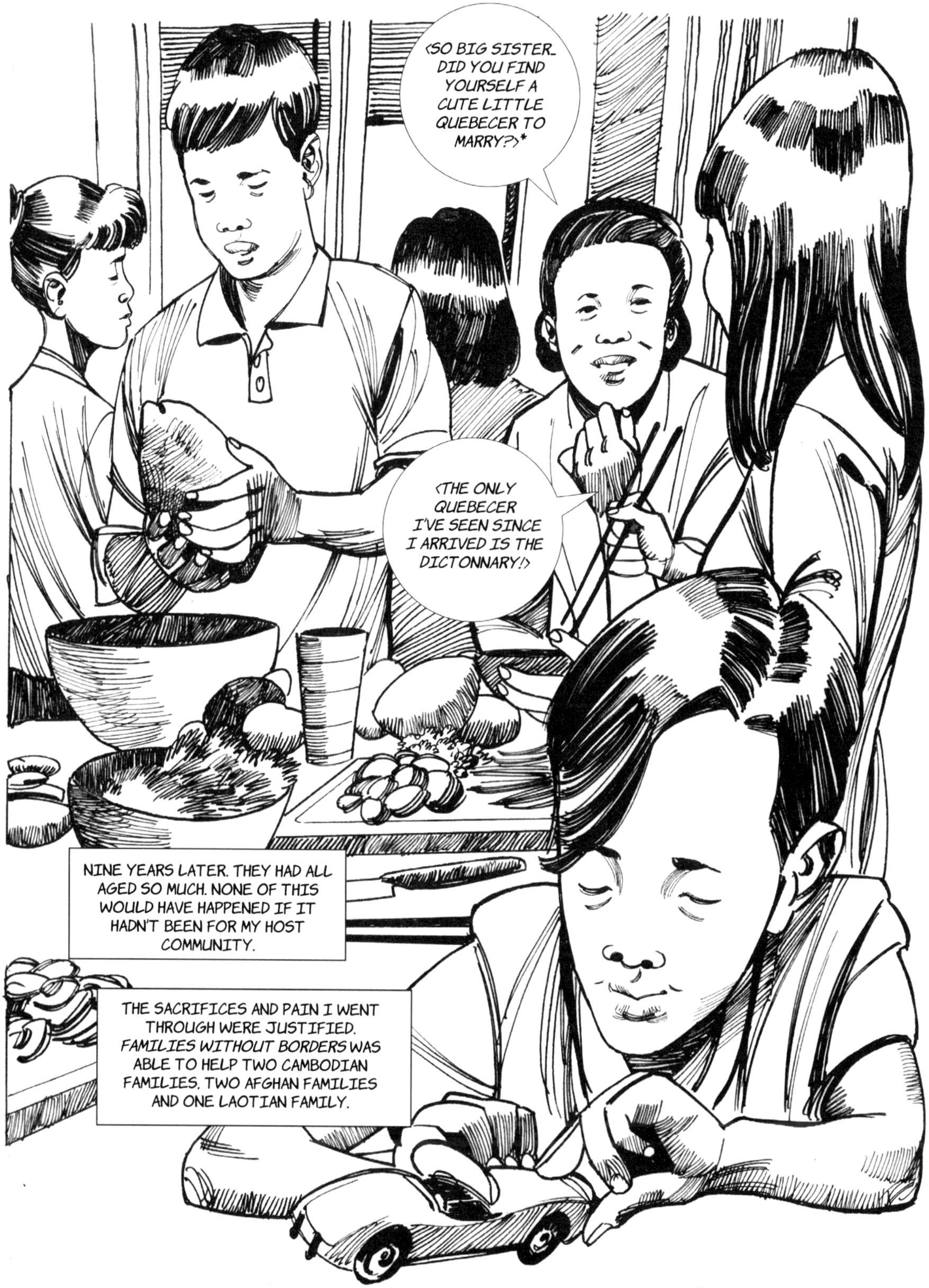
<SO BIG SISTER, DID YOU FIND YOURSELF A CUTE LITTLE QUEBECER TO MARRY?>*
<THE ONLY QUEBECER I'VE SEEN SINCE I ARRIVED IS THE DICTONNARY!>
NINE YEARS LATER. THEY HAD ALL AGED SO MUCH. NONE OF THIS WOULD HAVE HAPPENED IF IT HADN'T BEEN FOR MY HOST COMMUNITY.
THE SACRIFICES AND PAIN I WENT THROUGH WERE JUSTIFIED. *FAMILIES WITHOUT BORDERS* WAS ABLE TO HELP TWO CAMBODIAN FAMILIES, TWO AFGHAN FAMILIES AND ONE LAOTIAN FAMILY.

*TRANSLATED FROM VIETNAMESE

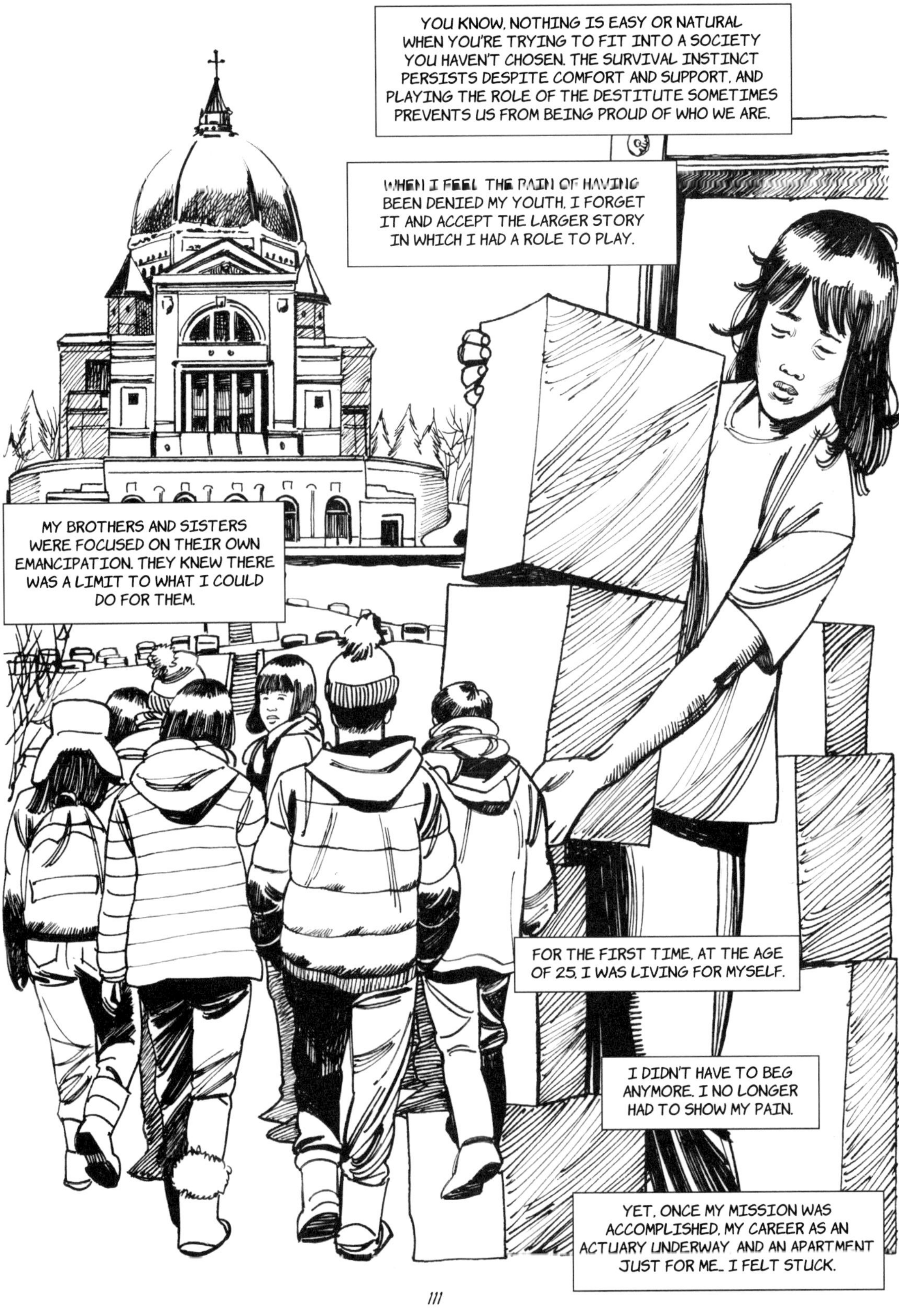
YOU KNOW, NOTHING IS EASY OR NATURAL WHEN YOU'RE TRYING TO FIT INTO A SOCIETY YOU HAVEN'T CHOSEN. THE SURVIVAL INSTINCT PERSISTS DESPITE COMFORT AND SUPPORT, AND PLAYING THE ROLE OF THE DESTITUTE SOMETIMES PREVENTS US FROM BEING PROUD OF WHO WE ARE.
WHEN I FEEL THE PAIN OF HAVING BEEN DENIED MY YOUTH, I FORGET IT AND ACCEPT THE LARGER STORY IN WHICH I HAD A ROLE TO PLAY.
MY BROTHERS AND SISTERS WERE FOCUSED ON THEIR OWN EMANCIPATION. THEY KNEW THERE WAS A LIMIT TO WHAT I COULD DO FOR THEM.
FOR THE FIRST TIME, AT THE AGE OF 25, I WAS LIVING FOR MYSELF.
I DIDN'T HAVE TO BEG ANYMORE. I NO LONGER HAD TO SHOW MY PAIN.
YET, ONCE MY MISSION WAS ACCOMPLISHED, MY CAREER AS AN ACTUARY UNDERWAY, AND AN APARTMENT JUST FOR ME... I FELT STUCK.

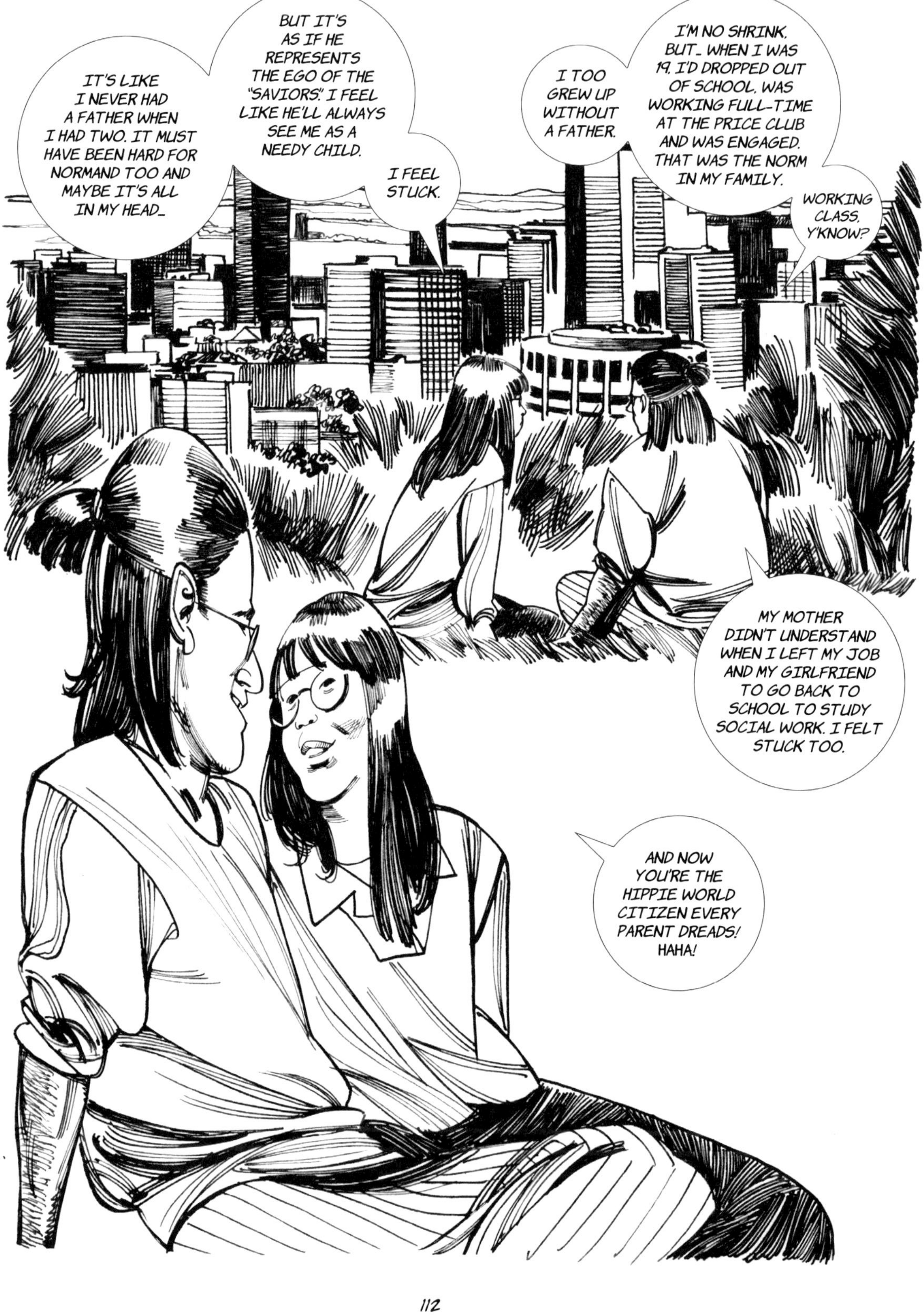

IT'S LIKE I NEVER HAD A FATHER WHEN I HAD TWO. IT MUST HAVE BEEN HARD FOR NORMAND TOO AND MAYBE IT'S ALL IN MY HEAD…
BUT IT'S AS IF HE REPRESENTS THE EGO OF THE "SAVIORS." I FEEL LIKE HE'LL ALWAYS SEE ME AS A NEEDY CHILD.
I FEEL STUCK.
I TOO GREW UP WITHOUT A FATHER.
I'M NO SHRINK, BUT… WHEN I WAS 19, I'D DROPPED OUT OF SCHOOL, WAS WORKING FULL-TIME AT THE PRICE CLUB AND WAS ENGAGED. THAT WAS THE NORM IN MY FAMILY.
WORKING CLASS, Y'KNOW?
MY MOTHER DIDN'T UNDERSTAND WHEN I LEFT MY JOB AND MY GIRLFRIEND TO GO BACK TO SCHOOL TO STUDY SOCIAL WORK. I FELT STUCK TOO.
AND NOW YOU'RE THE HIPPIE WORLD CITIZEN EVERY PARENT DREADS! HAHA!

I MET SERGE THROUGH
HIS SISTER, WHO WAS PLAYING
CUPID FOR HER BROTHER.

HE WAS AN INTERESTING SPECIMEN.
A QUEBECER FROM ABITIBI WHO
RELOCATED TO MONTREAL NORTH
IN HIS YOUTH.

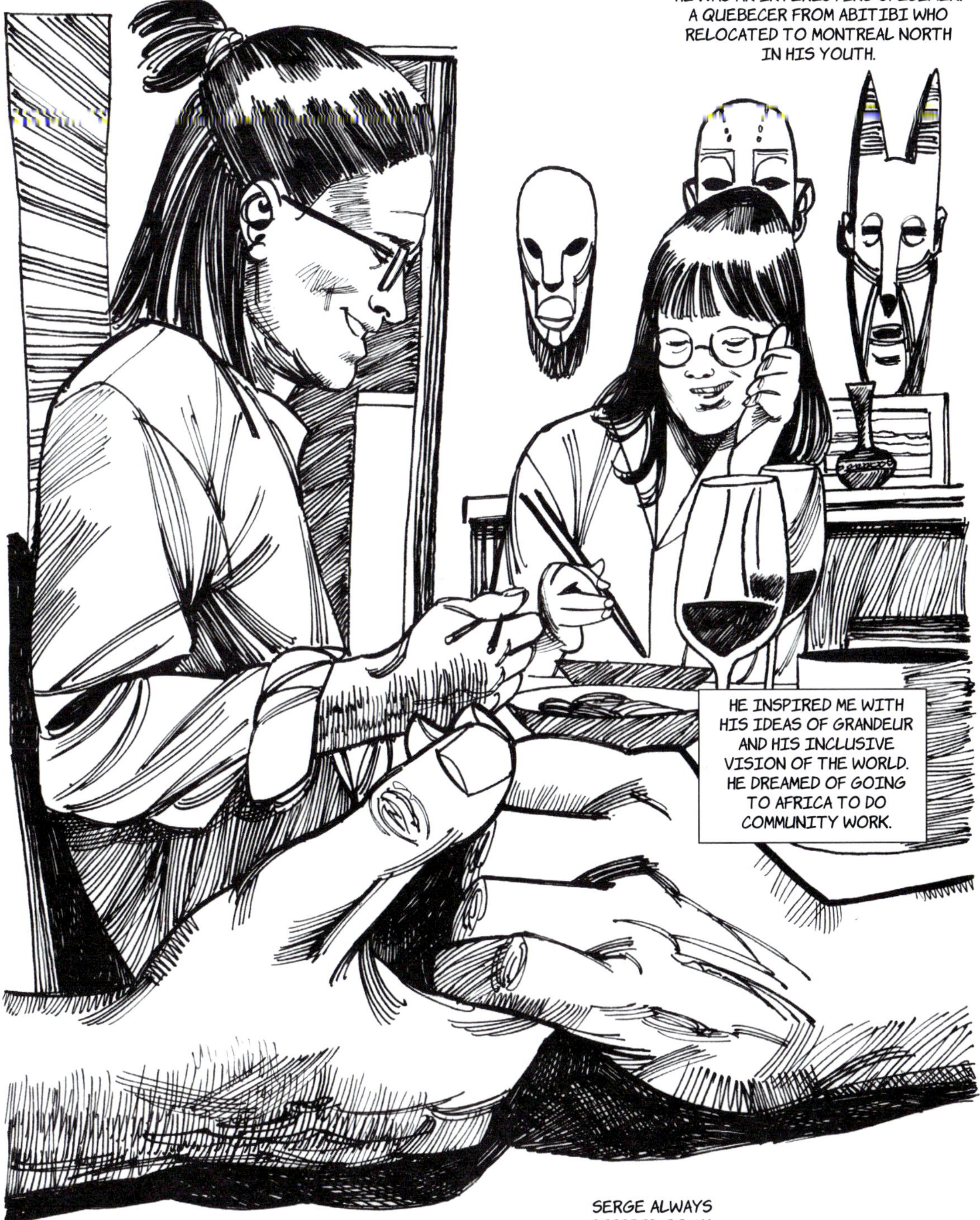
HE INSPIRED ME WITH HIS IDEAS OF GRANDEUR AND HIS INCLUSIVE VISION OF THE WORLD. HE DREAMED OF GOING TO AFRICA TO DO COMMUNITY WORK.

SERGE ALWAYS
OFFERED EQUAL
RESPECT TO EVERYONE.

IT GAVE
ME HOPE.

JULY 11, 1990

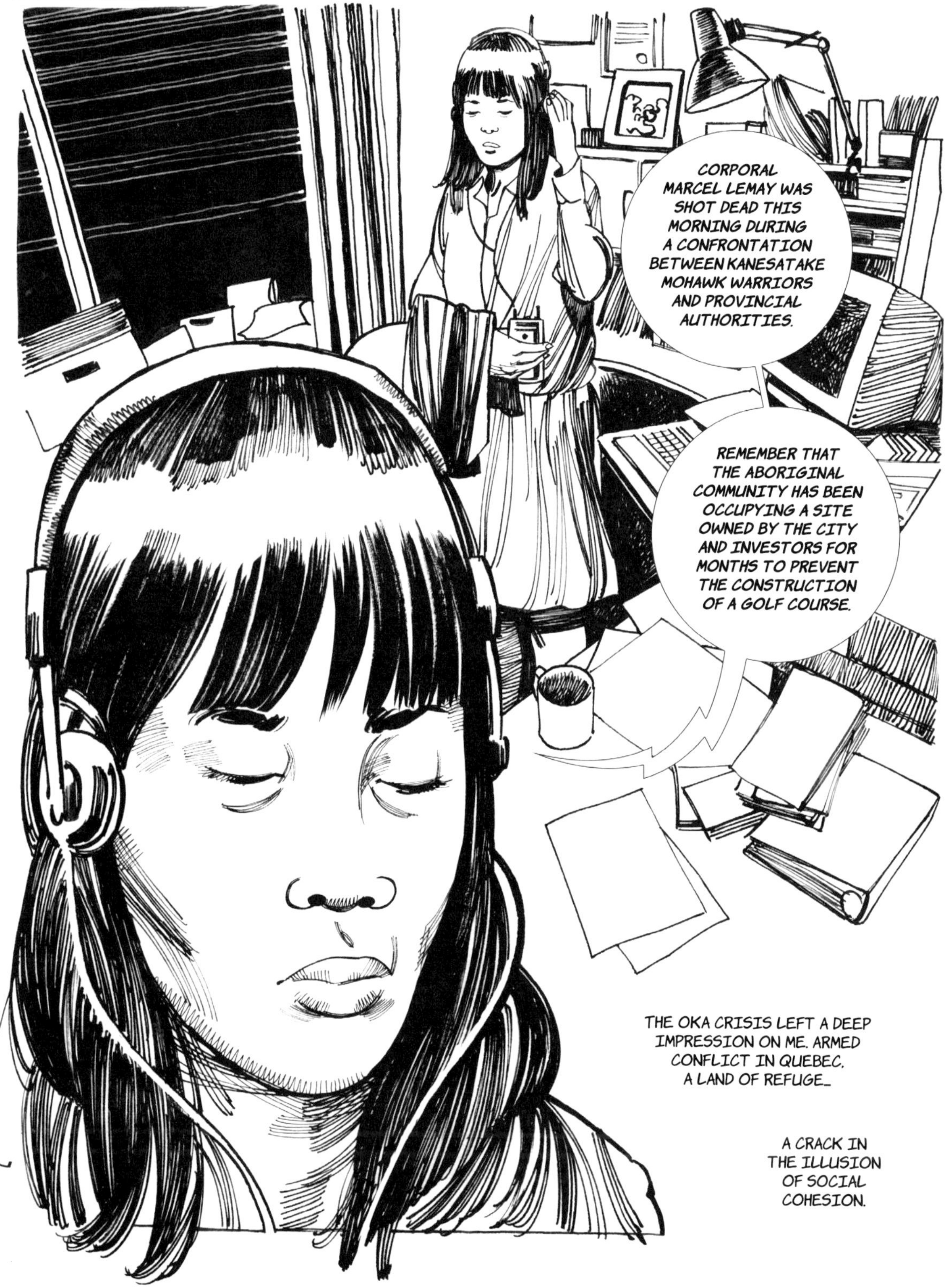
CORPORAL MARCEL LEMAY WAS SHOT DEAD THIS MORNING DURING A CONFRONTATION BETWEEN KANESATAKE MOHAWK WARRIORS AND PROVINCIAL AUTHORITIES.
REMEMBER THAT THE ABORIGINAL COMMUNITY HAS BEEN OCCUPYING A SITE OWNED BY THE CITY AND INVESTORS FOR MONTHS TO PREVENT THE CONSTRUCTION OF A GOLF COURSE.

THE OKA CRISIS LEFT A DEEP IMPRESSION ON ME. ARMED CONFLICT IN QUEBEC, A LAND OF REFUGE...

A CRACK IN THE ILLUSION OF SOCIAL COHESION.

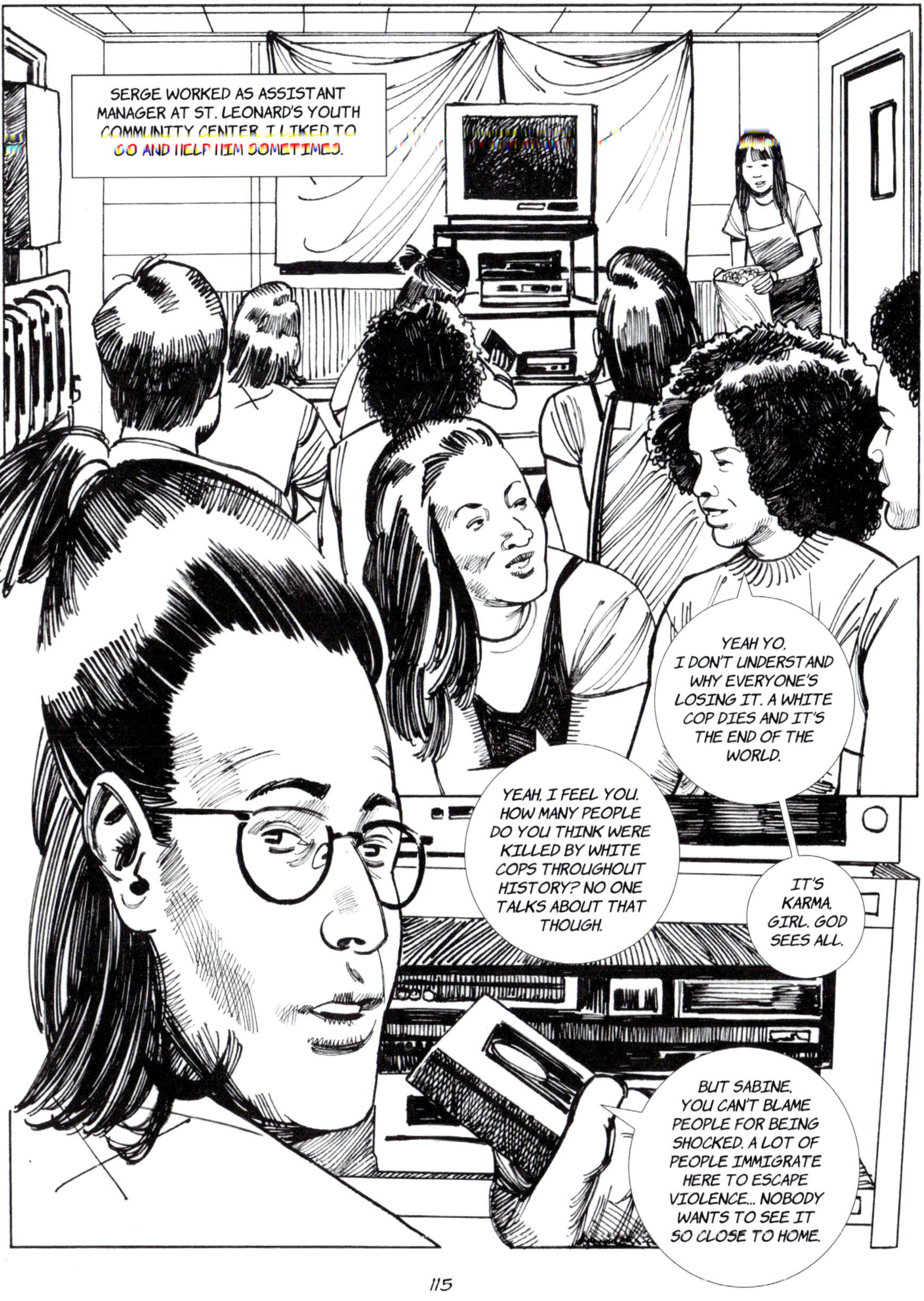
SERGE WORKED AS ASSISTANT MANAGER AT ST. LEONARD'S YOUTH COMMUNITY CENTER. I LIKED TO GO AND HELP HIM SOMETIMES.
YEAH YO, I DON'T UNDERSTAND WHY EVERYONE'S LOSING IT. A WHITE COP DIES AND IT'S THE END OF THE WORLD.
YEAH, I FEEL YOU. HOW MANY PEOPLE DO YOU THINK WERE KILLED BY WHITE COPS THROUGHOUT HISTORY? NO ONE TALKS ABOUT THAT THOUGH.
IT'S KARMA, GIRL. GOD SEES ALL.
BUT SABINE, YOU CAN'T BLAME PEOPLE FOR BEING SHOCKED. A LOT OF PEOPLE IMMIGRATE HERE TO ESCAPE VIOLENCE... NOBODY WANTS TO SEE IT SO CLOSE TO HOME.

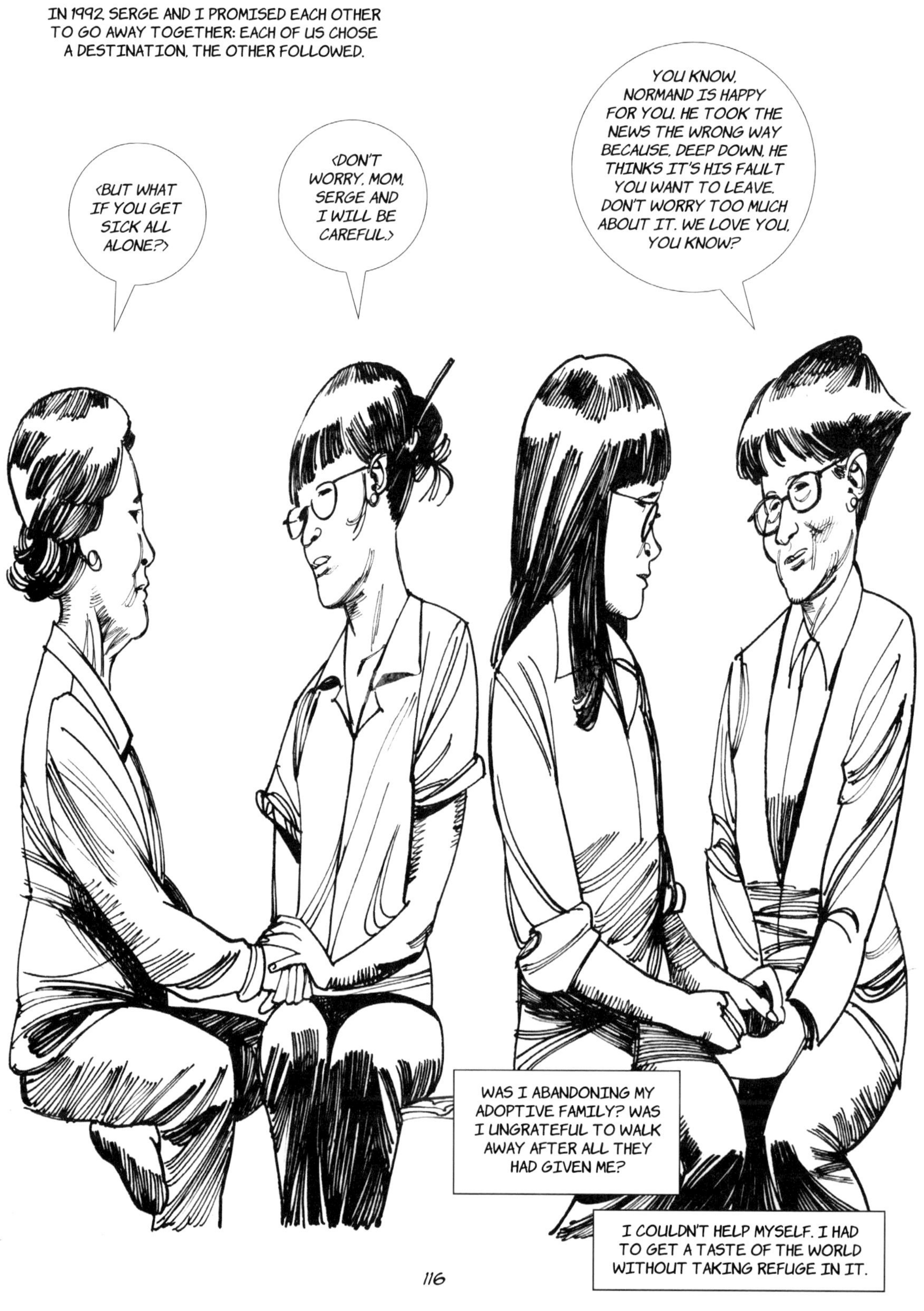
IN 1992, SERGE AND I PROMISED EACH OTHER TO GO AWAY TOGETHER: EACH OF US CHOSE A DESTINATION, THE OTHER FOLLOWED.
<BUT WHAT IF YOU GET SICK ALL ALONE?>
<DON'T WORRY, MOM. SERGE AND I WILL BE CAREFUL.>
YOU KNOW, NORMAND IS HAPPY FOR YOU. HE TOOK THE NEWS THE WRONG WAY BECAUSE, DEEP DOWN, HE THINKS IT'S HIS FAULT YOU WANT TO LEAVE. DON'T WORRY TOO MUCH ABOUT IT. WE LOVE YOU, YOU KNOW?
WAS I ABANDONING MY ADOPTIVE FAMILY? WAS I UNGRATEFUL TO WALK AWAY AFTER ALL THEY HAD GIVEN ME?
I COULDN'T HELP MYSELF. I HAD TO GET A TASTE OF THE WORLD WITHOUT TAKING REFUGE IN IT.

CHAPTER 5

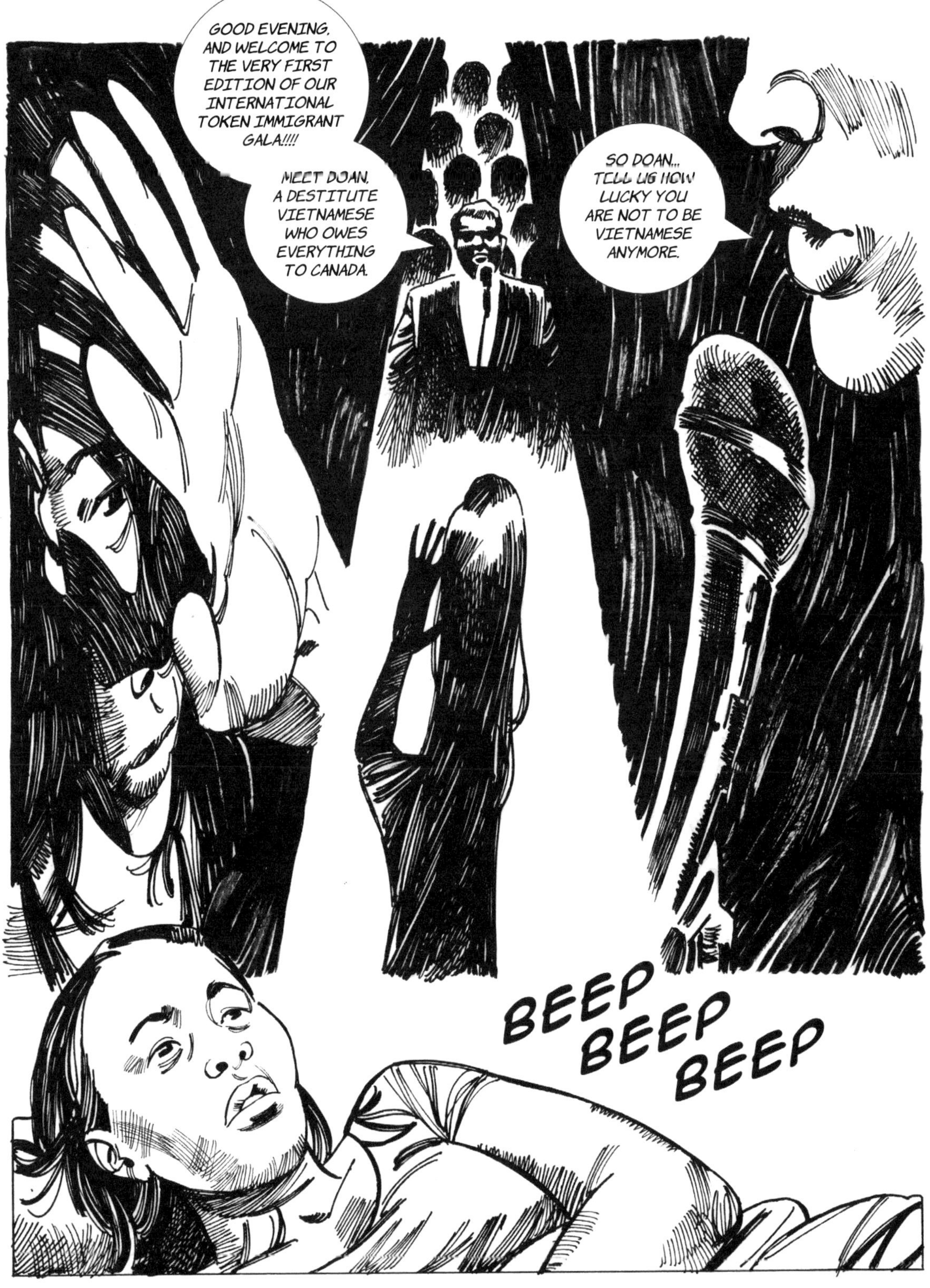
GOOD EVENING, AND WELCOME TO THE VERY FIRST EDITION OF OUR INTERNATIONAL TOKEN IMMIGRANT GALA!!!!
MEET DOAN, A DESTITUTE VIETNAMESE WHO OWES EVERYTHING TO CANADA.
SO DOAN... TELL US HOW LUCKY YOU ARE NOT TO BE VIETNAMESE ANYMORE.
BEEP BEEP BEEP

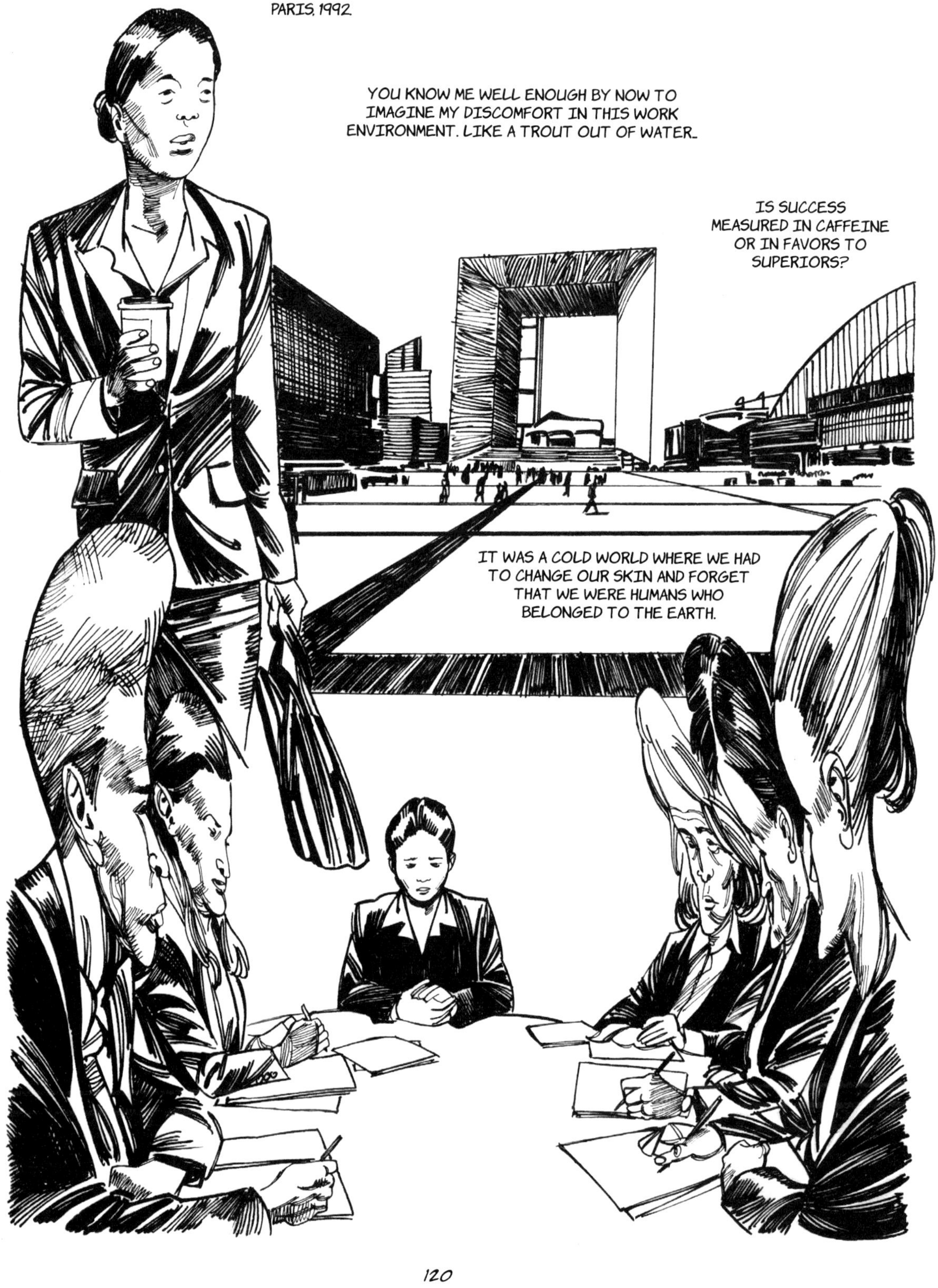
PARIS, 1992
YOU KNOW ME WELL ENOUGH BY NOW TO IMAGINE MY DISCOMFORT IN THIS WORK ENVIRONMENT. LIKE A TROUT OUT OF WATER…
IS SUCCESS MEASURED IN CAFFEINE OR IN FAVORS TO SUPERIORS?
IT WAS A COLD WORLD WHERE WE HAD TO CHANGE OUR SKIN AND FORGET THAT WE WERE HUMANS WHO BELONGED TO THE EARTH.

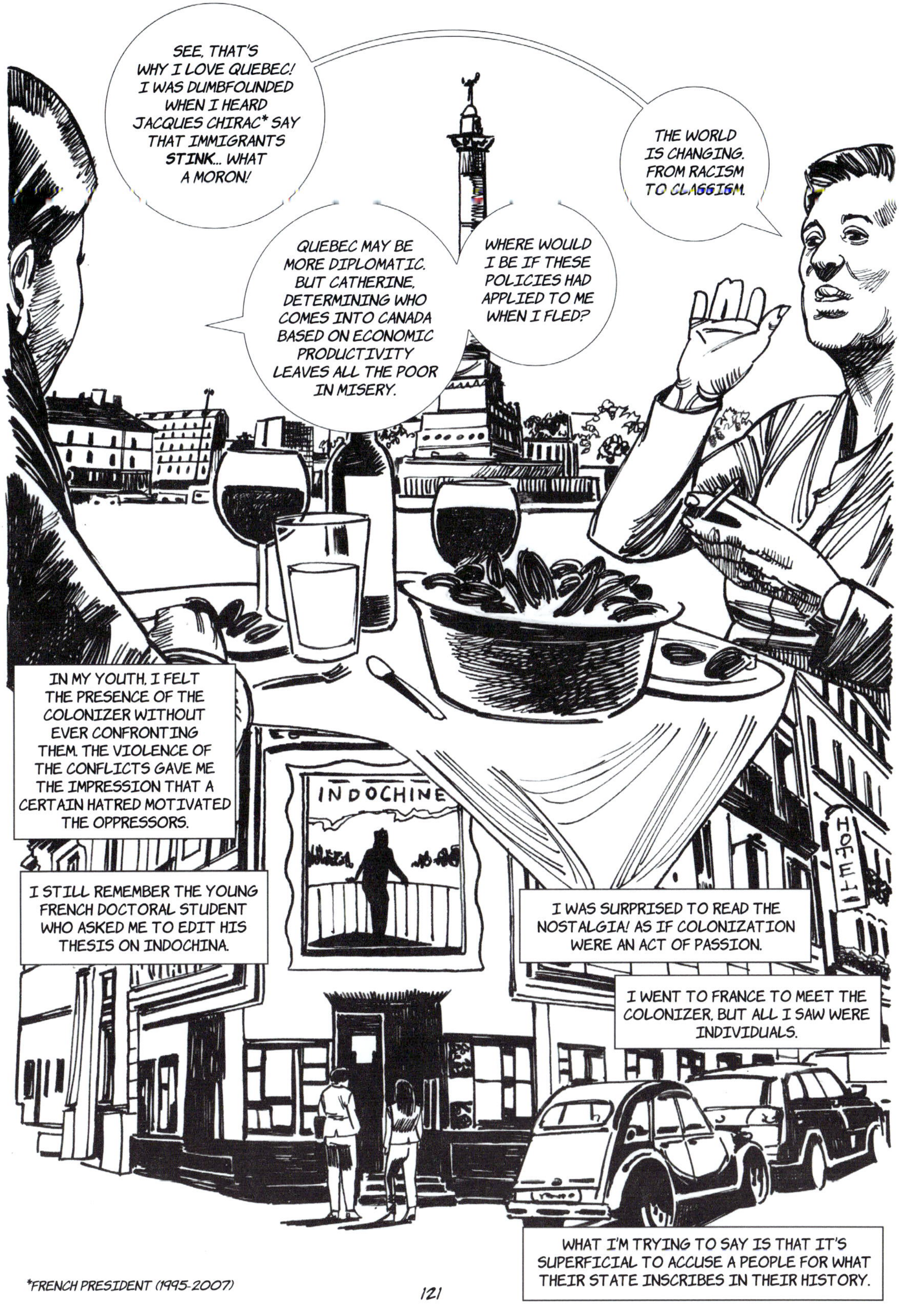
SEE, THAT'S WHY I LOVE QUEBEC! I WAS DUMBFOUNDED WHEN I HEARD JACQUES CHIRAC* SAY THAT IMMIGRANTS STINK... WHAT A MORON!
THE WORLD IS CHANGING. FROM RACISM TO CLASSISM.
QUEBEC MAY BE MORE DIPLOMATIC. BUT CATHERINE, DETERMINING WHO COMES INTO CANADA BASED ON ECONOMIC PRODUCTIVITY LEAVES ALL THE POOR IN MISERY.
WHERE WOULD I BE IF THESE POLICIES HAD APPLIED TO ME WHEN I FLED?
IN MY YOUTH, I FELT THE PRESENCE OF THE COLONIZER WITHOUT EVER CONFRONTING THEM. THE VIOLENCE OF THE CONFLICTS GAVE ME THE IMPRESSION THAT A CERTAIN HATRED MOTIVATED THE OPPRESSORS.
INDOCHINE
HOTEL
I STILL REMEMBER THE YOUNG FRENCH DOCTORAL STUDENT WHO ASKED ME TO EDIT HIS THESIS ON INDOCHINA.
I WAS SURPRISED TO READ THE NOSTALGIA! AS IF COLONIZATION WERE AN ACT OF PASSION.
I WENT TO FRANCE TO MEET THE COLONIZER, BUT ALL I SAW WERE INDIVIDUALS.
WHAT I'M TRYING TO SAY IS THAT IT'S SUPERFICIAL TO ACCUSE A PEOPLE FOR WHAT THEIR STATE INSCRIBES IN THEIR HISTORY.

*FRENCH PRESIDENT (1995-2007)

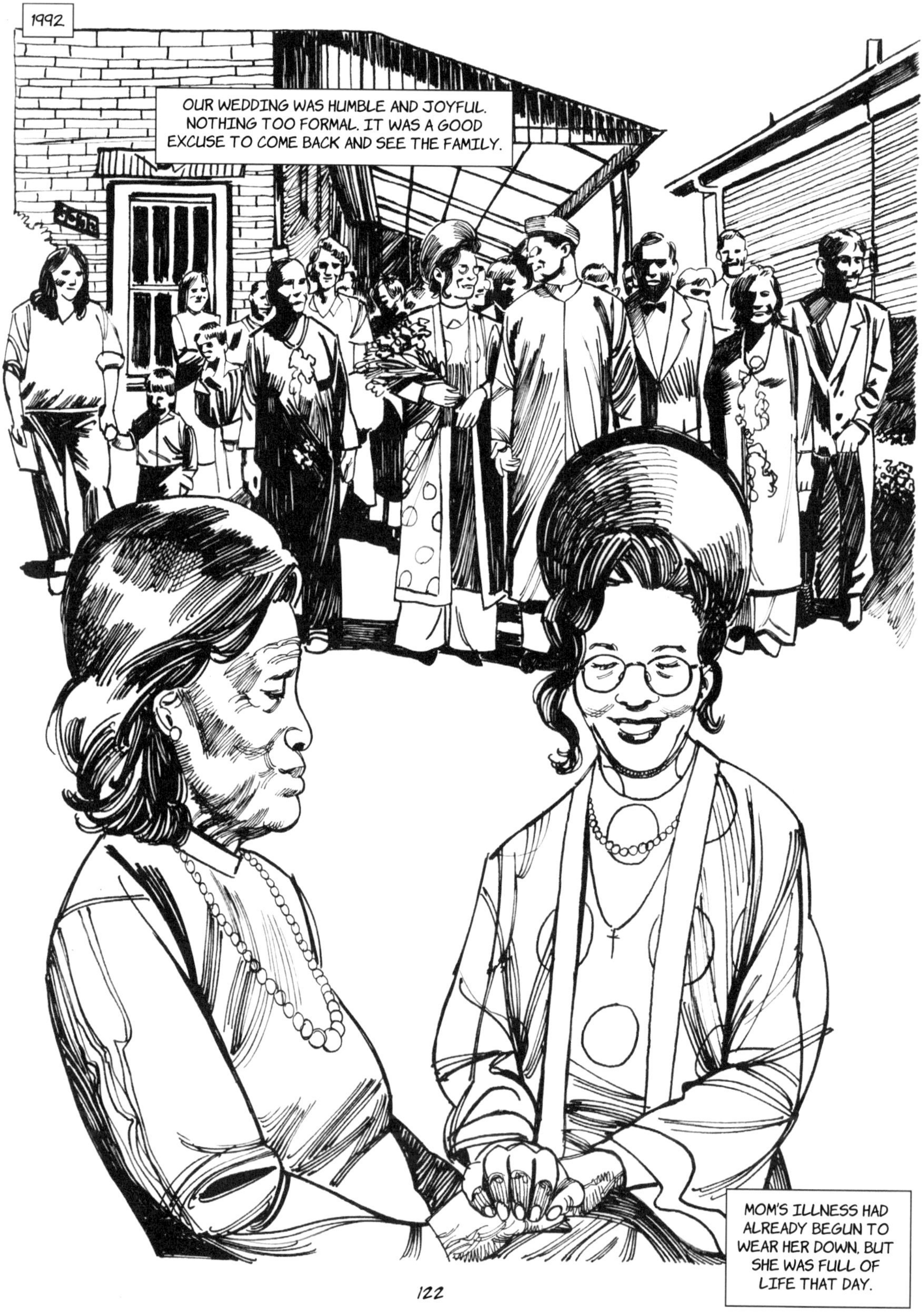
1992
OUR WEDDING WAS HUMBLE AND JOYFUL. NOTHING TOO FORMAL. IT WAS A GOOD EXCUSE TO COME BACK AND SEE THE FAMILY.
MOM'S ILLNESS HAD ALREADY BEGUN TO WEAR HER DOWN, BUT SHE WAS FULL OF LIFE THAT DAY.

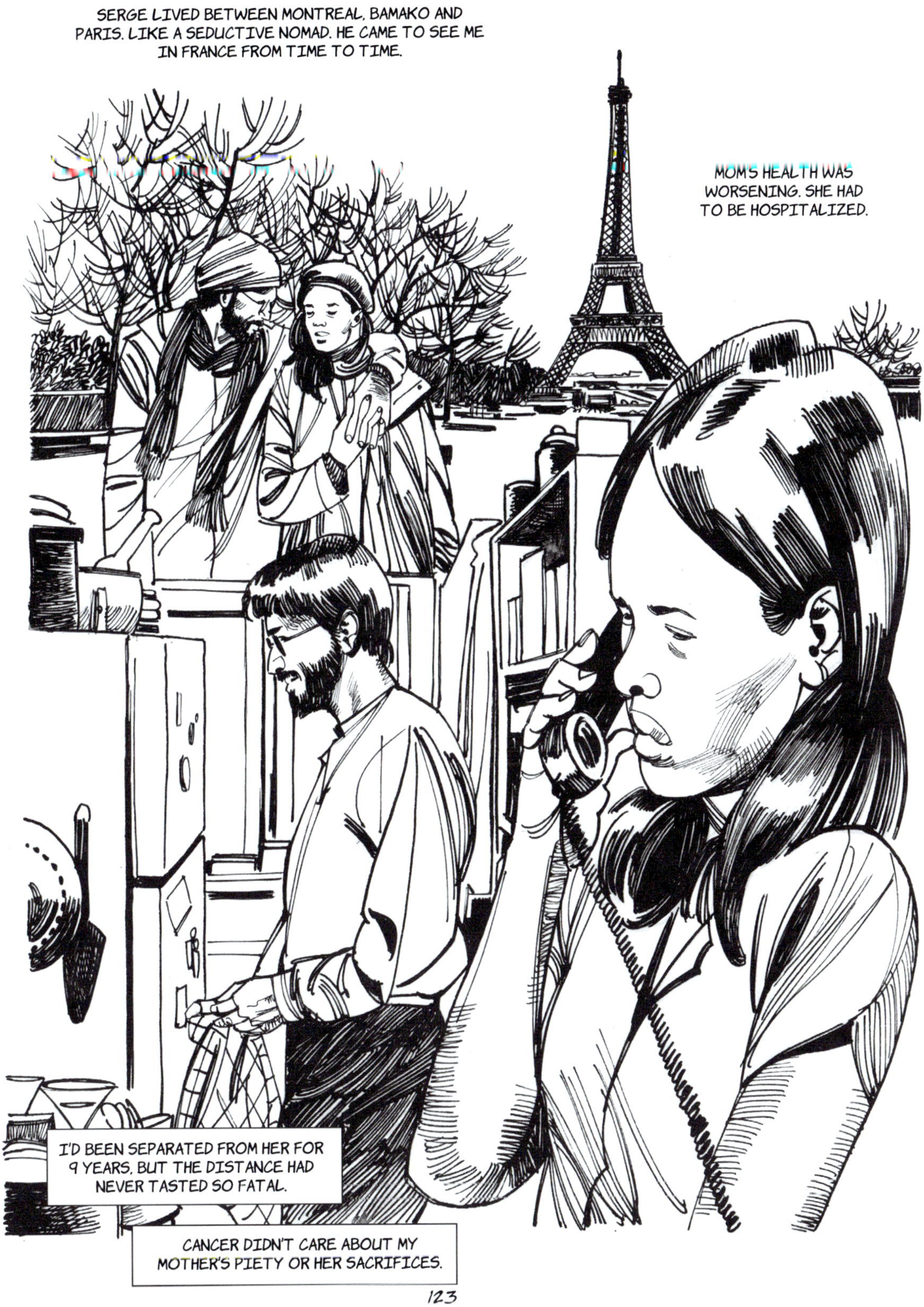
SERGE LIVED BETWEEN MONTREAL, BAMAKO AND PARIS. LIKE A SEDUCTIVE NOMAD. HE CAME TO SEE ME IN FRANCE FROM TIME TO TIME.
MOM'S HEALTH WAS WORSENING. SHE HAD TO BE HOSPITALIZED.
I'D BEEN SEPARATED FROM HER FOR 9 YEARS, BUT THE DISTANCE HAD NEVER TASTED SO FATAL.
CANCER DIDN'T CARE ABOUT MY MOTHER'S PIETY OR HER SACRIFICES.

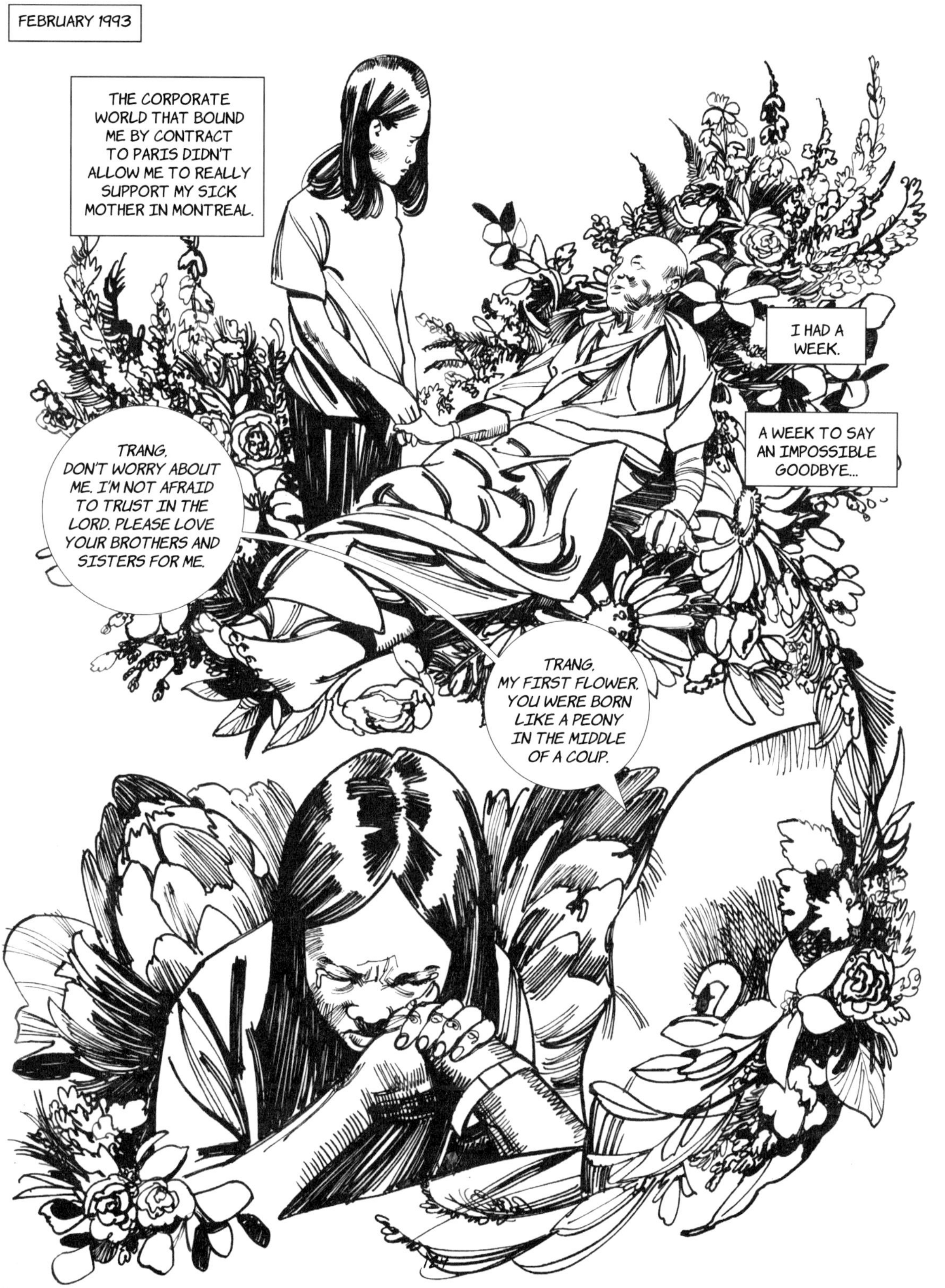
FEBRUARY 1993
THE CORPORATE WORLD THAT BOUND ME BY CONTRACT TO PARIS DIDN'T ALLOW ME TO REALLY SUPPORT MY SICK MOTHER IN MONTREAL.
I HAD A WEEK.
A WEEK TO SAY AN IMPOSSIBLE GOODBYE...
TRANG, DON'T WORRY ABOUT ME. I'M NOT AFRAID TO TRUST IN THE LORD. PLEASE LOVE YOUR BROTHERS AND SISTERS FOR ME.
TRANG, MY FIRST FLOWER, YOU WERE BORN LIKE A PEONY IN THE MIDDLE OF A COUP.

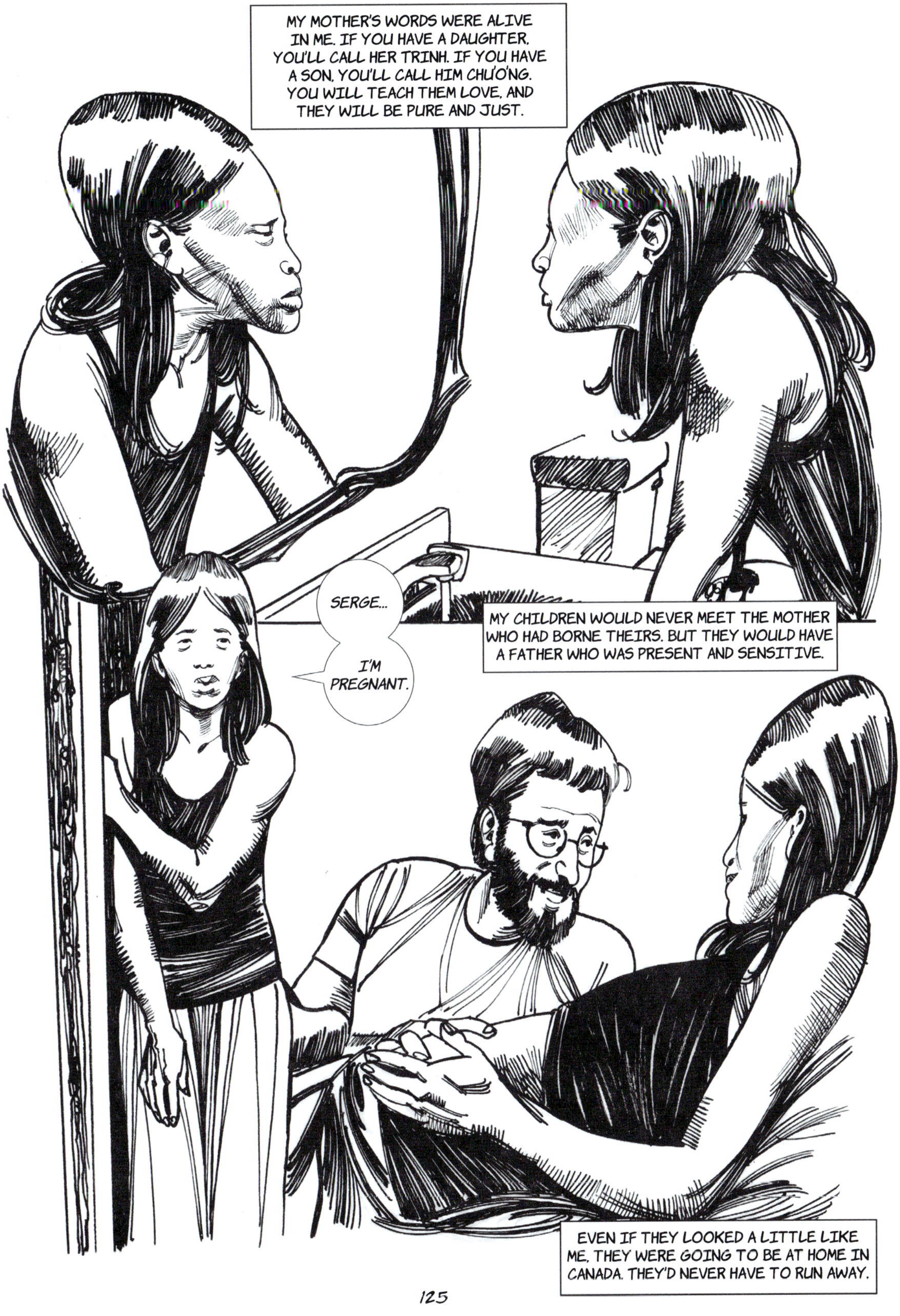
MY MOTHER'S WORDS WERE ALIVE IN ME. IF YOU HAVE A DAUGHTER, YOU'LL CALL HER TRINH. IF YOU HAVE A SON, YOU'LL CALL HIM CHƯƠNG. YOU WILL TEACH THEM LOVE, AND THEY WILL BE PURE AND JUST.
SERGE...
I'M PREGNANT.
MY CHILDREN WOULD NEVER MEET THE MOTHER WHO HAD BORNE THEIRS. BUT THEY WOULD HAVE A FATHER WHO WAS PRESENT AND SENSITIVE.
EVEN IF THEY LOOKED A LITTLE LIKE ME, THEY WERE GOING TO BE AT HOME IN CANADA. THEY'D NEVER HAVE TO RUN AWAY.

JULY 18, 1994

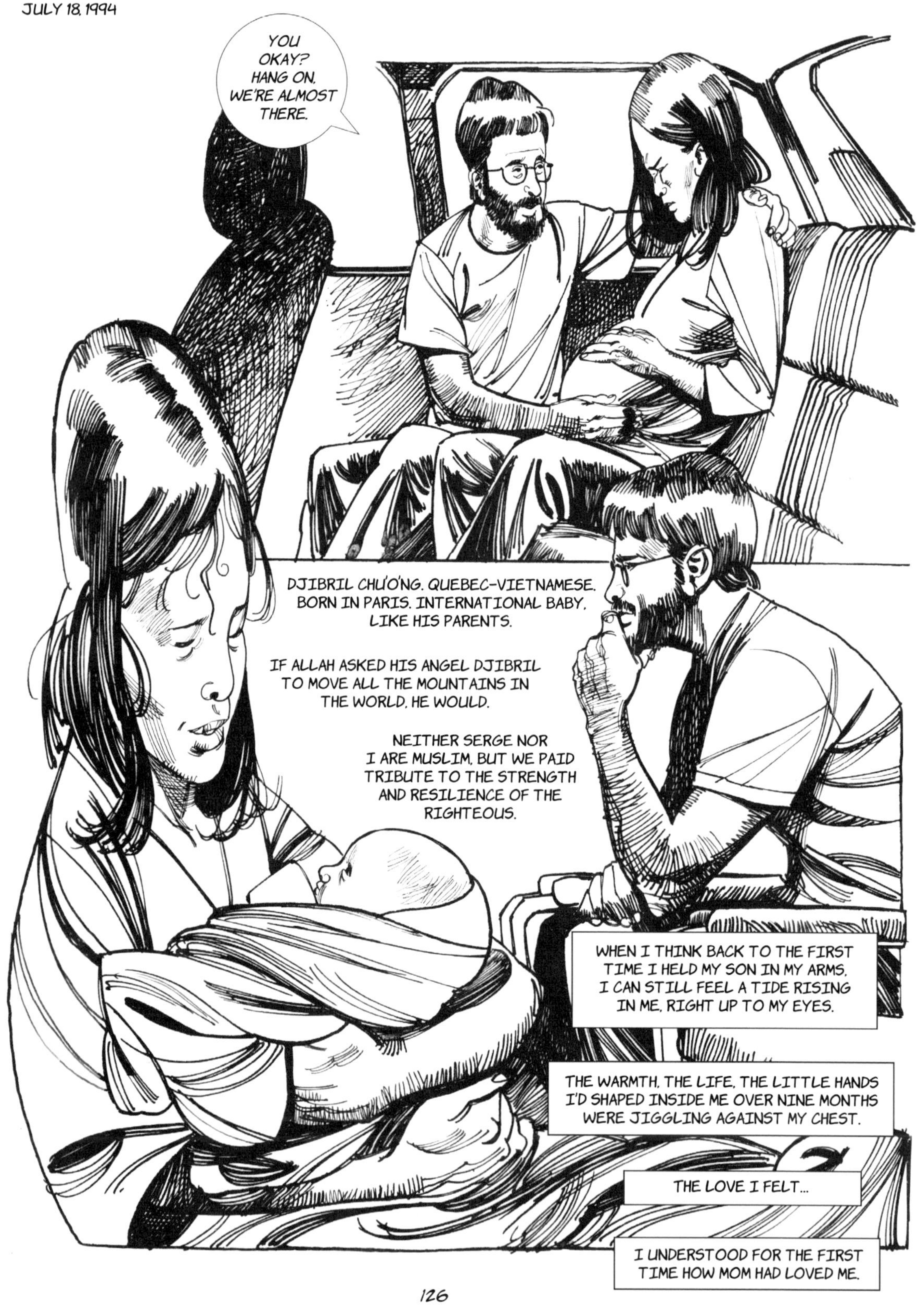
YOU OKAY? HANG ON. WE'RE ALMOST THERE.
DJIBRIL CHƯƠNG. QUEBEC-VIETNAMESE. BORN IN PARIS. INTERNATIONAL BABY, LIKE HIS PARENTS.
IF ALLAH ASKED HIS ANGEL DJIBRIL TO MOVE ALL THE MOUNTAINS IN THE WORLD, HE WOULD.
NEITHER SERGE NOR I ARE MUSLIM, BUT WE PAID TRIBUTE TO THE STRENGTH AND RESILIENCE OF THE RIGHTEOUS.
WHEN I THINK BACK TO THE FIRST TIME I HELD MY SON IN MY ARMS, I CAN STILL FEEL A TIDE RISING IN ME, RIGHT UP TO MY EYES.
THE WARMTH, THE LIFE, THE LITTLE HANDS I'D SHAPED INSIDE ME OVER NINE MONTHS WERE JIGGLING AGAINST MY CHEST.
THE LOVE I FELT...
I UNDERSTOOD FOR THE FIRST TIME HOW MOM HAD LOVED ME.

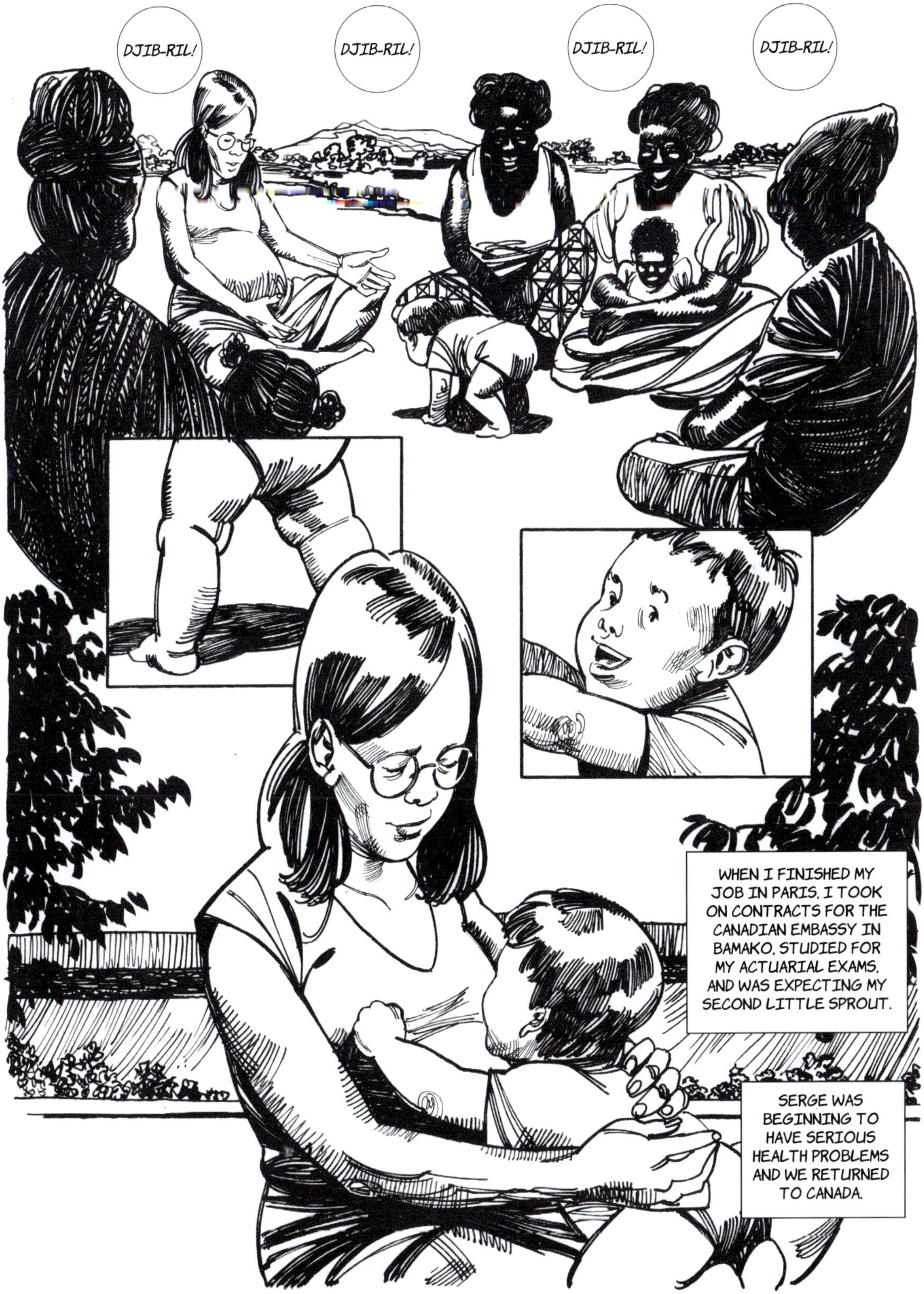
DJIB-RIL!
DJIB-RIL!
DJIB-RIL!
DJIB-RIL!
WHEN I FINISHED MY JOB IN PARIS, I TOOK ON CONTRACTS FOR THE CANADIAN EMBASSY IN BAMAKO, STUDIED FOR MY ACTUARIAL EXAMS, AND WAS EXPECTING MY SECOND LITTLE SPROUT.
SERGE WAS BEGINNING TO HAVE SERIOUS HEALTH PROBLEMS AND WE RETURNED TO CANADA.

MAY 23, 1996

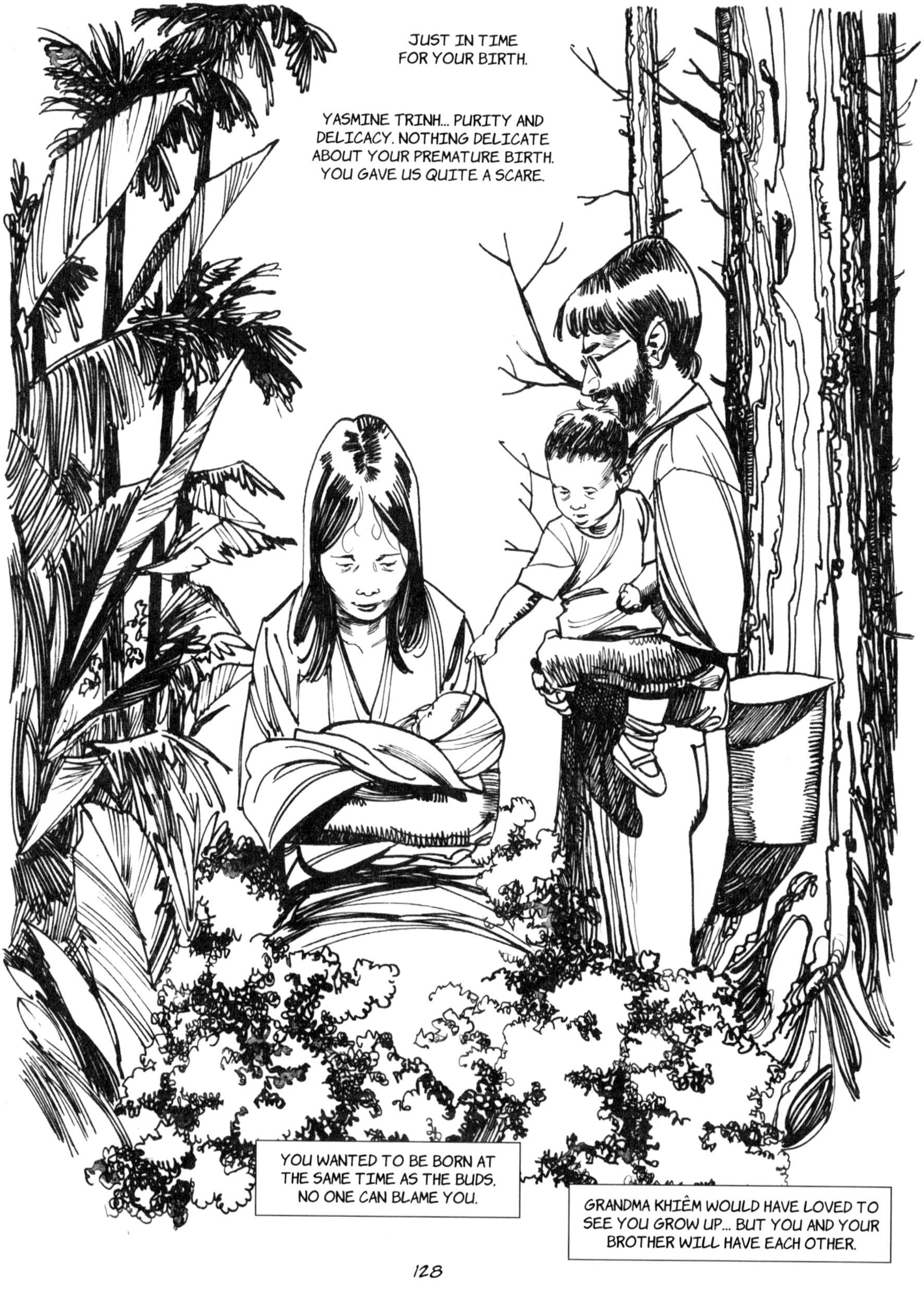
JUST IN TIME FOR YOUR BIRTH.
YASMINE TRINH... PURITY AND DELICACY. NOTHING DELICATE ABOUT YOUR PREMATURE BIRTH. YOU GAVE US QUITE A SCARE.
YOU WANTED TO BE BORN AT THE SAME TIME AS THE BUDS, NO ONE CAN BLAME YOU.
GRANDMA KHIÊM WOULD HAVE LOVED TO SEE YOU GROW UP... BUT YOU AND YOUR BROTHER WILL HAVE EACH OTHER.

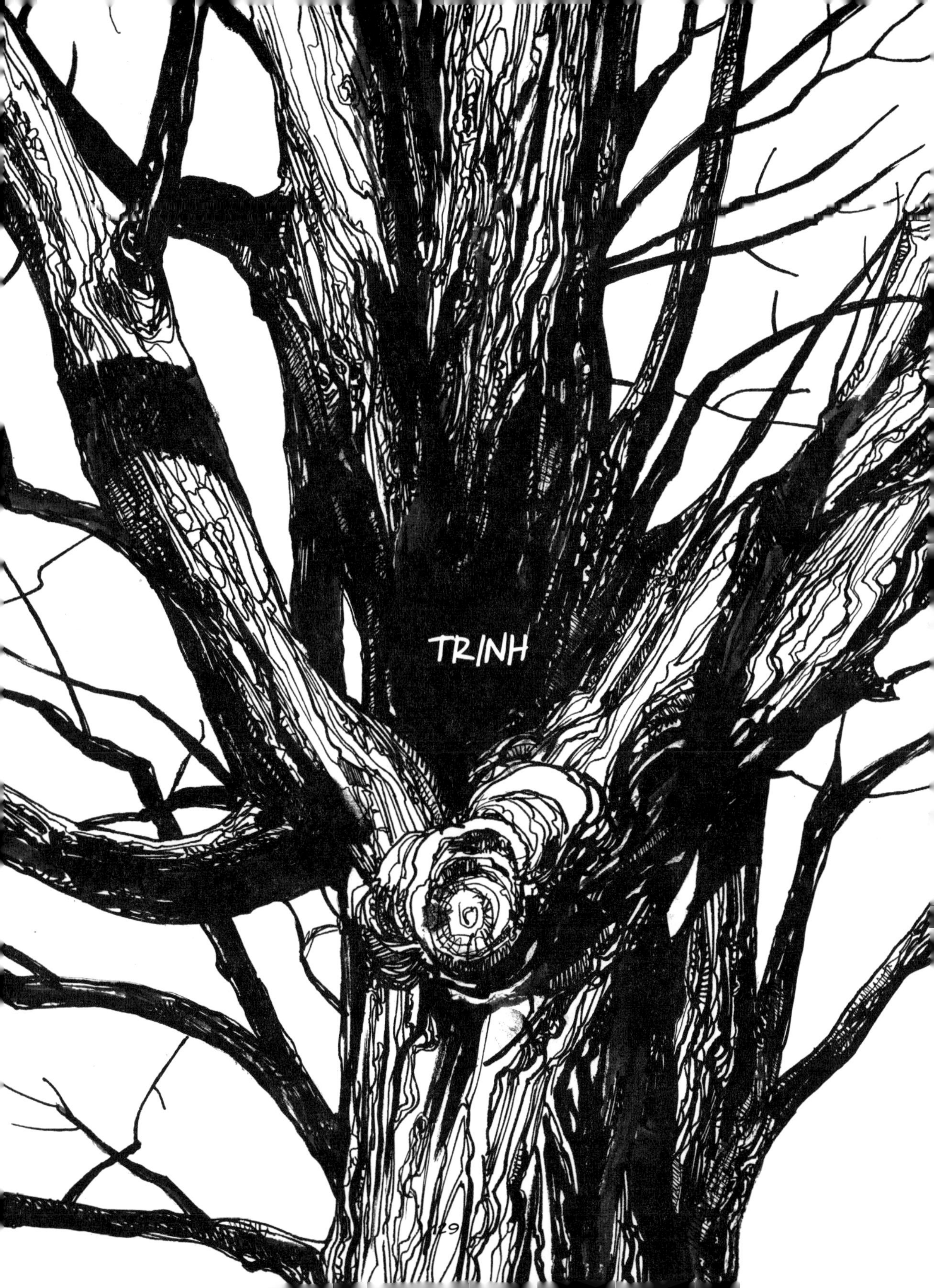
TRINH

CHAPTER 1

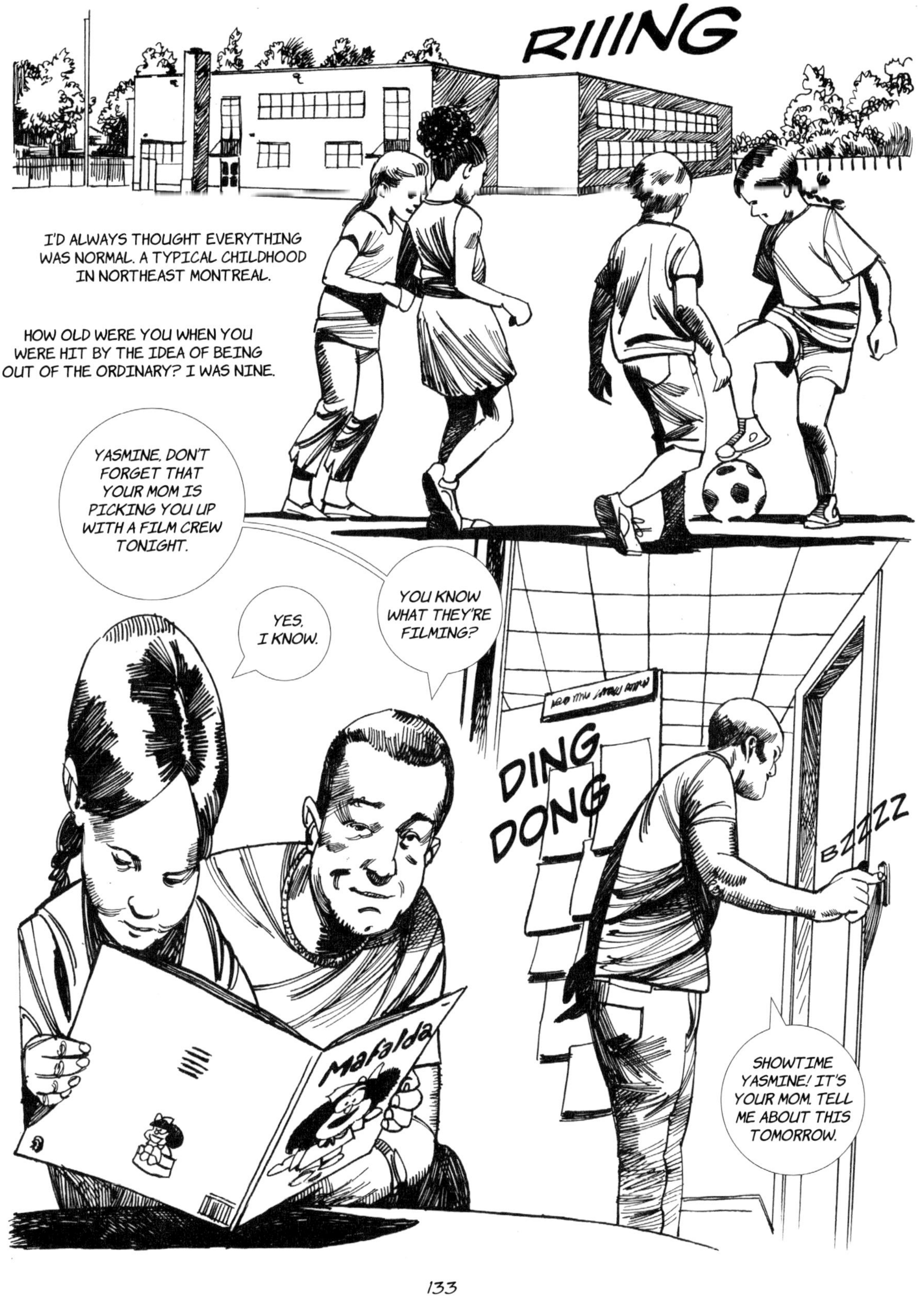
RIIING
I'D ALWAYS THOUGHT EVERYTHING WAS NORMAL. A TYPICAL CHILDHOOD IN NORTHEAST MONTREAL.
HOW OLD WERE YOU WHEN YOU WERE HIT BY THE IDEA OF BEING OUT OF THE ORDINARY? I WAS NINE.
YASMINE, DON'T FORGET THAT YOUR MOM IS PICKING YOU UP WITH A FILM CREW TONIGHT.
YES, I KNOW.
YOU KNOW WHAT THEY'RE FILMING?
Mafalda
DING DONG
BZZZZ
SHOWTIME YASMINE! IT'S YOUR MOM. TELL ME ABOUT THIS TOMORROW.

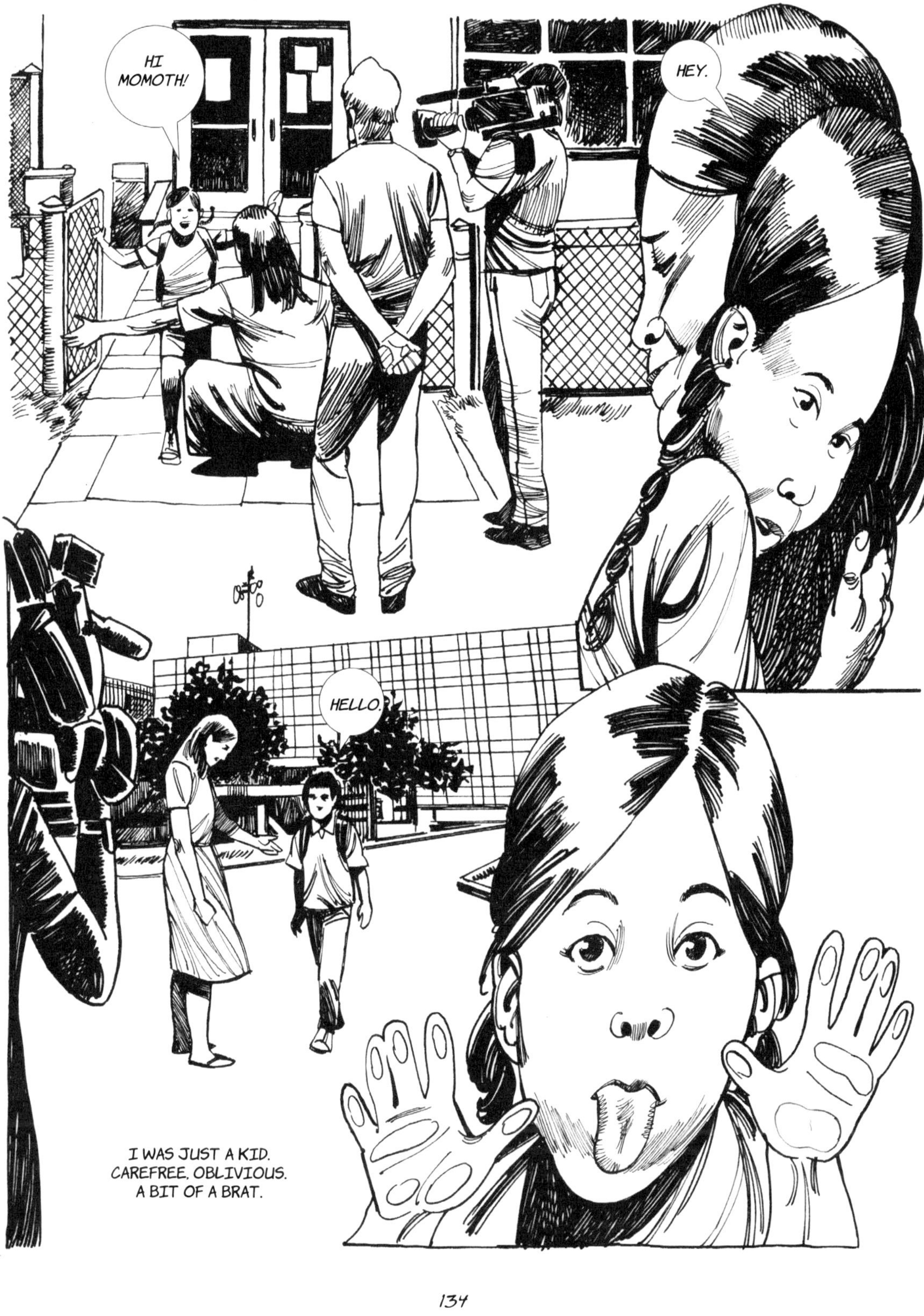
HI MOMOTH!
HEY.
HELLO.
I WAS JUST A KID.
CAREFREE. OBLIVIOUS.
A BIT OF A BRAT.

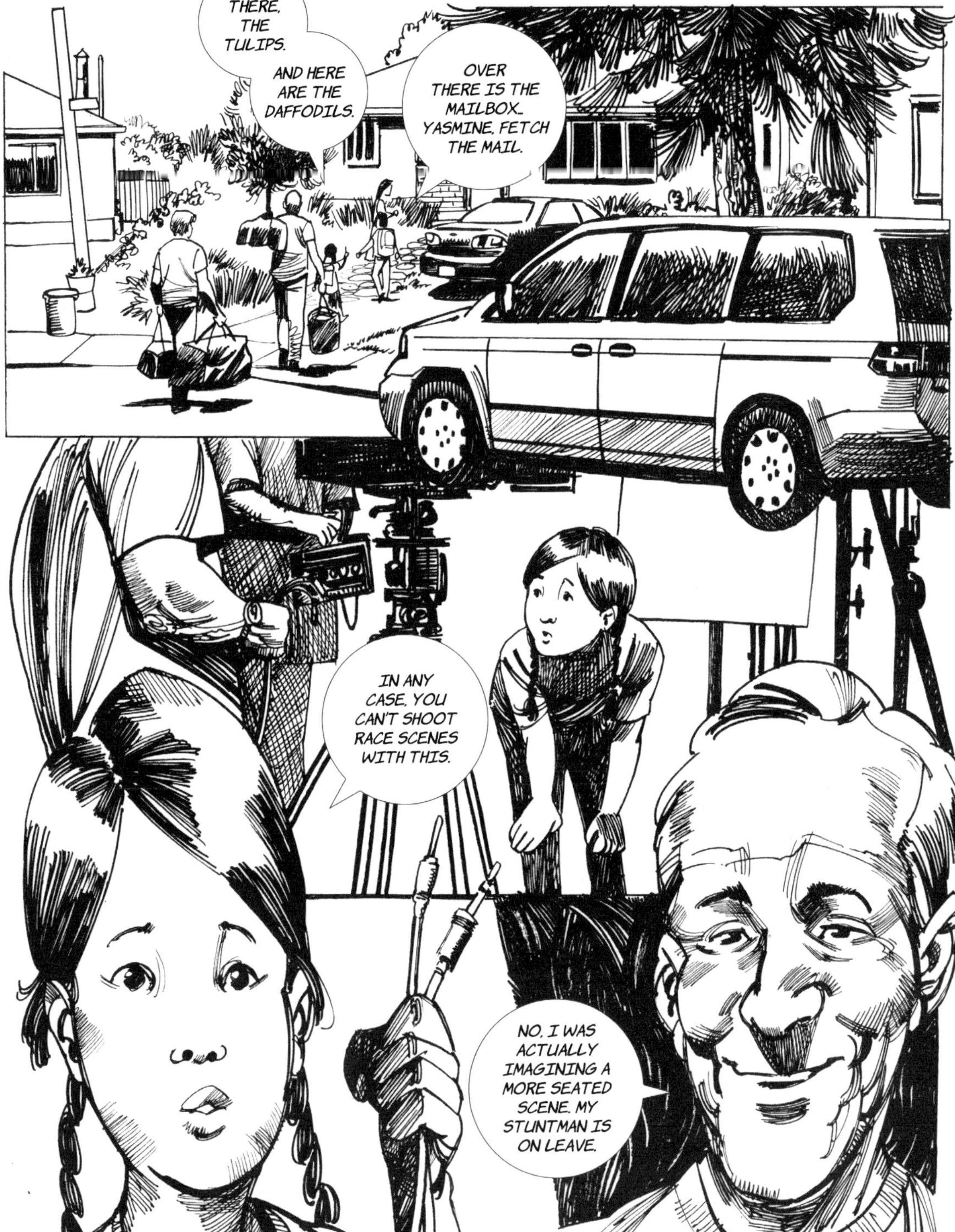
THERE, THE TULIPS.
AND HERE ARE THE DAFFODILS.
OVER THERE IS THE MAILBOX... YASMINE, FETCH THE MAIL.
IN ANY CASE, YOU CAN'T SHOOT RACE SCENES WITH THIS.
NO, I WAS ACTUALLY IMAGINING A MORE SEATED SCENE. MY STUNTMAN IS ON LEAVE.
GUY SIMONEAU, DOCUMENTARY FILMMAKER. THIS MAN IS THE EPITOME OF EMPATHY.

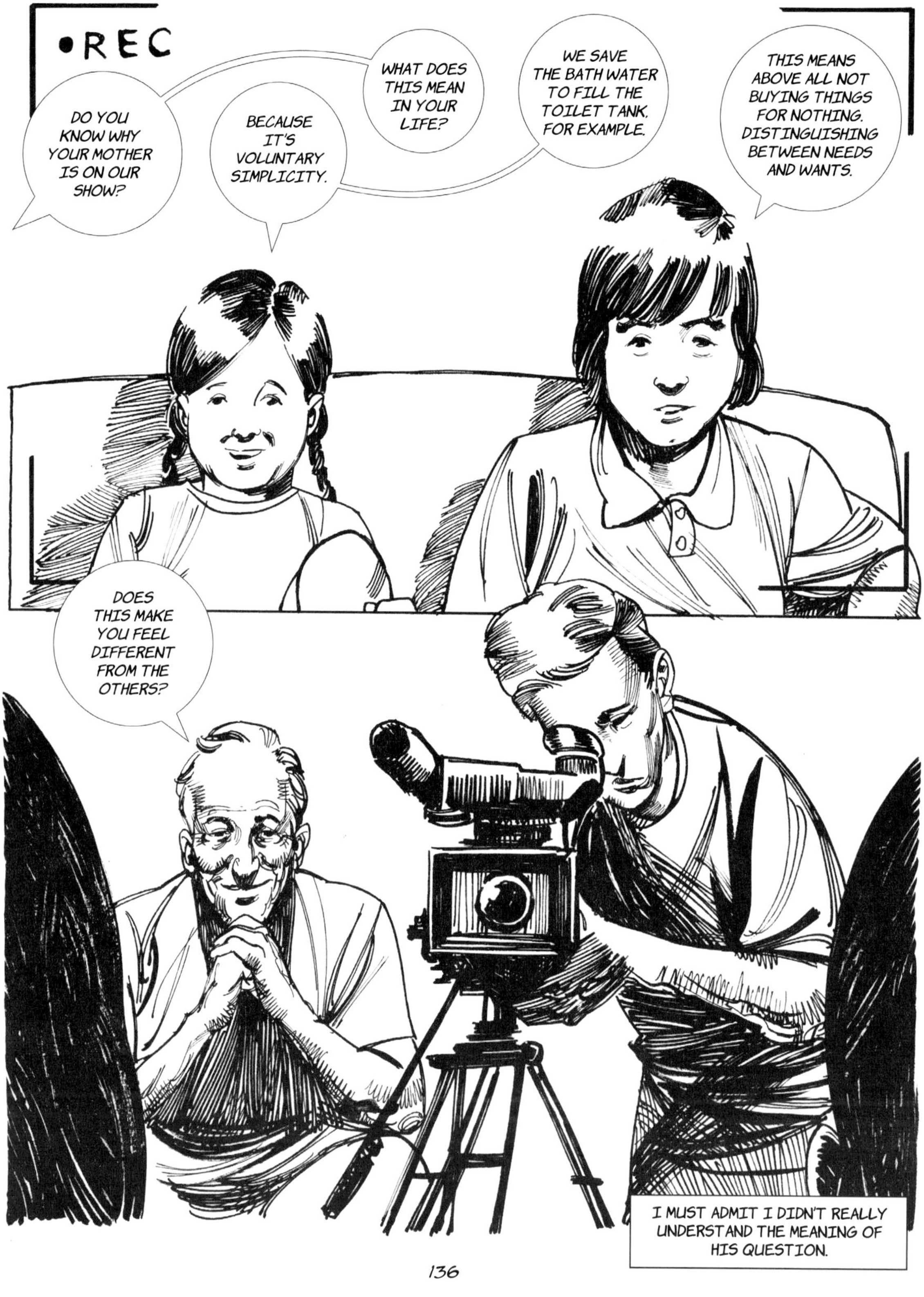
REC
DO YOU KNOW WHY YOUR MOTHER IS ON OUR SHOW?
BECAUSE IT'S VOLUNTARY SIMPLICITY.
WHAT DOES THIS MEAN IN YOUR LIFE?
WE SAVE THE BATH WATER TO FILL THE TOILET TANK, FOR EXAMPLE.
THIS MEANS ABOVE ALL NOT BUYING THINGS FOR NOTHING. DISTINGUISHING BETWEEN NEEDS AND WANTS.
DOES THIS MAKE YOU FEEL DIFFERENT FROM THE OTHERS?
I MUST ADMIT I DIDN'T REALLY UNDERSTAND THE MEANING OF HIS QUESTION.

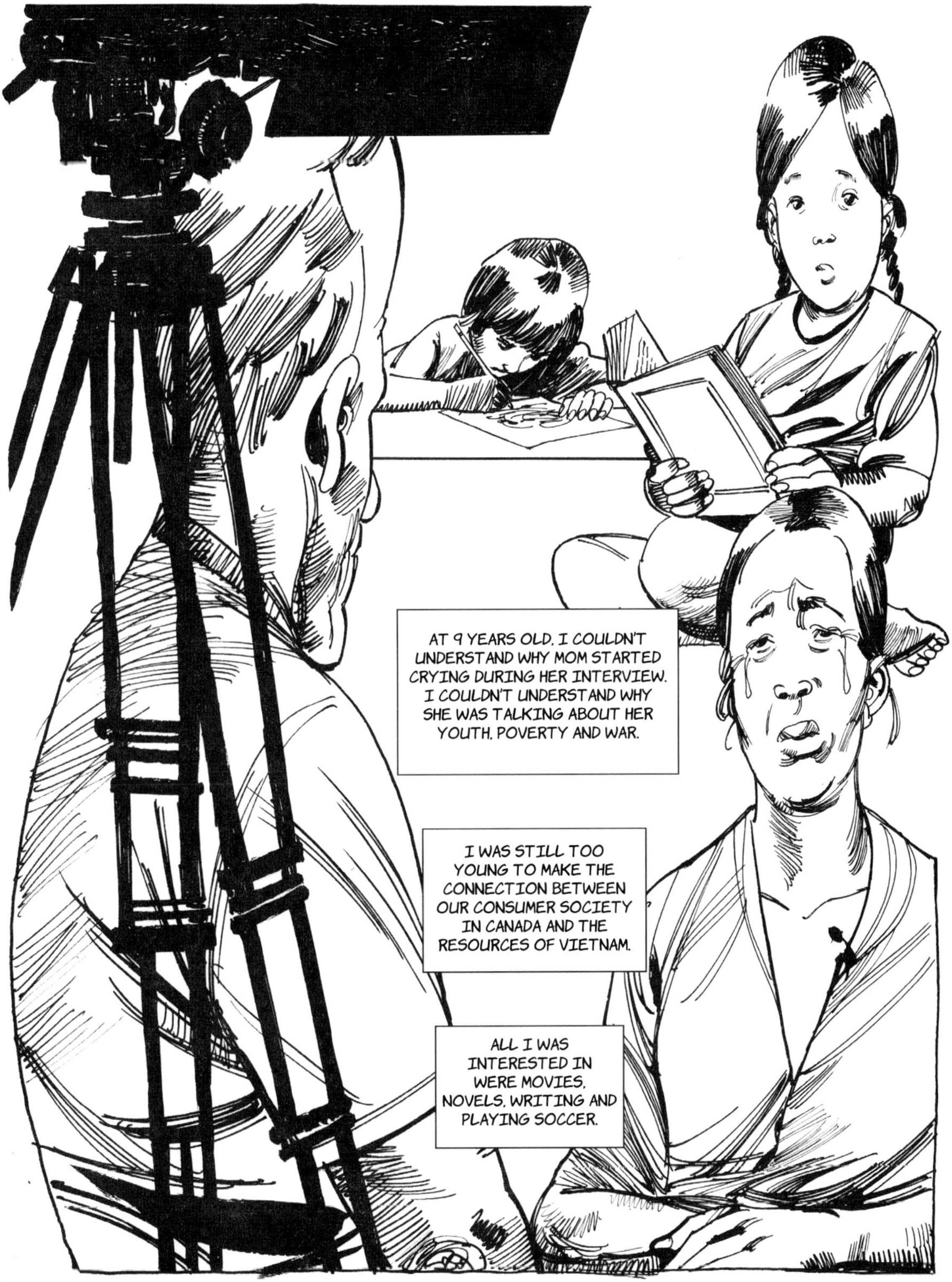
AT 9 YEARS OLD, I COULDN'T UNDERSTAND WHY MOM STARTED CRYING DURING HER INTERVIEW. I COULDN'T UNDERSTAND WHY SHE WAS TALKING ABOUT HER YOUTH, POVERTY AND WAR.
I WAS STILL TOO YOUNG TO MAKE THE CONNECTION BETWEEN OUR CONSUMER SOCIETY IN CANADA AND THE RESOURCES OF VIETNAM.
ALL I WAS INTERESTED IN WERE MOVIES, NOVELS, WRITING AND PLAYING SOCCER.

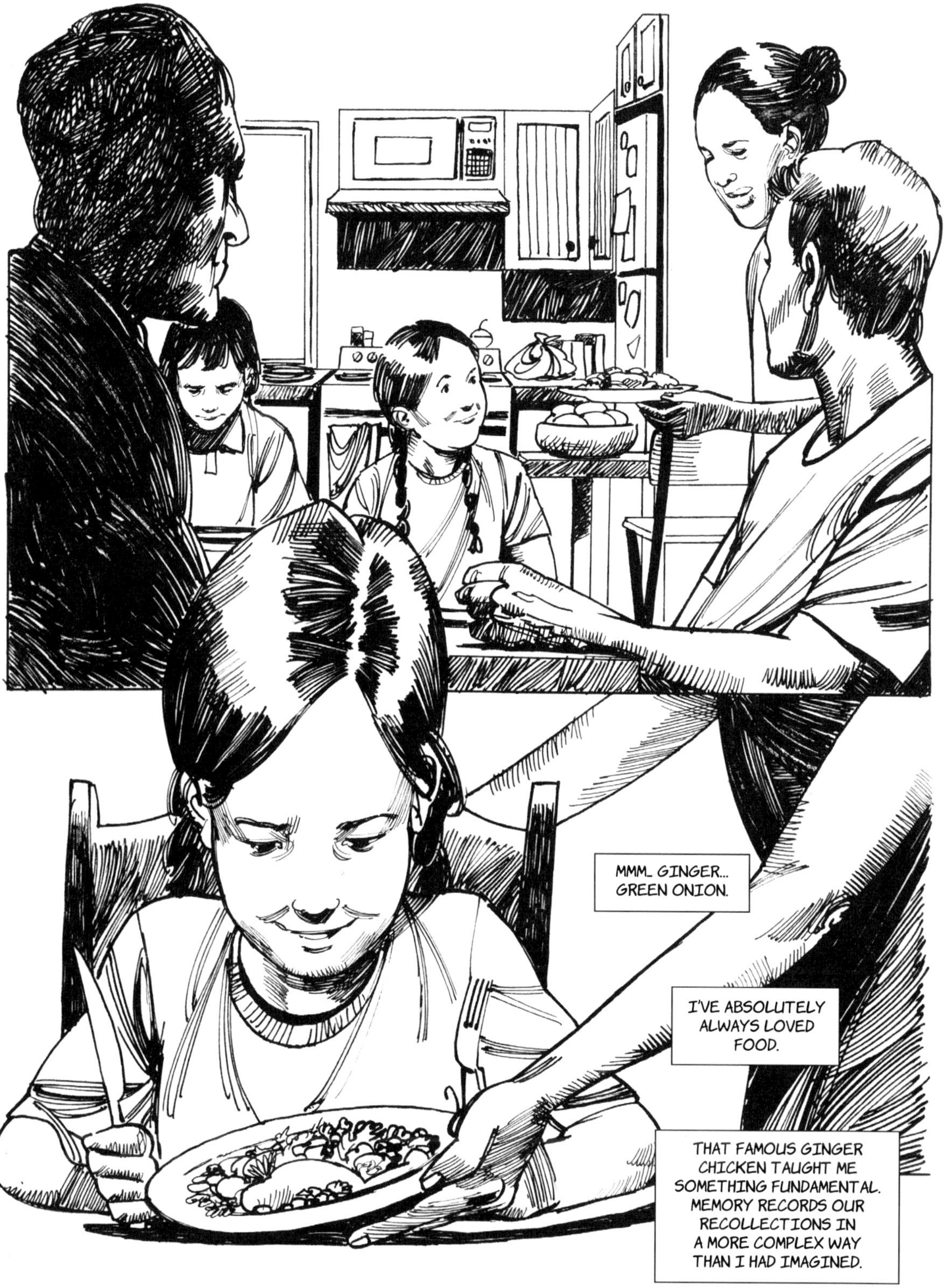
MMM… GINGER…
GREEN ONION.
I'VE ABSOLUTELY ALWAYS LOVED FOOD.
THAT FAMOUS GINGER CHICKEN TAUGHT ME SOMETHING FUNDAMENTAL. MEMORY RECORDS OUR RECOLLECTIONS IN A MORE COMPLEX WAY THAN I HAD IMAGINED.

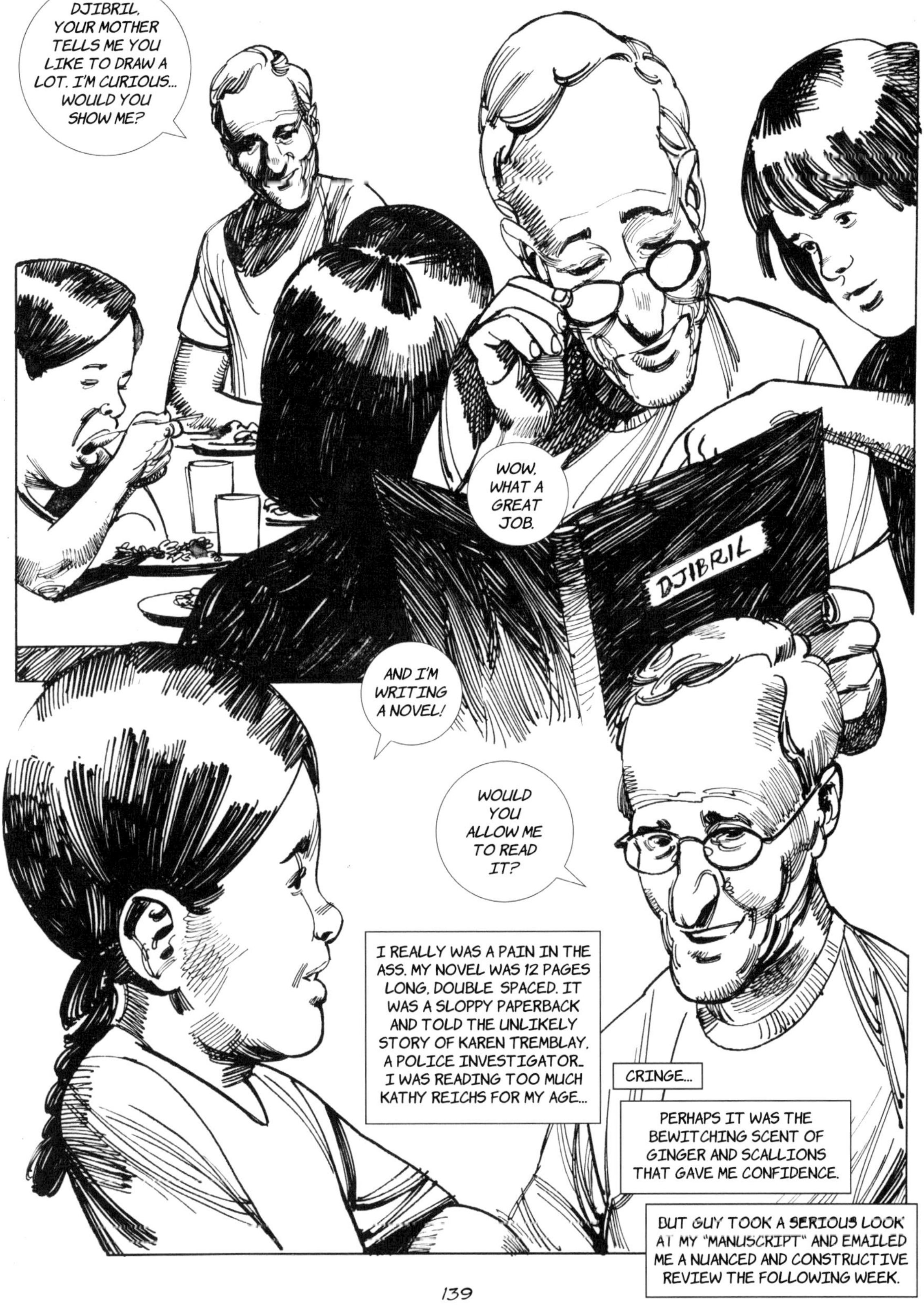

DJIBRIL, YOUR MOTHER TELLS ME YOU LIKE TO DRAW A LOT. I'M CURIOUS... WOULD YOU SHOW ME?
WOW, WHAT A GREAT JOB.
DJIBRIL
AND I'M WRITING A NOVEL!
WOULD YOU ALLOW ME TO READ IT?
I REALLY WAS A PAIN IN THE ASS. MY NOVEL WAS 12 PAGES LONG, DOUBLE SPACED. IT WAS A SLOPPY PAPERBACK AND TOLD THE UNLIKELY STORY OF KAREN TREMBLAY, A POLICE INVESTIGATOR. I WAS READING TOO MUCH KATHY REICHS FOR MY AGE...
CRINGE...
PERHAPS IT WAS THE BEWITCHING SCENT OF GINGER AND SCALLIONS THAT GAVE ME CONFIDENCE.
BUT GUY TOOK A SERIOUS LOOK AT MY "MANUSCRIPT" AND EMAILED ME A NUANCED AND CONSTRUCTIVE REVIEW THE FOLLOWING WEEK.

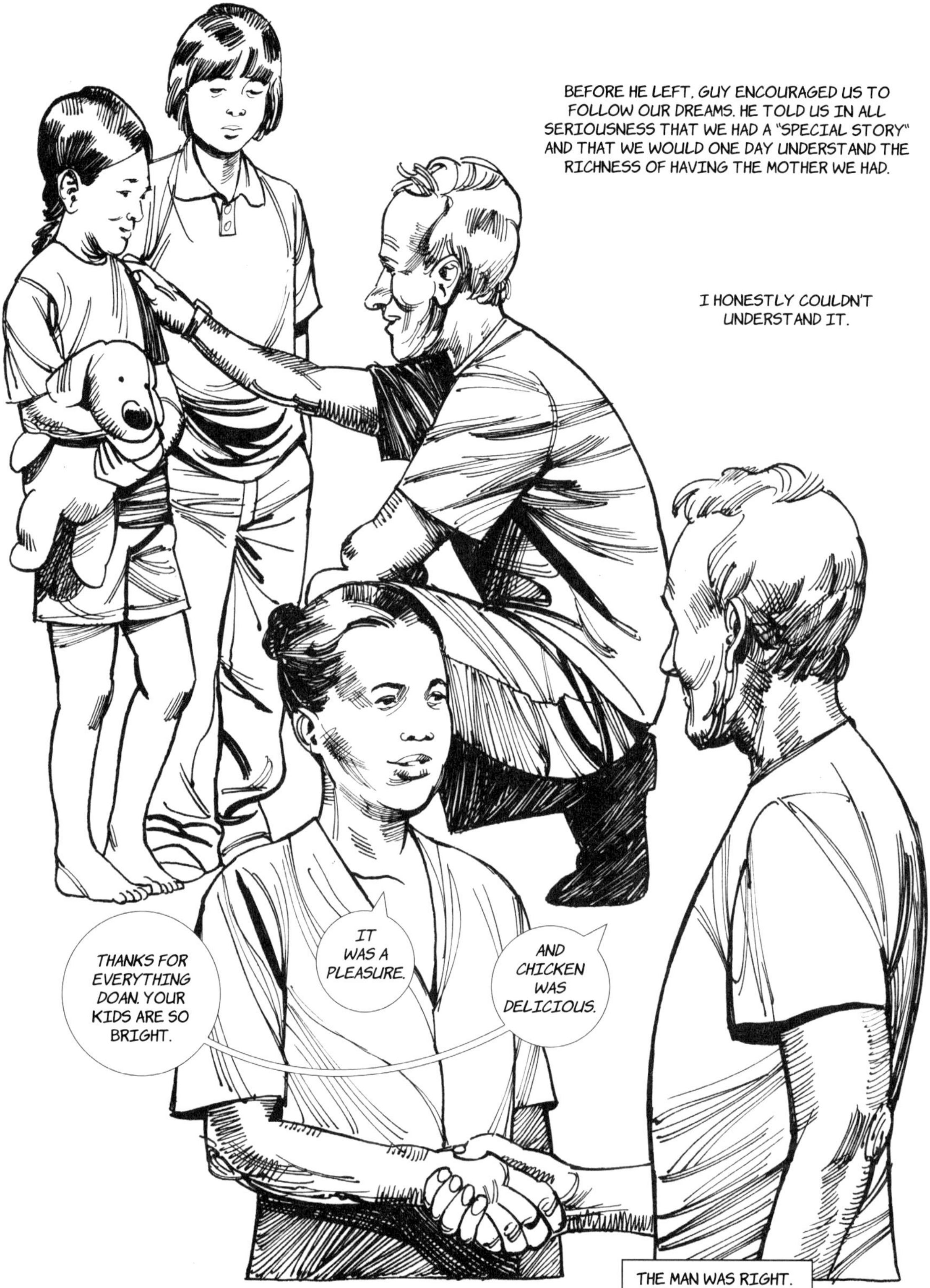
BEFORE HE LEFT, GUY ENCOURAGED US TO FOLLOW OUR DREAMS. HE TOLD US IN ALL SERIOUSNESS THAT WE HAD A "SPECIAL STORY" AND THAT WE WOULD ONE DAY UNDERSTAND THE RICHNESS OF HAVING THE MOTHER WE HAD.
I HONESTLY COULDN'T UNDERSTAND IT.
THANKS FOR EVERYTHING DOAN. YOUR KIDS ARE SO BRIGHT.
IT WAS A PLEASURE.
AND CHICKEN WAS DELICIOUS.
THE MAN WAS RIGHT. DE-LI-CIOUS.

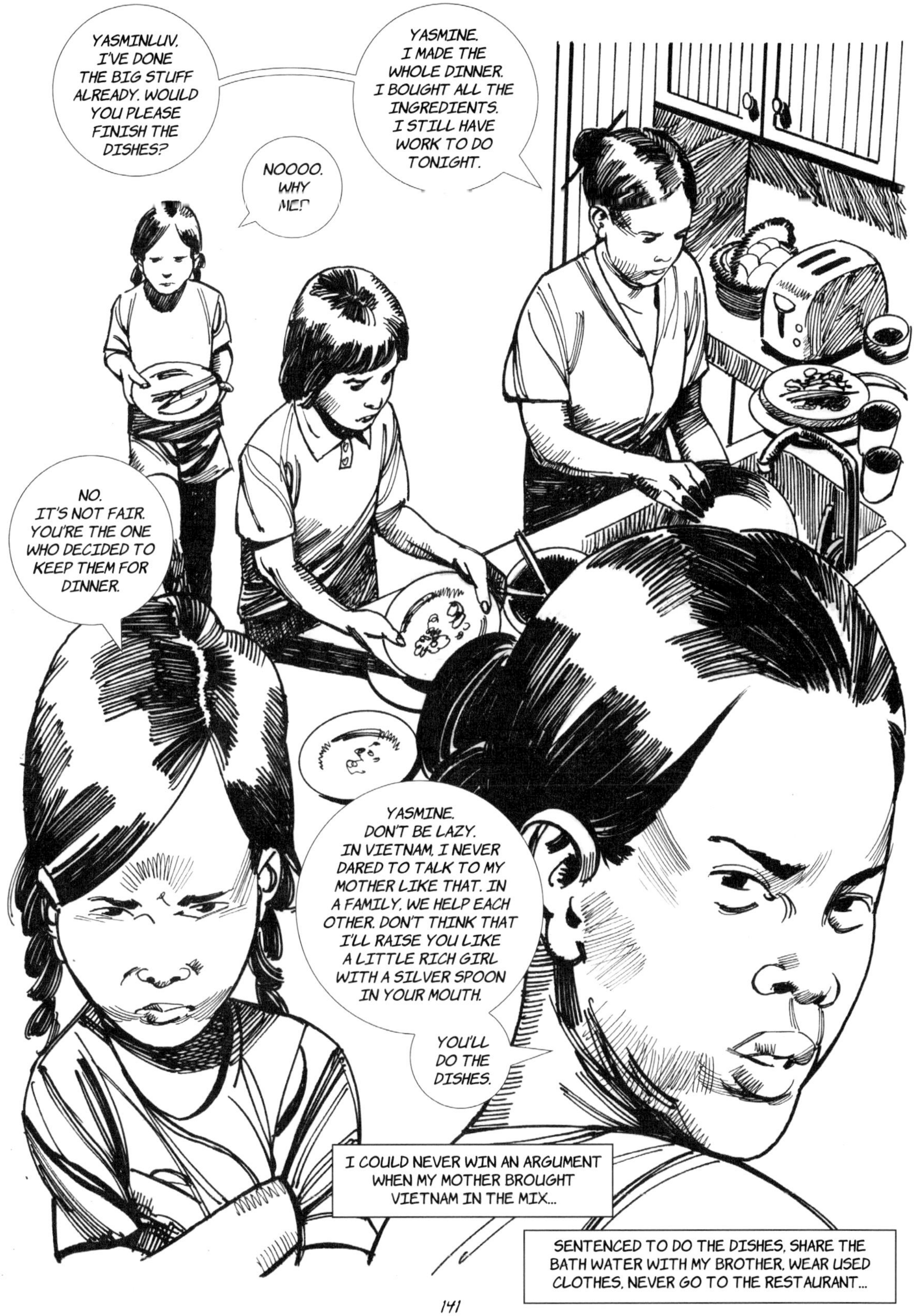
YASMINLUV, I'VE DONE THE BIG STUFF ALREADY. WOULD YOU PLEASE FINISH THE DISHES?
YASMINE. I MADE THE WHOLE DINNER. I BOUGHT ALL THE INGREDIENTS. I STILL HAVE WORK TO DO TONIGHT.
NOOOO. WHY ME?
NO. IT'S NOT FAIR. YOU'RE THE ONE WHO DECIDED TO KEEP THEM FOR DINNER.
YASMINE. DON'T BE LAZY. IN VIETNAM, I NEVER DARED TO TALK TO MY MOTHER LIKE THAT. IN A FAMILY, WE HELP EACH OTHER. DON'T THINK THAT I'LL RAISE YOU LIKE A LITTLE RICH GIRL WITH A SILVER SPOON IN YOUR MOUTH.
YOU'LL DO THE DISHES.
I COULD NEVER WIN AN ARGUMENT WHEN MY MOTHER BROUGHT VIETNAM IN THE MIX...
SENTENCED TO DO THE DISHES, SHARE THE BATH WATER WITH MY BROTHER, WEAR USED CLOTHES, NEVER GO TO THE RESTAURANT...

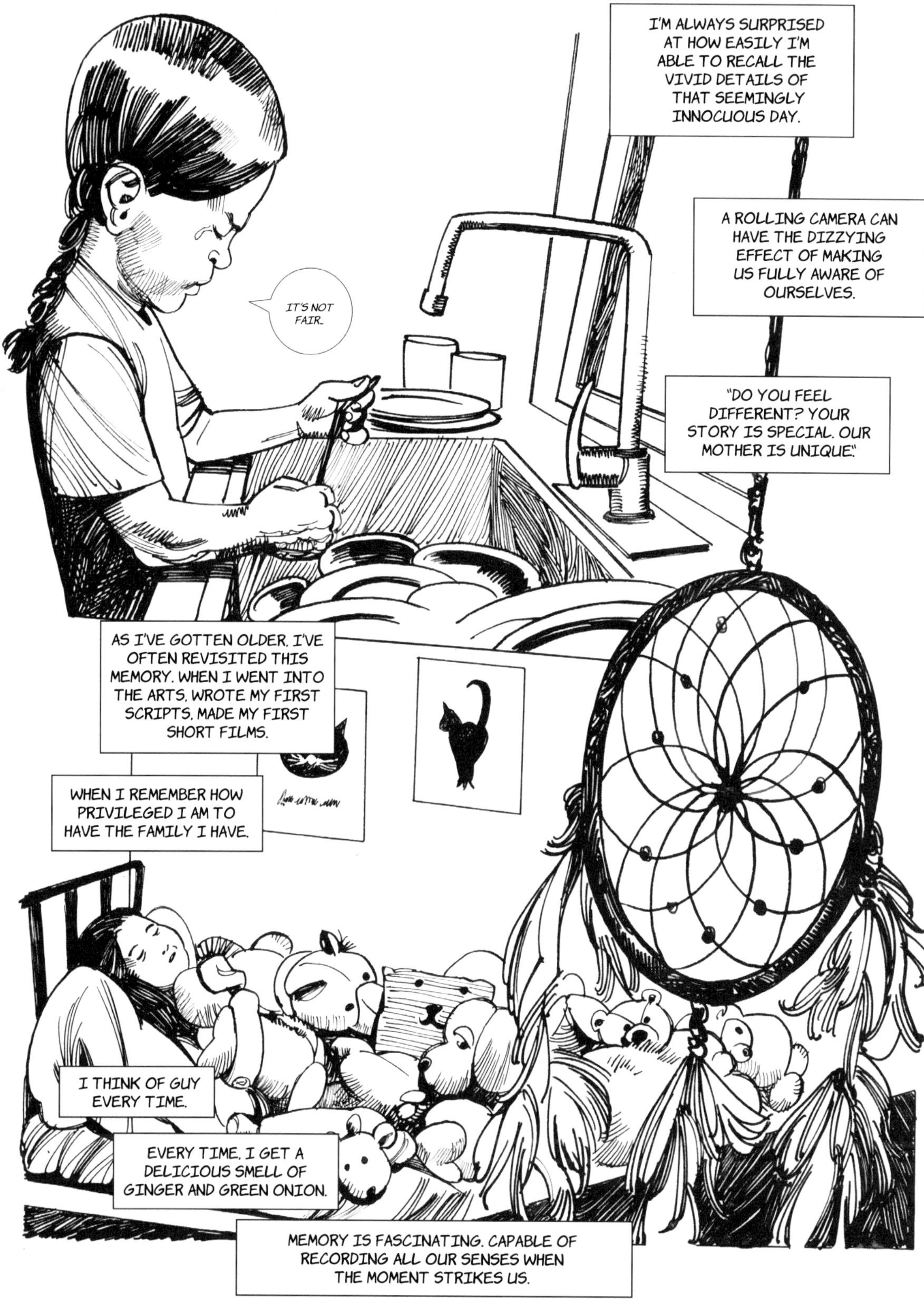
I'M ALWAYS SURPRISED AT HOW EASILY I'M ABLE TO RECALL THE VIVID DETAILS OF THAT SEEMINGLY INNOCUOUS DAY.
IT'S NOT FAIR...
A ROLLING CAMERA CAN HAVE THE DIZZYING EFFECT OF MAKING US FULLY AWARE OF OURSELVES.
"DO YOU FEEL DIFFERENT? YOUR STORY IS SPECIAL. OUR MOTHER IS UNIQUE."
AS I'VE GOTTEN OLDER, I'VE OFTEN REVISITED THIS MEMORY. WHEN I WENT INTO THE ARTS, WROTE MY FIRST SCRIPTS, MADE MY FIRST SHORT FILMS.
WHEN I REMEMBER HOW PRIVILEGED I AM TO HAVE THE FAMILY I HAVE.
I THINK OF GUY EVERY TIME.
EVERY TIME, I GET A DELICIOUS SMELL OF GINGER AND GREEN ONION.
MEMORY IS FASCINATING. CAPABLE OF RECORDING ALL OUR SENSES WHEN THE MOMENT STRIKES US.

CHAPITRE 2

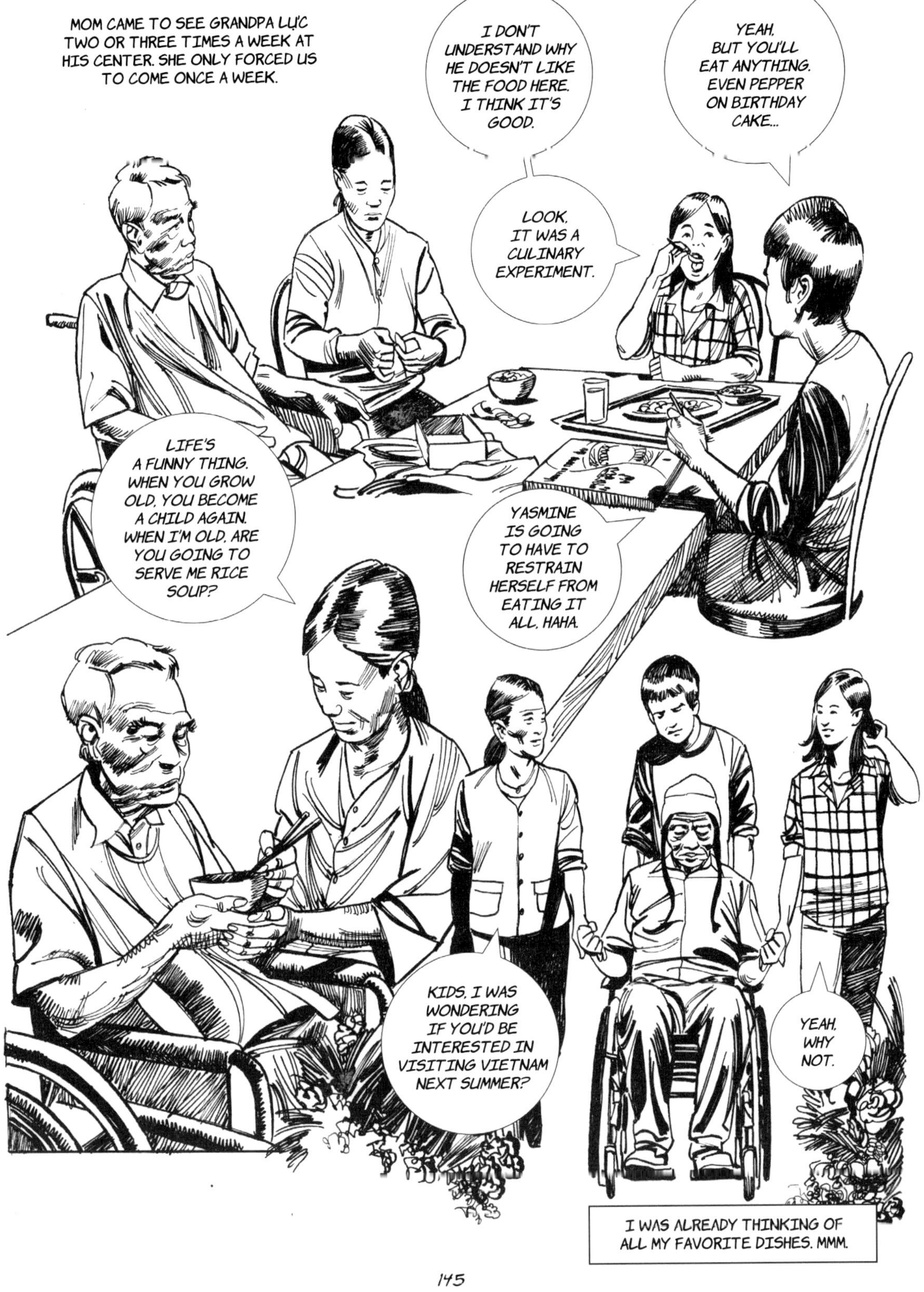
MOM CAME TO SEE GRANDPA LỰC TWO OR THREE TIMES A WEEK AT HIS CENTER. SHE ONLY FORCED US TO COME ONCE A WEEK.
I DON'T UNDERSTAND WHY HE DOESN'T LIKE THE FOOD HERE. I THINK IT'S GOOD.
YEAH, BUT YOU'LL EAT ANYTHING. EVEN PEPPER ON BIRTHDAY CAKE...
LOOK, IT WAS A CULINARY EXPERIMENT.
LIFE'S A FUNNY THING. WHEN YOU GROW OLD, YOU BECOME A CHILD AGAIN. WHEN I'M OLD, ARE YOU GOING TO SERVE ME RICE SOUP?
YASMINE IS GOING TO HAVE TO RESTRAIN HERSELF FROM EATING IT ALL, HAHA.
KIDS, I WAS WONDERING IF YOU'D BE INTERESTED IN VISITING VIETNAM NEXT SUMMER?
YEAH, WHY NOT.
I WAS ALREADY THINKING OF ALL MY FAVORITE DISHES. MMM.

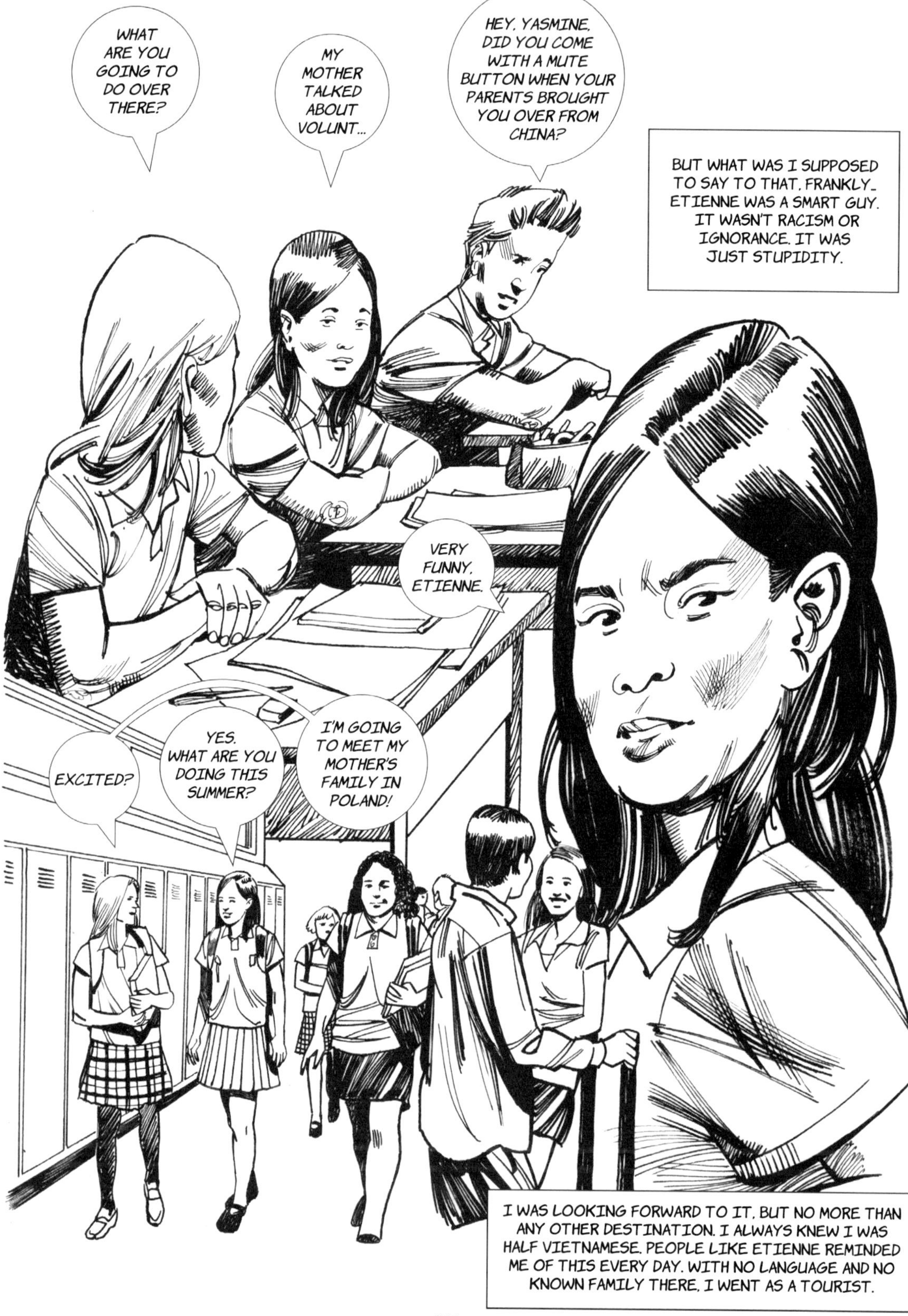
WHAT ARE YOU GOING TO DO OVER THERE?
MY MOTHER TALKED ABOUT VOLUNT...
HEY, YASMINE, DID YOU COME WITH A MUTE BUTTON WHEN YOUR PARENTS BROUGHT YOU OVER FROM CHINA?
BUT WHAT WAS I SUPPOSED TO SAY TO THAT, FRANKLY... ETIENNE WAS A SMART GUY. IT WASN'T RACISM OR IGNORANCE. IT WAS JUST STUPIDITY.
VERY FUNNY, ETIENNE.
EXCITED?
YES. WHAT ARE YOU DOING THIS SUMMER?
I'M GOING TO MEET MY MOTHER'S FAMILY IN POLAND!
I WAS LOOKING FORWARD TO IT, BUT NO MORE THAN ANY OTHER DESTINATION. I ALWAYS KNEW I WAS HALF VIETNAMESE. PEOPLE LIKE ETIENNE REMINDED ME OF THIS EVERY DAY. WITH NO LANGUAGE AND NO KNOWN FAMILY THERE, I WENT AS A TOURIST.

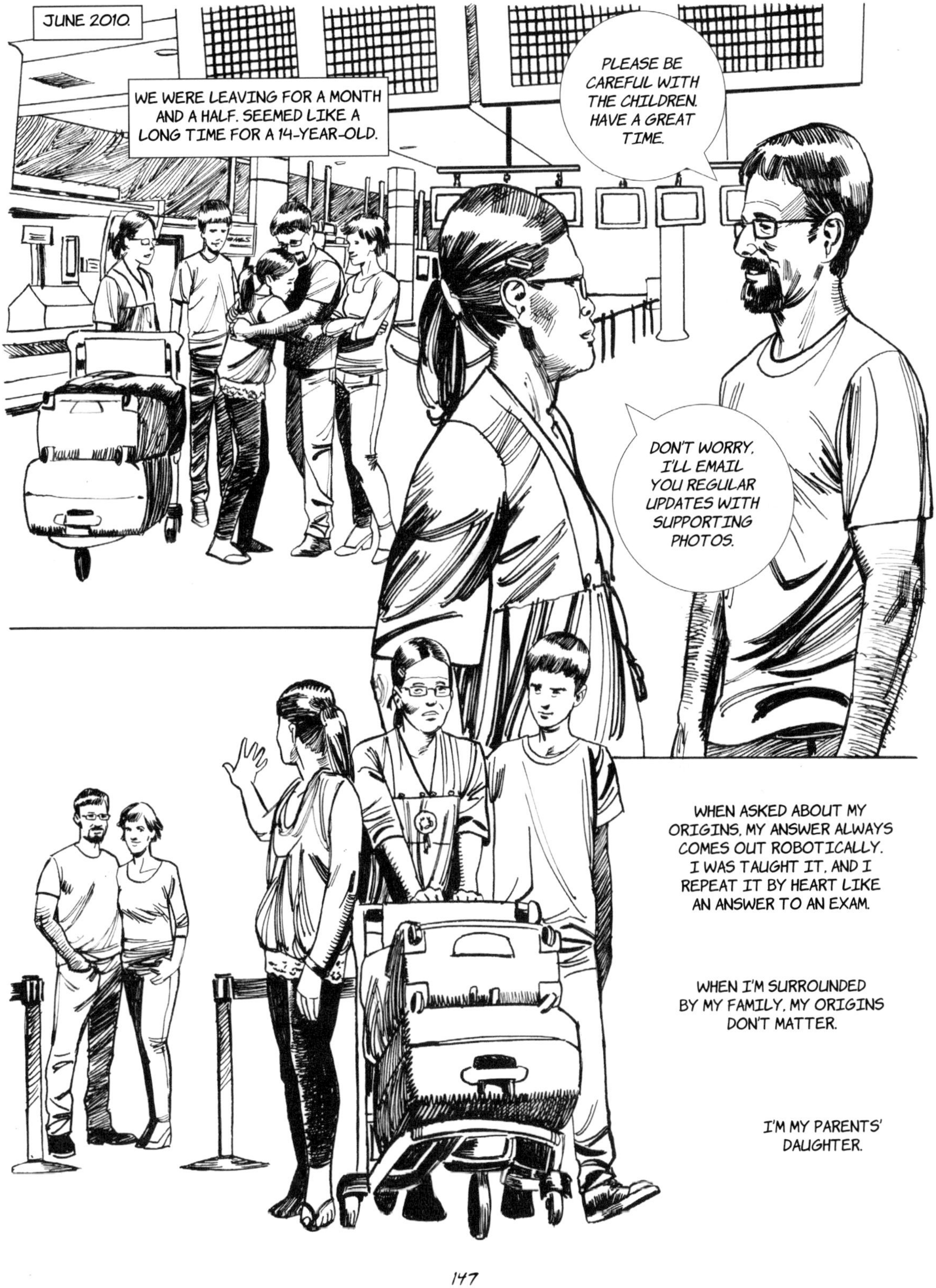
JUNE 2010.
WE WERE LEAVING FOR A MONTH AND A HALF. SEEMED LIKE A LONG TIME FOR A 14-YEAR-OLD.
PLEASE BE CAREFUL WITH THE CHILDREN. HAVE A GREAT TIME.
DON'T WORRY, I'LL EMAIL YOU REGULAR UPDATES WITH SUPPORTING PHOTOS.
WHEN ASKED ABOUT MY ORIGINS, MY ANSWER ALWAYS COMES OUT ROBOTICALLY. I WAS TAUGHT IT, AND I REPEAT IT BY HEART LIKE AN ANSWER TO AN EXAM.
WHEN I'M SURROUNDED BY MY FAMILY, MY ORIGINS DON'T MATTER.
I'M MY PARENTS' DAUGHTER.

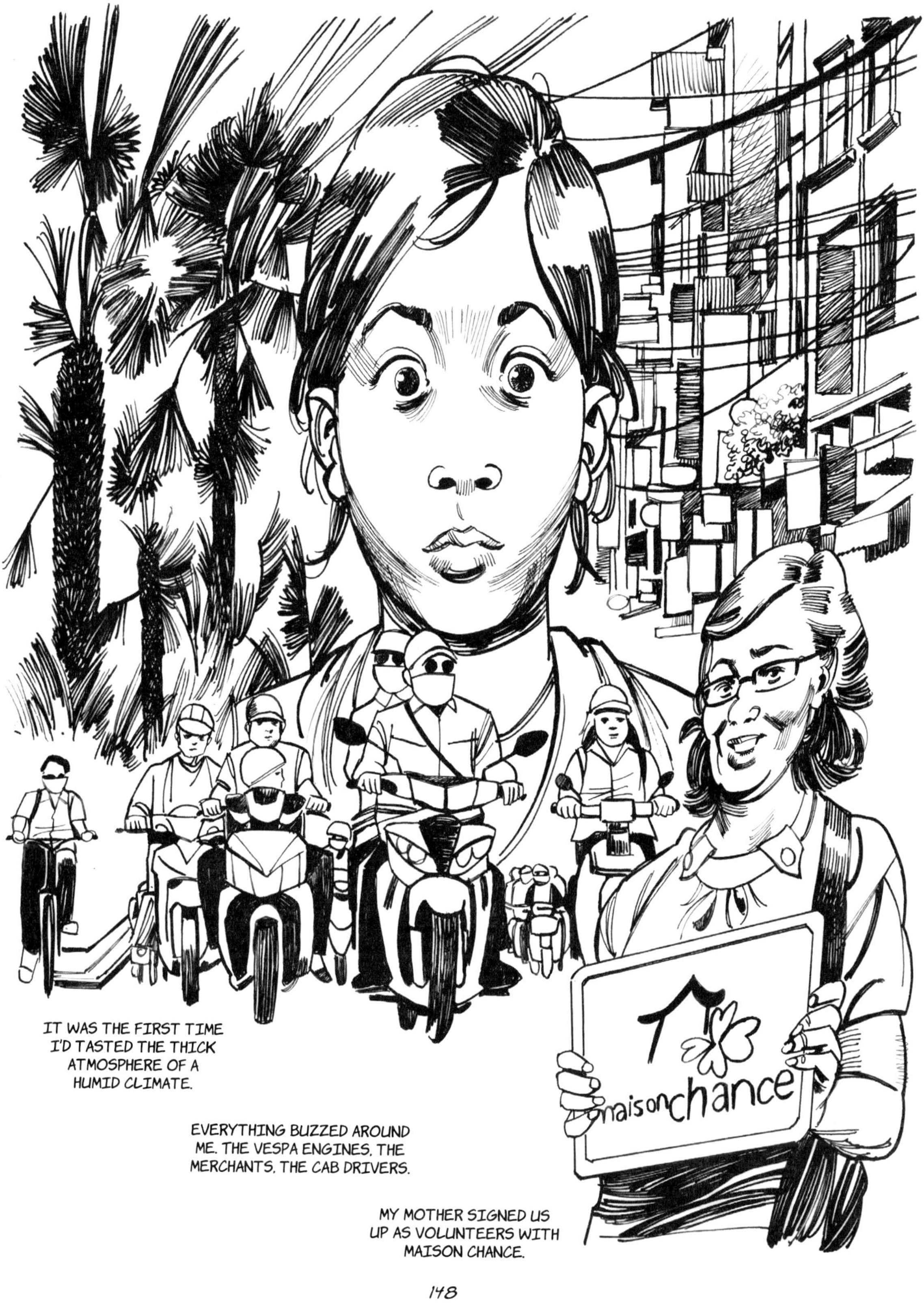
IT WAS THE FIRST TIME I'D TASTED THE THICK ATMOSPHERE OF A HUMID CLIMATE.
EVERYTHING BUZZED AROUND ME. THE VESPA ENGINES, THE MERCHANTS, THE CAB DRIVERS.
maisonchance
MY MOTHER SIGNED US UP AS VOLUNTEERS WITH MAISON CHANCE.

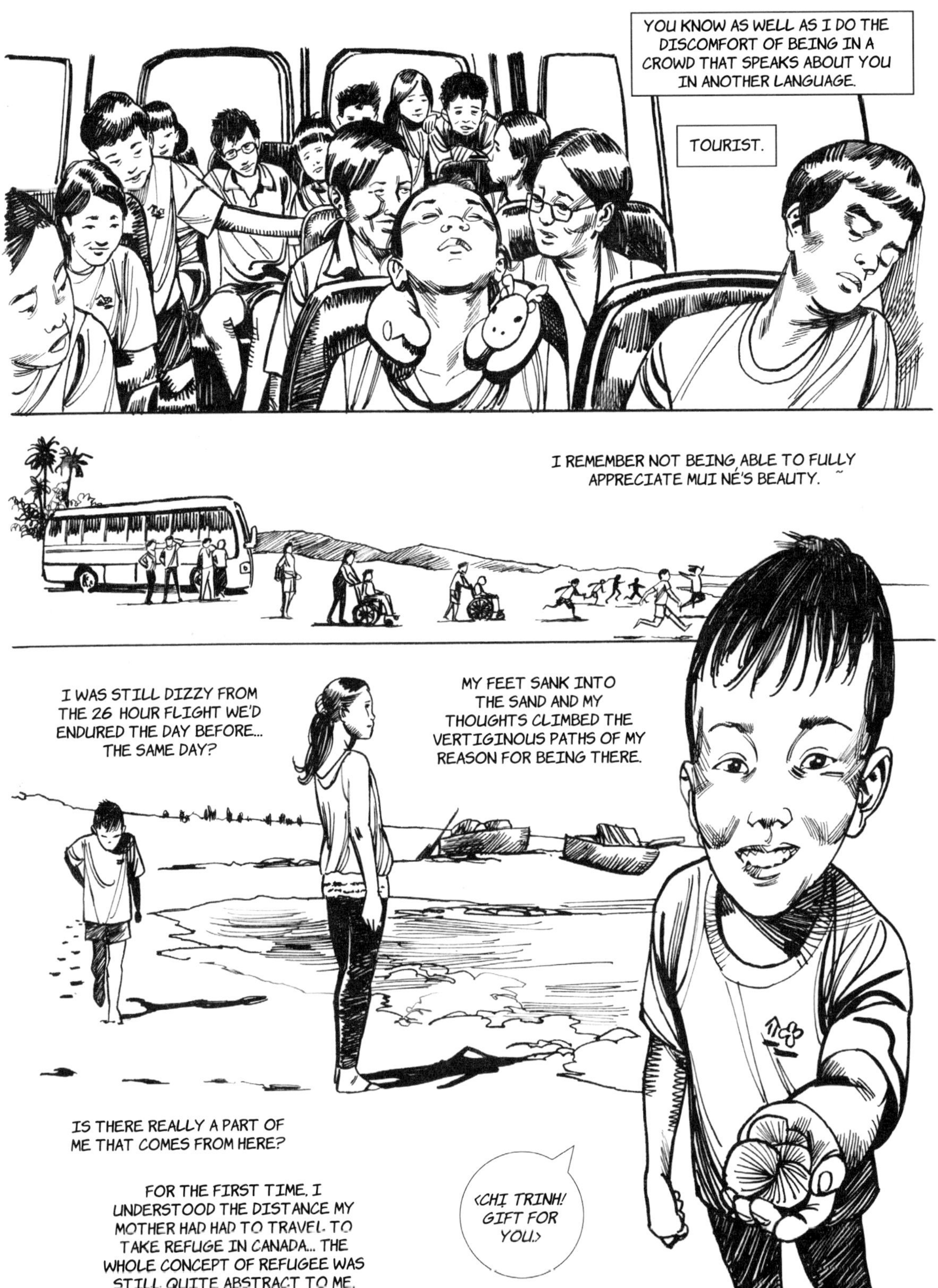
YOU KNOW AS WELL AS I DO THE DISCOMFORT OF BEING IN A CROWD THAT SPEAKS ABOUT YOU IN ANOTHER LANGUAGE.
TOURIST.
I REMEMBER NOT BEING ABLE TO FULLY APPRECIATE MUI NÉ'S BEAUTY.
I WAS STILL DIZZY FROM THE 26 HOUR FLIGHT WE'D ENDURED THE DAY BEFORE... THE SAME DAY?
MY FEET SANK INTO THE SAND AND MY THOUGHTS CLIMBED THE VERTIGINOUS PATHS OF MY REASON FOR BEING THERE.
IS THERE REALLY A PART OF ME THAT COMES FROM HERE?
FOR THE FIRST TIME, I UNDERSTOOD THE DISTANCE MY MOTHER HAD HAD TO TRAVEL TO TAKE REFUGE IN CANADA... THE WHOLE CONCEPT OF REFUGEE WAS STILL QUITE ABSTRACT TO ME.
<CHỊ TRINH! GIFT FOR YOU.>

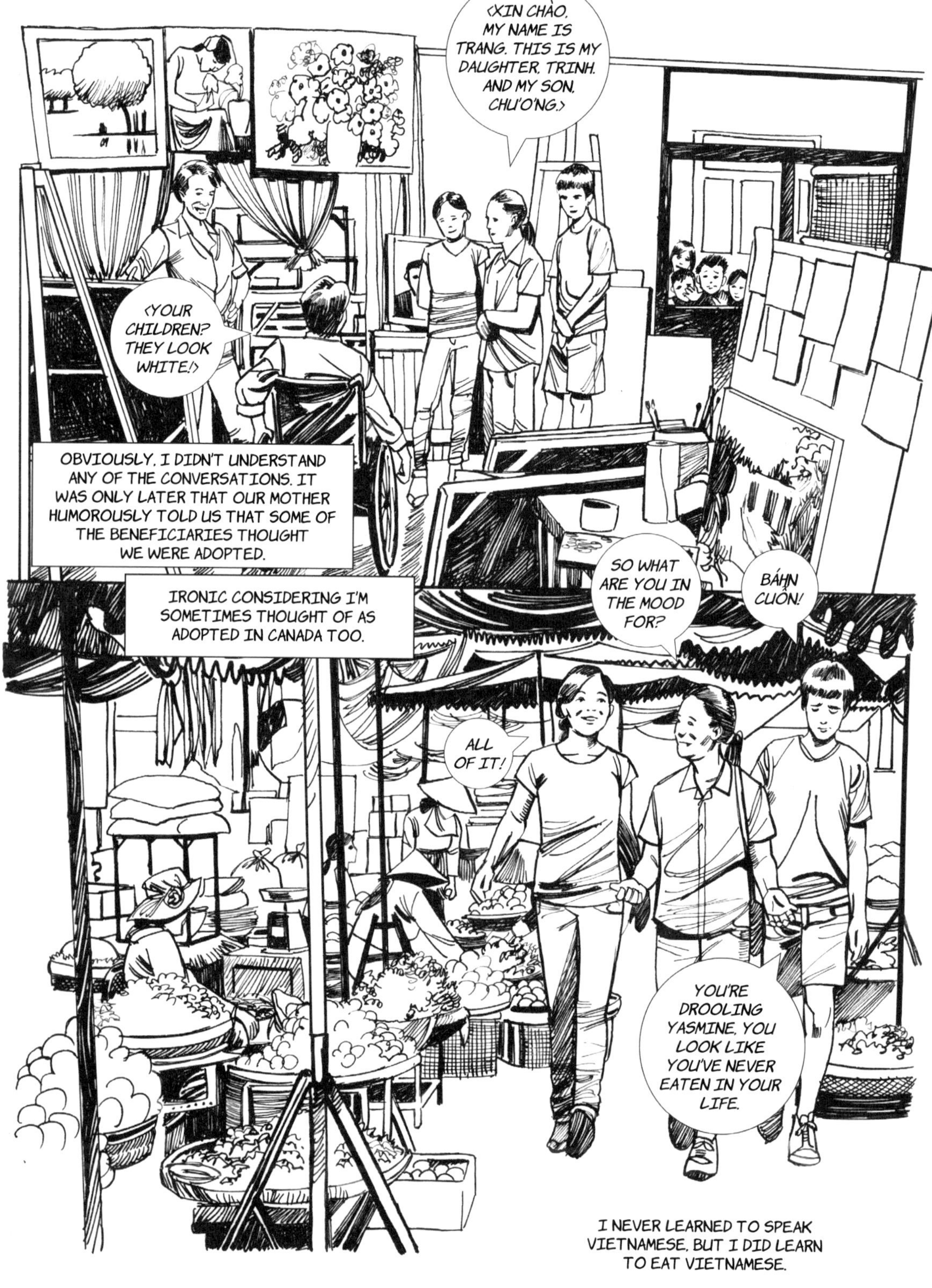
<XIN CHÀO, MY NAME IS TRANG. THIS IS MY DAUGHTER, TRINH. AND MY SON, CHƯƠNG.>
<YOUR CHILDREN? THEY LOOK WHITE!>
OBVIOUSLY, I DIDN'T UNDERSTAND ANY OF THE CONVERSATIONS. IT WAS ONLY LATER THAT OUR MOTHER HUMOROUSLY TOLD US THAT SOME OF THE BENEFICIARIES THOUGHT WE WERE ADOPTED.
IRONIC CONSIDERING I'M SOMETIMES THOUGHT OF AS ADOPTED IN CANADA TOO.
SO WHAT ARE YOU IN THE MOOD FOR?
BÁHN CUỐN!
ALL OF IT!
YOU'RE DROOLING YASMINE. YOU LOOK LIKE YOU'VE NEVER EATEN IN YOUR LIFE.
I NEVER LEARNED TO SPEAK VIETNAMESE, BUT I DID LEARN TO EAT VIETNAMESE.

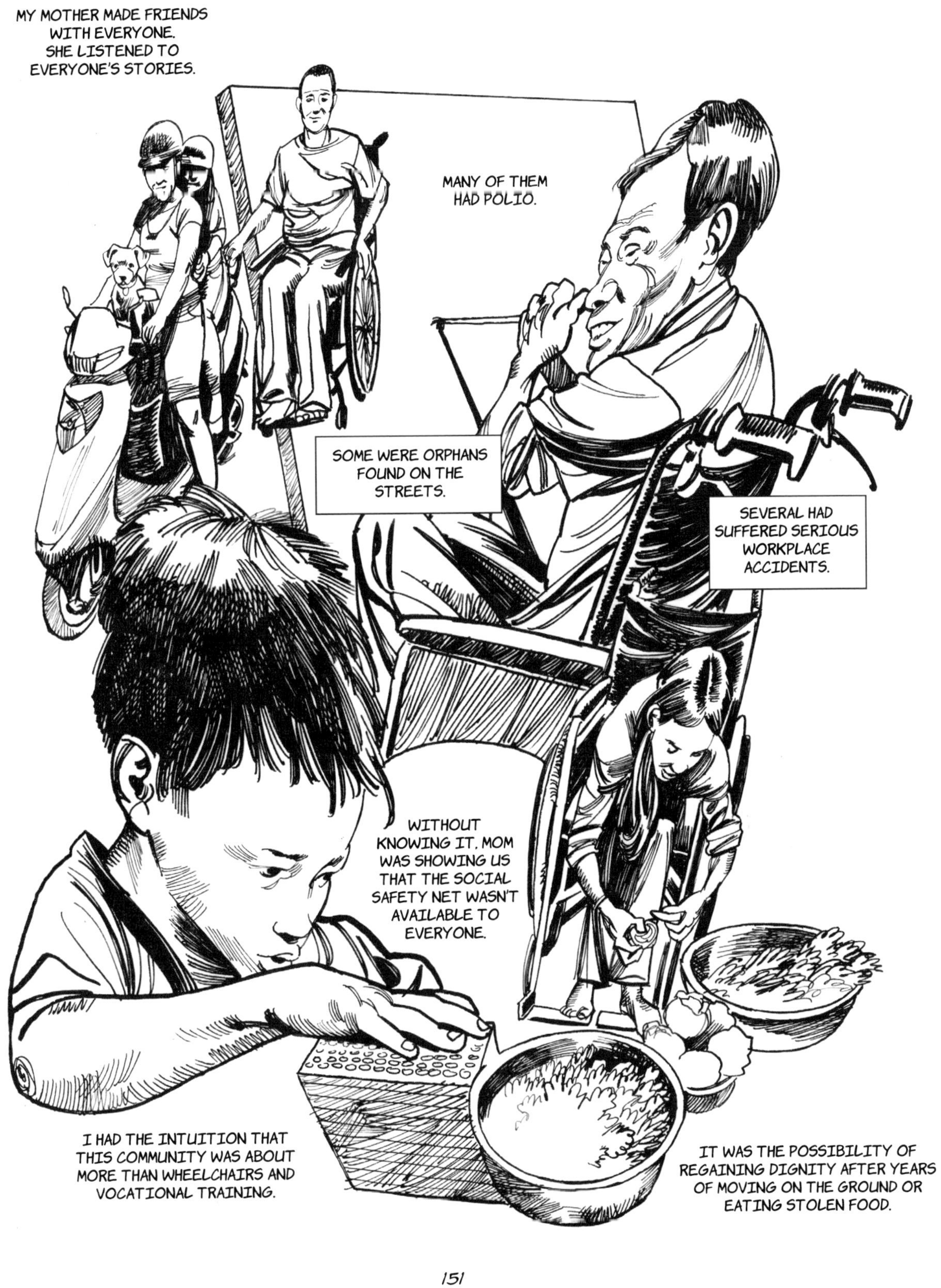
MY MOTHER MADE FRIENDS WITH EVERYONE. SHE LISTENED TO EVERYONE'S STORIES.
MANY OF THEM HAD POLIO.
SOME WERE ORPHANS FOUND ON THE STREETS.
SEVERAL HAD SUFFERED SERIOUS WORKPLACE ACCIDENTS.
WITHOUT KNOWING IT, MOM WAS SHOWING US THAT THE SOCIAL SAFETY NET WASN'T AVAILABLE TO EVERYONE.
I HAD THE INTUITION THAT THIS COMMUNITY WAS ABOUT MORE THAN WHEELCHAIRS AND VOCATIONAL TRAINING.
IT WAS THE POSSIBILITY OF REGAINING DIGNITY AFTER YEARS OF MOVING ON THE GROUND OR EATING STOLEN FOOD.

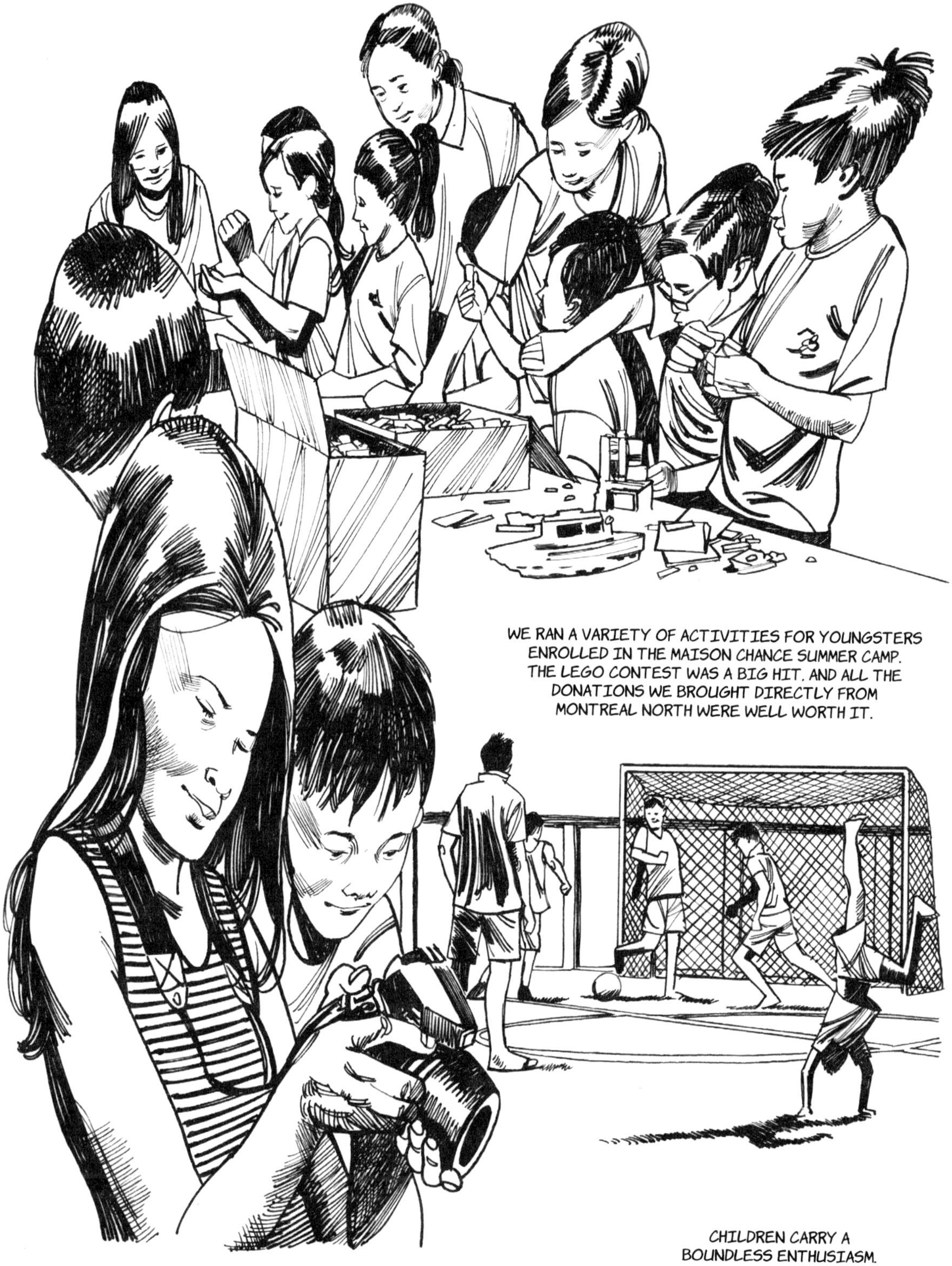
WE RAN A VARIETY OF ACTIVITIES FOR YOUNGSTERS ENROLLED IN THE MAISON CHANCE SUMMER CAMP. THE LEGO CONTEST WAS A BIG HIT, AND ALL THE DONATIONS WE BROUGHT DIRECTLY FROM MONTREAL NORTH WERE WELL WORTH IT.

AS THE WEEKS WENT BY, I CAME TO UNDERSTAND THAT LANGUAGE WASN'T NECESSARY FOR COMMUNICATION.

I'VE COME TO LOVE THESE CURIOUS LITTLE CREATURES.

CHILDREN CARRY A BOUNDLESS ENTHUSIASM. I COULD SEE IN THEM THE CHILDHOOD I MIGHT HAVE HAD IF I'D BEEN BORN ON THE OTHER SIDE OF MY HERITAGE.

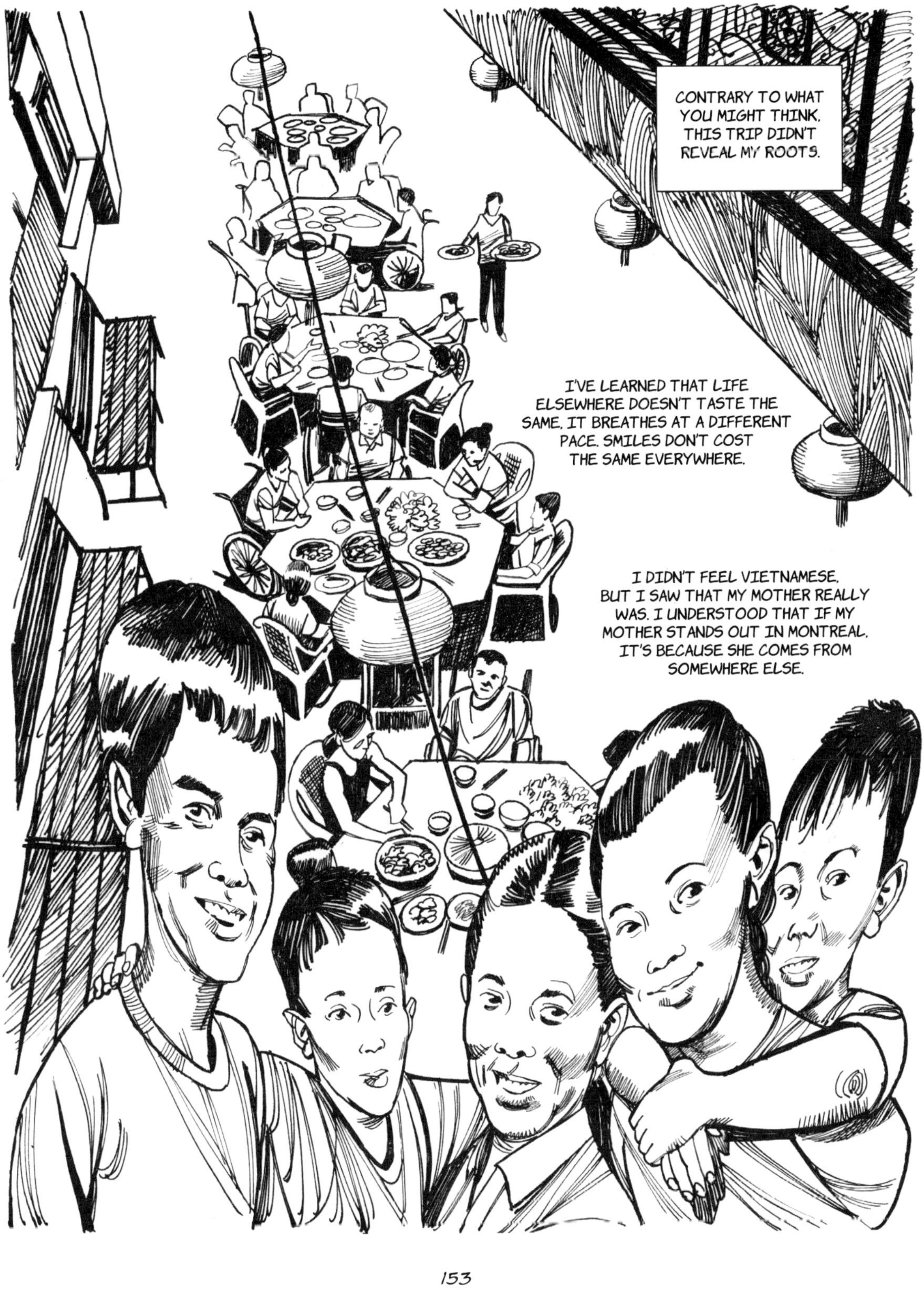
CONTRARY TO WHAT YOU MIGHT THINK, THIS TRIP DIDN'T REVEAL MY ROOTS.
I'VE LEARNED THAT LIFE ELSEWHERE DOESN'T TASTE THE SAME. IT BREATHES AT A DIFFERENT PACE. SMILES DON'T COST THE SAME EVERYWHERE.
I DIDN'T FEEL VIETNAMESE, BUT I SAW THAT MY MOTHER REALLY WAS. I UNDERSTOOD THAT IF MY MOTHER STANDS OUT IN MONTREAL, IT'S BECAUSE SHE COMES FROM SOMEWHERE ELSE.

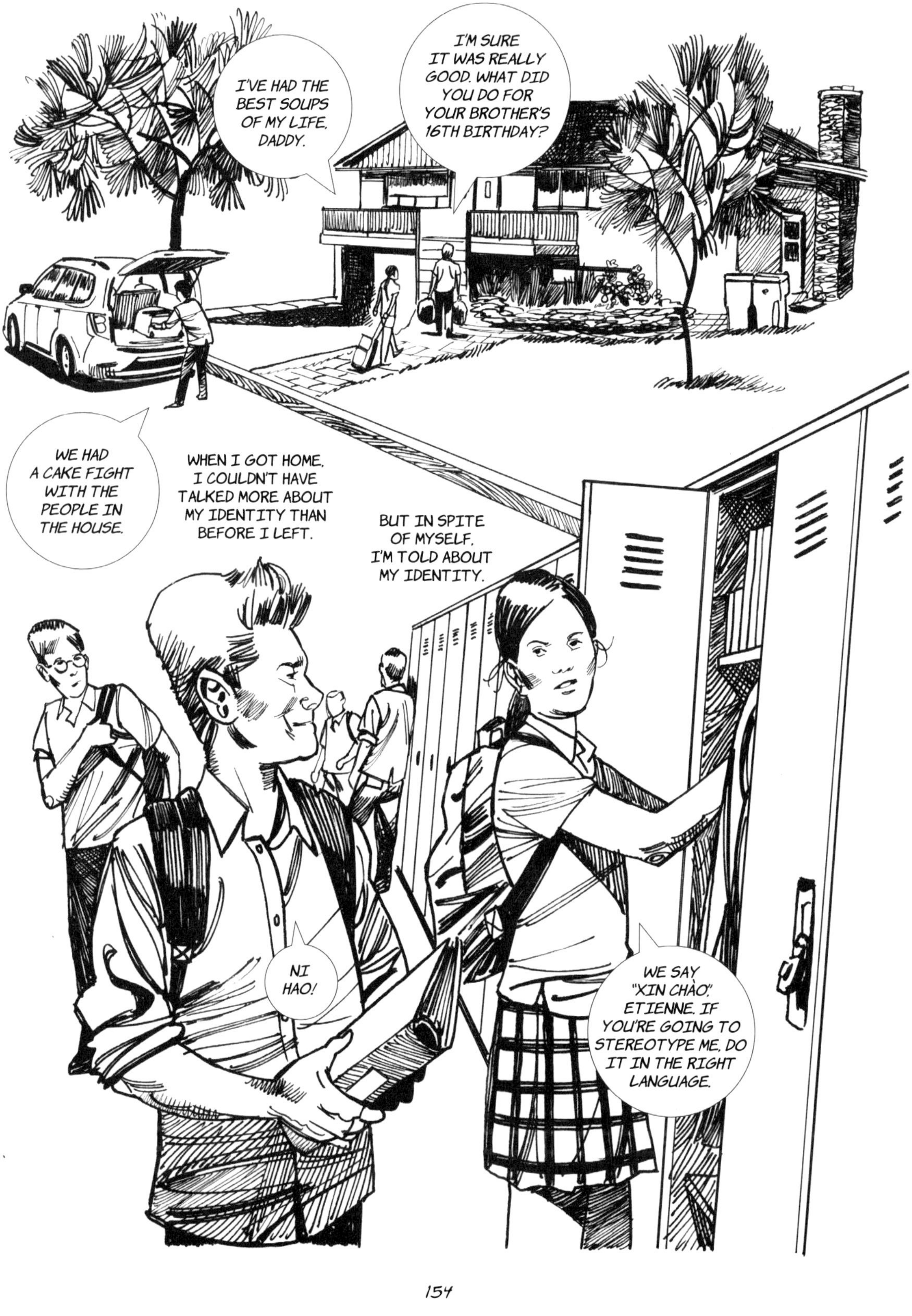
I'VE HAD THE BEST SOUPS OF MY LIFE, DADDY.
I'M SURE IT WAS REALLY GOOD. WHAT DID YOU DO FOR YOUR BROTHER'S 16TH BIRTHDAY?
WE HAD A CAKE FIGHT WITH THE PEOPLE IN THE HOUSE.
WHEN I GOT HOME, I COULDN'T HAVE TALKED MORE ABOUT MY IDENTITY THAN BEFORE I LEFT.
BUT IN SPITE OF MYSELF, I'M TOLD ABOUT MY IDENTITY.
NI HAO!
WE SAY "XIN CHÀO", ETIENNE. IF YOU'RE GOING TO STEREOTYPE ME, DO IT IN THE RIGHT LANGUAGE.

CHAPTER 3

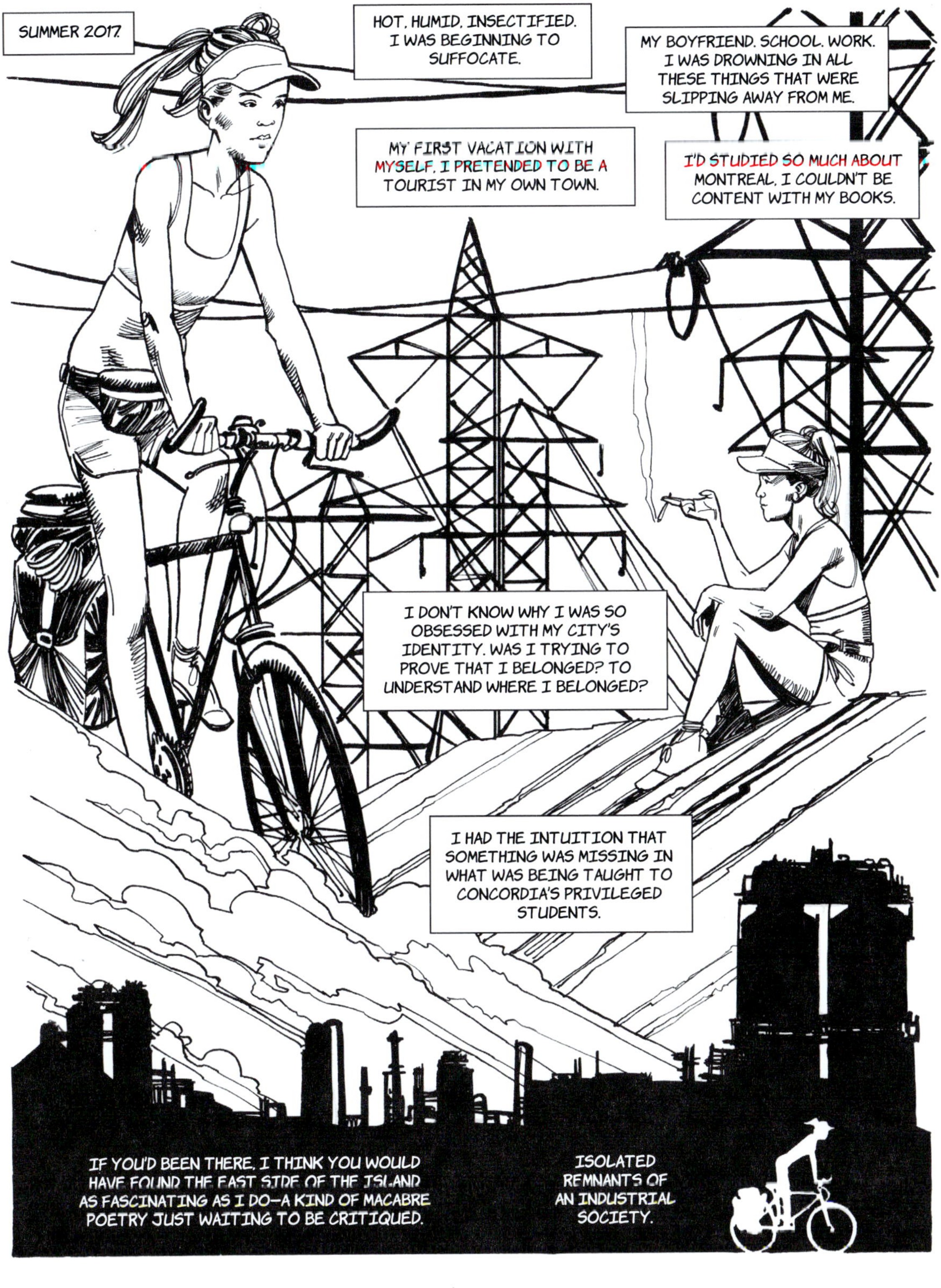
SUMMER 2017.
HOT, HUMID, INSECTIFIED. I WAS BEGINNING TO SUFFOCATE.
MY BOYFRIEND. SCHOOL. WORK. I WAS DROWNING IN ALL THESE THINGS THAT WERE SLIPPING AWAY FROM ME.
MY FIRST VACATION WITH MYSELF. I PRETENDED TO BE A TOURIST IN MY OWN TOWN.
I'D STUDIED SO MUCH ABOUT MONTREAL, I COULDN'T BE CONTENT WITH MY BOOKS.
I DON'T KNOW WHY I WAS SO OBSESSED WITH MY CITY'S IDENTITY. WAS I TRYING TO PROVE THAT I BELONGED? TO UNDERSTAND WHERE I BELONGED?
I HAD THE INTUITION THAT SOMETHING WAS MISSING IN WHAT WAS BEING TAUGHT TO CONCORDIA'S PRIVILEGED STUDENTS.
IF YOU'D BEEN THERE, I THINK YOU WOULD HAVE FOUND THE EAST SIDE OF THE ISLAND AS FASCINATING AS I DO—A KIND OF MACABRE POETRY JUST WAITING TO BE CRITIQUED.
ISOLATED REMNANTS OF AN INDUSTRIAL SOCIETY.

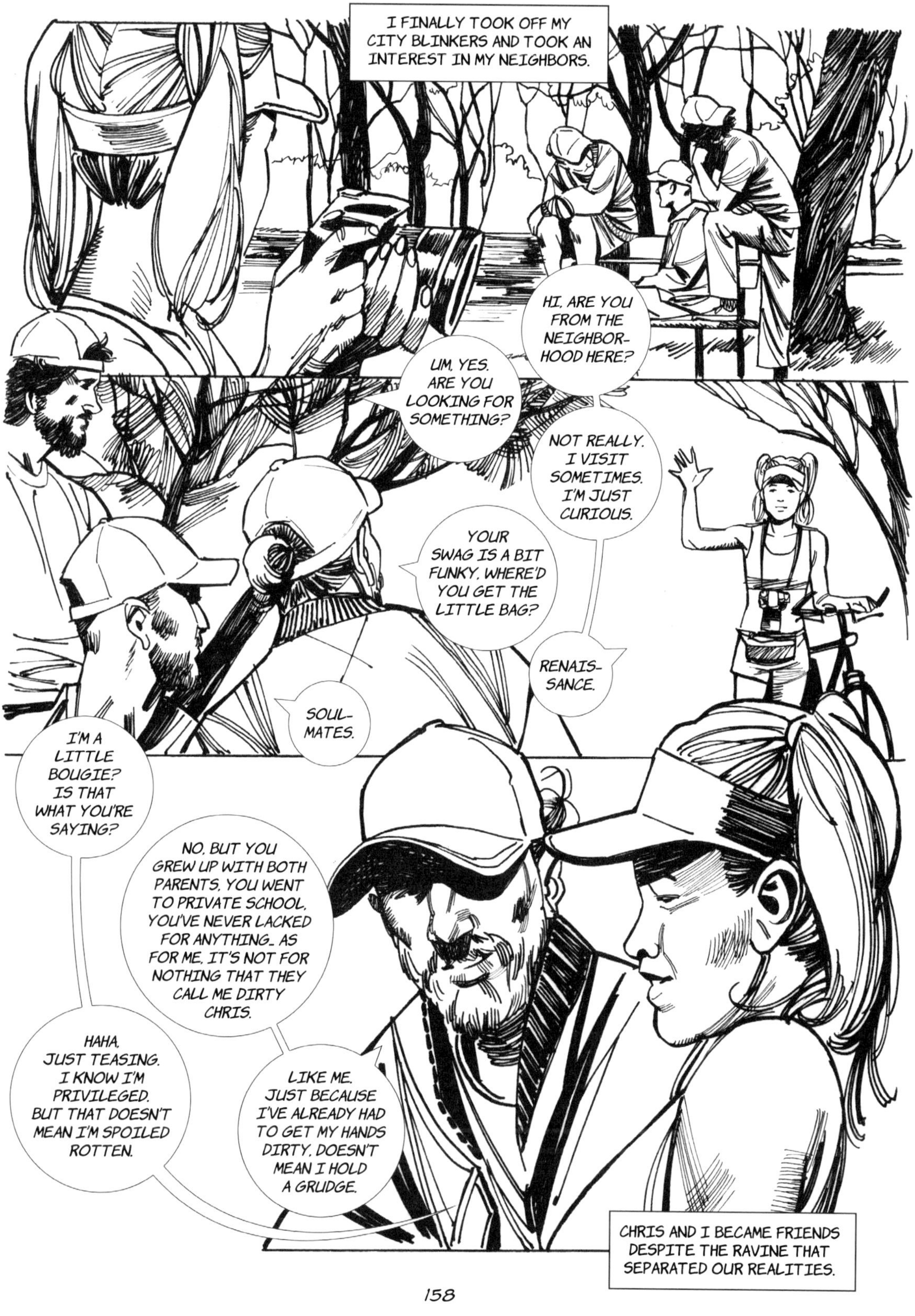
I FINALLY TOOK OFF MY CITY BLINKERS AND TOOK AN INTEREST IN MY NEIGHBORS.
HI, ARE YOU FROM THE NEIGHBOR-HOOD HERE?
UM, YES. ARE YOU LOOKING FOR SOMETHING?
NOT REALLY. I VISIT SOMETIMES. I'M JUST CURIOUS.
YOUR SWAG IS A BIT FUNKY, WHERE'D YOU GET THE LITTLE BAG?
RENAIS-SANCE.
SOUL-MATES.
I'M A LITTLE BOUGIE? IS THAT WHAT YOU'RE SAYING?
NO, BUT YOU GREW UP WITH BOTH PARENTS, YOU WENT TO PRIVATE SCHOOL, YOU'VE NEVER LACKED FOR ANYTHING... AS FOR ME, IT'S NOT FOR NOTHING THAT THEY CALL ME DIRTY CHRIS.
HAHA, JUST TEASING. I KNOW I'M PRIVILEGED. BUT THAT DOESN'T MEAN I'M SPOILED ROTTEN.
LIKE ME. JUST BECAUSE I'VE ALREADY HAD TO GET MY HANDS DIRTY, DOESN'T MEAN I HOLD A GRUDGE.
CHRIS AND I BECAME FRIENDS DESPITE THE RAVINE THAT SEPARATED OUR REALITIES.

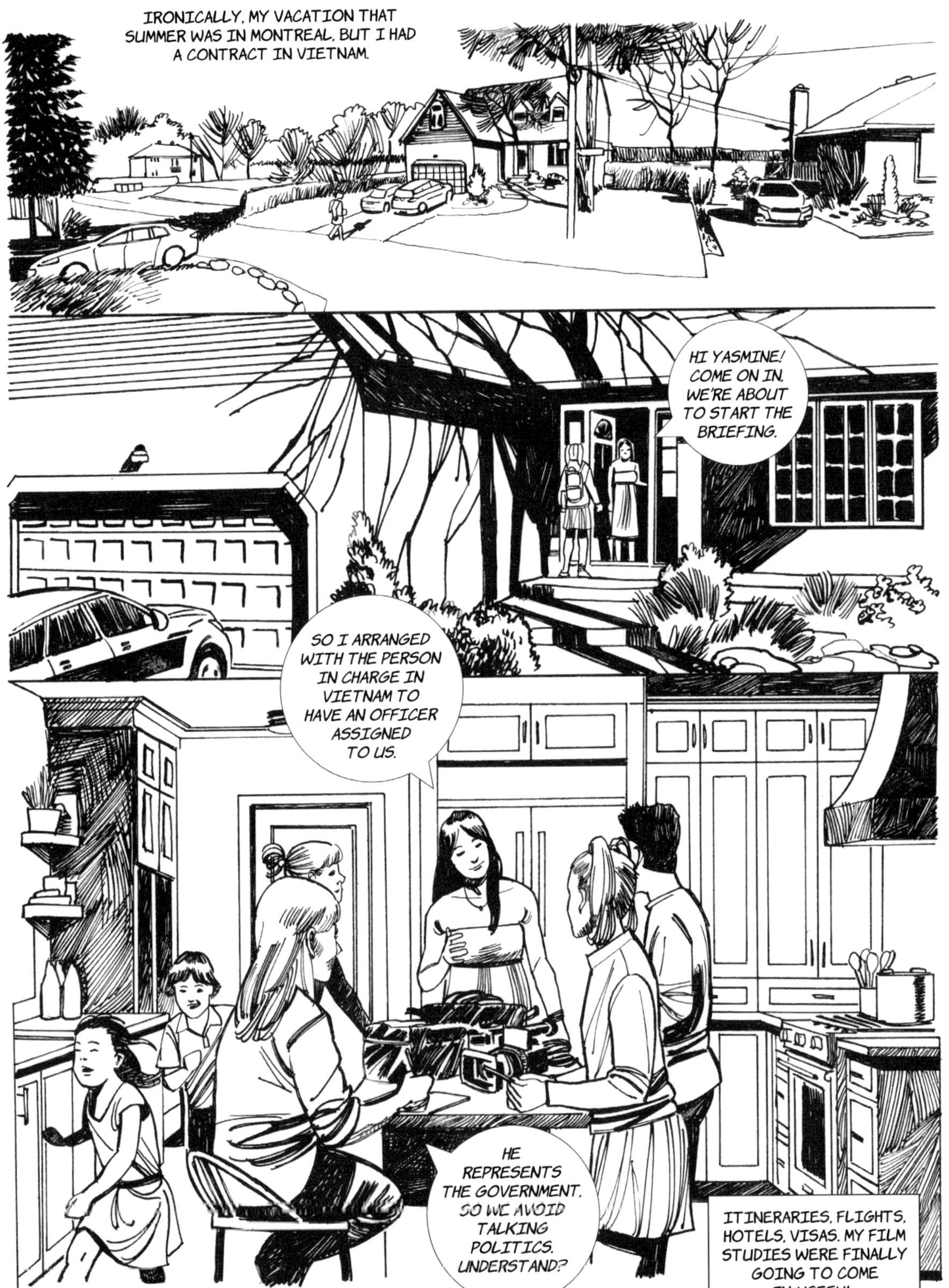
IRONICALLY, MY VACATION THAT SUMMER WAS IN MONTREAL, BUT I HAD A CONTRACT IN VIETNAM.
HI YASMINE! COME ON IN, WE'RE ABOUT TO START THE BRIEFING.
SO I ARRANGED WITH THE PERSON IN CHARGE IN VIETNAM TO HAVE AN OFFICER ASSIGNED TO US.
HE REPRESENTS THE GOVERNMENT, SO WE AVOID TALKING POLITICS. UNDERSTAND?
ITINERARIES, FLIGHTS, HOTELS, VISAS. MY FILM STUDIES WERE FINALLY GOING TO COME IN USEFUL.

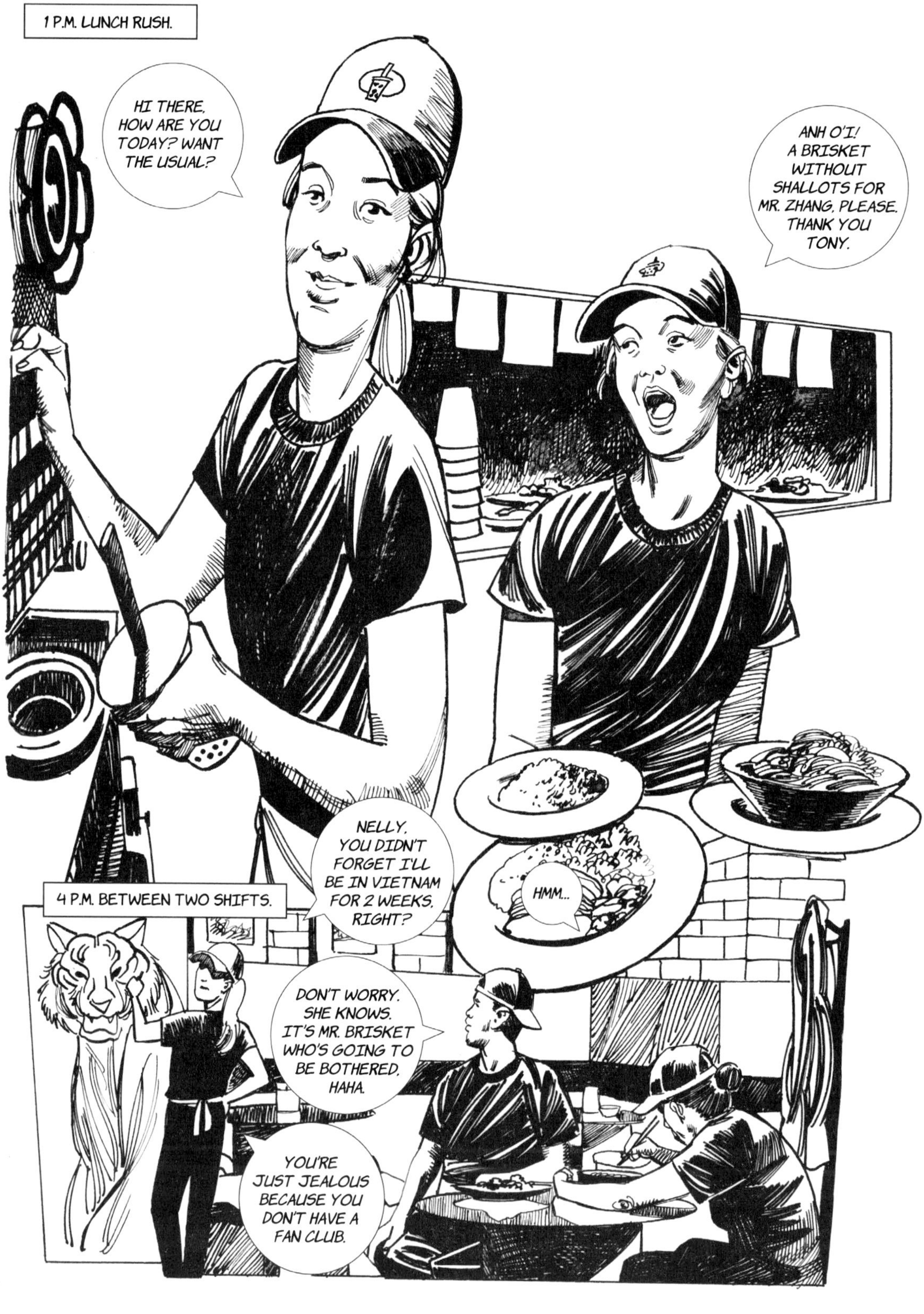
1 P.M. LUNCH RUSH.
HI THERE. HOW ARE YOU TODAY? WANT THE USUAL?
ANH O'I! A BRISKET WITHOUT SHALLOTS FOR MR. ZHANG, PLEASE. THANK YOU TONY.
HMM...
4 P.M. BETWEEN TWO SHIFTS.
NELLY. YOU DIDN'T FORGET I'LL BE IN VIETNAM FOR 2 WEEKS, RIGHT?
DON'T WORRY. SHE KNOWS. IT'S MR. BRISKET WHO'S GOING TO BE BOTHERED, HAHA.
YOU'RE JUST JEALOUS BECAUSE YOU DON'T HAVE A FAN CLUB.

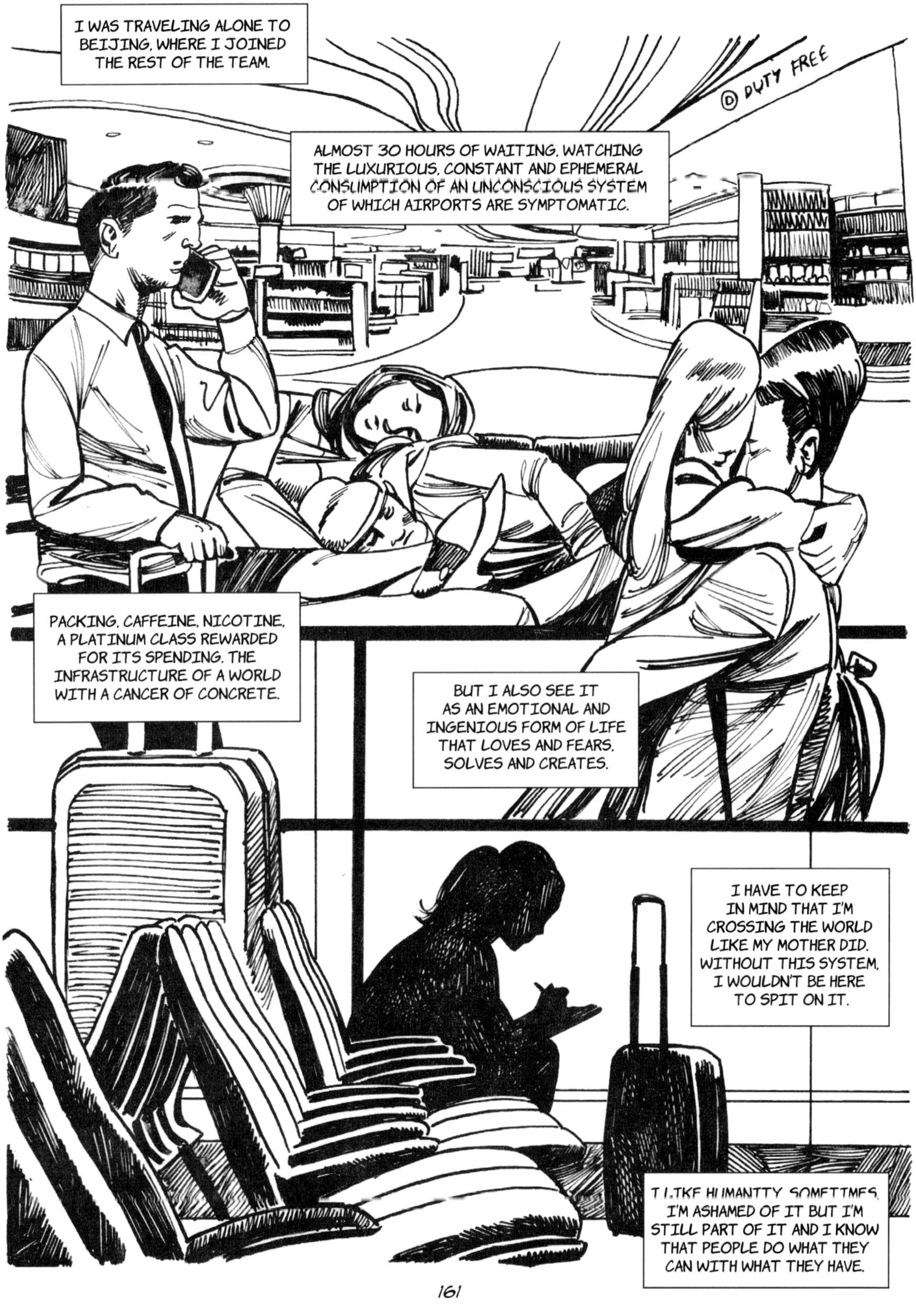
I WAS TRAVELING ALONE TO BEIJING, WHERE I JOINED THE REST OF THE TEAM.
DUTY FREE
ALMOST 30 HOURS OF WAITING, WATCHING THE LUXURIOUS, CONSTANT AND EPHEMERAL CONSUMPTION OF AN UNCONSCIOUS SYSTEM OF WHICH AIRPORTS ARE SYMPTOMATIC.
PACKING, CAFFEINE, NICOTINE, A PLATINUM CLASS REWARDED FOR ITS SPENDING. THE INFRASTRUCTURE OF A WORLD WITH A CANCER OF CONCRETE.
BUT I ALSO SEE IT AS AN EMOTIONAL AND INGENIOUS FORM OF LIFE THAT LOVES AND FEARS, SOLVES AND CREATES.
I HAVE TO KEEP IN MIND THAT I'M CROSSING THE WORLD LIKE MY MOTHER DID. WITHOUT THIS SYSTEM, I WOULDN'T BE HERE TO SPIT ON IT.
I LIKE HUMANITY SOMETIMES. I'M ASHAMED OF IT BUT I'M STILL PART OF IT AND I KNOW THAT PEOPLE DO WHAT THEY CAN WITH WHAT THEY HAVE.

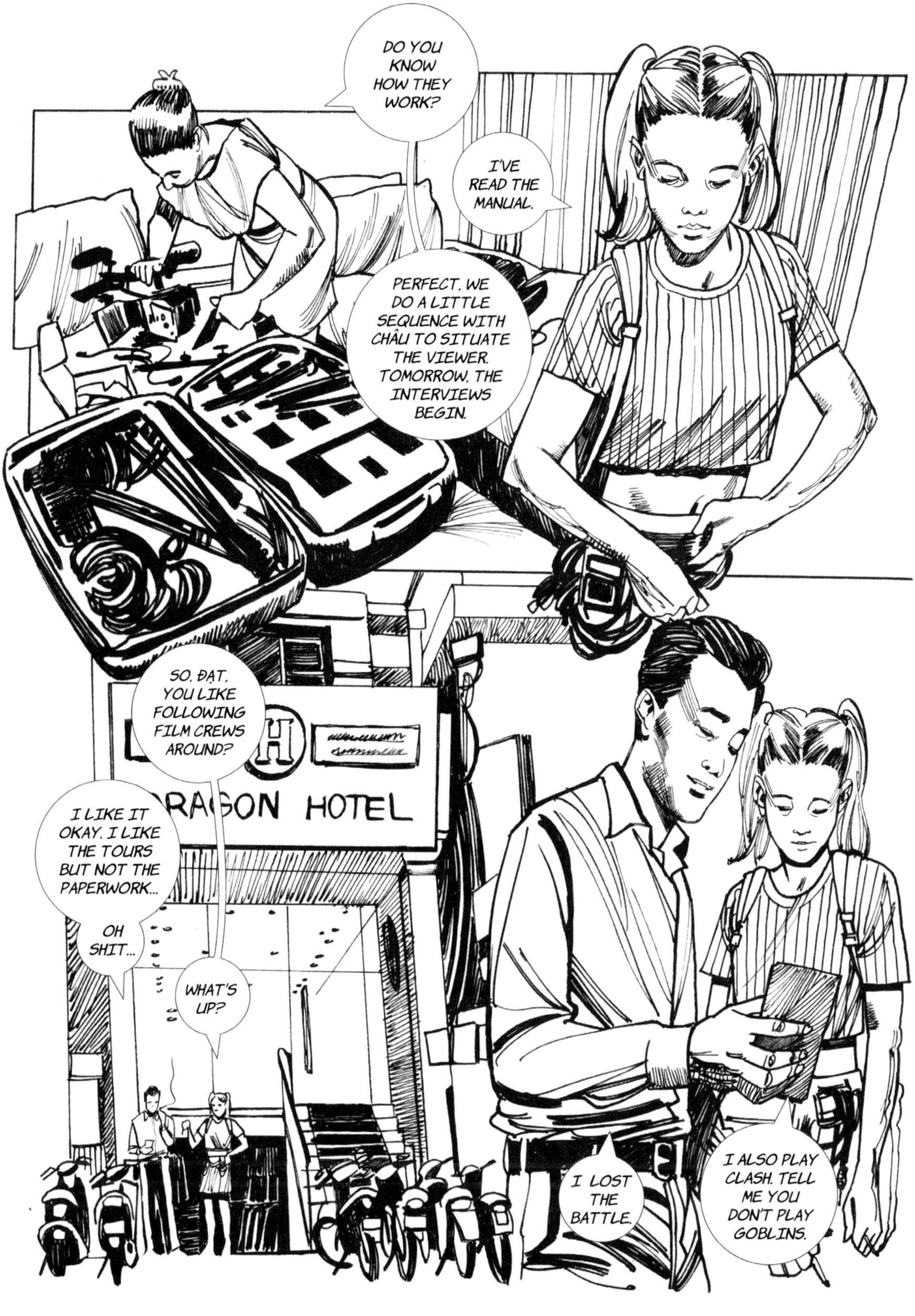
DO YOU KNOW HOW THEY WORK?
I'VE READ THE MANUAL.
PERFECT. WE DO A LITTLE SEQUENCE WITH CHÂU TO SITUATE THE VIEWER. TOMORROW, THE INTERVIEWS BEGIN.
RAGON HOTEL
SO, ĐẠT, YOU LIKE FOLLOWING FILM CREWS AROUND?
I LIKE IT OKAY. I LIKE THE TOURS BUT NOT THE PAPERWORK...
OH SHIT...
WHAT'S UP?
I LOST THE BATTLE.
I ALSO PLAY CLASH. TELL ME YOU DON'T PLAY GOBLINS.

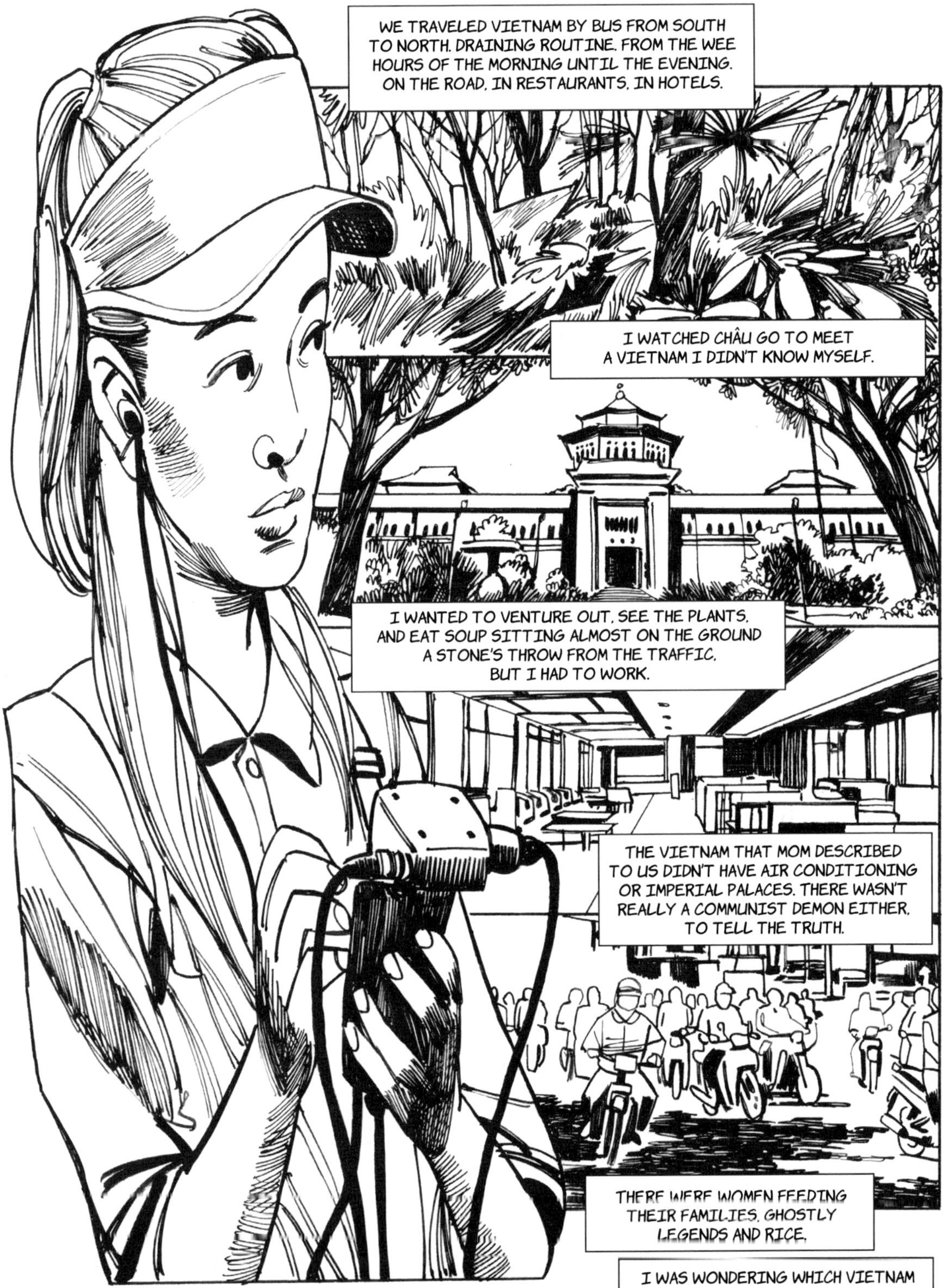
WE TRAVELED VIETNAM BY BUS FROM SOUTH TO NORTH. DRAINING ROUTINE. FROM THE WEE HOURS OF THE MORNING UNTIL THE EVENING. ON THE ROAD, IN RESTAURANTS, IN HOTELS.
I WATCHED CHÂU GO TO MEET A VIETNAM I DIDN'T KNOW MYSELF.
I WANTED TO VENTURE OUT, SEE THE PLANTS, AND EAT SOUP SITTING ALMOST ON THE GROUND A STONE'S THROW FROM THE TRAFFIC, BUT I HAD TO WORK.
THE VIETNAM THAT MOM DESCRIBED TO US DIDN'T HAVE AIR CONDITIONING OR IMPERIAL PALACES. THERE WASN'T REALLY A COMMUNIST DEMON EITHER, TO TELL THE TRUTH.
THERE WERE WOMEN FEEDING THEIR FAMILIES, GHOSTLY LEGENDS AND RICE.
I WAS WONDERING WHICH VIETNAM WOULD BE REPRESENTED IN THE FILM.

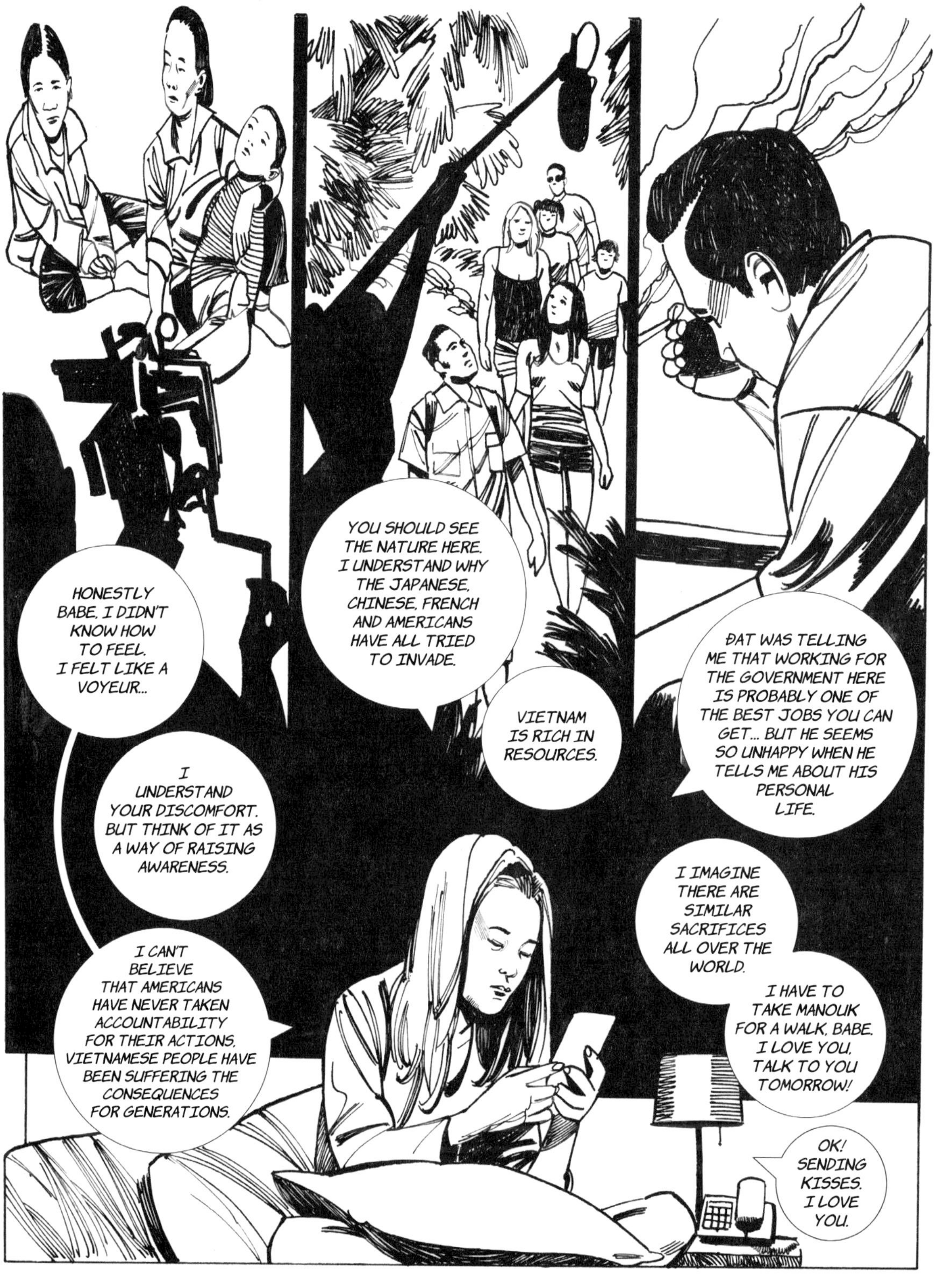
HONESTLY BABE, I DIDN'T KNOW HOW TO FEEL. I FELT LIKE A VOYEUR...
YOU SHOULD SEE THE NATURE HERE. I UNDERSTAND WHY THE JAPANESE, CHINESE, FRENCH AND AMERICANS HAVE ALL TRIED TO INVADE.
VIETNAM IS RICH IN RESOURCES.
ĐAT WAS TELLING ME THAT WORKING FOR THE GOVERNMENT HERE IS PROBABLY ONE OF THE BEST JOBS YOU CAN GET... BUT HE SEEMS SO UNHAPPY WHEN HE TELLS ME ABOUT HIS PERSONAL LIFE.
I UNDERSTAND YOUR DISCOMFORT. BUT THINK OF IT AS A WAY OF RAISING AWARENESS.
I CAN'T BELIEVE THAT AMERICANS HAVE NEVER TAKEN ACCOUNTABILITY FOR THEIR ACTIONS. VIETNAMESE PEOPLE HAVE BEEN SUFFERING THE CONSEQUENCES FOR GENERATIONS.
I IMAGINE THERE ARE SIMILAR SACRIFICES ALL OVER THE WORLD.
I HAVE TO TAKE MANOUK FOR A WALK, BABE. I LOVE YOU, TALK TO YOU TOMORROW!
OK! SENDING KISSES. I LOVE YOU.

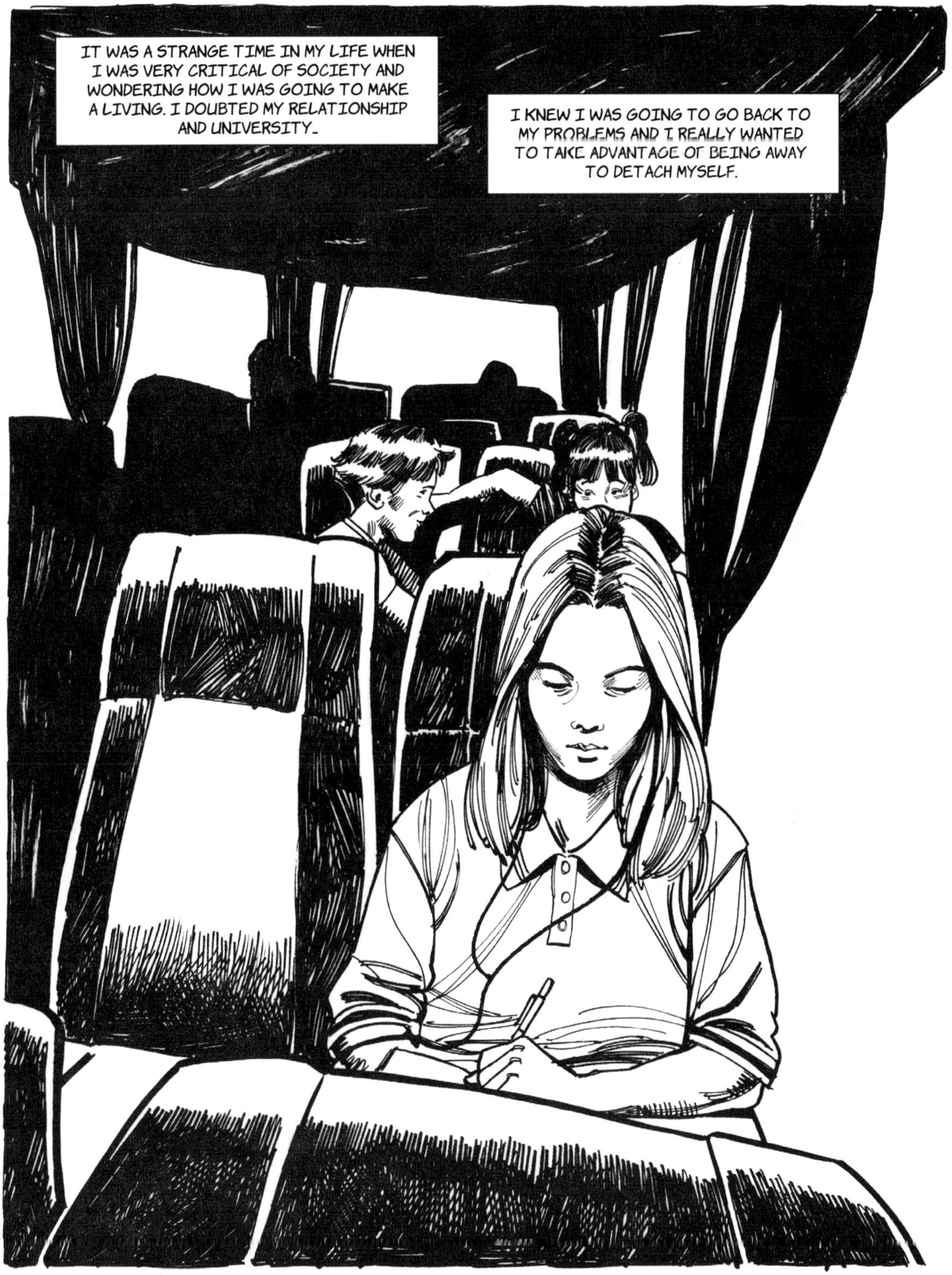
IT WAS A STRANGE TIME IN MY LIFE WHEN I WAS VERY CRITICAL OF SOCIETY AND WONDERING HOW I WAS GOING TO MAKE A LIVING. I DOUBTED MY RELATIONSHIP AND UNIVERSITY...
I KNEW I WAS GOING TO GO BACK TO MY PROBLEMS AND I REALLY WANTED TO TAKE ADVANTAGE OF BEING AWAY TO DETACH MYSELF.

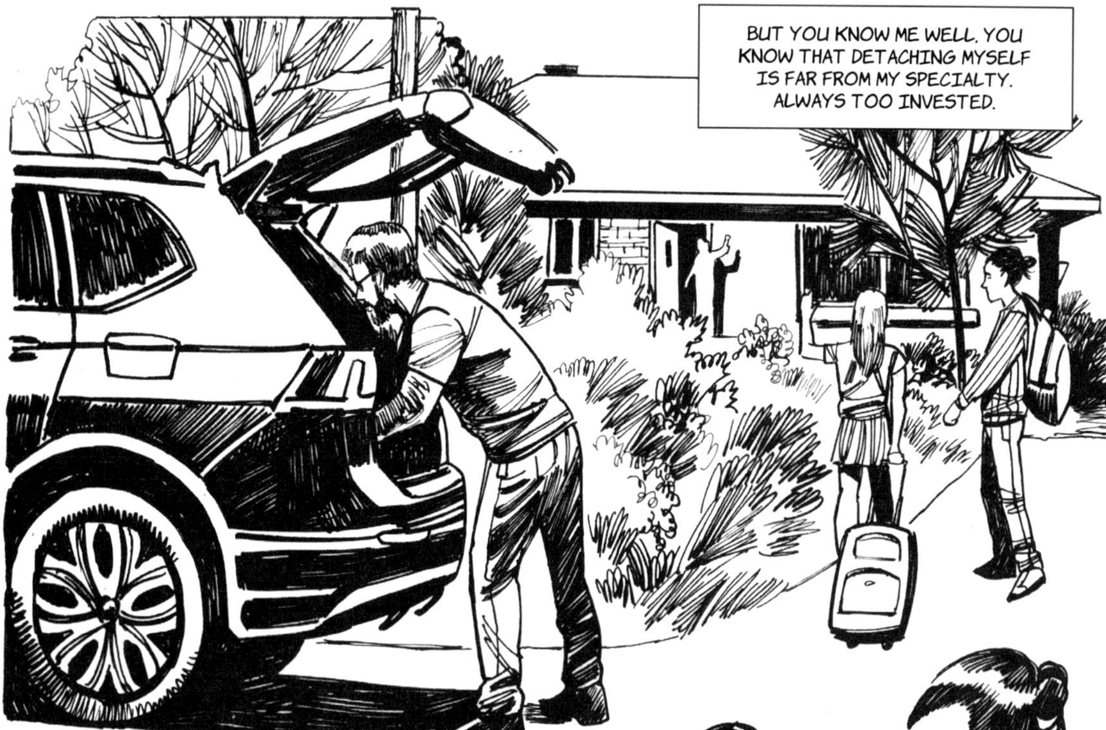
BUT YOU KNOW ME WELL. YOU KNOW THAT DETACHING MYSELF IS FAR FROM MY SPECIALTY. ALWAYS TOO INVESTED.

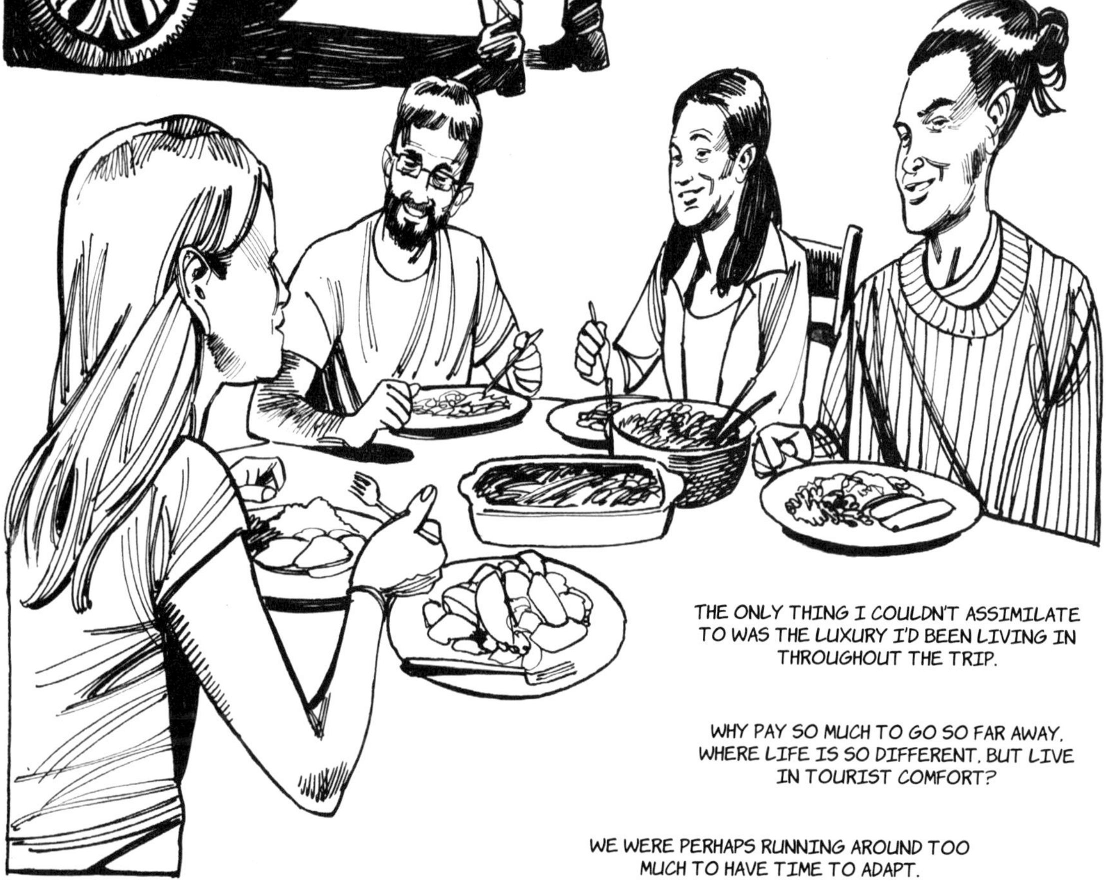
THE ONLY THING I COULDN'T ASSIMILATE TO WAS THE LUXURY I'D BEEN LIVING IN THROUGHOUT THE TRIP.
WHY PAY SO MUCH TO GO SO FAR AWAY, WHERE LIFE IS SO DIFFERENT, BUT LIVE IN TOURIST COMFORT?
WE WERE PERHAPS RUNNING AROUND TOO MUCH TO HAVE TIME TO ADAPT.

CHAPTER 4

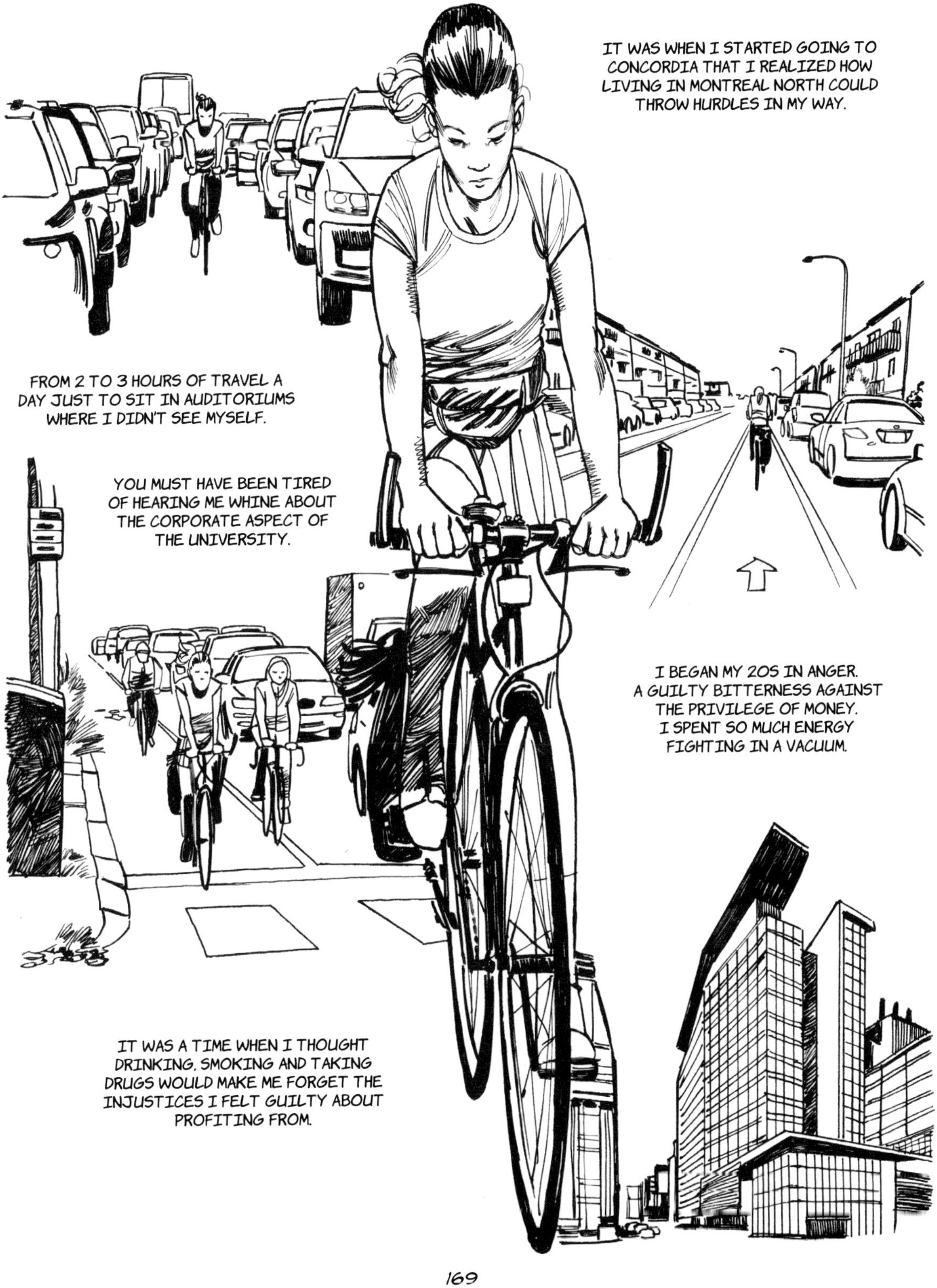
IT WAS WHEN I STARTED GOING TO CONCORDIA THAT I REALIZED HOW LIVING IN MONTREAL NORTH COULD THROW HURDLES IN MY WAY.
FROM 2 TO 3 HOURS OF TRAVEL A DAY JUST TO SIT IN AUDITORIUMS WHERE I DIDN'T SEE MYSELF.
YOU MUST HAVE BEEN TIRED OF HEARING ME WHINE ABOUT THE CORPORATE ASPECT OF THE UNIVERSITY.
I BEGAN MY 20S IN ANGER. A GUILTY BITTERNESS AGAINST THE PRIVILEGE OF MONEY. I SPENT SO MUCH ENERGY FIGHTING IN A VACUUM.
IT WAS A TIME WHEN I THOUGHT DRINKING, SMOKING AND TAKING DRUGS WOULD MAKE ME FORGET THE INJUSTICES I FELT GUILTY ABOUT PROFITING FROM.

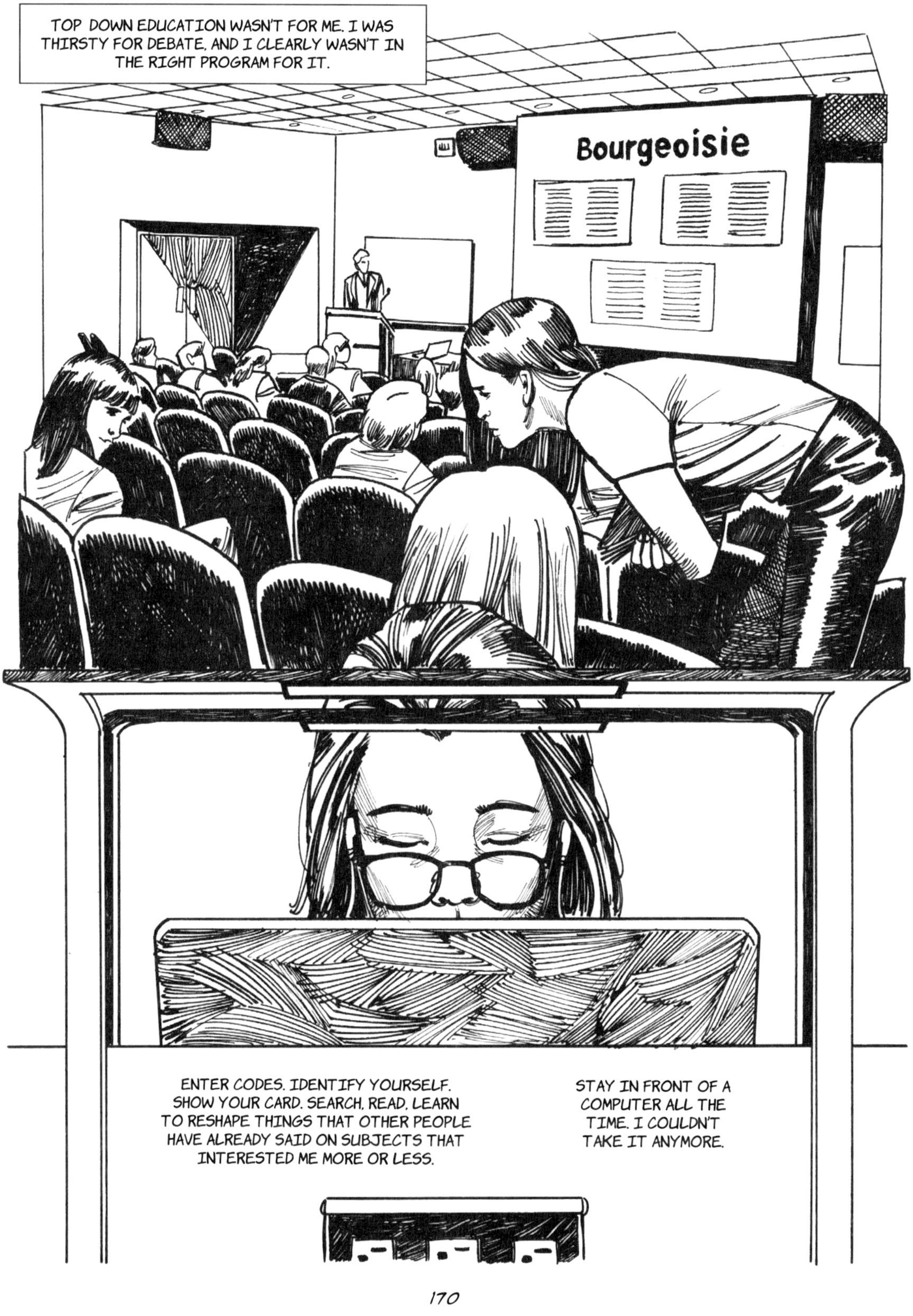
TOP DOWN EDUCATION WASN'T FOR ME. I WAS THIRSTY FOR DEBATE, AND I CLEARLY WASN'T IN THE RIGHT PROGRAM FOR IT.
Bourgeoisie
ENTER CODES. IDENTIFY YOURSELF. SHOW YOUR CARD. SEARCH, READ, LEARN TO RESHAPE THINGS THAT OTHER PEOPLE HAVE ALREADY SAID ON SUBJECTS THAT INTERESTED ME MORE OR LESS.
STAY IN FRONT OF A COMPUTER ALL THE TIME. I COULDN'T TAKE IT ANYMORE.

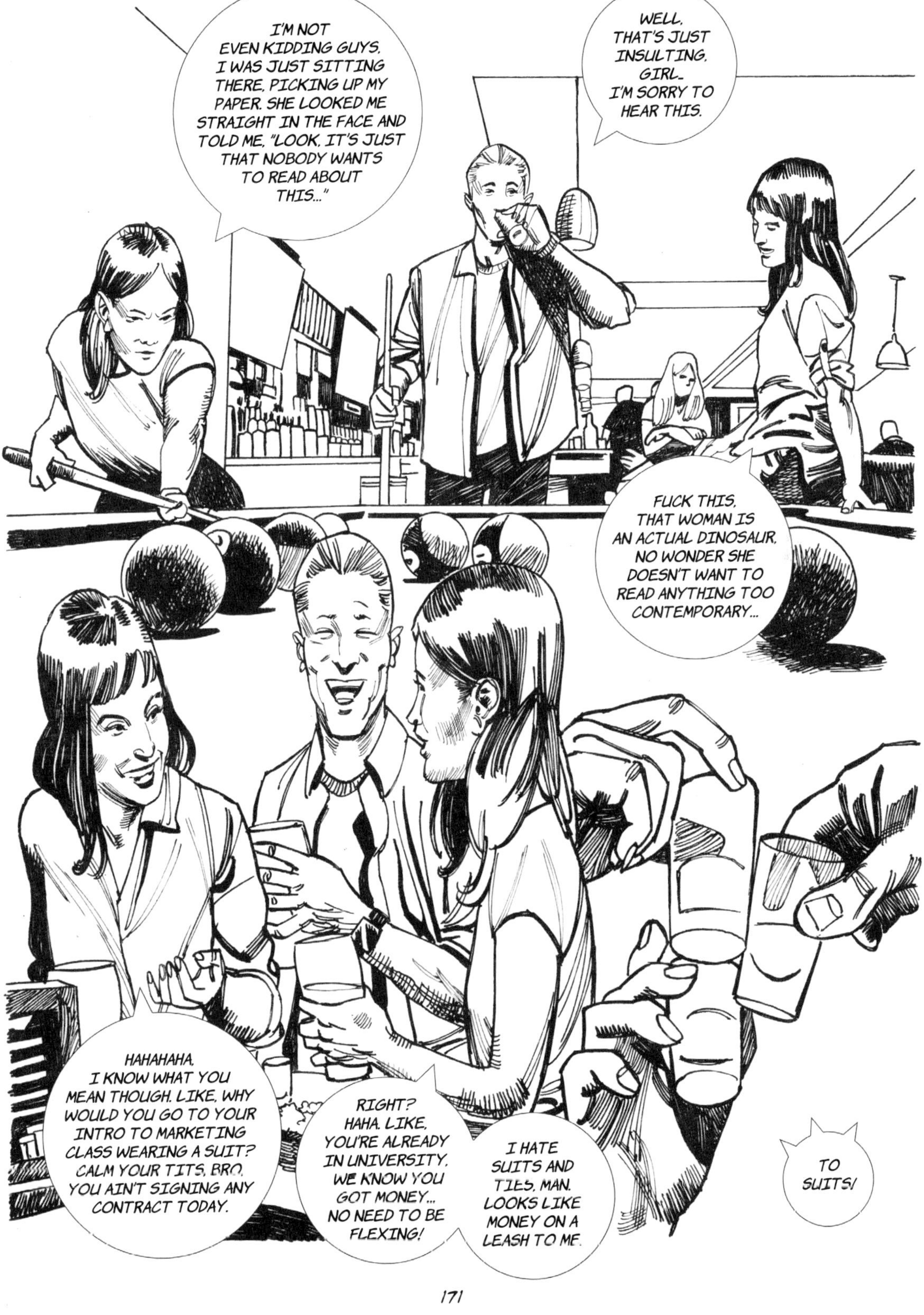
I'M NOT EVEN KIDDING GUYS. I WAS JUST SITTING THERE, PICKING UP MY PAPER. SHE LOOKED ME STRAIGHT IN THE FACE AND TOLD ME, "LOOK, IT'S JUST THAT NOBODY WANTS TO READ ABOUT THIS..."
WELL, THAT'S JUST INSULTING, GIRL. I'M SORRY TO HEAR THIS.
FUCK THIS, THAT WOMAN IS AN ACTUAL DINOSAUR, NO WONDER SHE DOESN'T WANT TO READ ANYTHING TOO CONTEMPORARY...
HAHAHAHA, I KNOW WHAT YOU MEAN THOUGH. LIKE, WHY WOULD YOU GO TO YOUR INTRO TO MARKETING CLASS WEARING A SUIT? CALM YOUR TITS, BRO, YOU AIN'T SIGNING ANY CONTRACT TODAY.
RIGHT? HAHA. LIKE, YOU'RE ALREADY IN UNIVERSITY, WE KNOW YOU GOT MONEY... NO NEED TO BE FLEXING!
I HATE SUITS AND TIES, MAN. LOOKS LIKE MONEY ON A LEASH TO ME.
TO SUITS!

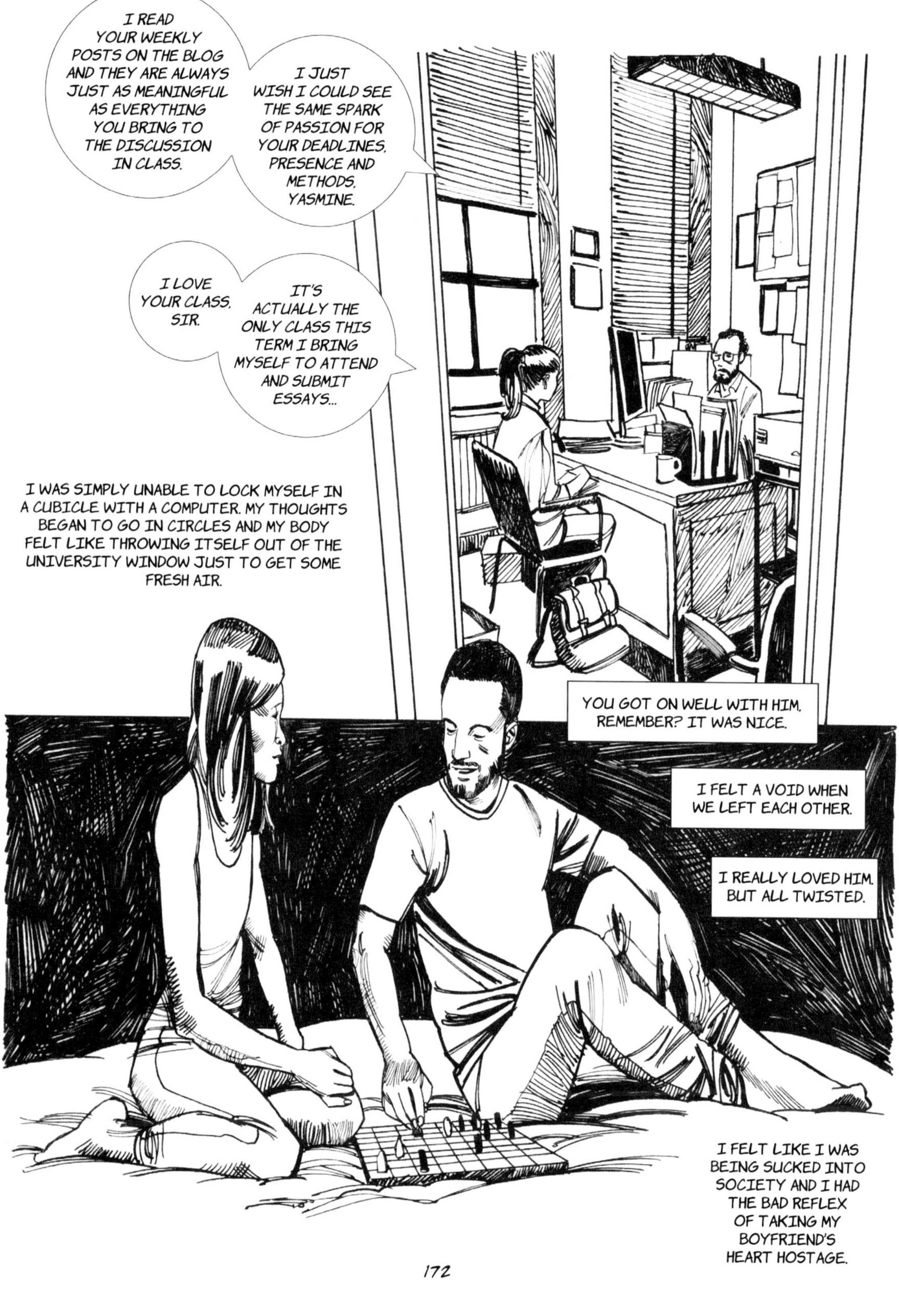
I READ YOUR WEEKLY POSTS ON THE BLOG AND THEY ARE ALWAYS JUST AS MEANINGFUL AS EVERYTHING YOU BRING TO THE DISCUSSION IN CLASS.
I JUST WISH I COULD SEE THE SAME SPARK OF PASSION FOR YOUR DEADLINES, PRESENCE AND METHODS, YASMINE.
I LOVE YOUR CLASS, SIR.
IT'S ACTUALLY THE ONLY CLASS THIS TERM I BRING MYSELF TO ATTEND AND SUBMIT ESSAYS...
I WAS SIMPLY UNABLE TO LOCK MYSELF IN A CUBICLE WITH A COMPUTER. MY THOUGHTS BEGAN TO GO IN CIRCLES AND MY BODY FELT LIKE THROWING ITSELF OUT OF THE UNIVERSITY WINDOW JUST TO GET SOME FRESH AIR.
YOU GOT ON WELL WITH HIM, REMEMBER? IT WAS NICE.
I FELT A VOID WHEN WE LEFT EACH OTHER.
I REALLY LOVED HIM. BUT ALL TWISTED.
I FELT LIKE I WAS BEING SUCKED INTO SOCIETY AND I HAD THE BAD REFLEX OF TAKING MY BOYFRIEND'S HEART HOSTAGE.

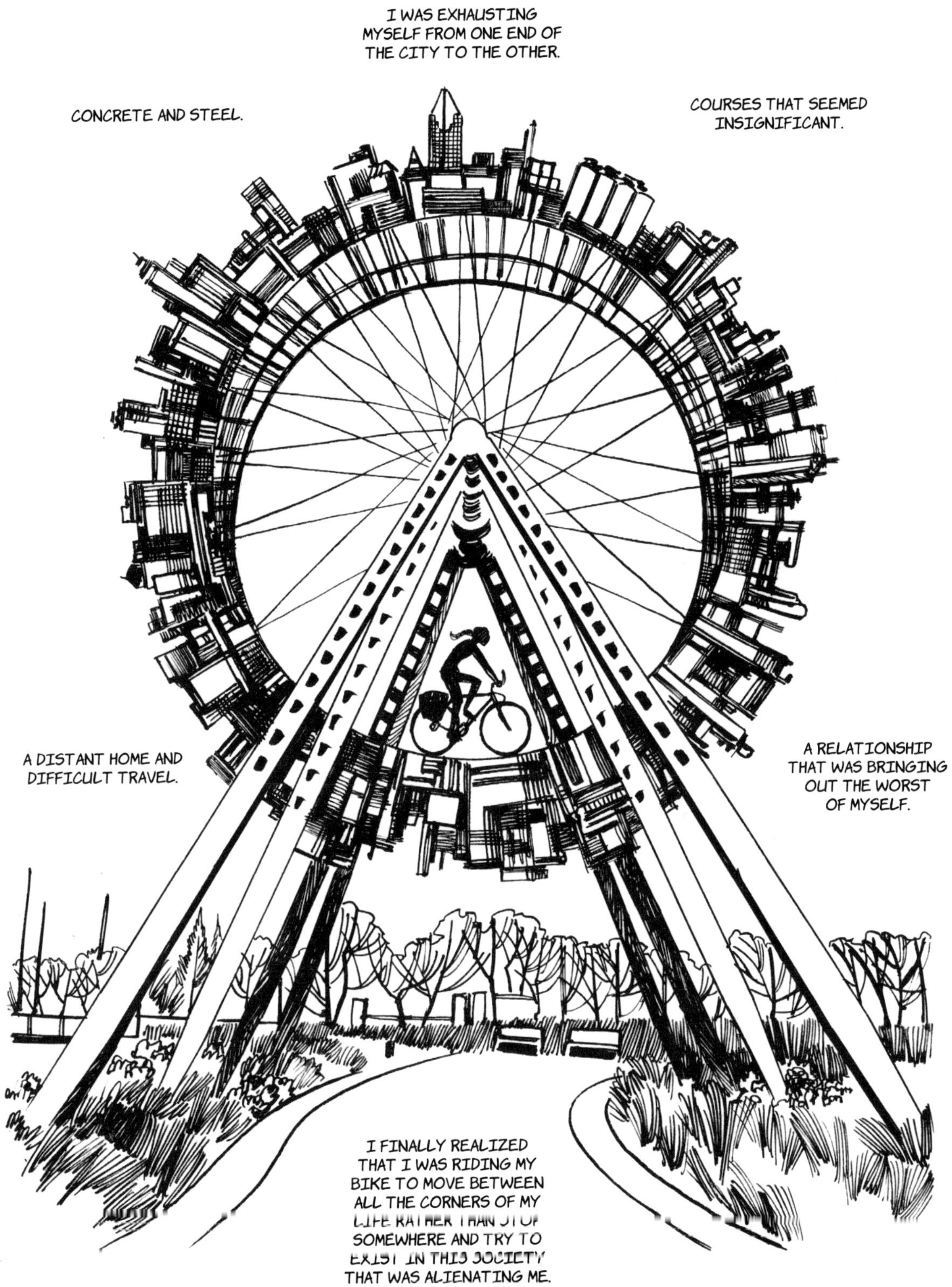
I WAS EXHAUSTING MYSELF FROM ONE END OF THE CITY TO THE OTHER.
CONCRETE AND STEEL.
COURSES THAT SEEMED INSIGNIFICANT.
A DISTANT HOME AND DIFFICULT TRAVEL.
A RELATIONSHIP THAT WAS BRINGING OUT THE WORST OF MYSELF.
I FINALLY REALIZED THAT I WAS RIDING MY BIKE TO MOVE BETWEEN ALL THE CORNERS OF MY LIFE RATHER THAN STOP SOMEWHERE AND TRY TO EXIST IN THIS SOCIETY THAT WAS ALIENATING ME.

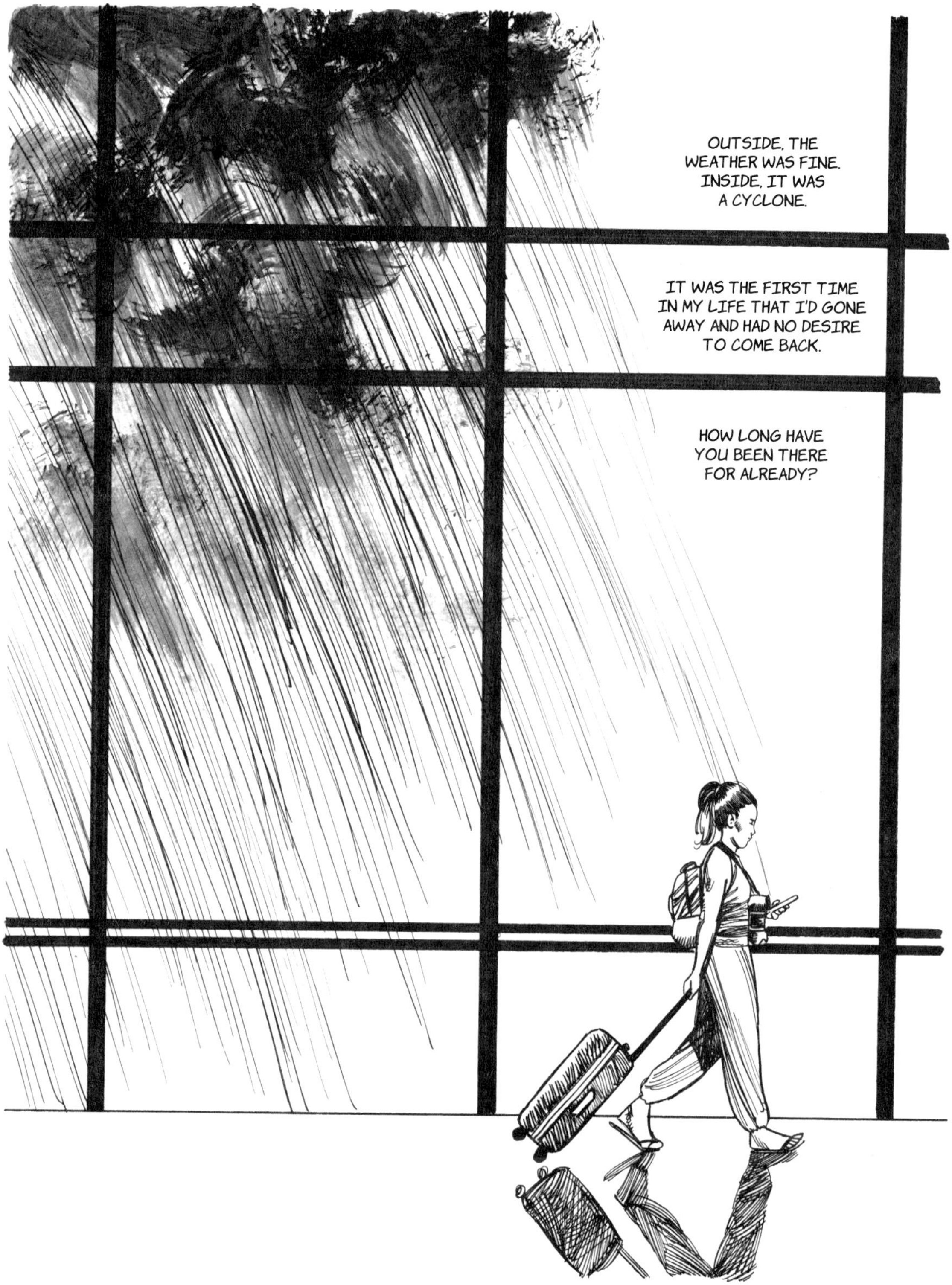
OUTSIDE, THE WEATHER WAS FINE. INSIDE, IT WAS A CYCLONE.
IT WAS THE FIRST TIME IN MY LIFE THAT I'D GONE AWAY AND HAD NO DESIRE TO COME BACK.
HOW LONG HAVE YOU BEEN THERE FOR ALREADY?

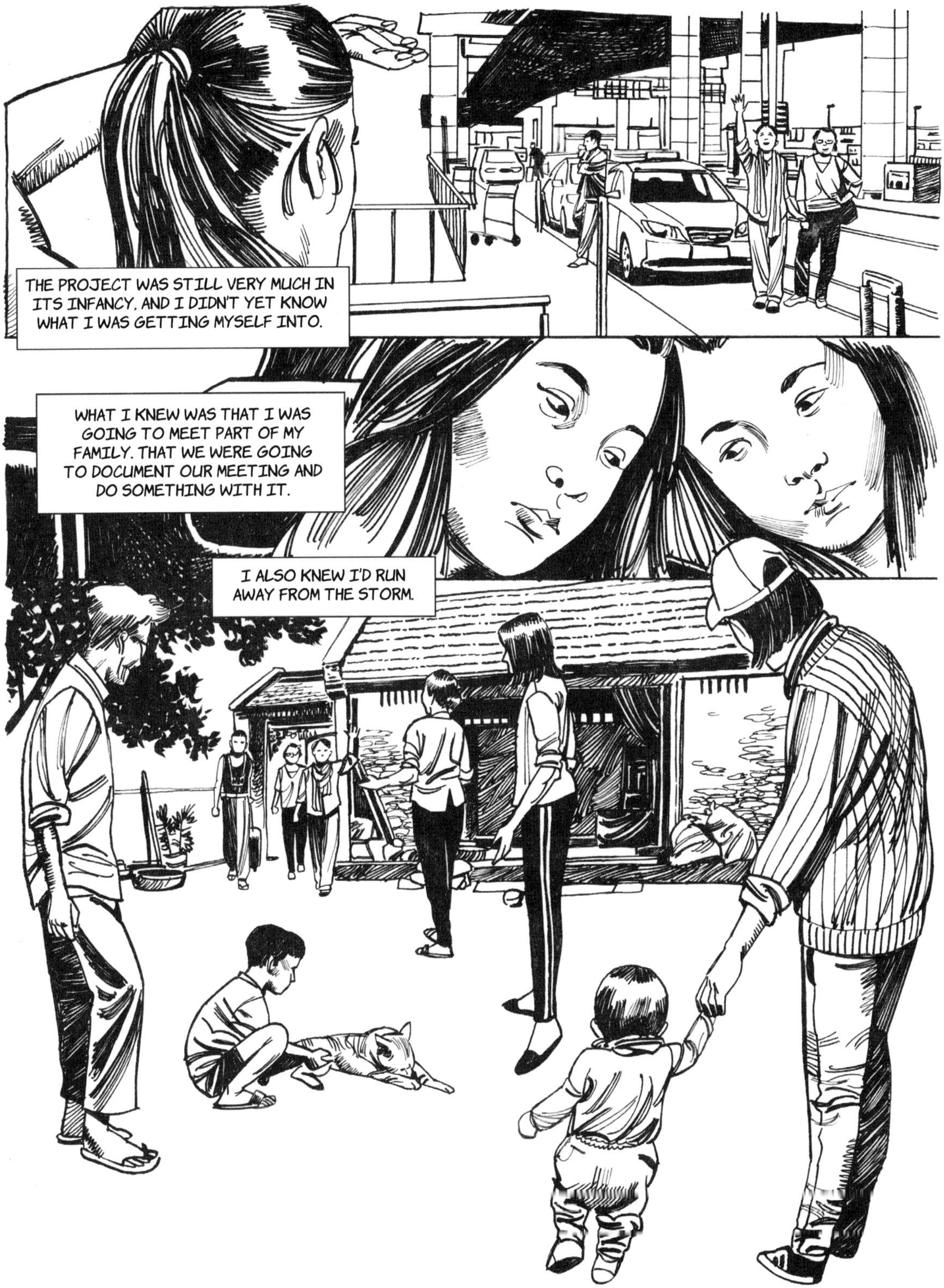
THE PROJECT WAS STILL VERY MUCH IN ITS INFANCY, AND I DIDN'T YET KNOW WHAT I WAS GETTING MYSELF INTO.
WHAT I KNEW WAS THAT I WAS GOING TO MEET PART OF MY FAMILY. THAT WE WERE GOING TO DOCUMENT OUR MEETING AND DO SOMETHING WITH IT.
I ALSO KNEW I'D RUN AWAY FROM THE STORM.

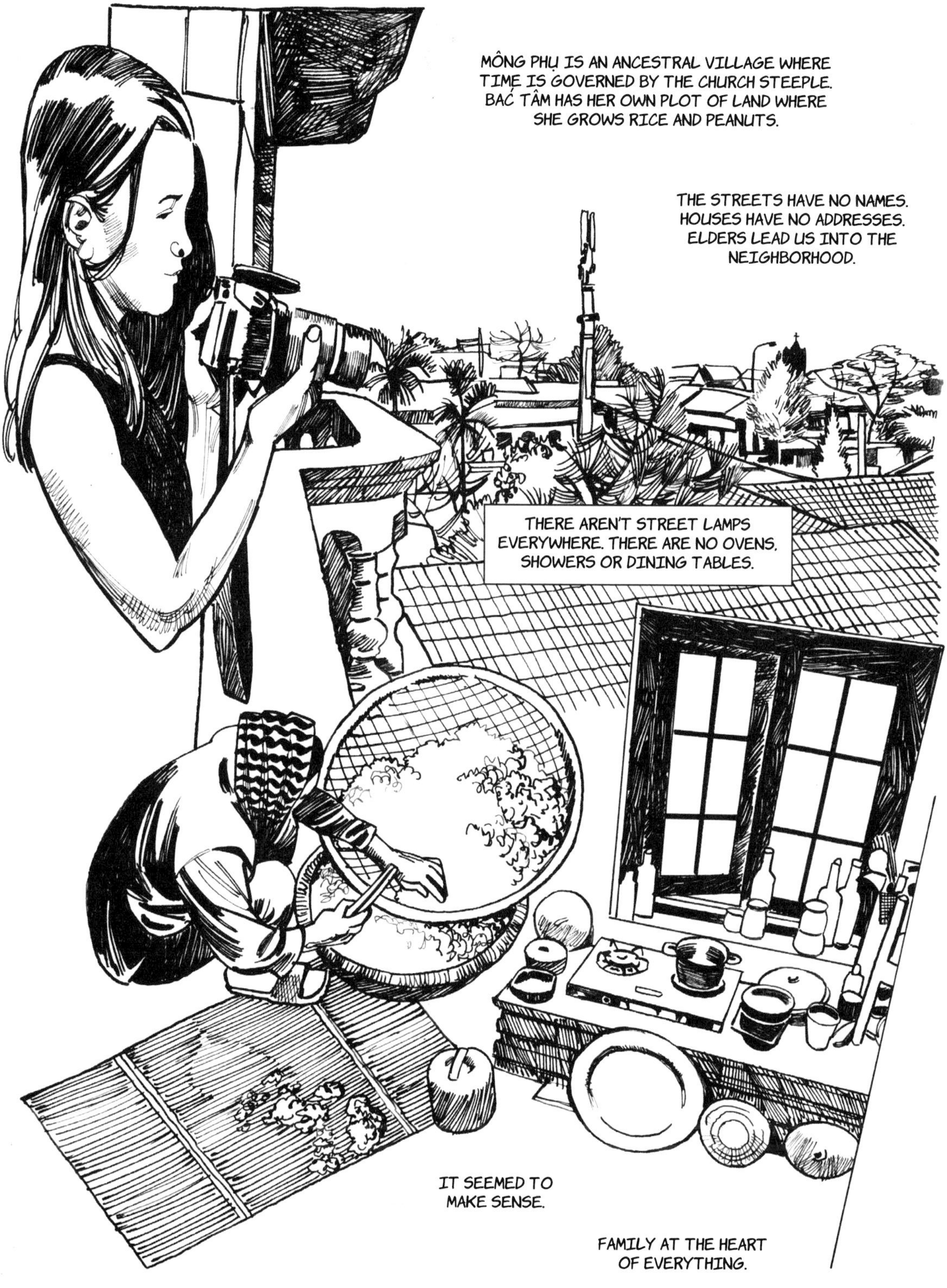
MÔNG PHỤ IS AN ANCESTRAL VILLAGE WHERE TIME IS GOVERNED BY THE CHURCH STEEPLE. BÁC TÂM HAS HER OWN PLOT OF LAND WHERE SHE GROWS RICE AND PEANUTS.
THE STREETS HAVE NO NAMES. HOUSES HAVE NO ADDRESSES. ELDERS LEAD US INTO THE NEIGHBORHOOD.
THERE AREN'T STREET LAMPS EVERYWHERE. THERE ARE NO OVENS, SHOWERS OR DINING TABLES.
IT SEEMED TO MAKE SENSE.
FAMILY AT THE HEART OF EVERYTHING.

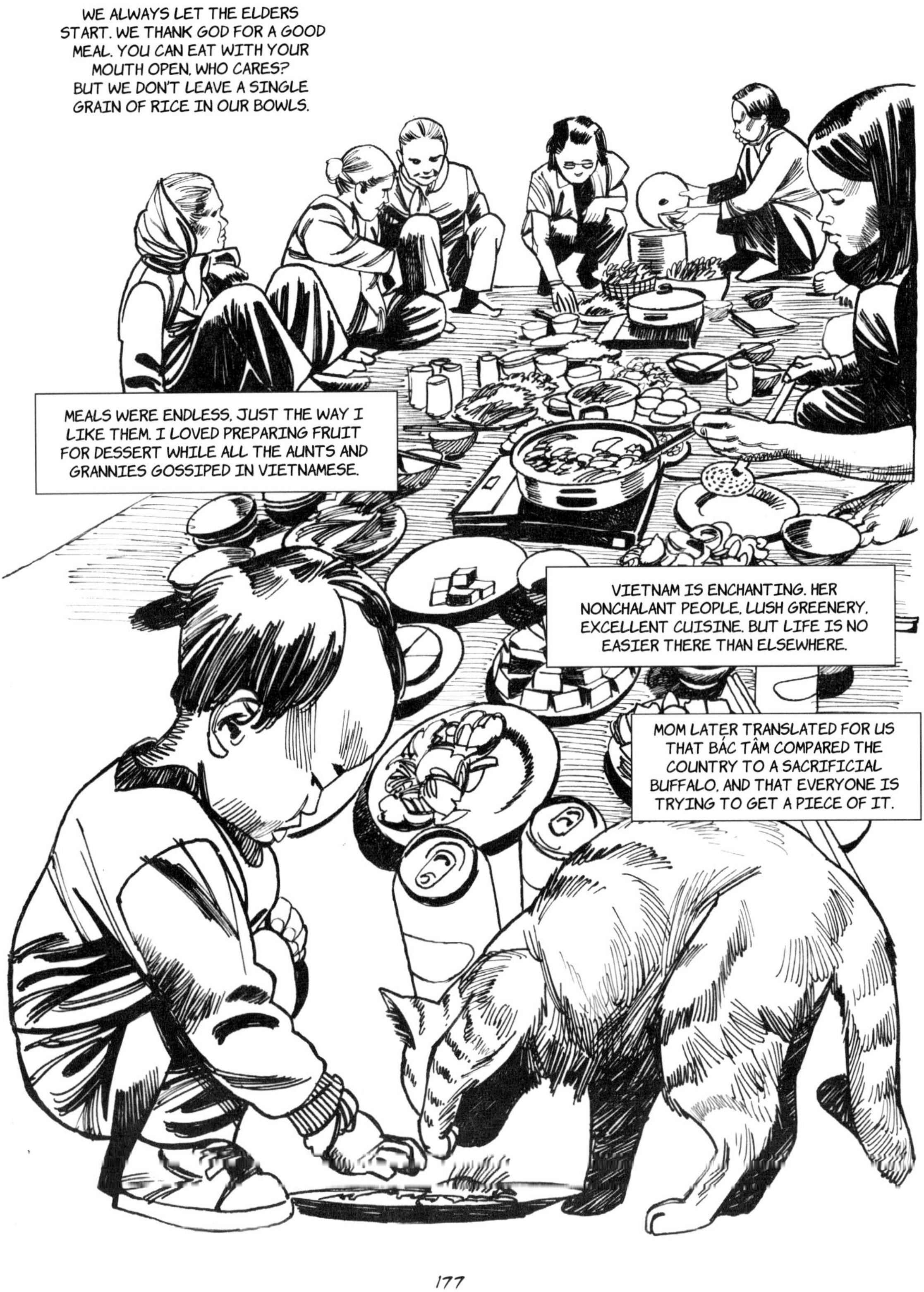
WE ALWAYS LET THE ELDERS START. WE THANK GOD FOR A GOOD MEAL. YOU CAN EAT WITH YOUR MOUTH OPEN, WHO CARES? BUT WE DON'T LEAVE A SINGLE GRAIN OF RICE IN OUR BOWLS.
MEALS WERE ENDLESS, JUST THE WAY I LIKE THEM. I LOVED PREPARING FRUIT FOR DESSERT WHILE ALL THE AUNTS AND GRANNIES GOSSIPED IN VIETNAMESE.
VIETNAM IS ENCHANTING. HER NONCHALANT PEOPLE, LUSH GREENERY, EXCELLENT CUISINE. BUT LIFE IS NO EASIER THERE THAN ELSEWHERE.
MOM LATER TRANSLATED FOR US THAT BÁC TÂM COMPARED THE COUNTRY TO A SACRIFICIAL BUFFALO, AND THAT EVERYONE IS TRYING TO GET A PIECE OF IT.

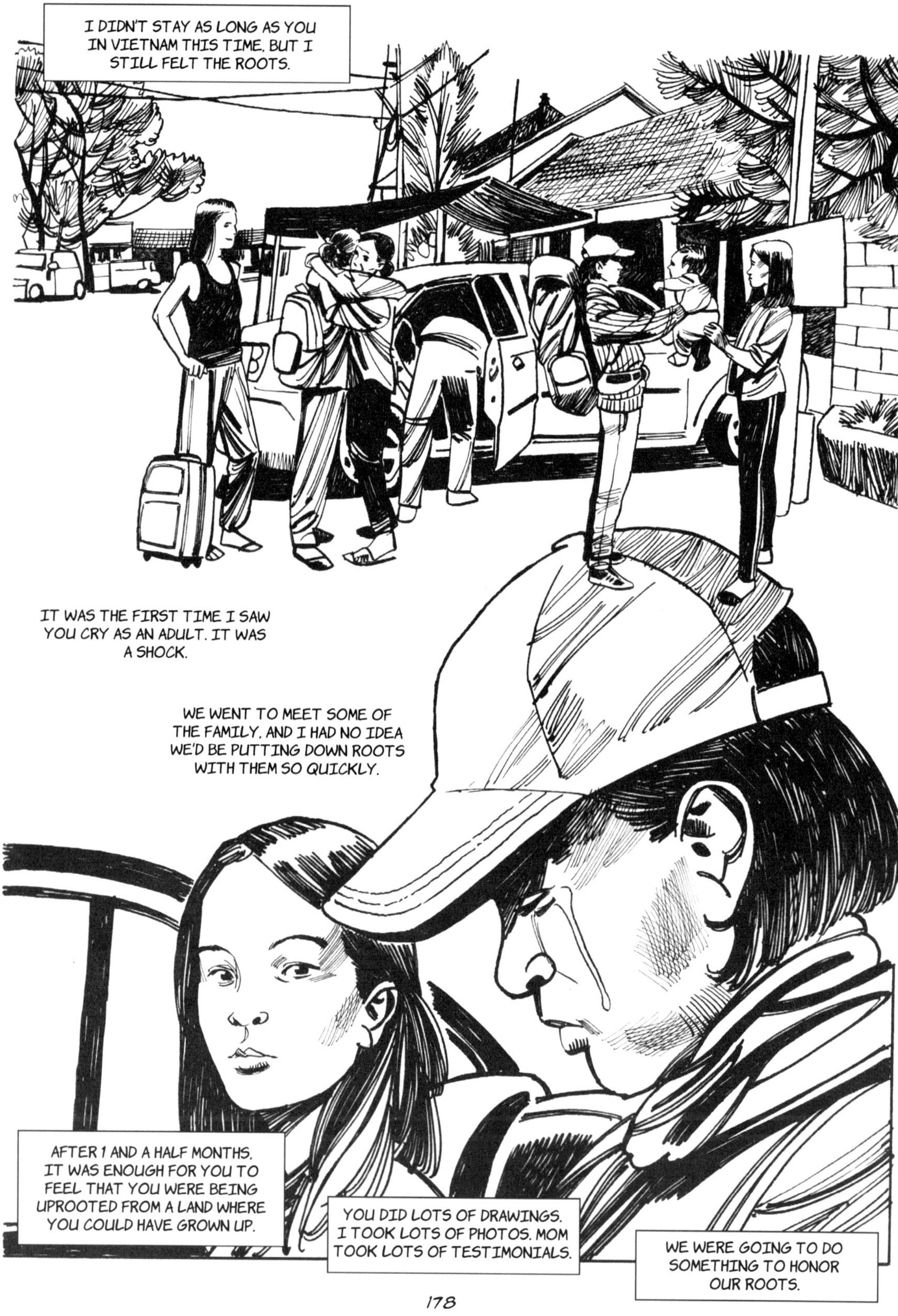
I DIDN'T STAY AS LONG AS YOU IN VIETNAM THIS TIME, BUT I STILL FELT THE ROOTS.
IT WAS THE FIRST TIME I SAW YOU CRY AS AN ADULT. IT WAS A SHOCK.
WE WENT TO MEET SOME OF THE FAMILY, AND I HAD NO IDEA WE'D BE PUTTING DOWN ROOTS WITH THEM SO QUICKLY.
AFTER 1 AND A HALF MONTHS, IT WAS ENOUGH FOR YOU TO FEEL THAT YOU WERE BEING UPROOTED FROM A LAND WHERE YOU COULD HAVE GROWN UP.
YOU DID LOTS OF DRAWINGS. I TOOK LOTS OF PHOTOS. MOM TOOK LOTS OF TESTIMONIALS.
WE WERE GOING TO DO SOMETHING TO HONOR OUR ROOTS.

CHAPTER 5

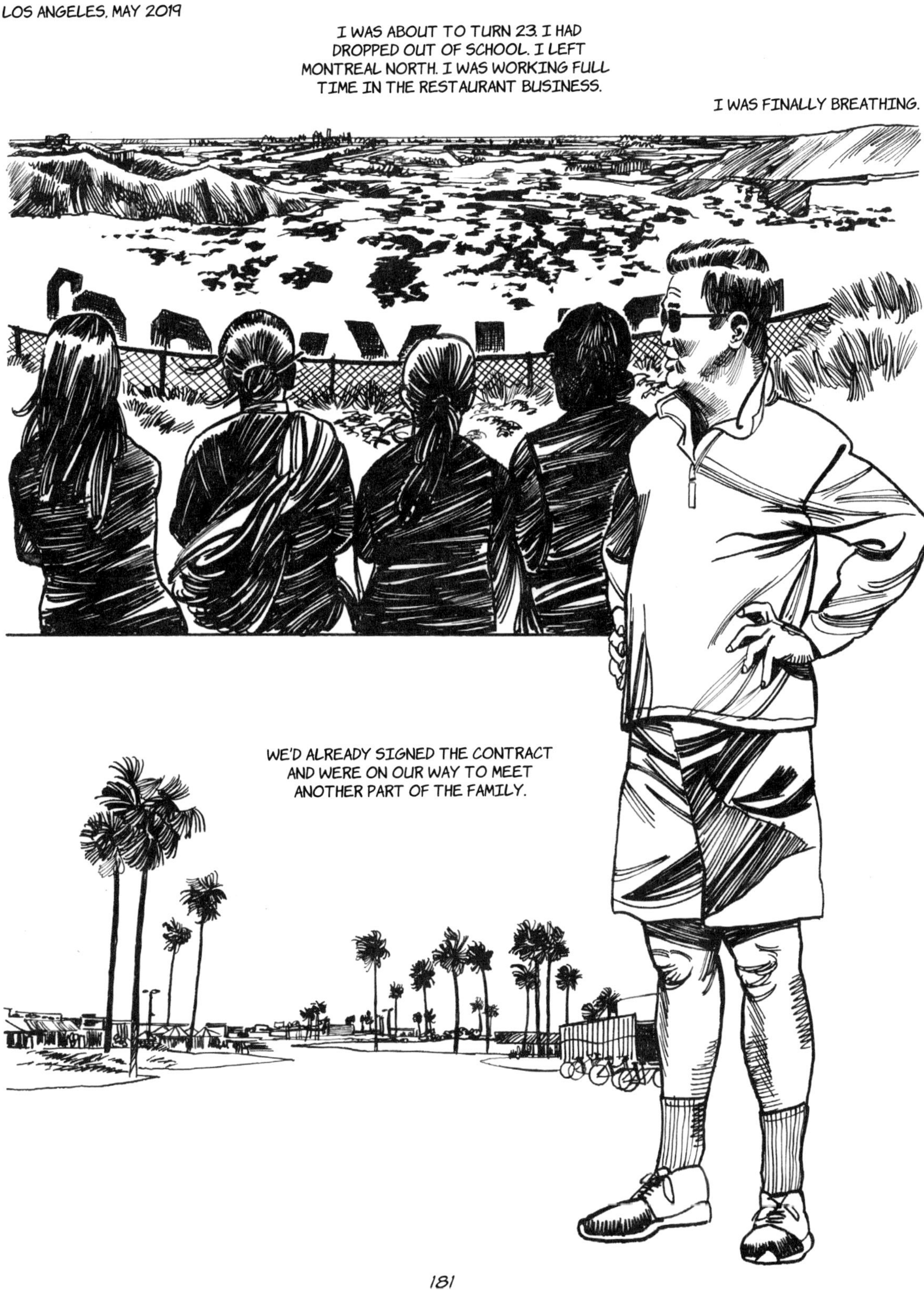
LOS ANGELES, MAY 2019
I WAS ABOUT TO TURN 23. I HAD DROPPED OUT OF SCHOOL. I LEFT MONTREAL NORTH. I WAS WORKING FULL TIME IN THE RESTAURANT BUSINESS.
I WAS FINALLY BREATHING.
WE'D ALREADY SIGNED THE CONTRACT AND WERE ON OUR WAY TO MEET ANOTHER PART OF THE FAMILY.

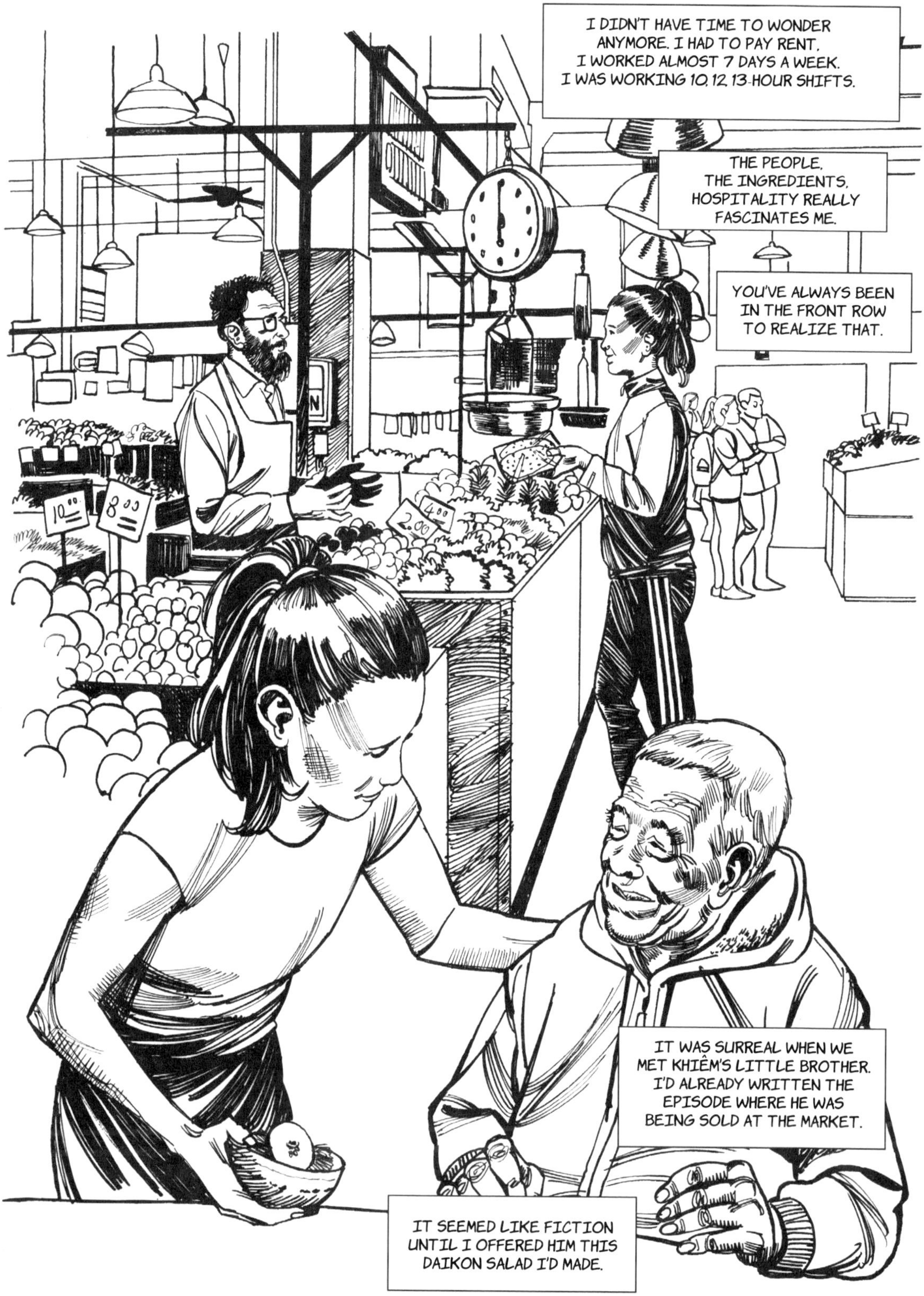
I DIDN'T HAVE TIME TO WONDER ANYMORE. I HAD TO PAY RENT. I WORKED ALMOST 7 DAYS A WEEK. I WAS WORKING 10, 12, 13-HOUR SHIFTS.
THE PEOPLE. THE INGREDIENTS. HOSPITALITY REALLY FASCINATES ME.
YOU'VE ALWAYS BEEN IN THE FRONT ROW TO REALIZE THAT.
10.00
8.00
4.00
2.00
IT WAS SURREAL WHEN WE MET KHIÊM'S LITTLE BROTHER. I'D ALREADY WRITTEN THE EPISODE WHERE HE WAS BEING SOLD AT THE MARKET.
IT SEEMED LIKE FICTION UNTIL I OFFERED HIM THIS DAIKON SALAD I'D MADE.

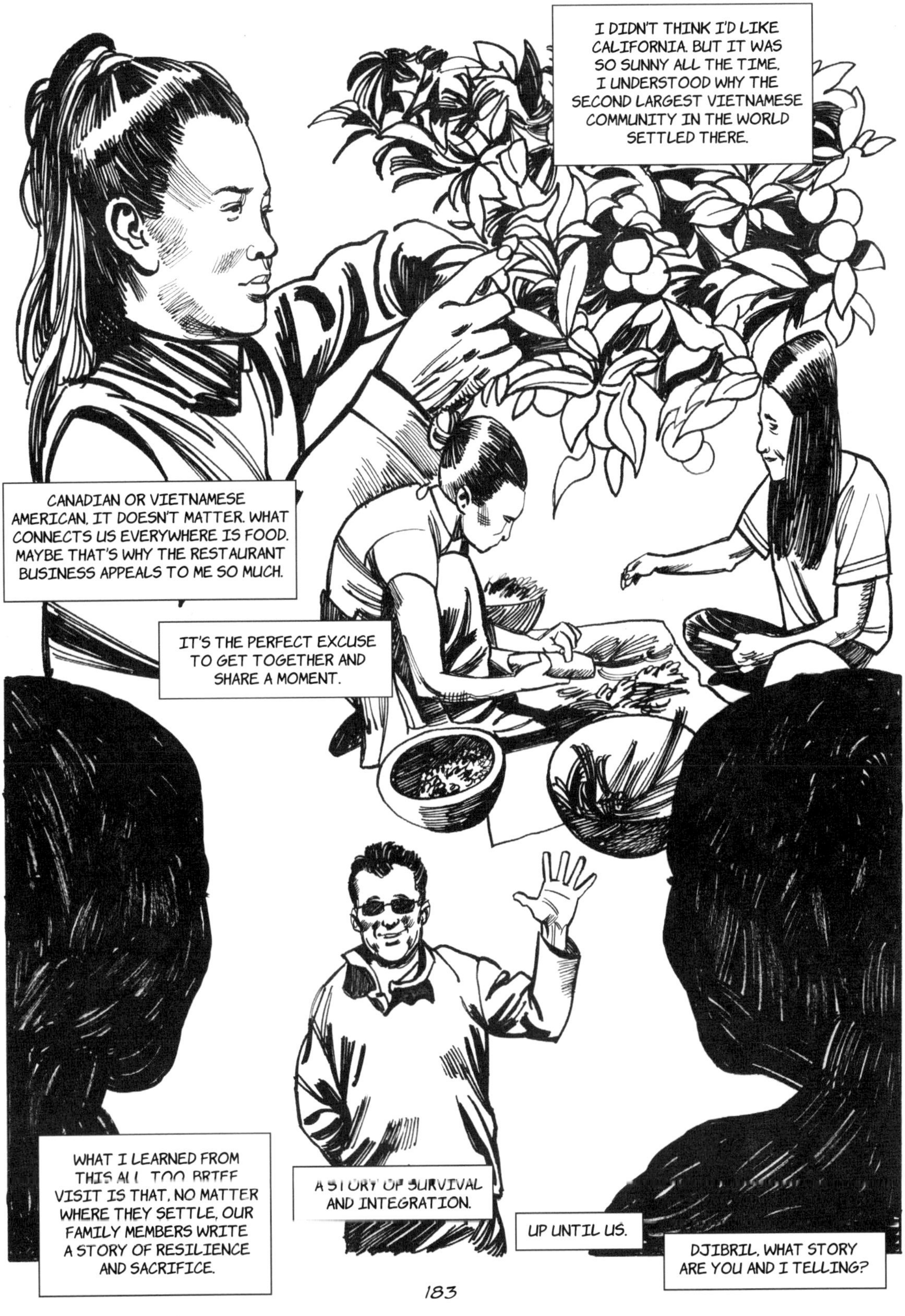
I DIDN'T THINK I'D LIKE CALIFORNIA. BUT IT WAS SO SUNNY ALL THE TIME. I UNDERSTOOD WHY THE SECOND LARGEST VIETNAMESE COMMUNITY IN THE WORLD SETTLED THERE.
CANADIAN OR VIETNAMESE AMERICAN, IT DOESN'T MATTER. WHAT CONNECTS US EVERYWHERE IS FOOD. MAYBE THAT'S WHY THE RESTAURANT BUSINESS APPEALS TO ME SO MUCH.
IT'S THE PERFECT EXCUSE TO GET TOGETHER AND SHARE A MOMENT.
WHAT I LEARNED FROM THIS ALL TOO BRIEF VISIT IS THAT, NO MATTER WHERE THEY SETTLE, OUR FAMILY MEMBERS WRITE A STORY OF RESILIENCE AND SACRIFICE.
A STORY OF SURVIVAL AND INTEGRATION.
UP UNTIL US.
DJIBRIL, WHAT STORY ARE YOU AND I TELLING?

HOCHELAGA MAISONNEUVE, WINTER 2020

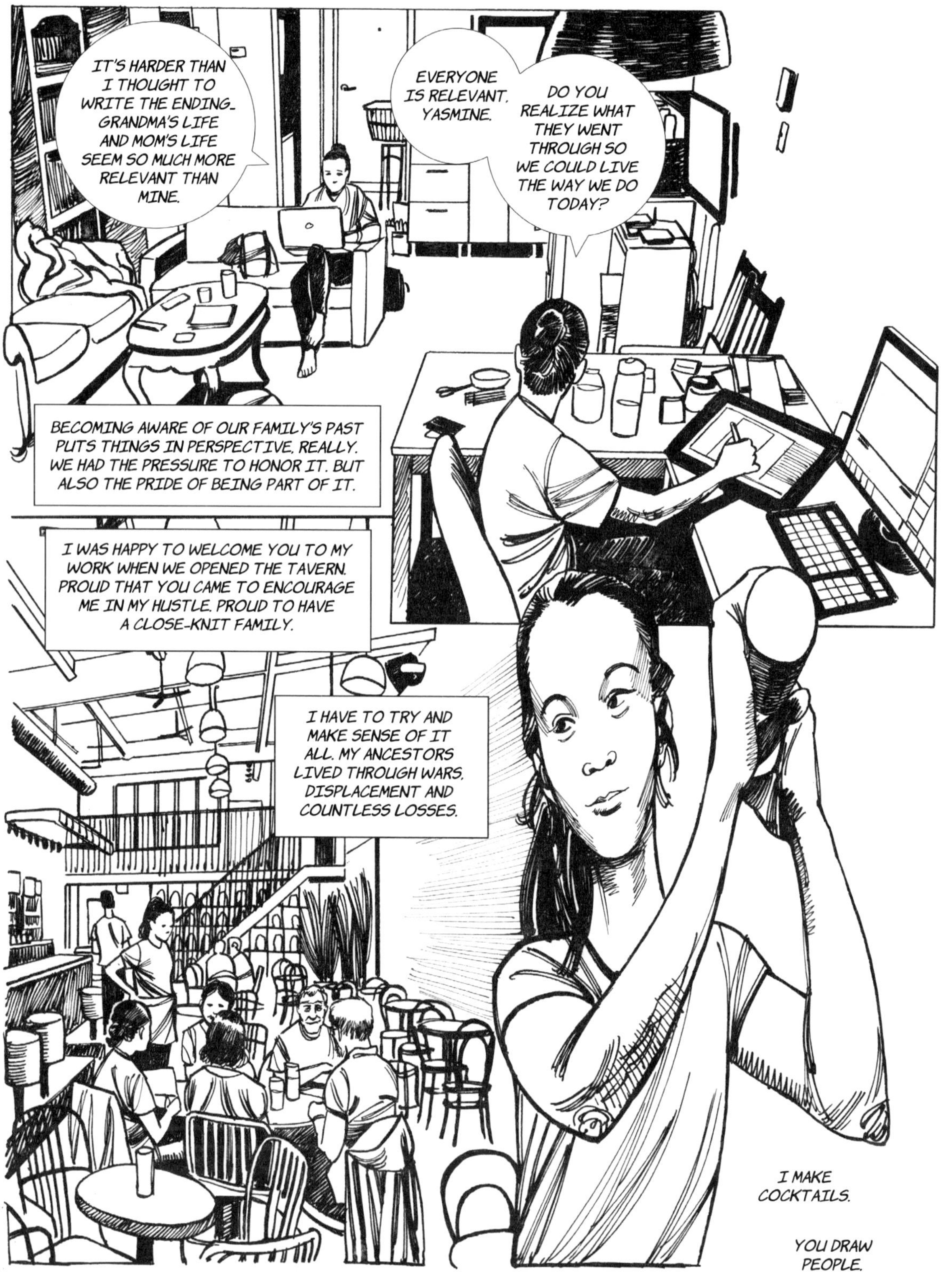
IT'S HARDER THAN I THOUGHT TO WRITE THE ENDING. GRANDMA'S LIFE AND MOM'S LIFE SEEM SO MUCH MORE RELEVANT THAN MINE.
EVERYONE IS RELEVANT, YASMINE.
DO YOU REALIZE WHAT THEY WENT THROUGH SO WE COULD LIVE THE WAY WE DO TODAY?
BECOMING AWARE OF OUR FAMILY'S PAST PUTS THINGS IN PERSPECTIVE, REALLY. WE HAD THE PRESSURE TO HONOR IT. BUT ALSO THE PRIDE OF BEING PART OF IT.
I WAS HAPPY TO WELCOME YOU TO MY WORK WHEN WE OPENED THE TAVERN. PROUD THAT YOU CAME TO ENCOURAGE ME IN MY HUSTLE. PROUD TO HAVE A CLOSE-KNIT FAMILY.
I HAVE TO TRY AND MAKE SENSE OF IT ALL. MY ANCESTORS LIVED THROUGH WARS, DISPLACEMENT AND COUNTLESS LOSSES.
I MAKE COCKTAILS.
YOU DRAW PEOPLE.

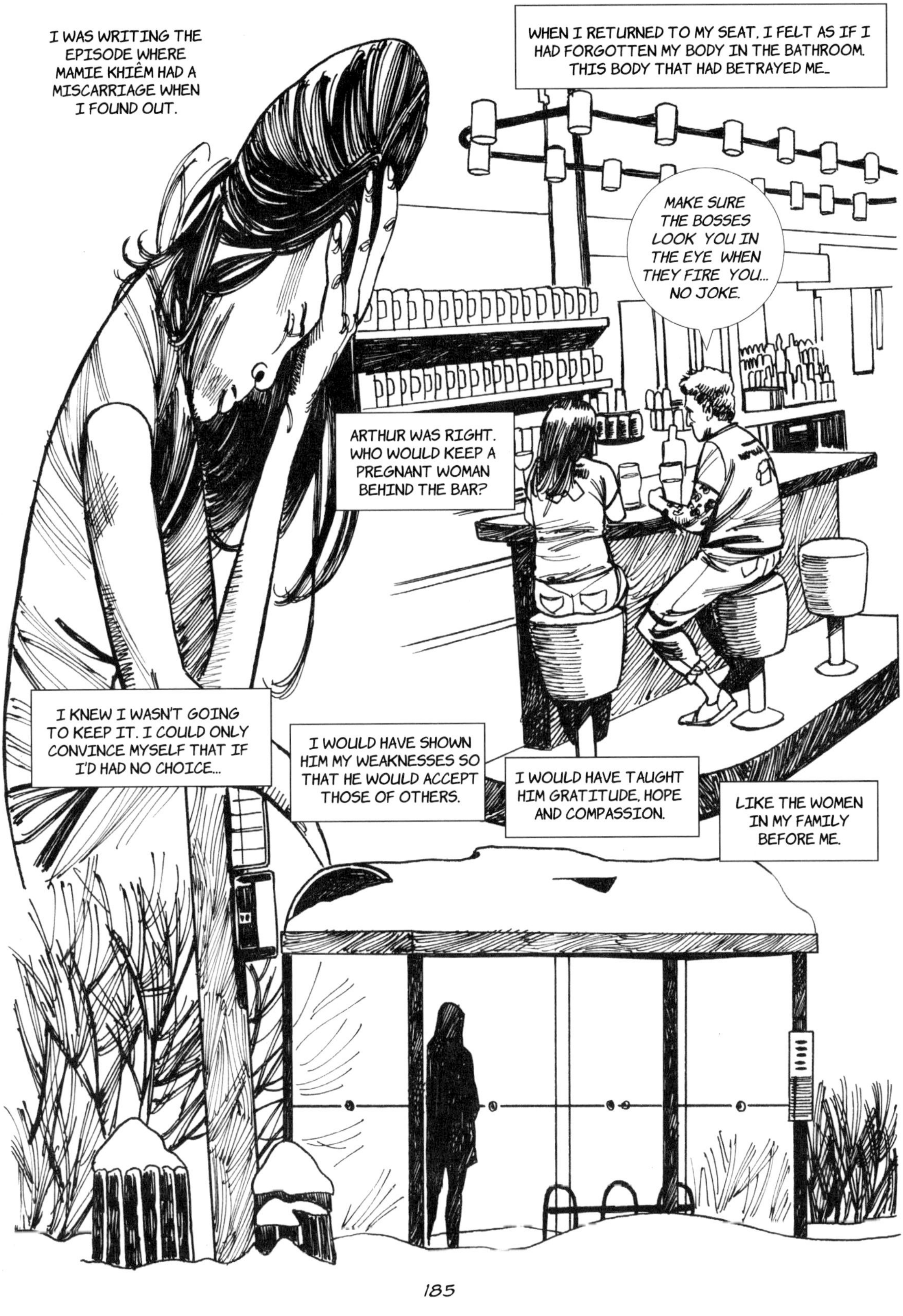
I WAS WRITING THE EPISODE WHERE MAMIE KHIÊM HAD A MISCARRIAGE WHEN I FOUND OUT.
WHEN I RETURNED TO MY SEAT, I FELT AS IF I HAD FORGOTTEN MY BODY IN THE BATHROOM. THIS BODY THAT HAD BETRAYED ME...
MAKE SURE THE BOSSES LOOK YOU IN THE EYE WHEN THEY FIRE YOU... NO JOKE.
ARTHUR WAS RIGHT. WHO WOULD KEEP A PREGNANT WOMAN BEHIND THE BAR?
I KNEW I WASN'T GOING TO KEEP IT. I COULD ONLY CONVINCE MYSELF THAT IF I'D HAD NO CHOICE...
I WOULD HAVE SHOWN HIM MY WEAKNESSES SO THAT HE WOULD ACCEPT THOSE OF OTHERS.
I WOULD HAVE TAUGHT HIM GRATITUDE, HOPE AND COMPASSION.
LIKE THE WOMEN IN MY FAMILY BEFORE ME.

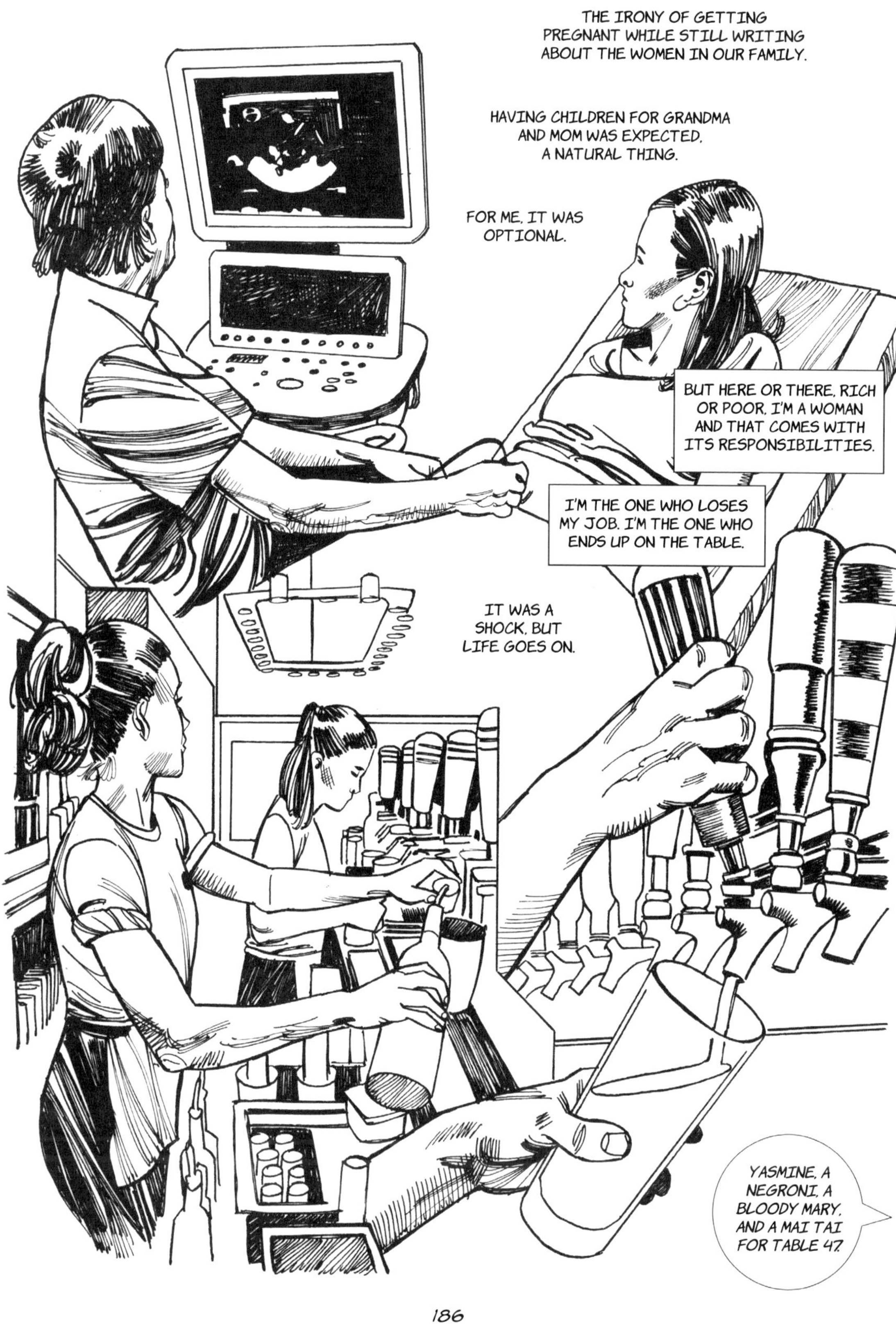
THE IRONY OF GETTING PREGNANT WHILE STILL WRITING ABOUT THE WOMEN IN OUR FAMILY.
HAVING CHILDREN FOR GRANDMA AND MOM WAS EXPECTED, A NATURAL THING.
FOR ME, IT WAS OPTIONAL.
BUT HERE OR THERE, RICH OR POOR, I'M A WOMAN AND THAT COMES WITH ITS RESPONSIBILITIES.
I'M THE ONE WHO LOSES MY JOB. I'M THE ONE WHO ENDS UP ON THE TABLE.
IT WAS A SHOCK, BUT LIFE GOES ON.
YASMINE, A NEGRONI, A BLOODY MARY, AND A MAI TAI FOR TABLE 47.

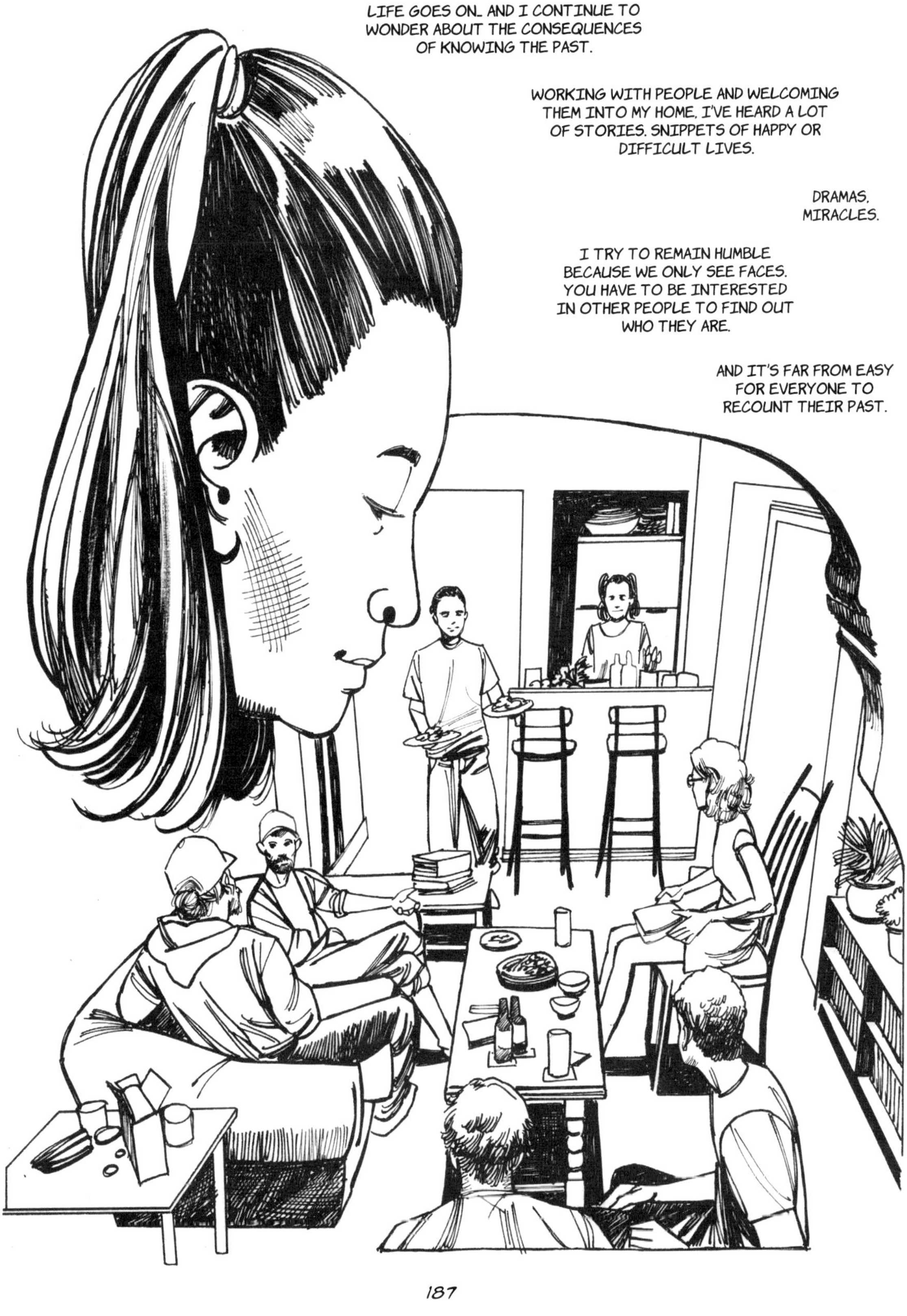
LIFE GOES ON... AND I CONTINUE TO WONDER ABOUT THE CONSEQUENCES OF KNOWING THE PAST.
WORKING WITH PEOPLE AND WELCOMING THEM INTO MY HOME, I'VE HEARD A LOT OF STORIES. SNIPPETS OF HAPPY OR DIFFICULT LIVES.
DRAMAS, MIRACLES.
I TRY TO REMAIN HUMBLE BECAUSE WE ONLY SEE FACES. YOU HAVE TO BE INTERESTED IN OTHER PEOPLE TO FIND OUT WHO THEY ARE.
AND IT'S FAR FROM EASY FOR EVERYONE TO RECOUNT THEIR PAST.

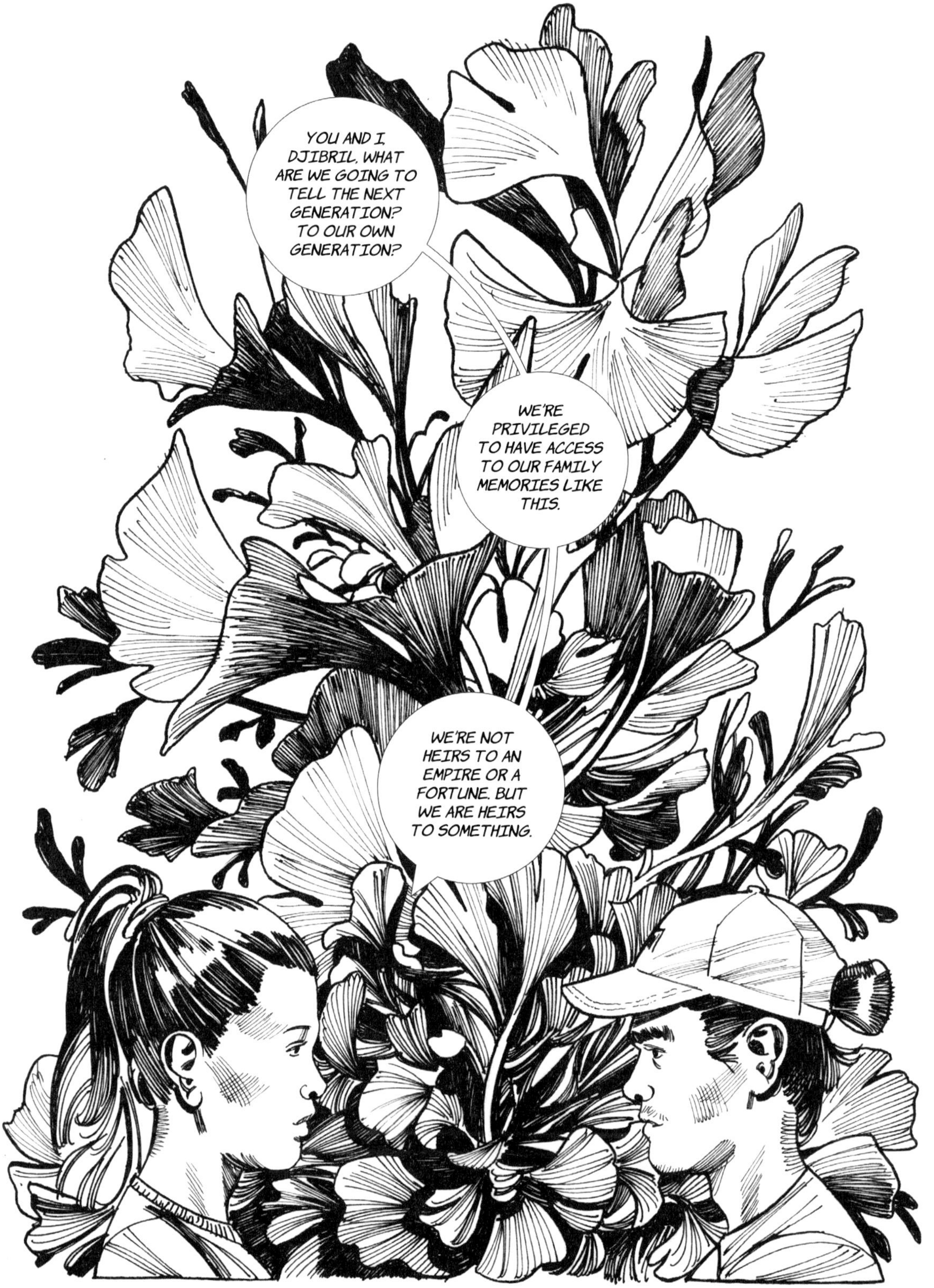
YOU AND I, DJIBRIL, WHAT ARE WE GOING TO TELL THE NEXT GENERATION? TO OUR OWN GENERATION?
WE'RE PRIVILEGED TO HAVE ACCESS TO OUR FAMILY MEMORIES LIKE THIS.
WE'RE NOT HEIRS TO AN EMPIRE OR A FORTUNE. BUT WE ARE HEIRS TO SOMETHING.

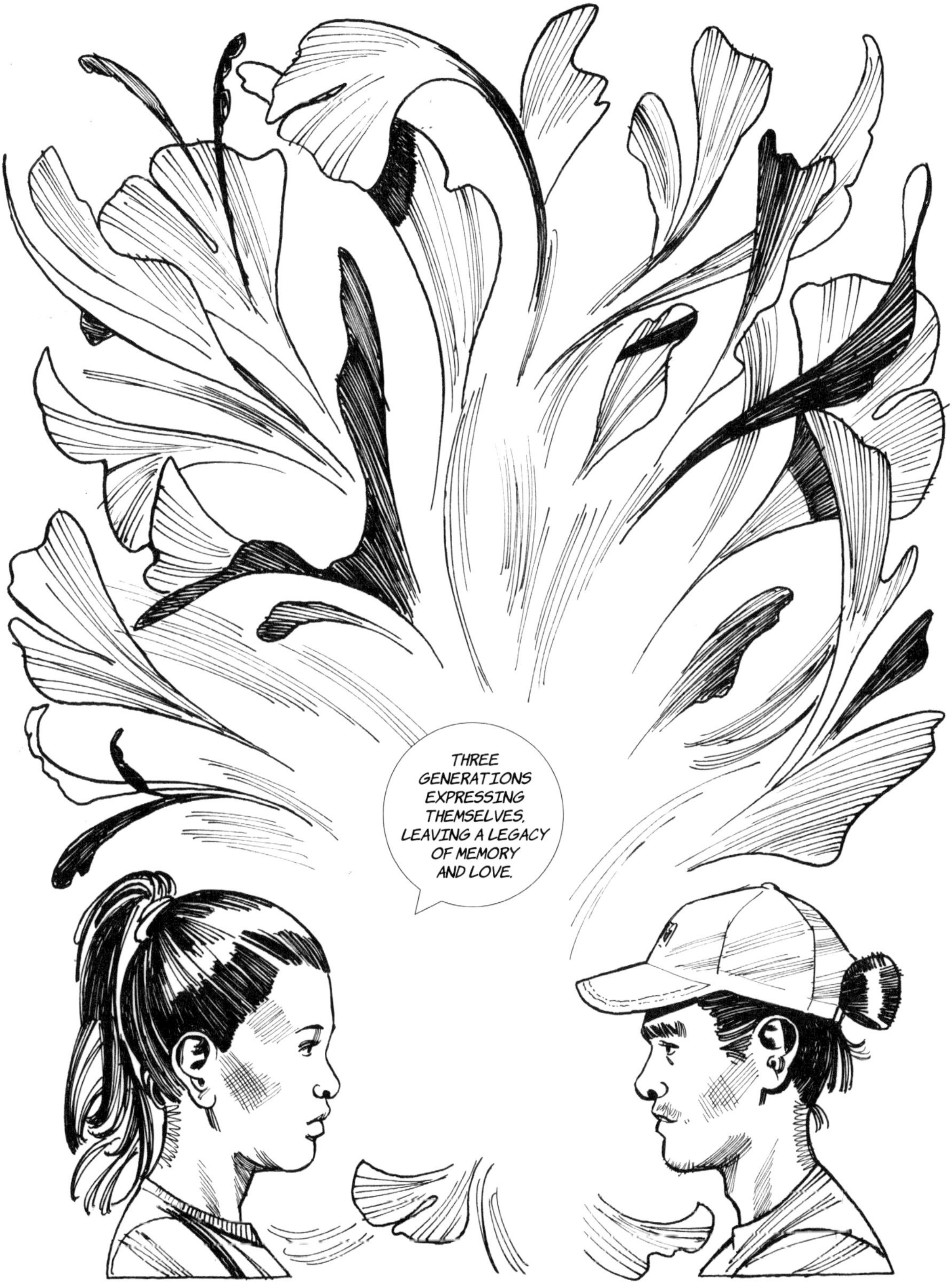
THREE GENERATIONS EXPRESSING THEMSELVES, LEAVING A LEGACY OF MEMORY AND LOVE.

WHAT DO WE KNOW ABOUT DAD'S SIDE?

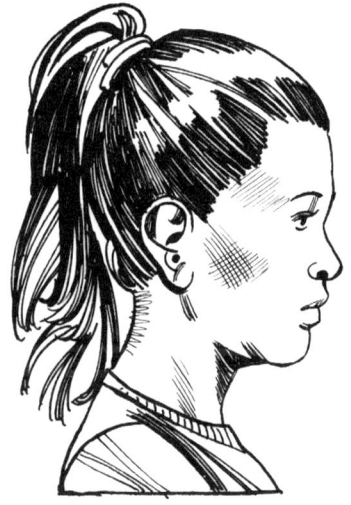

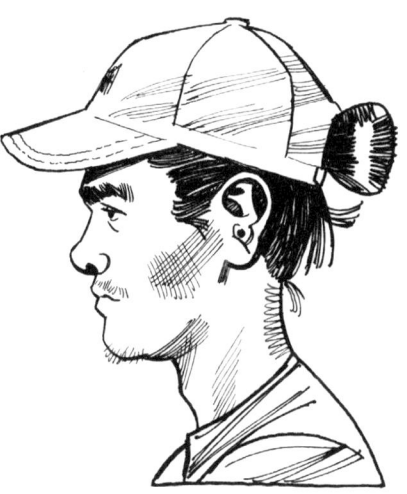

VIETNAM: A Thirty-Year War

Situated at the heart of Asia, Vietnam has always attracted great powers. China ruled Vietnam as a southern province for almost a thousand years. Once freed from Chinese rule in the 10th century, Vietnam extended its own empire southwards into the Mekong Delta, at the expense of its Cham, Cambodian and Laotian neighbors. In the 19th century, another imperial power arrived on the scene, this time a European one: France. The French sought to increase their trade with China and extend their empire into Asia. They conquered Vietnam in the latter half of the 19th century and incorporated it, along with the equally subjugated Laos and Cambodia, into the new colonial state they set up: French Indochina.

But the French presence was not without rivalry. In the 1930s, as the world headed towards the Second World War, the Japanese began to take a greater interest in this Vietnamese junction. When hostilities broke out in Europe and the Germans occupied France, the Japanese immediately entered Indochina. While the French government, displaced in Vichy, had agreed to work with the Germans in Europe, the Japanese did not overthrow the French in Indochina. In this phoney war, Vietnam belonged to both the French and Japanese empires, stretching from northern China to Singapore in the south.

As elsewhere in Asia, the Japanese occupation weighed heavily on local communities. Vietnam was no exception. The Japanese requisitioned rice to feed their army. By 1944, the demands were such that a terrible famine loomed in central and northern Vietnam. Bad weather and Allied bombing made matters worse (it was impossible to transport rice from the south to the north). Between 1944 and 1945, a total of at least one million Vietnamese peasants died of starvation—men and women, old people and young children. This famine created a wave of anger that the Hồ Chí Minh-led Nationalists would use to seize power once the war was over, in August 1945.

Who exactly was Hồ Chí Minh? Real name Nguyễn Sinh Cung, Hồ was born in 1890 in central Vietnam. Disappointed by the French's unfulfilled promises of reform, and determined to win Vietnam's independence, he turned to communism in the 1920s. In 1930, he founded the Indochinese Communist Party (now Vietnamese) and waited for the right moment to seize power. The Second World War offered the right conditions. In 1941, he created the famous "Việt Minh" national front for Vietnamese independence. The opportunity to seize power came in 1945 when the Japanese overthrew the French in Indochina in March, before surrendering themselves to the Allies on August 15. In the time that followed when no one was in power, the Việt Minh established itself in Hanoi on August 19, before taking over the provinces in the following weeks, propelled by the wave of anger generated by the famine. On September 2, 1945, in Hanoi, Hồ Chí Minh declared Vietnam's independence for the first time since the 19th century. Thus, the Democratic Republic of Vietnam was born.

Charles de Gaulle's "New France", which replaced Vichy, had no intention of giving up its Indochinese empire so easily. Humiliated during the Second World War, the French saw the opportunity to once again weigh in as a great power in world affairs by recapturing Indochina. De Gaulle sent his representatives to Indochina to re-establish French sovereignty. The problem, however, was that Hồ Chí Minh insisted on the reality of his "New Vietnam". Two diametrically opposed conceptions of the country's future collided... War was inevitable. It broke out in Saigon on September 23, 1945, then across the country a year later when negotiations failed. Driven out of the cities, Hồ and his allies ran the national government from the countryside. Isolated from the outside world for the first half of the war, they used guerrilla warfare against the French army like a tiger fighting an elephant. Frontal battles were to be avoided, as the French would have been able to concentrate their firepower on the young, ill-equipped and poorly-trained Vietnamese army. The key was to hit the enemy with ambushes before retreating into the jungle. However, the nature of the war changed in 1950, when Mao Tse-tung's Communist China supported Hồ's Vietnam diplomatically, militarily and economically. Thanks to Chinese aid, Hồ's Communist Party asserted itself at the head of the government. The Vietnamese army, meanwhile, received the modern weapons it needed to wage conventional war against the French. Between 1950 and 1954, the People's Army of Vietnam fought several battles against the French, including General Võ Nguyên Giáp's famous victory over the French army at Diên Biên Phu. Rather than continue the war, the French and Vietnamese agreed to negotiate an end to the conflict at a conference in Geneva. On July 21, they signed a ceasefire and agreed that the country would be temporarily divided into two territories at the 17° parallel: Hồ's Vietnam occupied the northern part, where the capital of Hanoi was located. In the south, a second Vietnam, the one the French had created in 1949 under the aegis of ex-emperor Bảo Đại, took hold. The French, like Hồ Chí Minh, were counting on the organization of elections in 1956 to determine which of the two Vietnams was to lead a unified and completely independent country.

Then the Americans entered the picture, opposing the project. They had supported the French and Bảo Đại's Vietnam since 1950 in a bid to stem the expansion of Sino-Soviet communism into Southeast Asia. It was out of the question for Washington to let Hồ take all of Vietnam by election. The emperor's prime minister, Ngô Đình Diệm, shared this view. Together, the Americans and Ngô Đình Diệm refused to hold elections. In 1955, Diem replaced Bảo Đại following rigged elections and declared the creation of the Republic of Vietnam with Saigon as its capital. The Americans supported him as they had supported the French previously. Their aim remained the same: to hinder Communist expansion into Southeast Asia. Elections never took place. Washington helped the Republic of Vietnam militarily, economically and diplomatically. President Eisenhower accepted that Vietnam would remain divided, like Korea, Germany and China (communist on the mainland, non-communist in Taiwan).

The Vietnamese Communists obviously didn't share this view. In 1959, they resumed the war they had waged against the French since 1945. At first, they proceeded in small, cautious steps. For example, the opening of the Hồ Chí Minh trail that year enabled them to send arms, troops and cadres discreetly into the South to assist a new national front. Hanoi hoped that, thanks to this aid, a well-fought guerrilla war and Ngô Đình Diệm's unpopularity, the Republic of Diệm could fall without the Americans having to intervene directly. Diệm, for his part, intended to create a centralized, economically strong nation-state, equipped with an army, capable of facing down the Communists. He ruled the South with an iron fist, but not without creating numerous adversaries among his own allies. Grumbling in the countryside worsened when he forcibly relocated hundreds of thousands of peasants to strategic hamlets isolated from the Communists. The latter exploited peasant resistance to Diệm's methods and, in the process, extended Communist control across the South. Worried, the Americans advised caution to Diệm. All in vain! In the summer of 1963, while Diệm was harshly suppressing Buddhist demonstrations, a handful of generals informed the Americans of their intention to overthrow the president before the Communists took over the entire South. The White House, under President John F. Kennedy, gave its approval. In early November, Ngô Đình Diệm was overthrown and assassinated. Shortly afterwards, Kennedy died.

The new American president, Lyndon B. Johnson, had to decide what to do in Vietnam. Either the Americans intervened directly to stop communism by sending in the army, or Washington accepted Hồ's leadership of Vietnam, which it had declared independent in 1945. As we know, Johnson chose to intervene directly. The so-called Vietnam War began in 1964 when the Americans bombed the North (Operation Rolling Thunder), convinced that Communist ships had fired on an American vessel operating in the Gulf of Tonkin. Troops landed in March 1965. Three years later, 500,000 American troops were present in Vietnam. Until 1973, the Americans fought alongside the Republican Army of the South against the forces of Hồ Chí Minh. During the Tet (New Year) holiday in early 1968, Hanoi ordered an offensive against the major cities of the South, including Saigon and Huế. They lost militarily, but the offensive made it clear that the war was not won. Johnson refused to run for president again.

Richard M. Nixon won the election and entered the White House in January 1969. With support from Henry Kissinger, he wanted to withdraw the US army from Vietnam. The new American president was convinced that he could protect South Vietnam through air power and the expansion of the Southern army. But he didn't see his impeachment coming when the Watergate affair reached its climax in 1974. In early 1975, the troops of Hồ Chí Minh (who died in 1969) rolled the dice and attacked the South, convinced that the Americans would not intervene. They were right. On April 30, 1975, Saigon fell to Võ Nguyên Giáp's army. The Vietnam that Hồ had declared independent in September 1945 became a reality, officially unified under the aegis of the Vietnamese Communist Party in 1976. For those who had opposed communism, the worst had just happened. The Communists controlled Vietnam, as well as Cambodia and Laos.

During these events, hundreds of thousands of people fled Vietnam, and it is this remarkable story that is the subject of Yasmine and Djibril Phan's comic strip today.

Christopher Goscha
Professor of International Relations
University of Quebec at Montreal

Khiêm during her novitiate (Congregation of the Lovers of the Cross, Phát Diệm, 1954)

Teacher Khiêm (Đà Lạt, 1958)

Khiêm and Lục's Wedding (Gia Định, 1963)

Lục, Trang and Khiêm (Gia Định, 1965)

Khiêm and Lục on Bus 32 (Montreal North, 1991)

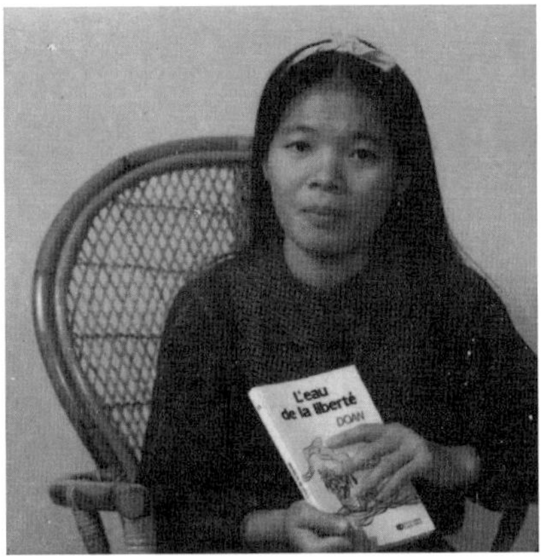
L'eau
de la liberté
DOAN

Trang at the release of "L'eau de la liberté"
(Montreal North, 1984)

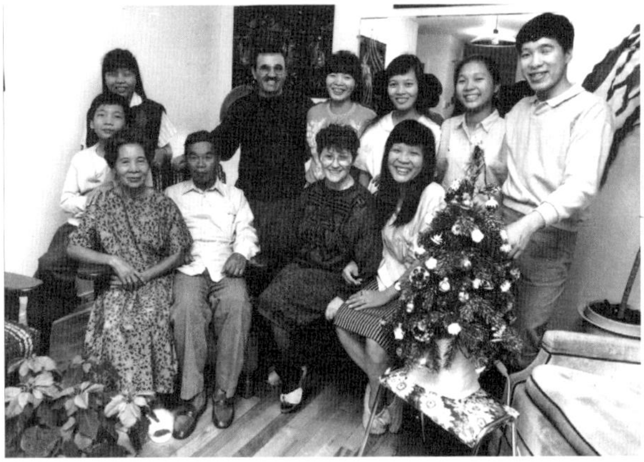

The first Christmas following the Phan family reunion
(Montreal North, 1988)

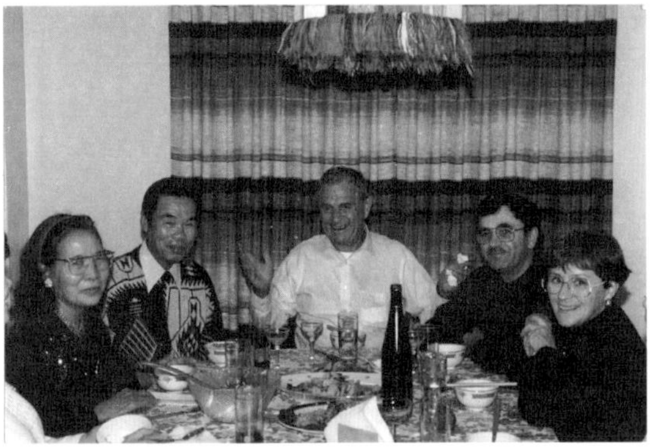

Khiêm, Lục, Marcel de la Sablonnière, Normand
and Therese (Montreal North, 1989)

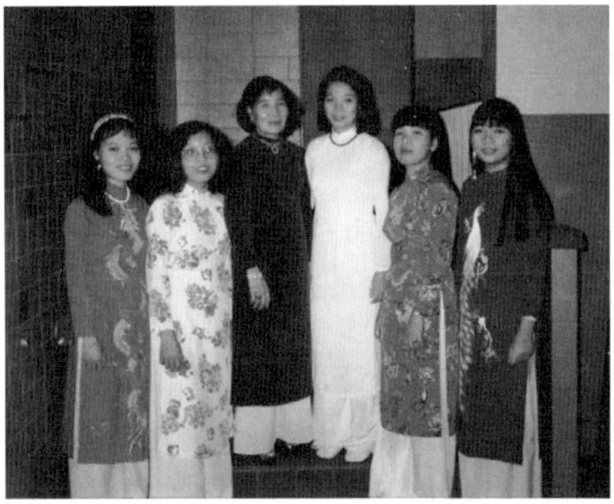

Khiêm and her 5 daughters at the 10th anniversary
of Famille Sans Frontière (Montreal, 1991)

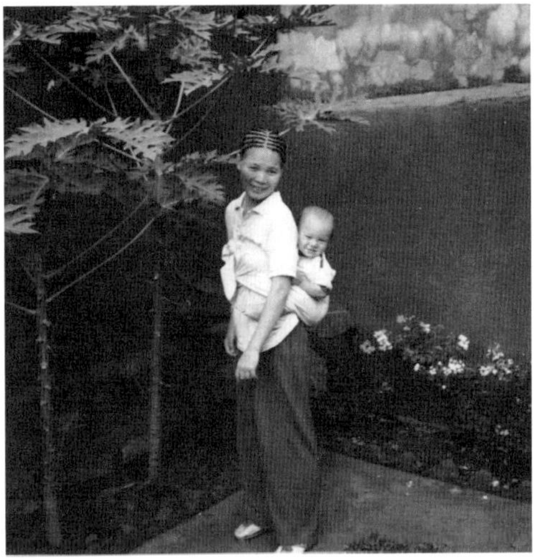

Trang and Djibril (Bamako, 1995)

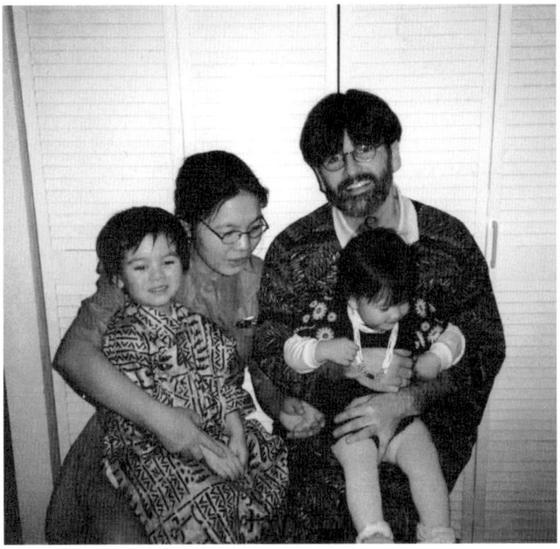

The Phan-Morissette family at Christmas (Montreal, 1997)

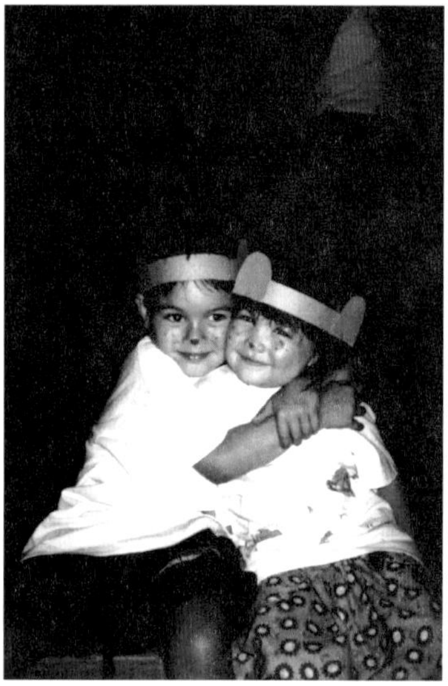

Djibril and Yasmine (Montreal, 2000)

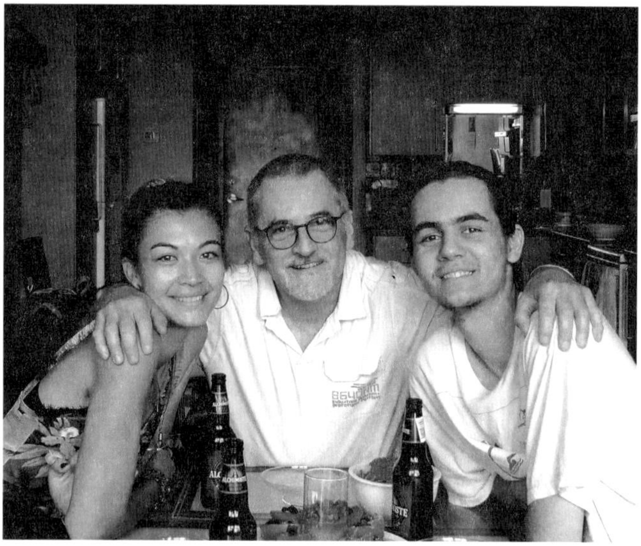

Yasmine, Serge and Djibril (Hochelaga, 2018)

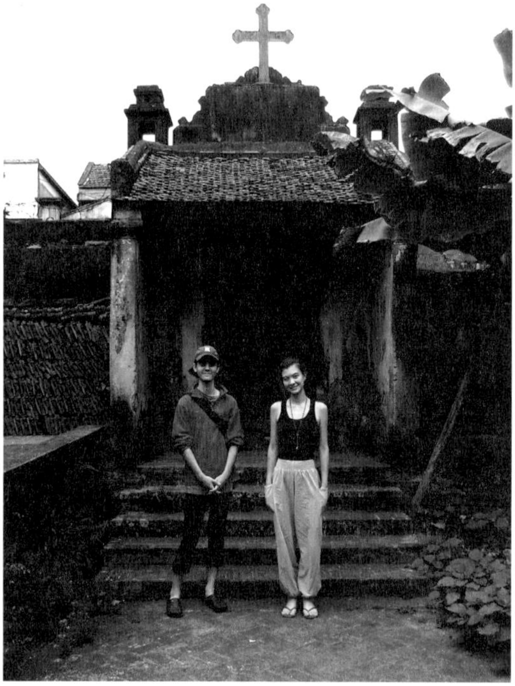

Djibril and Yasmine (Mông Phụ, 2018)

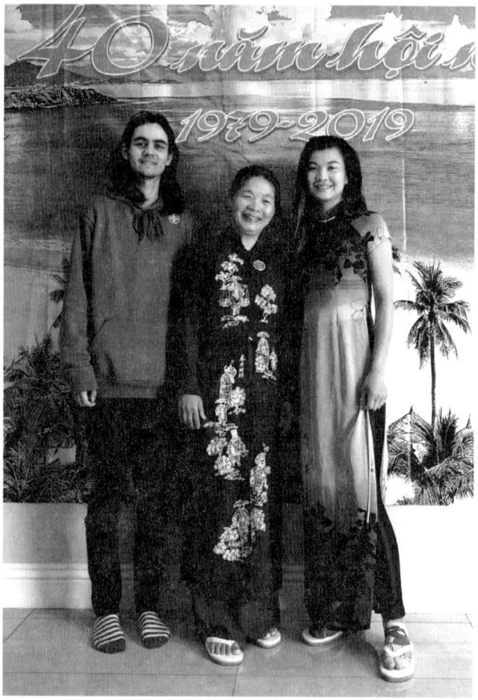
40 năm hội
1979-2019

Djibril, Trang and Yasmine (Westminster, California, 2019)

ACKNOWLEDGEMENTS

This project would never have been possible without the invaluable collaboration of many people. Many thanks to Professor Christopher Goscha, who readily agreed to provide historical context. Thanks to Rebecca and Christian, of Glénat, for instantly believing in the project. Thanks to my grandmother Therese for answering my questions.

Thanks to all those who appear in the story for enriching my journey. Special thanks to Bác Tâm and her family, who welcomed us with open hearts during our visit to Mông Phụ. Thanks also to Uncle Vũ and his family for warmly opening the door of their home in South El Monte to us.

Thanks to Doan Trang Phan, our mother, without whom Khiêm would have remained unknown to us.

Thanks to Serge Morissette, our loving father, the voice of my reason, an unconditional support in all our projects.

Our parents made it easy for us to explore our dual cultural identity.

Above all, thanks to Djibril, my brother, for suggesting this project. Our shared creative universe is as precious to me as our relationship, and will continue to be cultivated with new projects. It's an honor to put my writing at the service of your drawings.

WORKS REFERENCED

L'eau de la liberté, Doan, Éditions Paulines, 1984

Escape from Vietnam, the story of Doan, translated by Carmen Landry, Optimum Publishing International Inc., 1988

Immigration, phénomène souhaitable et inévitable, Pierre Vincent, Québec/Amérique, 1994

Đường Lâm, Village historique, work translated and published in French by the Institut des métiers de la ville, decentralized cooperation office between the Île-de-France Region and the Hanoi City People's Committee, June 2012.

Vietnam, le chagrin de la paix, Alain S. de Sacy, Librairie Vuibert, 2002

Maison Chance, un avenir pour les moins chanceux au Vietnam, Tim Aline Rebeaud, Favre, 2013

Boat people, Personal stories from the Vietnamese exodus 1975-1996, edited by Carina Hoang, Carina Hoang Communications, 2010

La culture du riz dans le delta du Tonkin, René Dumont, Prince of Songkla University, édition de 1995

La force de la faiblesse, Normand Longchamps, Éditeur De L'apotheose, 2017

Le sympathisant, Viet Thanh Nguyen, Belfond, 2017

Vietnam: A New History, Christopher Goscha, Basic Books, 2016

Indochine ou Vietnam?, Christopher Goscha, Vendémiaire, 2015

Légendes des terres sereines, Duy Khiêm Pham, Éditions Mercure de France, 1998

Mémoires de Viet Kieu tome 2 (graphic novel) - little Saigon, Clément Baloup, La Boîte à Bulles, 2012

The Best We could Do (graphic novel), Thi Bui, Chez Iceman, 2018